Commencement-Level:

PHYSICAL SETTING CHEMISTRY

STAREVIEW

CHEMISTRY

Authors
Nicholas R. Romano
Philip K. Cameron

Editors
Wayne Garnsey & Paul Stich
Fran Harrison, Associate Editor

Artwork & Graphics
Eugene B. Fairbanks & Wayne Garnsey

N&N Publishing Company, Inc.
18 Montgomery Street   Middletown, NY 10940-5116

For Ordering & Information
1-800-NN 4 TEXT
Website: www.nn4text.com   email: nn4text@nandnpublishing.com

DEDICATION & THANKS

Dedicated to our students, with the sincere hope that this book will further enhance their education and better prepare them with an appreciation and understanding of their role in the care and protection of Earth.

SPECIAL THANKS

Nicholas Romano:
Dedicated with much appreciation and thanks
to Shirley and Marietta Romano Mendler.

Philip Cameron:
Dedicated to my wife Elsa, sons Philip and Daniel, and my colleagues at John Jay High School for their constant support, help, and understanding during the development of this book.

SPECIAL CREDITS

We thank these dedicated educational professionals for their hard work, subject and curricula contributions, and technical proofing of our *Physical Setting: Chemistry STAReview*:

Sr. Kathleen McKinney, CSJ, Ed.D
Ms. Fran Harrison
Dr. Wayne Moreau
Ms. Paula Ranous
Mr. William Schoen
Ms. Judith Shuback
Mr. Brian Timm

front cover photo: © PhotoDisc

© Copyright 2002, **Revised 2005**

N&N Publishing Company, Inc.

phone: 1-800-NN 4 TEXT
website: www.nn4text.com   email: nn4text@nandnpublishing.com
SAN # - 216-4221   ISBN # - 0935487-75-1

5 6 7 8 9 0 BookMart 2010 2009 2008 2007 2006 2005

TABLE OF CONTENTS

*PI identifies the Performance Indicators

CONTEXT OF THE
PHYSICAL SETTING: CHEMISTRY

UNIT 4 – CHEMICAL BONDING 083

Key Idea 5 – Energy and matter interact through forces that result in changes in motion.

UNIT 5 – PHYSICAL BEHAVIOR OF MATTER 105

Key Idea 4 – Energy exists in many forms, and when these forms change, energy is conserved.

UNIT 6 – KINETICS / EQUILIBRIUM 157

Key Idea 3 – Matter is made up of particles whose properties determine the observable characteristics of matter and its reactivity.

To the Student & Teacher

PHYSICAL SETTING: CHEMISTRY STAREVIEW is written based on the new standards and assessments for chemistry. It is a comprehensive review of the Key Ideas, Major Understandings, Performance Indicators, Process Skills, and Real World Connections as set forth in the University of the State of New York Education Department: *Physical Setting: Chemistry Core Curriculum*.

"Open First"

The student should upon receiving this *STAReview* begin by reading this section: "To the Student."

- Start by reviewing the Table of Contents (previous 4 pages). This will give an overview of the major topics reviewed in this book.

- Now, become familiar with Unit 13 (page 335) Index & Glossary. This section is an extensive listing of the key chemical terms that one needs to know in order to understand the material. A brief definition or explanation of the term is given together with cross-referenced pages to direct the student to additional material directly related to the term.

Organization

The book is organized "conceptually," but the review is linked through the following organizational parts.

- **Standards** are the overall, general goals that apply to all scientific and indeed most general learning. For example, each Standard contains several goals, such as "Analysis, Scientific Inquiry, and Engineering Design in order to pose questions, seek answers, and develop solutions."

- Within each Standard, **Key Ideas** are used to further define the generalized objectives to be reached. For example, Standard 1 has several Key Ideas such as Key Idea 1 within the Scientific Inquiry part of Standard 1, that is, "to develop explanations of natural phenomena in a continuing, creative process."

- For each Key Idea there are several **Process Skills** which specifically identify what processes the student must learn in order to demonstrate the particular Key Ideas of a general Standard. These Skills are identified and found in all Units followed by explanations of the Skill and questions to test the student's abilities in preparation for the final, year-end test.

- Associated with both Standards and their Key Ideas are the **Performance Indicators**. These tell the student specifically what he/she is expected to know in order to answer correctly the questions on the final, year-end test. In other words, the specific objectives of the testing. These are identified at the beginning of each Unit and again at the end of each unit with the Part A, B, and C questions.

- Finally, there are the **Major Understandings**. Each Performance Indicator has specific concepts and chemical understandings to learn. This is the "meat and potatoes" of *Physical Setting: Chemistry STAReview*. These Major Understandings are first listed at the beginning of each Unit, are further developed in the text, examples, sample problems, and illustrations that follow, and are tested through out the Unit in the Skills and at the end of each Unit in Parts A, B, and C.

MEANING OF SYMBOLS

Symbols are critical in chemistry. So, the authors have developed a mini-help system. Stars are used to help navigate the student through the more complex Major Understandings in chemistry.

Stars indicate two important things: Some starred material may not be *specifically* referred to in the *Core Curriculum*, but this text is needed for better understanding of major chemical concepts. Also, stars may note special material that further explains Major Understandings, Skills, and Real World Connections.

In addition, the ☆ followed by a page number, directs the student to related material. These stars can help either by (1) providing a page reference to where that concept is further explained, or (2) give the student additional information making total understanding better.

FINALLY, STUDY

Success comes through study. The authors and editors of *Physical Setting: Chemistry STAReview* are teachers. This book has been written to provide the student with the best "outside help" possible. But, it can only help the student, if the student uses it consistently, with purpose, and focused study.

We wish you good studying and success on your final, year-end test.

UNIT 1
ATOMIC CONCEPTS

KEY IDEA **3** MATTER IS MADE UP OF PARTICLES WHOSE PROPERTIES DETERMINE THE OBSERVABLE CHARACTERISTICS OF MATTER AND ITS REACTIVITY

PERFORMANCE INDICATOR 3.1 *EXPLAIN THE PROPERTIES OF MATERIALS IN TERMS OF THE ARRANGEMENT AND PROPERTIES OF THE ATOMS THAT COMPOSE THEM.*

UNIT 1 – MAJOR UNDERSTANDINGS

☆ 3.1a The modern model of the atom has evolved over a long period of time through the work of many scientists.

☆ 3.1b Each atom has a nucleus, with an overall positive charge, surrounded by negatively charged electrons.

☆ 3.1c Subatomic particles contained in the nucleus include protons and neutrons.

☆ 3.1d The proton is positively charged, and the neutron has no charge. The electron is negatively charged.

☆ 3.1e Protons and electrons have equal but opposite charges. The number of protons equals the number of electrons in an atom.

☆ 3.1f The mass of each proton and each neutron is approximately equal to one atomic mass unit. An electron is much less massive than a proton or a neutron.

☆ 3.1g The number of protons in an atom (atomic number) identifies the element. The sum of the protons and neutrons in an atom (mass number) identifies an isotope. Common notations that represent isotopes include: ^{14}C, $^{14}_{6}C$, carbon-14, C-14.

☆ 3.1h In the wave-mechanical model (electron cloud model) the electrons are in orbitals which are defined as the regions of the most probable

UNIT 1
ATOMIC CONCEPTS

This unit is related to Key Idea 3 for the text and
Performance Indicator 3.1 for the assessments.

INTRODUCTION
A BRIEF CHRONOLOGICAL HISTORY OF
THE EARLY DEVELOPMENT OF ATOMIC STRUCTURE

Understanding why atoms are in constant motion requires understanding the characteristics of atomic structure. The modern model of
the atom has evolved over a long period of time through the work of
many early scientists. Included are the following events:

480 BC –   **Democritus** used the word atom – meaning indivisible in Greek – to
describe a substance.

1661 –   **Robert Boyle** published ***The Skeptical Chemist*** in which he stated that
substances are made up of elements which cannot be decomposed into simpler substances.

1772 –   **Antoine Laurent Lavoisier (Father of Modern Chemistry)** used quantitative methods to demonstrate ***Law of Conservation of Matter***.

1803 –   **John Dalton (Father of Atomic Theory)** stated
- all matter is composed of atoms
- all atoms of any one element have the same properties
- atoms cannot be created, destroyed, or subdivided
- when atoms of different elements combine they do so in
  whole number ratios and form a chemical compound
- when elements undergo a chemical reaction the atoms
  rearrange, combine, or separate

UNIT 1 – MAJOR UNDERSTANDINGS (CONTINUED)

electron location (ground
state)

☆ 3.1i Each electron in an atom
has its own distinct amount of
energy.

☆ 3.1j When an electron in an
atom gains a specific amount
of energy, the electron is at a
higher energy state (excited
state).

☆ 3.1k When an electron returns
from a higher energy state to a
lower energy state, a specific
amount of energy is emitted.
This emitted energy can be
used to identify an element.

☆ 3.1l The outermost electrons in
an atom are called the
valence electrons. In general,
the number of valence
electrons affects the chemical
properties of an element.

☆ 3.1m Atoms of an element
that contain the same number
of protons but a different
number of neutrons are called
isotopes of that element.

☆ 3.1n The average atomic mass
of an element is the weighted
average of the masses of its
naturally occurring isotopes.

1871 –	**Dmitri Ivanovich Mendeleev** created a periodic table using atomic mass as a priority arrangement.
1874 –	**G. D. Stoney** named the atom's negative particles **electrons**.
1879 –	**Sir William Crookes** invented the **cathode ray tube**, leading to the vacuum picture tube, found in television.
1897 –	**Sir J. J. Thomson** determined the mass to charge ratio of the electron.
1901 –	**Max Karl Ernst Ludwig Planck** proposed that radiant energy has a particulate as well as a wave nature.
1903 –	**Marie Curie**, Polish-born French chemist, shared a 1903 Nobel Prize with her husband, Pierre Curie and Henri Becquerel for research on radioactivity; in 1911, won a 2nd Nobel Prize for her discovery of radium and polonium.
1905 –	**Albert Einstein** proposed that mass and energy are related in the equation $E = mc^2$
1909 –	**Robert A. Millikan** determined the charge on the electron.
1911 –	**Ernest Rutherford** proposed that the atom is "mostly empty space with a tiny positive center made of protons and negative electrons orbiting it."
–	**J. J. Thomson** noted that particles from the surface of metals irradiated in a vacuum were identical to electrons.
1913 –	**Niels Henrik David Bohr** used **Rutherford's nuclear atom concept** and **Plancks' quantum theory** to propose a solar system model of the atom.
1921 –	**Albert Einstein** received **Nobel Prize** for discovering **Photoelectric Law**.
1923 –	**Louis deBroglie** stated that all matter like radiant energy has both particulate and wave characteristics.
1925 –	**Werner K. Heisenberg** proposed the **Uncertainty Principle**.
1926 –	**Erwin Schrödinger** proposed the **Wave-Mechanical Model** of the atom by using a 100 year old wave function equation by **William Hamilton** in addition to his own ideas.
1932 –	**Sir James Chadwick** discovered neutrons in the nucleus.

Note: Many more significant scientific discoveries, including more concerning the atoms, have been made during the past century, several of these are discussed in (S) **REAL WORLD CONNECTIONS**.

A - NATURE OF THE ATOM

An **atom** is a unit of matter, the smallest unit of an element, having all the characteristics of that element and consisting of a dense, central, positively charged nucleus surrounded by a system of electrons.

Our concept of the nature of the atom has undergone change and will most likely continue to do so into the future. However, one concept remains unchanged – any atomic theory must be based on the structure of the atom and its various fundamental or subatomic particles. Experimentally, it has been shown that the volume of the atom is primarily made up of negatively charged whirling electrons. The mass of the atom is located in a central core particle called the **nucleus**, which contains all the atom's positive charge.

B - SUBATOMIC PARTICLES

An **electron** ($_{-1}^{0}e$) has a mass of approximately $1/1836$ of a proton and a unit negative charge (**-1**). The mass of an electron is considered negligible; however, they do account for the volume of the atom.

Particles that compose the nucleus are called **nucleons** and include:

- **Protons** ($_{+1}^{1}\textbf{p}$) – A proton has a mass of approximately one atomic mass unit and a unit positive charge (**+1**). Although protons and neutrons are the only nuclear particles that have been identified in an intact nucleus, other particles have been identified among the breakdown products of certain nuclear disintegration. The relationship of these particles to the structure and stability of the nucleus is the subject of much current research. In an atom, the number of protons equals the number of electrons, and the number of protons in an atom (atomic number) identifies the element.

- **Neutrons** ($_{0}^{1}\textbf{n}$) – A neutron also has a mass of approximately one atomic mass unit. It has a unit charge of zero (**0**); therefore, the name "neutron." It is found in the nucleus along with the proton.

Since protons (**p+**) and electrons (**e-**) have equal but opposite charges, all atoms are considered neutral (**0**).

C – ATOMIC STRUCTURE

Atoms differ in the amount of protons and neutrons in the nucleus and in the configuration of the electrons surrounding the nucleus. Most of the atom consists of empty space. Ernest Rutherford's gold foil experiments showed an atom to be mostly empty space with the size of the nucleus very small compared to the atom's size.

NUCLEUS

The mass of the atom is concentrated almost entirely in the nucleus, which is the basis for determining:

- **Atomic Number** – The atomic number indicates the number of protons in the nucleus. It is the number of protons that identifies the element.

- **Isotopes** – Isotopes are atoms with the same atomic number (number of protons) but a different number of neutrons. This difference in the number of neutrons affects the mass of an atom but does not affect its chemical identity.

Note: For an element the number of protons in the nucleus remains constant, but the number of neutrons may vary. The most common isotope of carbon has six protons and six neutrons in its nucleus. It can be written ^{12}C or $_{6}^{12}C$ or Carbon-12 or C-12. However, there are less common isotopes of carbon such as C-14 and C-15. They also contain six protons in the nucleus but C-14 contains eight neutrons in its nucleus and C-15 contains nine neutrons in its nucleus.

- **Mass number** – The mass number indicates the total number of protons and neutrons. Since the masses of the protons and neutrons are approximately one, the mass number approximates the total mass of the isotope. The number of neutrons in an atom can be calculated by subtracting the atomic number from the mass number.

  The sum of the protons and neutrons in an atom (mass number) identifies an isotope. Common notations that represent isotopes include: ^{14}C, $^{14}_{6}$C, carbon-14, C-14.

- **Atomic mass** – The mass of a neutral atom, called its atomic mass, is measured in **atomic mass units** (**amu**s), which are standardized on the isotope carbon-12 ($^{12}_{6}$C). This isotope of carbon is equal to 12.000 atomic mass units. Therefore, the definition for an atomic mass unit can be stated as one twelfth ($^1/_{12}$) of a carbon-12 ($^{12}_{6}$C) atom.

  The atomic mass of an element, given in the *Reference Tables for Physical Setting: Chemistry*, is the weighted average mass of the naturally occurring isotopes of that element. Since most elements occur naturally as mixtures of isotopes, this average is weighted according to the proportions in which the isotopes occur. This accounts for fractional atomic masses found in the reference tables. For example, the element hydrogen exists in three different isotopes:

  protium ($^1_1$H) occurs about 99.0% of the time in nature.

  deuterium ($^2_1$H) occurs about 0.6% of the time in nature.

  tritium ($^3_1$H) occurs about 0.4% of the time in nature.

SKILLS 3.1X *INTERPRET AND WRITE ISOTOPIC NOTATION.*

1   Which pair of atoms are isotopes of element X?

   (1) $^{226}_{90}$X and $^{226}_{91}$X   (3) $^{226}_{91}$X and $^{227}_{90}$X

   (2) $^{226}_{91}$X and $^{227}_{91}$X   (4) $^{226}_{90}$X and $^{227}_{91}$X

2   Which atoms represent different isotopes of the same element?

   (1) $^{39}_{18}$Ar and $^{39}_{19}$K   (3) $^{12}_{6}$C and $^{13}_{6}$C

   (2) $^{58}_{27}$Co and $^{59}_{28}$Ni   (4) $^{35}_{17}$Cl and $^{35}_{17}$Cl

3   Which pair must represent isotopes of the same element?

   (1) $^{120}_{51}$X and $^{120}_{52}$X   (3) $_{21}$X^{2+} and $_{19}$X^{2+}

   (2) $^{38}_{18}$X and $^{39}_{18}$X   (4) $_{26}$X^{2+} and $_{26}$X^{3+}

In general, the mass number is determined by rounding off the atomic mass of the element to the nearest whole number. For example, the atomic mass of a single atom (isotope) such as neon-20 is 19.992 amu, while the atomic mass of the element neon (which is the weighted average of all its natural isotopes) is 20.183 amu. The masses of atoms, multiplied by their occurrence, average out to be 1.000797 amu.

SKILLS 3.1XI *GIVEN THE ATOMIC MASS, DETERMINE THE MOST ABUNDANT ISOTOPE.*

COMPUTING THE AVERAGE WEIGHT (MASS) OF AN ELEMENT

The average atomic weight of an element, as given the *Periodic Table of the Elements*, is the average of the weights of the atoms in a naturally occurring mixture of the isotopes of the element, if any. Computation of some of these average weights is an interesting mathematical extension which leads to an understanding of the process.

Example: Data in the various chemical handbooks indicate that the occurrences of the principal isotopes of magnesium are:

Mg^{24} – 79.3 percent of atomic mass 23.9924
Mg^{25} – 10.1 percent of atomic mass 24.9938
Mg^{26} – 10.6 percent of atomic mass 25.9898

It is obvious that the average atomic mass (chemical atomic weight) is between 24 and 26 and closer to 24. The weighted average is computed as:

Mg^{24} – 23.9924 x .793 = 19.026
Mg^{25} – 24.9938 x .101 = 2.524
Mg^{26} – 25.9898 x .106 = 2.755
                                          24.305

This corresponds to the weight given in the table.

SKILLS 3.1XII *CALCULATE THE ATOMIC MASS OF AN ELEMENT GIVEN THE MASSES AND RATIOS OF NATURALLY OCCURRING ISOTOPES.*

4   Compute the average atomic weights of the following additional elements: Complete the following table:

Element	Percent in Nature	Relative Atomic Mass		Average Atomic Mass
copper-63	69.17	62.939598	=_____	
copper-65	30.83	64.927793	=_____	(average)_____
uranium-235	0.720	235.043924	=_____	
uranium-238	99.280	238.051000	=_____	(average)_____
hydrogen-1	99.985	1.007825	=_____	
hydrogen-2	0.015	2.0140	=_____	(average)_____

The **gram atomic mass** (the mass of one mole of atoms) of an element is the mass in grams of **Avogadro's number** (approx. 6.0225 x 10^{23}) of atoms of that element as it occurs naturally. It is numerically equal to the atomic mass. Examples:

1 gram atomic mass of carbon-12 has a mass of 12 grams.
1 gram atomic mass of sodium-23 has a mass of 23 grams.

SKILLS 3.1I *USE MODELS TO DESCRIBE THE STRUCTURE OF ATOMS.*
The use of ball and stick model kits serve to illustrate the three dimensional character of the atom. However, it must be stressed that most orbitals are not circular in shape.

Draw simple "stick models" (in 3-D if possible)
of combined atoms, such as H_2O (shown at the right):

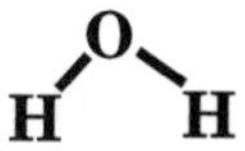

5 Question: CH_4

6 Question: CF_4

7 Question: CO_2

D – ATOMIC MODELS

BOHRS' PLANETARY MODEL

All atoms possess energy which causes them to vibrate. In 1901, Max Karl Ernst Ludwig Planck proposed that atoms absorb energy only in discrete amounts called **quanta**. A single quanta is called a quantum of energy.

Planck also proposed an equation that relates the energy of a vibrating atom to its frequency: $E = h\nu$. Where E is energy in ergs, ν (Greek letter "nu") is frequency in reciprocal seconds sec^{-1}, and h is a fundamental constant of nature, called **Planck's constant**. Its value is **6.63 x 10^{34} Joules/second**. This equation proposed that high frequency violet light waves have more energy than low frequency red light waves. He also proposed that energy is not given off or absorbed in a continuous flow – but in small packets of quanta.

The model for atomic structure of the elements has passed through many stages of development. Less than a century ago, Danish physicist Niels Bohr made one proposal for the model.

Although not currently used by chemists to describe atomic structure, the significance of the Bohr model of the atom is that Bohr's model is concerned with the first applications of the quantum mechanical concepts to atomic structure.

In the Bohr model (at the right), electrons were considered to revolve around the nucleus in one of several concentric circular orbits, similar to the solar system.

In the Bohr model of an atom, the principal energy level approximates how far the electron is from the nucleus and can be denoted by the letters K, L, M, N, O, P, Q, or by the numbers 1, 2, 3, 4, 5, 6, 7.

Bohr Model

E – ENERGY LEVELS

The energy levels of the electrons within an atom are represented by four (4) quantum numbers (see Wave Mechanical Model, page 18). They include:

Principal quantum number – The principal quantum number (n) represents the **principal energy level** (also referred to as shells). This number (n), is equal to the number of the principal energy level (as referred to under the Bohr atom) and is the same as the period number in the periodic table. For example, in the Bohr model, if the electron was described as being in the second shell, then its orbital model description would include a principal quantum number of 2.

Second quantum number – The second quantum number (l) represents **sublevels**. Additional spectral lines appearing in the spectrum of atoms heavier than hydrogen can be explained only by assuming that the principal energy levels are divided into sublevels.

The total number of possible sublevels for each principal energy level is equal to the number of the principal energy level (n). These sublevels are designated by the letters s, p, d, and f.

1) **Principal energy level 1** is made up of one energy sublevel called **1s**.

2) **Principal energy level 2** is made up of two sublevels called **2s** and **2p**.

3) **Principal energy level 3** is made up of three sublevels called **3s**, **3p**, and **3d**.

4) **Principal energy level 4** is made up of four sublevels called **4s**, **4p**, **4d**, and **4f**.

Within a given principal energy level, the lowest in energy is the "*s*" sublevel and the highest is the "*f*" sublevel. The number of the principal energy levels and one of the letters *s*, *p*, *d*, or *f* are used to describe the energy of an electron in a particular sublevel. (The number of occupied sublevels does not exceed four even when **n** is greater than 4.)

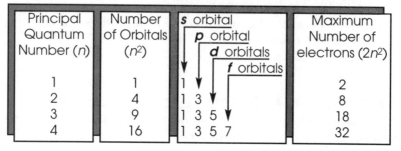

Principal Quantum Number (n)	Number of Orbitals (n^2)	*s* orbital *p* orbital *d* orbitals *f* orbitals	Maximum Number of electrons ($2n^2$)
1	1	1	2
2	4	1 3	8
3	9	1 3 5	18
4	16	1 3 5 7	32

Third quantum number – The third quantum number (m_l) represents **orbitals**. Each sublevel may consist of one or more orbitals with each orbital having a different spatial orientation. The maximum number of electrons possible in the various energy levels and their distribution are shown in the table above.

Each electron occupies an orbital, which can hold no more than two electrons. The number of orbitals within the same principal energy level (**n, principal quantum number**) is equal to (n^2, **number of orbitals**). When n is less than or equal to 4, the following sequence occurs:

1 The *s* sublevel consists of 1 orbital.
2 The *p* sublevel consists of 3 orbitals.
3 The *d* sublevel consists of 5 orbitals.
4 The *f* sublevel consists of 7 orbitals.

Fourth quantum number – The fourth quantum number (m_s) represents the spin of the electron. In order for two electrons to occupy the same orbital, they must have opposite spins.

SKILLS 3.1III *DETERMINE THE NUMBER OF PROTONS OR ELECTRONS IN AN ATOM OR ION (A CHARGED PARTICLE FORMED BY THE TRANSFER OF ELECTRONS) WHEN GIVEN ONE OF THESE VALUES.*

8 A Ca^{2+} ion differs from a Ca atom in that the Ca^{2+} ion has
(1) more protons
(2) fewer protons
(3) more electrons
(4) fewer electrons

9 What is the total number of electrons in a Mg^{2+} ion?
(1) 10
(2) 2
(3) 12
(4) 24

10 The nucleus of an atom consists of 8 protons and 6 neutrons. The total number of electrons present in a neutral atom of this element is
(1) 6
(2) 2
(3) 8
(4) 14

11 Any sodium atom must have the same number of
   (1) protons   (3) occupied principal energy levels
   (2) orbitals   (4) outermost electrons

12 What is the mass number of an atom which contains 21 electrons, 21 protons, and 24 neutrons?
   (1) 21   (2) 42   (3) 45   (4) 66

WAVE-MECHANICAL MODEL (ELECTRON CLOUD MODEL)

Although Bohr's model accounted for the lines of the hydrogen spectrum, it did not account for the spectra of heavier and more complicated atoms.

Electrons occupy orbitals that may differ in size, shape, or orientation in space. The term **orbital** refers to the average region of the most probable electron location. The orbital model differs from the Bohr model in that it does not represent electrons as moving in planetary orbits around the nucleus. Instead, it is defined so that no two electrons will have the same four (4) quantum numbers.

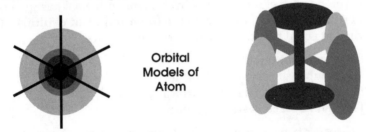

Orbital Models of Atom

Electrons in orbits near the nucleus are at lower energy levels than those in orbits more distant from the nucleus. When the electrons are in the lowest available energy levels, the atom is said to be in the "**ground state**."

When atoms absorb energy, electrons may shift to a higher energy level. At this higher energy level, the atom is said to be in an "**excited state**." The excited state is unstable, and the electrons fall back to lower ground state energy levels. In the process, they release energy equal to the energy difference of the two energy levels involved. This emitted energy can be used to identify the element.

13 Which is the electron configuration of an atom in the excited state?
   (1) $1s^2 2s^1$ (2) $1s^2 2s^2 2p^1$ (3) $1s^2 2s^2 2p^5$ (4) $1s^2 2s^2 2p^5 3s^1$

14 Which electron configuration represents an atom in an excited state?
  (1) $1s^22s^22p^63p^1$
  (3) $1s^22s^22p^63s^23p^2$
  (2) $1s^22s^22p^63s^23p^1$
  (4) $1s^22s^22p^63s^2$

15 Which electron configuration represents an atom in the excited state?
  (1) $1s^22s^1$ (2) $1s^22s^22p^4$ (3) $1s^22s^23s^1$ (4) $1s^22s^22p^63s^2$

16 Which is an electron configuration of a fluorine atom in an excited state?
  (1) $1s^22s^22p^4$ (2) $1s^22s^22p^5$ (3) $1s^22s^22p^43s^1$ (4) $1s^22s^22p^53s^1$

Spectral lines. When electrons in an atom in the excited state return to lower energy levels, the quanta of energy emitted is called **radiant energy**.

This radiant energy, made up of **quanta** (also called **photons**), has a wave characteristic with a specific frequency. Elements are identified by measuring the wavelength of the radiant energy being emitted. These waves are called spectral lines.

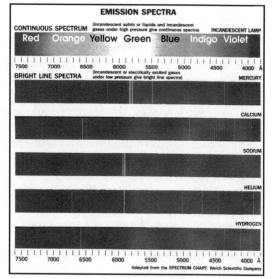

The study of spectral lines has provided much of the evidence regarding energy levels within the atom. This study is carried on with an instrument called the **spectroscope**, which investigates the wavelength of one type of radiant energy called **light**. A spectroscope separates light into specific bright line bands of color called a **spectrum**. Each element gives off a characteristic bright line spectra when investigated by a spectroscope and can therefore be identified by this method. Some examples of bright line spectral lines (measured in Å = **angstrom** is a unit of length equal to one hundred-millionth (10^{-8}) of a centimeter):

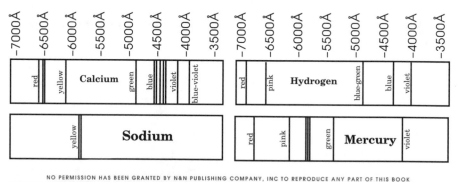

Directions: Use the following article to answer questions 17 through 19.

Article. In 1913, the Danish scientist, Niels Bohr used the concept of the atom proposed by Ernest Rutherford and the quantum theory proposed by Max Planck to develop the solar system model of the atom. For his work on atomic structure, Bohr was awarded the 1922 Nobel Prize in physics. His model is now obsolete. However, in 1913, this model was revolutionary, and led to the development of our modern atomic theory.

The Bohr model also helped to explain the spectral lines of hydrogen observed by the Swiss spectroscopist, Johann Balmer. Bohr envisioned electrons possessing discrete amounts of energy that correspond to the different energy levels found outside the nucleus of the atom. When they absorb energy, the electrons are promoted to higher levels of energy. This "excited" state is very unstable, and the electrons quickly drop back down to the lower level of energy from which they came. As they drop back down, photons of light that correspond to the different levels of energy are given off and produce the characteristic bright line spectrum for an element. Each element has its own characteristic bright line spectrum, because the atoms of each element have a unique number of electrons and protons.

17 Question: Describe one way the spectral lines observed by Balmer help to explain that each electron in an atom has its own distinct amount of energy.

18 Question: What evidence do scientists have that leads to the conclusion that electrons occupy different levels of energy in their positions outside the nucleus?

19 Question: Explain how an excited atom produces a bright line spectrum.

Directions: Identify the element for each of the bright line spectral line graphs in questions 20 through 22.

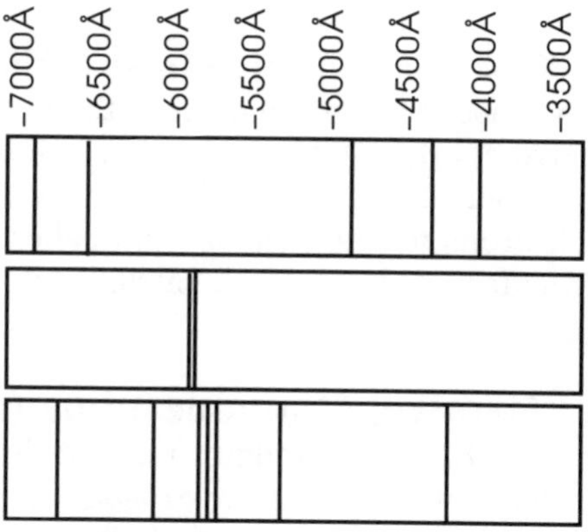

-7000Å -6500Å -6000Å -5500Å -5000Å -4500Å -4000Å -3500Å

20 Question: _____

21 Question: _____

22 Question: _____

F – VALENCE ELECTRON

The electrons in the outermost principal energy level of an atom are called the **valence electrons**. The chemical properties of an atom are related to the valence electrons. The term "**kernel**" is sometimes used to refer to the atom exclusive of the valence electrons. The kernel consists of the nucleus and all electrons except the valence electrons.

The valence electrons may be represented by Lewis **electron dot symbols** in which the kernel of the atom is represented by the letter symbol for the element and the valence electrons are represented by dots. For example, to the right is the electron dot diagram for a chlorine molecule (Cl_2).

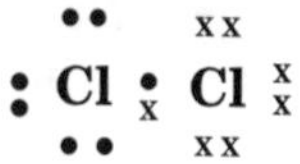

$$: Cl : Cl :$$

SKILLS 3.1 VIII *DRAW A LEWIS ELECTRON-DOT STRUCTURE OF AN ATOM.*

23 If X is the symbol of a noble gas atom in the ground state, its electron-dot symbol could be

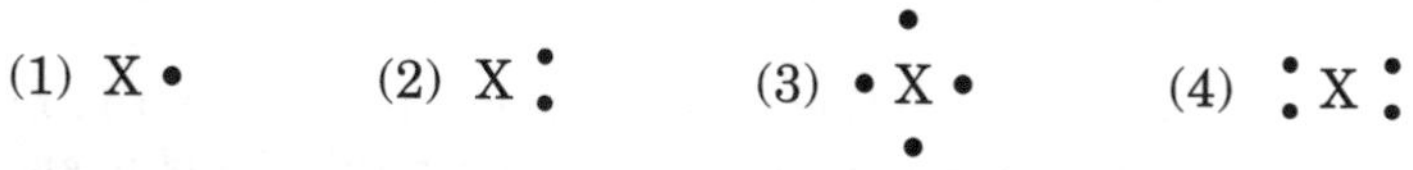

(1) X •   (2) X :   (3) • X •   (4) : X :

24 Which electron dot symbol could represent a noble gas?

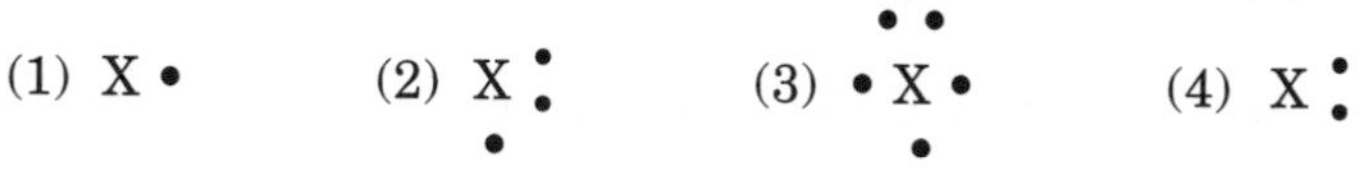

(1) X •   (2) X :   (3) • X •   (4) X :

25 Which is the correct electron dot symbol for an Aluminum atom in the ground state?

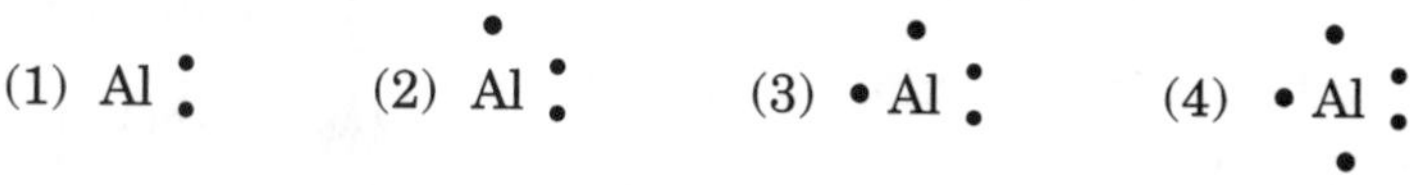

(1) Al :   (2) Al :   (3) • Al :   (4) • Al :

The chemical properties of an atom are dependent on the number of valence electrons available to react with other atoms and the strength of the **electrostatic force** which holds them to the nucleus.

As atoms increase in size, the amount of protons and electrons increase causing the nucleus to have greater mass and also a greater positive charge. With an increase in electrons the kernel holds a greater number of electron shells and the electrostatic attraction of the valence electrons to the nucleus diminishes. This allows the valence electrons to wander and be more chemically active.

ELECTRON CONFIGURATIONS (DISTRIBUTION OF ELECTRONS)

Electron configurations of the atoms in order of their atomic numbers starting with hydrogen can be built up by adding one electron at a time according to the following rules:

- No more than *two electrons* can be accommodated in any orbital. The two electrons in an orbital have *opposite spins*.

- The added electron is placed in the unfilled orbital of lowest energy.

- In a given sublevel, according to Hund's rule, a 2nd electron is not added to an orbital until each orbital in the sublevel contains one electron.

- No more than four orbitals are occupied in the outermost principal energy level of any atom except for palladium.

In an electron configuration, the number of electrons in a sublevel is shown by a superscript following the designation of the sublevel. For example:

Calcium is represented as: $1s^2\ 2s^2\ 2p^6\ 3s^2\ 3p^6\ 4s^2$ or $(Ar)\ 4s^2$

Sulfur is represented as: $1s^2\ 2s^2\ 2p^6\ 3s^2\ 3p^4$ or $(Ne)\ 3s^2\ 3p^4$

Missing in electron configuration (distribution) notation is the manner in which the electrons are distributed in the orbitals. This is shown with diagrams called orbital notation.

In each instance, an orbital is shown as either:

a an empty orbital with no electrons

b a half-filled orbital with one electron

c a full orbital with a maximum number of two electrons

Below, note the electron notation and orbital notation of a chlorine atom:

$$1s^2 \quad 2s^2 \quad 2p^6 \quad 3s^2 \quad 3p^5$$

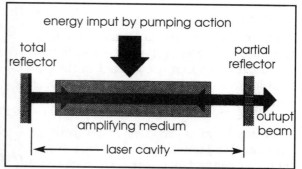

Atoms differ in the number of protons and neutrons in the nucleus and in the configuration (distribution) of electrons surrounding the nucleus.

SKILLS 3.1VII *DISTINGUISH BETWEEN VALENCE AND NON-VALENCE ELECTRONS GIVEN AN ELECTRON CONFIGURATION, E.G. 2-8-2.*

26 Which is the electron configuration of a neutral atom in the ground state with a total of six valence electrons?

(1) $1s^2\,2s^2\,2p^2$ (3) $1s^2\,2s^2\,2p^6$

(2) $1s^2\,2s^2\,2p^4$ (4) $1s^2\,2s^2\,2p^6\,3p^6$

27 The number of valence electrons in an atom with an electron configuration of $1s^2\,2s^2\,2p^6\,3s^2\,3p^4$ is

(1) 6   (2) 2   (3) 16   (4) 4

28 What is the total number of valence electrons in an atom of phosphorus in the ground state?

(1) 5   (2) 2   (3) 3   (4) 7

REAL WORLD CONNECTIONS

Lasers – Lasers make use of the wave effects of the electron and its ability to absorb and emit photons. Ruby is crystalline alumina (Al_2O_3) in which a small fraction of the Al^{3+} ions have been replaced by chromium ions (Cr^{3+}). It is the chromium ions that give rise to its red color and it is these ions that are irradiated with bright light from a xenon flashbulb. The stimulated electrons then proceed to build up and to emit photons in unison in what is called "stimulated emissions" giving those characteristics of a laser.

Flame tests – In the laboratory, as energy is applied to an element, the electrons are made "excited" and jump to a higher energy area. They then immediately return back to their ground state. When they return, they give off the energy they absorbed with an identifying wavelength of a specific color. The color can be used to identify the element. In the lab, this is done using a Bunsen burner as an energy source and salt solutions of various metals. By dipping a clean platinum wire into a salt solution of sodium, a yellow flame result. A solution of a potassium salt gives a violet color, and a solution of lithium gives a red or carmine color. In a lightbulb, this is done by using electricity as the energy source and stimulating a gas of an element in the glass vacuum tube.

Neon gas is an element which gives off three different colors. At about 6500 Angstroms, it gives off a red color. At about 6000 Angstroms, it give off a yellow color, and at about 5500 Angstroms, it gives off a green color.

Fireworks with their nitrate salts of lithium, sodium, and potassium perform the same exciting color display.

©PhotoDisc

Forensic analysis is an area in which identifying elements is crucial to a valid report on the presentation of evidence. Blood samples and other evidence are tested for the presence of certain elements.

Spectral analysis of stars is carried out with very sophisticated instruments to identify the proportion of hydrogen and helium and other gases that are present in the star in order to ascertain its age and other information.

When there is less fresh water draining into the Hudson River, the "salt front" [point of contact between salt water and fresh water], migrates up river from the Atlantic Ocean. The location of this boundary can be identified by Atomic Absorption Analysis (AAA). This process uses an instrument that vaporizes the solution and measures the intensity (brightness) of yellow light emitted from the excited sodium atoms. The process is used to determine the concentration of sodium in the solution.

ASSESSMENTS

PART A - MULTIPLE CHOICE

1 What is the atomic number of an element that has six protons and eight neutrons?
   (1) 6   (2) 2   (3) 8   (4) 14

2 Which statement about the mass of an electron is correct?
   (1) The mass of an electron is equal to the mass of a proton.
   (2) The mass of an electron is less than the mass of a proton.
   (3) The mass of an electron is equal to the mass of a neutron.
   (4) The mass of an electron is greater than the mass of a neutron.

3 What is the total number of protons and neutrons in an atom of $^{86}_{37}Rb$?
   (1) 37   (2) 49   (3) 86   (4) 123

4 What is the total number of valence electrons in an atom of boron in the ground state?
   (1) 1   (2) 7   (3) 3   (4) 5

5 Which electron configuration represents an atom in the excited state?
   (1) $1s^22s^22p^63s^2$ (3) $1s^22s^22p^6$
   (2) $1s^22s^22p^63s^1$ (4) $1s^22s^22p^53s^2$

6 What is the total number of electrons in an atom of an element with an atomic number of 18 and a mass number of 40?
   (1) 18   (2) 22   (3) 40   (4) 58

7 Which subatomic particle is found in the nucleus of all isotopes of hydrogen?
   (1) proton   (2) neutron   (3) electron   (4) positron

8 Which symbols represent atoms that are isotopes of each other?
   (1) ^{14}C and ^{14}N (3) ^{131}I and ^{131}I
   (2) ^{16}O and ^{18}O (4) ^{222}Rn and ^{222}Ra

9 Which diagram correctly represents a fluorine atom in an excited state?

   (1)   (3)

   (2)   (4)

10 Which orbital notation correctly represents the outermost principal energy level of a nitrogen atom in the ground state?

   (1)   (3)

   (2)   (4)

11 Which atom has an equal number of protons and neutrons?

   (1) $_1^1H$ (2) $_6^{12}C$ (3) $_9^{19}F$ (4) $_{19}^{39}K$

12 The atomic mass unit is defined as exactly one-twelfth of the mass of an atom of

   (1) $_6^{12}C$ (2) $_5^{11}B$ (3) $_{11}^{23}Na$ (4) $_{12}^{24}Mg$

13 What is the total number of nucleons (protons and neutrons) in an atom of Se?

   (1) 34   (2) 45   (3) 79   (4) 93

14 The atomic number of an atom is always equal to the total number of:

   (1) neutrons in the nucleus
   (2) protons in the nucleus
   (3) neutrons plus protons in the atom
   (4) protons plus electrons in the atom

15 Which of the following nuclei is an isotope of $\left(\begin{array}{c}10\ p\\11\ n\end{array}\right)$?

   (1) $\left(\begin{array}{c}10\ p\\9\ n\end{array}\right)$ (2) $\left(\begin{array}{c}11\ p\\10\ n\end{array}\right)$ (3) $\left(\begin{array}{c}9\ p\\11\ n\end{array}\right)$ (4) $\left(\begin{array}{c}11\ p\\12\ n\end{array}\right)$

16 Compared to an atom of $_6^{14}C$, an atom of $_6^{12}C$ has:

   (1) more protons   (3) more neutrons
   (2) fewer protons   (4) fewer neutrons

17 Which of the following atoms has the greatest nuclear charge?

   (1) N   (2) C   (3) H   (4) He

18 Isotopes of the same element must differ in their

   (1) atomic number   (3) number of electrons
   (2) mass number   (4) number of protons

19 An atom of potassium containing 23 neutrons has a mass number of

   (1) 19   (2) 20   (3) 23   (4) 42

20 Which particle has a negative charge?

   (1) neutron   (2) electron   (3) proton   (4) alpha particle

21 Which two particles have approximately the same mass?

   (1) neutron and electron   (3) proton and neutron
   (2) neutron and deuteron   (4) proton and electron

22 When an atom goes from the excited state to the ground state, the total energy of the atom

   (1) decreases   (2) increases   (3) remains the same

23 What is the maximum number of electrons that can occupy the second principal energy level?

   (1) 6   (2) 8   (3) 18   (4) 32

24 A neutral atom of an element has an electron configuration of 2-8-2. What is the total number of *p* electrons in this atom?

   (1) 6   (2) 2   (3) 10   (4) 12

25 Which principal energy level can hold a maximum of 18 electrons?
(1) 5   (2) 2   (3) 3   (4) 4

26 Which electron transition is accompanied by the emission of energy?
(1) $1s$ to $2s$ (2) $2s$ to $2p$ (3) $3p$ to $3s$ (4) $3p$ to $4p$

27 The total number of orbitals in the $4f$ sublevel is
(1) 1   (2) 5   (3) 3   (4) 7

28 The total number of d orbitals in the third principal energy level is
(1) 1   (2) 5   (3) 3   (4) 7

29 What is the total number of electrons in an atom with an atomic
number of 13 and a mass number of 27?
(1) 13   (2) 14   (3) 27   (4) 40

30 What is the maximum number of sublevels in the third principal
energy level?
(1) 1   (2) 2   (3) 3   (4) 4

31 What is the electron configuration for Be^{2+} ions?
(1) $1s^1$ (2) $1s^2$ (3) $1s^2\,2s^1$ (4) $1s^2\,2s^2$

32 What is the electron configuration of an O^{2-} in the ground state?
(1) 2-4   (2) 2-8   (3) 2-8-4   (4) 2-8-8

33 The number of completely filled orbitals in a fluorine atom in the
ground state is
(1) 5   (2) 6   (3) 9   (4) 4

34 Which orbital notation represents the outermost principal energy
level of a phosphorus atom in the ground state?

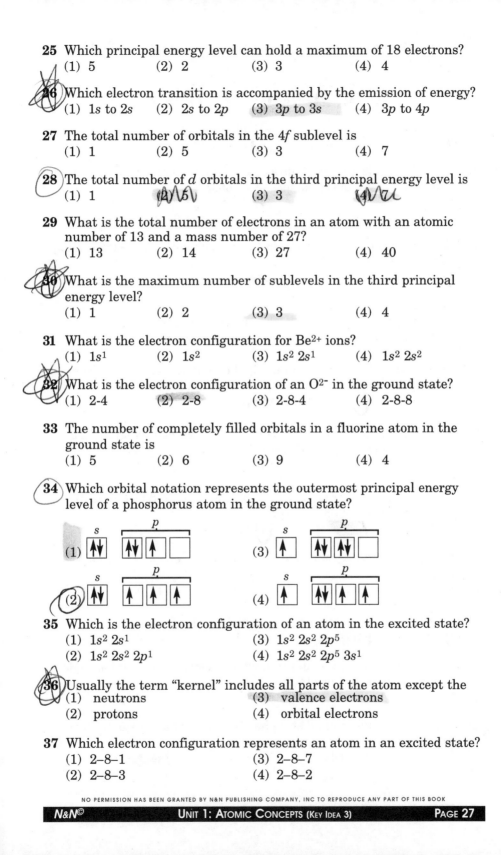

35 Which is the electron configuration of an atom in the excited state?
(1) $1s^2\,2s^1$ (3) $1s^2\,2s^2\,2p^5$
(2) $1s^2\,2s^2\,2p^1$ (4) $1s^2\,2s^2\,2p^5\,3s^1$

36 Usually the term "kernel" includes all parts of the atom except the
(1) neutrons   (3) valence electrons
(2) protons   (4) orbital electrons

37 Which electron configuration represents an atom in an excited state?
(1) 2–8–1   (3) 2–8–7
(2) 2–8–3   (4) 2–8–2

38 Which element forms the ion represented in the following orbital notation?

$$1s \quad 2s \quad \overline{2p} \quad 3s \quad \overline{3p}$$

| $\uparrow\downarrow$ | $\uparrow\downarrow$ | $\uparrow\downarrow$ $\uparrow\downarrow$ $\uparrow\downarrow$ | $\uparrow\downarrow$ | $\uparrow\downarrow$ $\uparrow\downarrow$ $\uparrow\downarrow$ |

(1) boron   (3) magnesium
(2) bromine   (4) potassium

39 Which is the electron configuration of a neutral atom in the ground state with a total of six valence electrons?
(1) $1s^2\,2s^2\,2p^2$ (3) $1s^2\,2s^2\,2p^6$
(2) $1s^2\,2s^2\,2p^4$ (4) $1s^2\,2s^2\,2p^6\,3s^2\,3p^6$

40 The number of valence electrons in an atom with an electron configuration of $1s^2\,2s^2\,2p^6\,3s^2\,3p^4$ is
(1) 6   (2) 2   (3) 16   (4) 4

41 Ca^{2+} differs from Ca in that the Ca^{2+} has
(1) more protons   (3) more electron
(2) fewer protons   (4) fewer electrons

42 What is the total number of principal energy levels that are completely filled in an atom of magnesium in the ground state?
(1) 1   (2) 2   (3) 3   (4) 4

43 What is the total number of occupied principal energy levels in a sodium atom in the ground state?
(1) 1   (2) 2   (3) 3   (4) 4

44 Which atom in the ground state has three unpaired electrons in its outermost principal energy level?
(1) Li   (2) B   (3) N   (4) Ne

45 Which atom in the ground state contains only one orbital that is partially occupied?
(1) Si   (2) Ne   (3) Ca   (4) Na

46 What is the total number of electrons in a Mg^{2+} ion?
(1) 10   (2) 2   (3) 12   (4) 24

47 In the ground state, the atoms of which element have an incomplete 3rd principal energy level?
(1) Zn   (2) Mn   (3) Kr   (4) Sr

48 Which atom in the ground state has five electrons in its outer level and ten electrons in its kernel?
(1) C   (2) Cl   (3) Si   (4) P

PART B - CONSTRUCTED-RESPONSE

Illustration A: Use the illustration below showing the electromagnetic spectrum and the corresponding energy levels to answer questions 1 and 2.

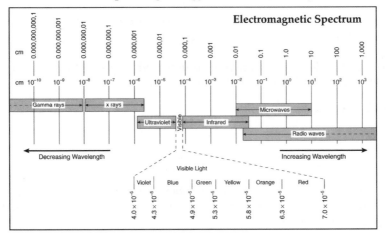

1 **Question**: Based upon the illustration above, identify the visible light color that has the greatest amount of energy. [1]

Red has the greatest number of energy.
(7.0×10⁻⁵)

2 **Question**: Describe how an electron can be promoted to a higher energy level than it normally occupies in the ground state. [1]

When an atom absorbs energy the electrons can shift to a higher level. But the electrons are unstable and can fall back down to a lower state again

Illustration B: Use the illustration of a Bohr Model at the right to answer questions 3 through 6.

Bohr Model: The first principal energy level contains two electrons, the second principal energy level contains eight electrons, and the third principal energy level contains one electron.

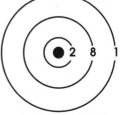

Bohr Model

3 **Question**: Identify the principal energy level that contains electrons which have the lowest amount of energy, and describe the shape of the atomic orbital(s) found in this principal energy level. [2]

The level 1 p principal energy level I has the lowest amount of energy. B/c it has only sublevel s that only has one orbital fitting only 2 e⁻

4 Question: Describe what happens when an electron becomes "excited." [1]

When an electron becomes excited it rises to the next energy level, where it is unstable and when the energy decreases the electron falls back to its natural level.

5 Question: Identify the element illustrated in the Bohr diagram based upon its electron configuration. [1]

The element is Na

6 Question: As the atom loses a valence electron, it will form a positive ion. Compare the size of the changed atom relative to the size of the original atom. [1]

The changed atom will be smaller than the original one.

PART C – EXTENDED CONSTRUCTED-RESPONSE

Article A: In 1911, Ernest Rutherford and his co-workers used positively charged alpha particles emitted from a radioactive substance to bombard a thin sheet of gold foil. Using fluorescent screens placed around the source, Rutherford was able to trace the path that the alpha particles took. To his surprise, most of the particles passed through the gold foil without being deflected. This led to his conclusion that the atom is mostly empty space. Some particles, however, bounced almost straight back, allowing Rutherford to conclude that each atom must contain a very small, dense core that is positively charged. He labeled this central portion of the atom the nucleus.

Henry Moseley was an English scientist who worked with Ernest Rutherford in the early part of the twentieth century. Moseley's experiments involved bombarding different metals with a beam of electrons. He noted that each different metal emitted X-rays of a characteristic frequency and that the heavier the element, the higher the frequency. He described this regular increase in frequency of the X-rays in terms of a regular increase of positive charge in the nuclei of the atoms. His experiments confirmed a hypothesis of Rutherford's that each atomic nucleus contains a unique number of positively charged particles (called protons) that we identify today as the atomic number.

1   **Question**: Explain why Rutherford concluded that the nucleus must be positively charged if it reflected the alpha particle straight backward. [1]

Alpha particles are positive so when the alpha particle was shot toward the nucleus + it reflected back he concluded the nucleus was positive b/c similiar charges do not attract each other.

2   **Question**: What lead Rutherford to conclude that the atom is mostly empty space? [1]

Rutherford concluded this because most of the particles went through the foil w/o it getting deflected back.

3   **Question**: Based upon the information in the article above, arrange the following elements in order of increasing X-ray frequency: Na, Li, Ca, Mg. [1]

Li, Na, Mg, Ca

Statement B: Elements are substances that are composed of atoms that have the same atomic number, or number of protons. In the unreacted (ground) state, each atom has the same number of electrons as protons. Atoms of an element that contain the same number of protons but a different number of neutrons are called isotopes of the element.

4   **Question**: Explain how the nuclei of C-12 and C-14 are different from one another and how they are similar to each other. [2]

5 **Question**: Even though they are isotopes, explain why the reactivity of C-14 is the same as that of C-12 in chemical reactions. [1]

Article C: In his "Uncertainty Principle," Heisenberg stated that it was impossible to determine the exact location and velocity of an electron at any given moment. As a result of his work, and that of others, the wave-mechanical model (electron-cloud model) of the atom was developed. This model differs from Bohr's solar system model in that the electrons are not only thought to occupy principle energy levels but sublevels of energy as well. These sublevels of energy contain orbitals that are defined as regions in space around the nucleus where the probability of finding an electron is the greatest. These regions of probability are mathematically generated and define the shape of the orbitals. The *s* orbital is spherical and the three *p* orbitals are dumbbell-shaped, oriented at 90° to each other.

Each atom in the ground state contains the same number of electrons as protons. Each electron has a **-1** charge and each proton has a **+1** charge which accounts for the fact that all atoms in the ground state have no overall charge.

By applying Wolfgang Pauli's Exclusion Principle which states that no more than two electrons of equal and opposite spin can occupy an orbital at any given time, and Hund's Rule which states that no orbital of a sublevel can contain two electrons until each orbital of that sublevel contains at least one electron in it, it is possible to determine the electron configuration of an atom.

6 **Question**: Using complete sentences, describe the shapes of the atomic orbitals found in the *s* and *p* sublevels of the atom. [1]

7 **Question**: Describe the orientation of the three *p* orbitals relative to each other. [1]

8 Question: Explain why each of the **2p** orbitals of a nitrogen atom in the ground state only has three half filled orbitals instead of one filled orbital, one half filled orbital, and one vacant orbital. [1]

9 Question: Explain why atoms in the ground state have no overall charge. [1]

10 Question: State one way that the modern model of the atom differs from Bohr's solar system model. [1]

11 Question: Describes what happens to an electron in terms of energy when it is promoted from a **3s** to a **3p** sublevel in the excited state. [1]

Article D: The many different organic molecules produced by carbon are made possible by the fact that carbon atoms are usually tetravalent. The electron configuration in the ground state only produces two half-filled orbitals in the **p** sublevel. However, due to **sp³** hybridization, carbon mixes the orbitals in its outer principal energy level and produces four half-filled orbitals, each with only one electron in it. These four half-filled orbitals are what make it possible for carbon always to form four bonds.

12 Question: Using the information supplied in the Periodic Table, state which outer principal energy level contains the valence electrons of carbon. [1]

Part D - Laboratory Skills

Identifying Metallic Ions Using a Flame Test

Background: The absorption of energy by an electron causes it to jump to a higher energy level. At this point, the atom is said to be in an excited state. When the electron returns to a ground state level it emits a photon of energy. If the frequency of the photon corresponds to those found in the visible spectrum, a specific colored light is seen. The identification of an element is made possible through the use of these spectral lines of color.

Normally the atoms of most elements require large amounts of energy to bring them to an excited state. However, some metallic ions can be excited by the flame of a Bunsen burner.

Procedure: It is possible to test for presence of some metallic elements by dipping a clean wire loop of platinum into solutions and then placing it into a Bunsen burner flame.

Observation: The color the wire exhibits can be used to identify the metallic ion present in the solution. Solutions of the salts of lithium (red), sodium (yellow), potassium (violet), calcium (yellowish-red), strontium (scarlet red), and barium (yellowish-green), may be used.

Application: After observing the various colors, a chemistry text or other reference can be used to make a chart, listing the wavelengths of each metallic element observed.

1   **Question**: After dipping a wire into a solution and heating it, a violet flame was produced. Which metallic ion was present?
    (1) calcium   (2) potassium (3) barium   (4) sodium

2   **Question**: A solution of sodium ions would give you what color in a flame test?
    (1) red   (2) blue   (3) yellow   (4) violet

3   **Question**: Use the Library and/or the *Handbook of Chemistry and Physics* to list a wavelength of each of the following:

    a   sodium

    b   potassium

    c   calcium

    d   strontium

    e   barium

UNIT 2
PERIODIC TABLE

KEY IDEA  **MATTER IS MADE UP OF PARTICLES WHOSE PROPERTIES DETERMINE THE OBSERVABLE CHARACTERISTICS OF MATTER AND ITS REACTIVITY**

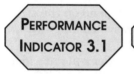

PERFORMANCE INDICATOR 3.1

PERFORMANCE INDICATOR
5.2 *EXPLAIN CHEMICAL BONDING IN TERMS OF THE BEHAVIOR OF ELECTRONS.*

UNIT 2 – MAJOR UNDERSTANDINGS

☆ 3.1y The placement or location of an element on the Periodic Table gives an indication of the physical and chemical properties of that element. The elements on the Periodic Table are arranged in order of increasing atomic number.

☆ 3.1g The number of protons in an atom (atomic number) identifies the element. The sum of the protons and neutrons in an atom (mass number) identifies an isotope. Common notations that represent isotopes include: ^{14}C, $^{14}_{6}C$, carbon-14, C-14.

☆ 3.1v Elements can be classified by their properties and located on the Periodic Table as metals,

nonmetals, metalloids (B, Si, Ge, As, Sb, Te), and noble gases.

☆ 3.1w Elements can be differentiated by physical properties. Physical properties of substances, such as density, conductivity, malleability, solubility, and hardness, differ among elements.

☆ 3.1x Elements can also be differentiated by chemical properties. Chemical properties describe how an element behaves during a chemical reaction.

☆ 3.1z For Groups 1, 2, and 13-18 on the *Periodic Table*, elements within the same group have the same number of valence electrons (helium is an

UNIT 2
PERIODIC TABLE

This unit is related to Key Idea 3 for the text and Performance Indicators 3.1 and 5.2 for the assessments.

INTRODUCTION

The *Periodic Table of the Elements* has passed through many stages of development, evolving into the present form. Observed regularity in the properties of elements led Dmitri Ivanovich Mendeleev and others to consider these regularities to be functions of the atomic mass. Henry Moseley established that properties of elements are periodic functions of the atomic number. This is known as the *Periodic Law*.

The atomic number is the basis of the arrangement in the present form of the *Periodic Table*. The properties of the elements depend on the structure of the atom and vary with the atomic number in a systematic way.

There are various notations by which **isotopes** of elements are identified. In the case of the element carbon, it should be written as $^{14}_{6}C$, ^{14}C, carbon-14, or C-14. The symbol C stands for carbon which has an atomic number of 6 because it has 6 protons in its nucleus. All that is needed is the mass number to identify which isotope of carbon is being studied. There are other isotopes of carbon such as $^{16}_{6}C$ or $^{15}_{6}C$. Note that the atomic number 6 is the same for all carbon isotopes. (For more information on atomic structure, see ☆ pg 12.)

UNIT 2 – MAJOR UNDERSTANDINGS (CONTINUED)

exception) and therefore similar chemical properties.

☆ 3.1aa The succession of elements within the same group demonstrates characteristic trends: differences in atomic radius, ionic radius, electronegativity, first ionization energy, metallic/nonmetallic properties.

☆ 3.1bb The succession of elements across the same period demonstrates characteristic trends: differences in atomic radius, ionic radius, electronegativity, first ionization energy, metallic/nonmetallic properties.

☆ 5.2f Some elements exist in two or more forms in the same phase. These forms differ in their molecular or crystal structure, and hence in their properties.

KEY

Atomic Mass → 12.0111 → Selected Oxidation States: -4, +2, +4

Symbol → **C**

Atomic Number → 6

Electron Configuration → 2-4

Relative atomic masses are based on $^{12}C = 12.000$

Note: Mass numbers in parentheses are mass numbers of the most stable or common isotope.

*The systematic names and symbols for elements of atomic numbers above 109 will be used until the approval of trivial names by IUPAC.

**Denotes the presence of (2-8-) for elements 72 and above

A – Development of Periodic Table

Metals

Metal atoms possess relatively low ionization energy (allowing them to lose electrons easily) and low electronegativity (restricting the gain of electrons). More than two-thirds of the elements are metals; the rest are metalloids (semimetals), nonmetals, and inert gases.

Metal atoms tend to lose electrons and to form positive ions when combining with other elements. Metallic properties are most pronounced in those elements on the lower left side of the *Periodic Table*. Metals usually possess the properties of high thermal and electrical conductivity, metallic luster, malleability (drawn into sheets), and ductility (drawn into wire). The metal mercury is a liquid at room temperature, but the other metals are all solids.

Alloys are mixtures of metals combined by heat or other means. This gives them improved characteristics such as stainless steel.

Nonmetals

Nonmetal atoms possess high ionization energies and have high electronegativity. Nonmetallic properties are most pronounced in those elements in the upper right corner of the *Periodic Table* (not including Group 18). Nonmetal atoms tend to gain electrons when in combination with metals or to share electrons when in combination with other elements. Nonmetals tend to be gases, molecular solids, or network solids. The exception is bromine which is a volatile (ability to change from liquid to gas) liquid at room temperature. Nonmetals in the solid phase tend to be brittle, to have low thermal and electrical conductivity, and to lack metallic luster. A good example is the element sulfur.

METALLOIDS (SEMIMETALS)

Note: *IUPAC* (*International Union of Pure and Applied Chemistry*) recommends that the term metalloid be abandoned because of language inconsistencies. Using the word semimetal may be better.

Metalloids (semimetals) are those elements that have some properties characteristic of metals and other properties characteristic of nonmetals. They are used in the manufacture of semiconductors. Examples of metalloids (semimetals) are boron, silicon, arsenic, tellurium, germanium, and antimony. They are solids.

SKILLS 3.1XIII *CLASSIFY ELEMENTS AS METALS, NONMETALS, METALLOIDS, OR NOBLE GASES BY THEIR PROPERTIES.*

1 Elements that have properties of both metals and nonmetals are called
   (1) alloys
   (2) metalloids (semimetals)
   (3) transition elements
   (4) isotopes

2 The properties of carbon are expected to be most similar to those of
   (1) boron   (3) silicon
   (2) aluminum   (4) phosphorus

3 Atoms of metallic elements tend to
   (1) gain electrons and form negative ions
   (2) gain electrons and form positive ions
   (3) lose electrons and form negative ions
   (4) lose electrons and form positive ions

4 Which element is considered malleable?
   (1) gold   (2) hydrogen   (3) sulfur   (4) radon

5 Which are two properties of most nonmetals?
   (1) low ionization energy and good electrical conductivity
   (2) high ionization energy and poor electrical conductivity
   (3) high ionization energy and good electrical conductivity
   (4) low ionization energy and poor electrical conductivity

SKILLS 3.1XVI *EXPLAIN THE PLACEMENT OF AN UNKNOWN ELEMENT IN THE PERIODIC TABLE BASED ON ITS PROPERTIES.*

A study of the *Periodic Table* leads to many generalizations (based on physical and chemical properties) which scientists have used to place elements into the *Periodic Table*. Some of these are listed here.

- Elements in the *Periodic Table* are arranged according to their atomic number.
- For any element in a period, the number of principal energy levels equals the period number.
- The atomic number increases from left to right and from top to bottom.
- Elements to the left of the heavy line running step-wise from boron to astitine are generally classed as metals. Elements to the right of the line are generally classed as nonmetals.
- Elements that border the heavy line running step-wise from boron to astatine exhibit intermediate properties and are known as metalloids, or semimetals (aluminum *can* exhibit different properties).
- Metals greatly outnumber nonmetals.
- Metals conduct heat better than nonmetals.
- Metals are better conductors of electricity than nonmetals (carbon is an exception).
- Hydrogen exhibits both metallic and nonmetallic properties and is often an exception to any generalization about its location on the Table.
- The boiling points of metals are generally higher than those of nonmetals.

Directions: Name at least three other generalizations that can be made concerning the placement of elements in the *Periodic Table*.

6 _____

_____

7 _____

_____

8 _____

_____

9 _____

_____

10 _____

_____

B - PROPERTIES OF ELEMENTS

Physical Properties readily discernible by the senses without changing the identity of the substance such as odor, color, hardness, shape (crystalline or amorphous), density, malleability, solubility, melting, and boiling points.

Chemical Properties are characteristics of substances that change due to activities such as burning, reacting with air, water, acids, bases, or combining other solvents. Their reactions are classed as active (vigorously), inactive (sluggishly), or inert (under ordinary conditions these do not react).

The horizontal rows of the *Periodic Table* are called **periods**, **rows**, or **series**. The properties of elements change systematically through a period. Period 2 examples include: Li, Be, B, C, N, O, F, and Ne. The vertical columns of the *Periodic Table* are called **groups** (**families**). The elements of a group exhibit similar or related properties. Group 17 examples include: F, Cl, Br, I, and At.

Most elements are solids at room temperature, except for the liquids Mercury and Bromine. Gases include Hydrogen, Oxygen, Nitrogen, Fluorine, Chlorine, and all of Group 18.

Some elements exist as **allotropes**. Allotropes are two or more forms of the same element that differ in their molecular or crystalline structure, and therefore in their properties. The classical example of an allotropic element is carbon. **Fullerenes** (**buckyballs**) of carbon are geometrically different than diamonds or graphite. Oxygen gas (O_2) has an allotrope called ozone (O_3).

SKILLS 3.1XVIII *DESCRIBE THE STATES OF THE ELEMENTS AT STP.*

Directions: Using your text or other resource, complete the table below describing the following characteristics of state for each element at STP (Standard Temperature and Pressure).

	Element	Color	State	Density	Solubility
11	Mercury	_____	_____	_____	_____
12	Sulfur	_____	_____	_____	_____
13	Chlorine	_____	_____	_____	_____
14	Silicon	_____	_____	_____	_____
15	Iodine	_____	_____	_____	_____
16	Bromine	_____	_____	_____	_____
17	Graphite	_____	_____	_____	_____

ATOMIC RADIUS

The radius of an atom is the closest distance to which one atom can approach another. Since each atom in a molecule or crystal is affected by the presence of other atoms, the radius of an atom will vary under certain specified circumstances.

The radius of a single atom cannot be measured easily because the electron probability distribution will not allow a single distance measurement. However, measurements can be made using large numbers of the same atoms (in molecules and crystals). This results in the atomic radius being a property of the combined atoms.

For example, the radius of adjacent atoms within the same molecule is defined as one-half the distance between the nuclei. However, in adjacent atoms in different but adjoining molecules, the radius will be a different distance. Also, different values will be measured when the types of movements that the atoms have attained are characterized as solid, liquid, or gas.

The atomic radius is very useful in determining density, solubility, melting point, and acid strength; therefore, it is considered a periodic property. Valid comparisons of properties can be made, if the atomic radius is specified as Covalent Radius, van der Waals Radius, or Atomic Radius in metals. High school chemistry problems should be solved using the covalent radius method unless otherwise specified.

Covalent Radius is the effective distance from the center of the nucleus to the outer valence shell of that atom in a typical covalent or coordinate bond.

Van der Waals Radius is half the internuclear distance or radius of closest approach of an atom with another atom with which it forms no bond.

Atomic Radius in metals is half the internuclear distance or radius in a crystalline metal.

The relationship between atomic radius and atomic number can be interpreted in terms of the arrangement of electrons in the orbitals of atoms and in terms of nuclear charge. Within a single period of the Periodic Table, the atomic radius generally decreases as the atomic number increases. Within any one period, the electrons in the outer orbitals are arranged around a **kernel** (core) containing the same number of filled levels.

As one proceeds from left to right in the period, the increase in nuclear charge – due to the increasing number of protons – pulls the electrons more tightly around the nucleus. This increased attraction more than balances the repulsion between the added electron and other electrons; therefore, the atomic radius is reduced.

The members of any group in the *Periodic Table* generally show an increase in atomic radius with an increase in the atomic number.

For a group of elements, the atoms of each successive member have a larger kernel containing more filled levels. Therefore, the electrons in the unfilled outer orbitals are farther from the nucleus. This results in an increase in atomic radius as the atomic number increases among the elements in a group.

IONIC RADIUS

A loss or gain of electrons by an atom causes a corresponding change in size.

*   Metal atoms lose one or more electrons when they form ions. Ionic radii of metals are smaller than the corresponding atomic radii.

*   Nonmetal atoms gain one or more electrons when they form ions. Ionic radii of nonmetals are larger than the corresponding atomic radii. Atomic and ionic radii are usually measured in Angstrom (Å) units ($1Å = 1 \times 10^{-10}$ meter).

ELECTRONEGATIVITY

Electronegativity is a measure of the ability of an atom to attract the electrons that form a bond between it and another atom. The values designated are based on an arbitrary scale on which fluorine, the most electronegative element, is assigned a value of 4.0.

Keep in mind that this electronegativity value does *not* necessarily measure the reactivity of the element. However, the scale can be used to predict the type of intramolecular (attractive forces inside the molecule) bond formed.

The **ionic** or **covalent** character of a bond can be approximated from the differences in electronegativity of the resulting species. Electronegativity differences of 1.7 or more indicate a bond that is predominately ionic in character. Differences of less than 1.7 indicate that the bond is predominately covalent. Some exceptions to this may be found. (For example, the metal hydrides, with an electronegativity difference of less than 1.7, are predominately ionic.)

IONIZATION ENERGY

Ionization energy is the amount of energy required to remove the most loosely bound electron from an atom in the gaseous phase. The *Reference Tables for Physical Setting: Chemistry* list the ionization energy in kilojoules./mole required for the removal of the first (outermost) electron. The second ionization energy refers to the removal of the second most loosely bound electron. Each successive ionization energy is greater than the previous one.

A KEY TO THE *PERIODIC TABLE*

When referring to any reproduction of the *Periodic Table of Elements*, the first item the student should look at is the key. The key of the *Periodic Table* is illustrated below.

KEY

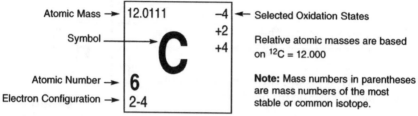

Atomic Mass → 12.0111   −4 ← Selected Oxidation States
                         +2
Symbol → **C**   +4   Relative atomic masses are based
                               on $^{12}C = 12.000$

Atomic Number → **6**   **Note:** Mass numbers in parentheses
Electron Configuration → 2-4   are mass numbers of the most
                               stable or common isotope.

C – CHEMISTRY OF A GROUP

The elements in the *Periodic Table* are divided into **orbital blocks *s*, *p*, *d*,** and *f* [☆ pg 16] and are further divided into **Groups 1** through **18**.

 REAL WORLD CONNECTIONS

The chemical properties of the elements in each group are related. Similarities in chemical properties within a group are associated with the similarity in the number of valence electrons.

Related chemical properties are illustrated by the similarity in the type of compound formed by the members of a group. For example, the elements in **Group 1** form chlorides having the general formula **MCl**, where **M** represents any member of the group. Elements in **Group 2** form chlorides having the general formula MCl_2. In general, the properties of elements in a group change progressively as the atomic number increases.

Properties of the members of the *s* and *p* orbital blocks [☆ pg 16] depend on the following

a) As one moves down a group, a new, fully occupied shell is added, giving the atom a larger atomic radius.

b) These newly occupied shells allow the "kernel" (all the occupied shells except the valence shell) to enlarge. The positive nuclear charge which holds the valence electrons must penetrate a "**screening**" or "**shielding effect**" caused by the electrons in the inner shells. This, coupled with the increased distance of the valence electron(s) from the nucleus, causes the nuclear attraction to diminish. Generally, it can be stated that the ionization energy of the valence electrons decreases as one proceeds down a group.

Exceptions in the properties of elements within a group do occur. For example, in Group 13, boron does not form an ion as do other members of the group. These anomalies occur most frequently among the elements in Period 2 because of the relative closeness of the valence electrons to the nucleus and the somewhat small screening or shielding effect of the two electrons in the 1s sublevel.

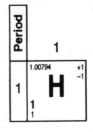

c) Going down a group, the electronegativity of the element generally decreases.

d) Going down a group, the elements tend to have more metallic properties.

Note: The relative tendency of the atoms to form compounds (sometimes called the reactivity of the element, see *Reference Table J*, pg 328) cannot be predicted from the electronegativity of the atom, but should be found from the *Table of Standard Electrode Potentials* [☆ pg 229].

GROUPS 1 AND 2

Properties of the elements in Groups 1 and 2 (*S-orbital block* [☆ pg 16]) – include

a) Groups 1 and 2 include the most reactive metals.

b) Elements in **Group 1** are called the **alkali metals**. *Note: Hydrogen is not an alkali metal.*

c) Elements in **Group 2** are called the **alkaline earth metals**.

d) Because of their reactivity, Groups 1 and 2 elements occur in nature only in compounds.

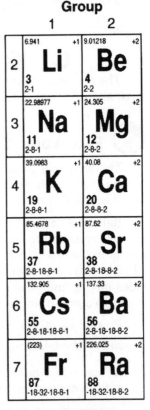

e) The elements in both groups have relatively low ionization energy and electronegativity. Therefore, they lose electrons readily to form ionic compounds that are somewhat stable.

f) Generally, the reactivity within both groups usually increase with an increase in atomic number. Exceptions to this occur in Group 1. The anomaly of lithium is due to the small size of the lithium atom and ion.

g) In the same period, each Group 1 metal is more active than the corresponding Group 2 metal.

h) The elements in both groups are usually reduced to their free state by the **electrolysis** of their fused compounds.

GROUPS 13 THROUGH 18

Properties of the elements in **Group 13** (*p*-orbital block [☆ pg 16] include:

a) All members have oxidation states of +3.

b) Boron is the only Group 13 element that has nonmetallic properties and is classified as a metalloid (semimetal).

c) Aluminum is the best known element of Group 13. It is a shiny easily workable, non-corroding metal.

d) Gallium, indium, and thallium are lustrous moderately reactive metals.

Properties of the elements in **Group 14** include:

a) The Group 14 elements progress from carbon (nonmetallic) to silicon and germanium (metalloids, semimetals) to tin and lead (metals). They have the oxidation states of +2, +4, and -4.

b) Carbon exists in **allotropic forms**, such as graphite, diamond, and buckyballs.

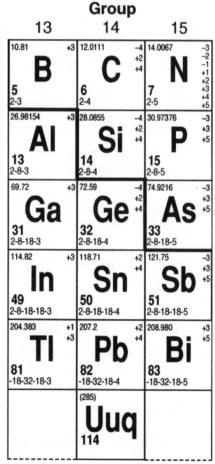

c) Silicon is a dull solid and the second most abundant element in the Earth's crust.

d) Germanium is used as a semiconductor in transistors.

e) Tin and lead are relatively inert metals.

Properties of the elements in **Group 15** include:

a) The elements in Group 15 show a marked progression from non-metallic to metallic properties with increasing atomic number.

b) Nitrogen and phosphorus are typical nonmetals; arsenic is classified as a metalloid (semimetal); bismuth is metallic in both appearance and properties.

c) The element nitrogen is relatively inactive at room temperature.

d) In general, the reactivity of nonmetals in the same group decreases with increasing atomic number.

e) Nitrogen exists as a diatomic molecule with a triple bond between the two atoms. The high energy required to break a triple bond (Example: $N \equiv N$) explains the relative inactivity of nitrogen.

f) Nitrogen compounds are essential constituents of all living matter (example: animal and plant proteins).

g) Generally, nitrogen compounds are relatively unstable.

h) The element phosphorus is more reactive than nitrogen at room temperature because nitrogen has a strong triple bond.

i) Phosphorus does not exist as a diatomic molecule at room temperature but exists as a tetratomic molecule, P_4.

j) Phosphorus compounds are essential constituents of all living matter.

Properties of the elements in **Group 16** include:

a) The elements in Group 16 show a marked progression from nonmetallic to metallic properties with an increase in atomic number.

b) Oxygen and sulfur are typical nonmetals; selenium and tellurium are classified as a metalloid (semimetal); polonium shows metallic properties.

Group 16

15.9994	−2
O	
8	
2-6	

32.06	−2
	+4
S	+6
16	
2-8-6	

78.96	−2
	+4
Se	+6
34	
2-8-18-6	

127.60	−2
	+4
Te	+6
52	
2-8-18-18-6	

(209)	+2
	+4
Po	
84	
-18-32-18-6	

(289)	
Uuh	
116	

c) The element oxygen is an active nonmetal.

d) Oxygen forms compounds with most elements. The existence of oxygen in its free state, in spite of its high reactivity, is explained by the continuous production of oxygen by plants during photosynthesis. Because of its high electronegativity, oxygen in compounds always shows a negative oxidation state unless combined with fluorine.

e) Sulfur is less reactive than oxygen.

f) Sulfur in compounds shows both $\overset{+1\ -2}{H_2S}$ and $\overset{+1\ +6\ -2}{H_2SO_4}$ negative and positive oxidation states.

g) Examples of elements, in Group 16, having allotropic forms are oxygen and sulfur (i.e. ozone O_3 and rhombic sulfur S_8).

h) Selenium and tellurium are rare elements.

i) Selenium and tellurium show negative oxidation states when combined with hydrogen. In most other compounds, they show positive oxidation states.

j) Polonium is a radioactive element that emits alpha particles. Polonium is a degradation product of uranium.

Group 17

Properties of elements in **Group 17** include:

a) The elements in Group 17 are typical nonmetals.

b) Group 17 is known as the **halogen group**.

c) Although the metallic character increases with increasing atomic number, none of the elements in the group is a metal. (Astatine is radioactive with a short half-life. It has not been found in nature, and its properties are not well known.)

d) The elements in Group 17 have relatively high electronegativity and high ionization energy as shown in *Reference Table S*.

e) **Fluorine** has the highest electronegativity of any element and in compounds can show only a negative oxidation state.

f) The other elements of the group may exhibit positive oxidation states in combination with more electronegative elements (for example, ClO_2^{-2}). The ease with which positive oxidation states of the halogens are formed increases with increasing atomic number.

g) The physical form of the free element at room temperature varies with increasing atomic number. At room temperature, fluorine and chlorine are gases, bromine is a liquid, and iodine a solid. Group 17 is the only group that contains all three phases of matter.

h) The change in physical form as the atomic radius increases is due to an increase in the number of van der Waals forces.

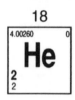

i) The elements are usually prepared from the corresponding halide ion by removing one of the electrons from the ion.

j) Because of their high reactivity, the halogens occur in nature only in compounds. Since fluorine is the most electronegative element, there is no chemical oxidizing agent that can oxidize the fluoride ion to fluorine. Fluorine is prepared by the electrolysis of its fused compounds. Chlorine, bromine, and iodine can be prepared by various chemical methods.

Properties of the elements in **Group 18** include:

a) Group 18 elements are **monatomic gases**. The atoms of these elements have complete outer shells, which result in an electron configuration of s^2p^6, and is a stable configuration. Therefore, they possess the highest *first ionization energies* in their Periods.

b) Group 18 elements are referred to by a variety of terms including **rare gases**, **"inert" gases**, and **noble gases**.

c) The term "inert" is no longer strictly applicable to this group, since it is possible to form compounds of krypton, xenon, and radon with fluorine and oxygen.

d) However, the term inert is still in general use and the electron configuration is quite generally referred to as the "inert gas structure."

Note: Helium is an exception in Group 18 with no *p* in its electron configuration.

SKILLS 3.1XV *DETERMINE THE GROUP OF AN ELEMENT, GIVEN THE CHEMICAL FORMULA OF A COMPOUND, E.G.,* XCl *or* XCl_2.

Directions: For the following list of six compounds, determine the group of an element **X**.

18 XO _____

19 NX _____

20 N_2X _____

21 XBr _____

22 KX _____

23 CaX_2 _____

SKILLS 3.1XIV *COMPARE AND CONTRAST PROPERTIES OF ELEMENTS WITHIN A GROUP OR PERIOD FOR GROUPS* 1, 2, 13 - 18 *ON THE PERIODIC TABLE.*

24 The Group 2 element having the largest atomic radius is found in Period
(1) 1   (2) 2   (3) 6   (4) 7

25 As the elements in Group 1 are considered in order of increasing atomic number, the atomic radius of each successive element increases. This is primarily due to an increase in the number of
(1) neutrons in nucleus   (3) electrons in outermost shell
(2) unpaired electrons   (4) principal energy levels

26 Given the same conditions, which of the following Group 17 elements has the least tendency to gain electrons?
(1) fluorine   (2) iodine   (3) bromine   (4) chlorine

27 Which of the following Group 17 elements has the highest melting point?
(1) fluorine   (2) chlorine   (3) bromine   (4) iodine

28 Alkali metals, alkaline earth metals, and halogens are elements found respectively in Groups
(1) 1, 2, and 18   (3) 1, 2, and 14
(2) 2, 13, and 18   (4) 1, 2, and 17

29 Which element in Group 16 has no stable isotopes?
(1) O   (2) S   (3) Po   (4) Te

30 In which group do the elements usually form oxides which have the general formula XO_2?
(1) 1   (2) 2   (3) 13   (4) 14

31 Which group contains the most active metals?
(1) 1   (2) 11   (3) 17   (4) 7

32 In which group do the elements usually form chlorides which have the general formula MCl_2?
(1) 1   (2) 2   (3) 17   (4) 18

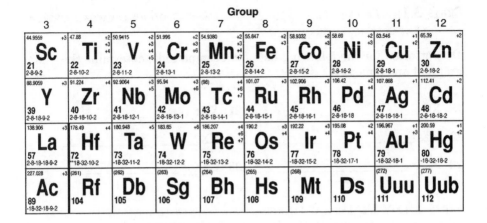

3	4	5	6	7	8	9	10	11	12
44.9559 +3 **Sc** 21 2-8-9-2	47.88 +2 +3 +4 **Ti** 22 2-8-10-2	50.9415 +2 +3 +4 +5 **V** 23 2-8-11-2	51.996 +2 +3 +6 **Cr** 24 2-8-13-1	54.9380 +2 +3 +4 +7 **Mn** 25 2-8-13-2	55.847 +2 +3 **Fe** 26 2-8-14-2	58.9332 +2 +3 **Co** 27 2-8-15-2	58.69 +2 +3 **Ni** 28 2-8-16-2	63.546 +1 +2 **Cu** 29 2-8-18-1	65.39 +2 **Zn** 30 2-8-18-2
88.9059 +3 **Y** 39 2-8-18-9-2	91.224 +4 **Zr** 40 2-8-18-10-2	92.9064 +3 +5 **Nb** 41 2-8-18-12-1	95.94 +3 +6 **Mo** 42 2-8-18-13-1	(98) +4 +6 +7 **Tc** 43 2-8-18-14-1	101.07 +3 **Ru** 44 2-8-18-15-1	102.906 +3 **Rh** 45 2-8-18-16-1	106.42 +2 +4 **Pd** 46 2-8-18-18	107.868 +1 **Ag** 47 2-8-18-18-1	112.41 +2 **Cd** 48 2-8-18-18-2
138.906 +3 **La** 57 2-8-18-18-9-2	178.49 +4 **Hf** 72 -18-32-10-2	180.948 +5 **Ta** 73 -18-32-11-2	183.85 +6 **W** 74 -18-32-12-2	186.207 +4 +6 +7 **Re** 75 -18-32-13-2	190.2 +3 +4 **Os** 76 -18-32-14-2	192.22 +3 **Ir** 77 -18-32-15-2	195.08 +2 +4 **Pt** 78 -18-32-17-1	196.967 +1 +3 **Au** 79 -18-32-18-1	200.59 +1 +2 **Hg** 80 -18-32-18-2
227.028 +3 **Ac** 89 -18-32-18-9-2	(261) **Rf** 104	(262) **Db** 105	(263) **Sg** 106	(264) **Bh** 107	(265) **Hs** 108	(268) **Mt** 109	(272) **Ds** 110	(272) **Uuu** 111	(277) **Uub** 112

TRANSITION ELEMENTS

A transition element is an element whose atom has an incomplete
d subshell or which gives rise to a **cation** or cations with an incomplete
d subshell. Properties of the elements in this group include:

a) Transition elements are those elements in which electrons from the
two outermost sublevels may be involved in a chemical reaction.
Because of this, these elements generally exhibit multiple positive
oxidation states.

b) The transition elements are found in *d*–orbital block [☆ pg 16],
Groups 3 through 11 of the *Periodic Table*.

c) The ions of transition elements usually appear colored, both in solid
compounds and in solution.

D – CHEMISTRY OF A PERIOD

A study of the orbital blocks *s* and *p* [☆ pg 16] elements in a period,
from left to right, leads to certain generalizations. In each period, as the
atomic number increases:

a) The radius of the atom generally decreases.

b) The ionization energy of the element generally increases.

c) The electronegativity of the element generally increases.

d) The elements generally change from very active metals, to less active
nonmetals, and, finally, to an "inert" monatomic gas molecule.

e) There is a transition from positive to negative oxidation states.
Elements near the center of the period may exhibit both positive and
negative oxidation states.

f) The metallic characteristics of the **s** and **p** orbital blocks [☆ pg 16] elements decrease.

g) The "rare earth" elements are found in the Lanthanoid Series and have atomic numbers 57 through 71.

E – NAMING ELEMENTS
WITH ATOMIC NUMBERS GREATER THAN 100

As of August 30, 1997, IUPAC (International Union of Pure Applied Chemistry) adopted nomenclature for the short-lived Transfermium elements 101 through 109:

Element	Name	Symbol	Element	Name	Symbol
101	Mendelevium	Md	106	Seaborgium	Sg
102	Nobelium	No	107	Bohrium	Bh
103	Lawrencium	Lr	108	Hassium	Hs
104	Rutherfordium	Rf	109	Meitnerium	Mt
105	Dubnium	Db	110*	Darmstadium	Ds

*IUPAC approved 08/16/03

 REAL WORLD CONNECTIONS

Use of different elements (e.g. use of semiconductors in solid state electronics and computer technology) – Metals are used in the construction industry because they form materials which are strong and yet light in weight such as the combination of magnesium and aluminum's molten sodium is used in nuclear reactors as a heat-transfer fluid. The transitional metals are used as semiconductors and as coloring agents. The non-metals of Group 17 are used in insecticides, water purification, and photography.

Alloys as superconductors – Many superconductor materials belong to the family of ceramic oxide whose empirical formula is $YBa_2Cu_3O_X$. Can you name the different elements in the formula?

OXYGEN V. OZONE

Oxygen (O_2) is a linear molecule with two atoms of oxygen forming a bond angle of 180°. It is an odorless, colorless, tasteless at STP. Because it is slightly more dense than air, it is not dissipated into the atmosphere and remains a life-sustaining factor on Earth's surface. It can be liquefied and also solidified at the correct temperature and pressure. Chemically, it forms oxides, peroxides, superoxides depending on its oxidation state.

Ozone (O_3) is a bent molecule whose three oxygen atoms form a bond angle of 117°. At STP, ozone is a blue gas with a very pungent odor and is poisonous (in the lower atmosphere). Its formation requires a two step process: first, energy is applied to an oxygen molecule and it breaks to form two free atoms of oxygen, which then react with two other oxygen molecules to reproduce two molecules of ozone. In the upper atmosphere, ozone molecules shield Earth from harmful, cancer causing ultraviolet rays.

ALLOTROPES OF CARBON

Coal is an uncrystallized form (amorphous) composed of carbon (at least 50%), some moisture, volatile substance, and incombustible substances (such as ash). It is used in the manufacture of natural gas.

Graphite is a layered form of carbon in which the carbon atoms are connected to each other by three bonds and are resonance single and double covalent bond structure. The fourth carbon bond is located in an orbital between the layers with weak London dispersion forces which allow the layers to slip along one another. This accounts for the greasy feel of graphite, which can be used as a lubricant. The bonds (in layers) are strong covalent bonds from which carbon fiber is made. Each carbon atom layer contains mobile electrons, allowing graphite to be used as a conductor of electricity.

Diamond has covalent, tightly bonded carbon atoms in a tetrahedral structure which gives the diamond its reputation of being the hardest material known. It has the highest density of all carbon substances. The valence electrons are all occupied forming the covalent bonds so they do not become mobile, making diamond poor electrical conductors.

Buckminsterfullerene is a relatively new class of spherically shaped carbon atoms. It consists of 60 carbon atoms in a truncated icosahedron shape that looks like a soccer ball and is highly electronegative. It is quite different from graphite and diamond. When exposed to strong ultraviolet light (as from lasers), these "buckyballs" **polymerize**, forming bonds between adjoining balls. Little is known about this form of carbon molecule, but it offers exciting promises.

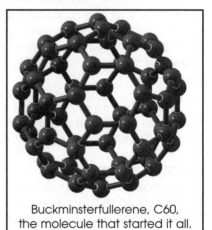

Buckminsterfullerene, C60, the molecule that started it all.

A variation of buckyballs are long hollow carbon tubes, called "bucky tubes." These tubes have been successfully introduced into scanning and tunneling microscopy as "sharp needles" for probing surfaces.

blue = right

PERFORMANCE INDICATOR 3.1
ASSESSMENTS

PART A - MULTIPLE CHOICE

1 Which of the following period 4 elements has the most metallic characteristics?
   (1) Ca   (2) Ge   (3) As   (4) Br

2 In general, atoms of transition elements in Period 5 are characterized by an incomplete
   (1) **3p** subshell   (3) **3d** subshell
   (2) **4p** subshell   (4) **4d** subshell

3 The elements in Period 3 all contain the same number of
   (1) protons   (3) valence electrons
   (2) neutrons   (4) occupied principal energy levels

4 Which element attains the structure of a noble gas when it becomes a 1+ ion?
   (1) K   (2) Ca   (3) F   (4) Ne

5 Which Group 15 element exists as a diatomic molecule at STP?
   (1) phosphorus   (3) bismuth
   (2) nitrogen   (4) arsenic

6 Which halogen is a solid at STP?
   (1) Br_2 (2) F_2 (3) Cl_2 (4) I_2

7 An element has a first ionization energy of 1,314 kilojoules/mole and an electronegativity of 3.4. It is classified as a
   (1) metal   (3) metalloid
   (2) nonmetal   (4) halogen

8 At which location in the *Periodic Table* would the most active metallic element be found?
   (1) in Group 1 at the top   (3) in Group 17 at the top
   (2) in Group 1 at the bottom   (4) in Group 17 at the bottom

9 Which reactant is most likely to have **d** electrons involved in a chemical reaction?
   (1) a halogen   (3) a transition element
   (2) a noble gas   (4) an alkali metal

10 Elements in a given period of the *Periodic Table* contain the same number of
   (1) protons in the nucleus   (3) electrons in the outermost level
   (2) neutrons in the nucleus   (4) occupied principal energy levels

11 Which compound forms a colored aqueous solution?
   (1) $CaCl_2$ (2) $CrCl_3$ (3) NaOH   (4) KBr

12 How does the size of a barium ion compare to the size of a barium atom?
(1) The ion is smaller because it has fewer electrons.
(2) The ion is smaller because it has more electrons.
(3) The ion is larger because it has fewer electrons.
(4) The ion is larger because it has more electrons.

13 Which element in Group 1 has the greatest tendency to lose an electron?
(1) cesium   (2) rubidium   (3) potassium   (4) sodium

14 The table at the right shows some properties of elements A, B, C, and D.

Which element is most likely a nonmetal?
(1) A
(2) B
(3) C
(4) D

Element	Ionization Energy	Electro-negativity	Conductivity of Heat and Electricity
A	low	low	low
B	low	low	high
C	high	high	low
D	high	high	high

15 Which metal is most likely obtained by the electrolysis of its fused salt?
(1) Au   (2) Ag   (3) Li   (4) Am

16 A diatomic element with a high first ionization energy would most likely be a
(1) nonmetal with a high electronegativity
(2) nonmetal with a low electronegativity
(3) metal with a high electronegativity
(4) metal with a low electronegativity

17 As the elements in Period 3 are considered from left to right, they tend to
(1) lose electrons more readily and increase in metallic character
(2) lose electrons more readily and increase in nonmetallic character
(3) gain electrons more readily and increase in metallic character
(4) gain electrons more readily and increase in nonmetallic character

18 Which element's ionic radius is smaller than its atomic radius?
(1) neon   (2) nitrogen   (3) sodium   (4) sulfur

19 Which is the most active nonmetal in the *Periodic Table of the Elements*?
(1) Na   (2) F   (3) I   (4) Cl

20 Which of the following particles has the smallest radius?
(1) Na^0 (2) K^0 (3) Na^+ (4) K^+

21 In a chemical reaction, which element forms an ion with a smaller radius than its atom?
(1) Mg   (2) Br   (3) O   (4) Ne

22 Which element in Group 15 has the most metallic character?
(1) nitrogen   (3) arsenic
(2) bismuth   (4) phosphorus

23 Which group contains elements in the solid, liquid, and gas phases at 25°C and 1 atm.
(1) 16   (2) 2   (3) 17   (4) 18

24 Which is the symbol of an alkaline earth element?
(1) Na   (2) Ne   (3) Ca   (4) Ce

25 What is the total number of electrons found in the valence shell of a halogen in the ground state?
(1) 1   (2) 2   (3) 7   (4) 8

26 The element found in Group 13 and in Period 2 is
(1) Be   (2) Mg   (3) B   (4) Al

27 An element that is liquid at STP is in Group
(1) 1   (2) 2   (3) 11   (4) 12

28 Beryllium is classified as
(1) an alkaline earth metal   (3) a transition element
(2) an alkali metal   (4) a noble gas

29 The reactivity of the metals in Groups 1 and 2 generally increases with
(1) increased ionization energy
(2) increased atomic radius
(3) decreased nuclear charge
(4) decreased mass

30 Which group contains the atom with the highest first ionization energy?
(1) 1   (2) 2   (3) 17   (4) 18

31 The pair of elements with the most similar chemical properties are
(1) Mg and S   (3) Mg and Ca
(2) Ca and Br   (4) S and Ar

32 Which element is a member of the halogen group?
(1) K   (2) B   (3) I   (4) S

33 Which group contains elements with a total of four electrons in the outermost principal energy level?
(1) 1   (2) 18   (3) 16   (4) 14

34 Which element exhibits a crystalline structure at STP?
(1) fluorine   (2) chlorine   (3) bromine   (4) iodine

35 Which is an alkaline earth metal?
(1) Mg   (2) Zn   (3) Li   (4) Pb

36 The S^{2-} ion differs from the S^0 atom in that the S^{2-} ion has a
   (1) smaller radius, fewer electrons
   (2) smaller radius, more electrons
   (3) larger radius, fewer electrons
   (4) larger radius, more electrons

37 A reason why fluorine has a higher ionization energy than oxygen is that fluorine has a
   (1) smaller nuclear charge   (3) smaller number of electrons
   (2) larger nuclear charge   (4) larger number of neutrons

PART B - CONSTRUCTED-RESPONSE

Directions: Refer to the *Periodic Table* (on page 37, also *Reference Table S*) showing the elements labeled with their atomic number.

1 **Question**: Describe how the atomic radius changes as you go from left to right in Period 2 of the *Periodic Table*. [1]

2 **Question**: Identify the number of the group that contains the most active nonmetals, and explain how the elements loose or gain an electron to behave as nonmetals during a chemical reaction. [2]

3 **Question**: Given the following elements: Ca, Fe, Ga, Br, identify which element will form aqueous solutions that are colored. [1]

4 **Question**: Describe how the first ionization energy changes as you go from the top to the bottom in Group 1 of the *Periodic Table*. [1]

5 **Question**: Describe how the electronegativity changes as you go from left to right in Period 2 of the *Periodic Table*. [1]

PART C – EXTENDED CONSTRUCTED-RESPONSE

Article A: The modern *Periodic Table* is arranged in order of increasing atomic number and can be looked at in terms of its horizontal rows called periods and its vertical columns called Groups (Families). As one looks at the *Periodic Table*, different trends can be observed.

Moving from left to right within a period, it is observed that the atomic radius decreases and that the electronegativity and first ionization energy generally increase. The trend, therefore, is one that moves from metals that lose electrons to form positive ions to nonmetals that gain electrons to form negative ions, to inert gases that do not react because they have a completed outer principal energy level. The number of the Period corresponds to the number of the outer principal energy level containing the valence electrons.

1 **Question**: Explain in terms of nuclear charge, atomic radius, and electronegativity why non-metallic characteristics increase as one proceeds across Period 2 of the *Periodic Table* from Li to F. [3]

2 **Question**: Describe the transition in terms of metallic vs. nonmetallic character as one goes from left to right in Period 2 of the *Periodic Table*. [1]

Article A (cont.): Moving from top to bottom within a Group, it can be observed that the atomic radius increases, the screening effect increases, and the first ionization energy and electronegativity decrease. As one moves from top to bottom within a Group, therefore, the ability of atoms to lose electrons increases and the ability of atoms to gain electrons decreases and one can observe an increase in metallic character and a decrease in nonmetallic character of the elements. The elements of each Group have similar chemical properties due to the fact that they have the same number of valence electrons in the outer principal energy level.

3 **Question**: Explain why the chemical properties of the elements in a given group of the *Periodic Table* are similar, but not identical to one another. [1]

4 **Question**: Explain in terms of atomic radius, screening effect, and ionization energy, why the metallic characteristics increase as one

proceeds from top to bottom within a given Group on the *Periodic Table*. [3]

Article B: A student must be aware that Groups 1 and 2, the alkali metals and alkaline earth metals, respectively, are groups of very active metals. The alkali metals are so active that they do not exist alone in nature but are found only in compounds with nonmetals. The transition elements are found to the right of the very active metals. These elements are less active metals and form compounds which are often colored when hydrated or placed into solution. Group 17 is the Halogen Group that consists of very active nonmetals and Group 18 are the noble or inert gases. These noble or inert gases do not usually react due to the fact that they have a completed outer principal energy level.

5   **Question**: Describe the chemical properties of the elements in the Group 1 (Alkali Metals). [1] Very reactive, only exist in compounds

6   **Question**: Describe the chemical properties of the elements in the Group 17 (Halogen Group). [1] Very active nonmetals

7   **Question**: Explain why the elements belonging to the Halogen Group always exhibit a –1 oxidation state when combining with metals. [1] It ~~gives about~~ takes in one electron all the time

8   **Question**: Using *Reference Table S* illustrating atomic radii of atoms, tell why the first ionization energy and electronegativity generally increase going across a Period but decrease when going down in a Group. [3]

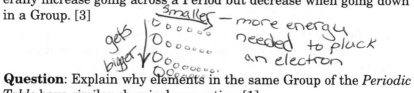

smaller — more energy needed to pluck an electron
gets bigger

9   **Question**: Explain why elements in the same Group of the *Periodic Table* have similar chemical properties. [1]
Same valence electrons

PART D – LABORATORY SKILLS

THE PERIODIC TABLE

Purpose: To illustrate Mendeleev's *Periodic Law*: "The physical and chemical properties of the elements are periodic functions of their atomic numbers."

Materials: *Periodic Table, Reference Tables for Physical Setting: Chemistry*, graph paper, pencil.

Procedure: Using your *Periodic Table* and *Reference Table S*, make vertical bar graphs of the first ionization energy and electronegativity for

a   Period 2 and Group 1 of the representative elements

b   the alkali metals, alkaline earth metals, and the Halogen Group

Observations and Analysis:

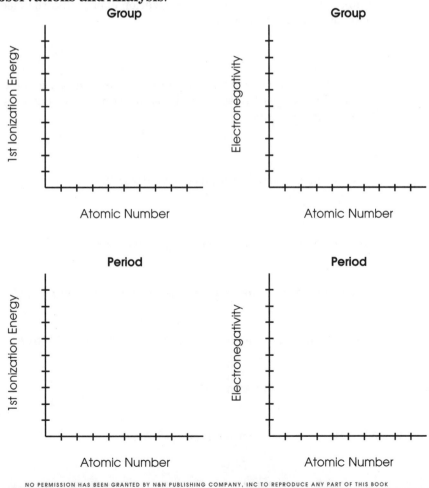

Conclusion:

1   As the atomic number of the elements increases in any given period, what happens to the first ionization energy and the electronegativity of the elements?

2   As the atomic number of the elements increases in any given period, what happens to the metallic and nonmetallic characteristics of the elements?

3   As the atomic number of the elements increases in any given group, what happens to the first ionization energy and the electronegativity of the elements?

4   As the atomic number of the elements increases in any given group, what happens to the metallic and nonmetallic characteristics of the elements?

5   Which element is the most electrogenative? Why?

6   Which element is the least electrogenative? Why?

7   Which element has the highest first ionization energy? Why?

8   Which element has the lowest first ionization energy? Why?

9   Which atom is the most metallic? Why?

10   Which atom is the most nonmetallic? Why?

UNIT 3
MOLES &
STOICHIOMETRY

KEY IDEA **3**

MATTER IS MADE UP OF PARTICLES WHOSE PROPERTIES DETERMINE THE OBSERVABLE CHARACTERISTICS OF MATTER AND ITS REACTIVITY

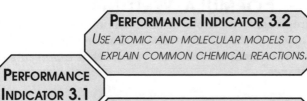

PERFORMANCE INDICATOR 3.2
USE ATOMIC AND MOLECULAR MODELS TO EXPLAIN COMMON CHEMICAL REACTIONS.

PERFORMANCE INDICATOR 3.1

PERFORMANCE INDICATOR 3.3
APPLY THE PRINCIPLE OF CONSERVATION OF MASS TO CHEMICAL REACTIONS.

UNIT 3 – MAJOR UNDERSTANDINGS

☆ 3.1cc A compound is a substance composed of two or more different elements that are chemically combined in a fixed proportion. A chemical compound can be broken down by chemical means. A chemical compound can be represented by a specific chemical formula and assigned a name based on the IUPAC system.

☆ 3.1ee Types of chemical formulas include empirical, molecular, and structural.

☆ 3.3d The empirical formula of a compound is the simplest whole-number ratio of atoms of the elements in a compound. It may be different from the molecular formula, which is the actual ratio of atoms in a molecule of that compound.

☆ 3.3a In all chemical reactions there is a conservation of mass, energy, and charge.

☆ 3.3c A balanced chemical equation represents conservation of atoms. The coefficients in a balanced

UNIT 3
MOLES & STOICHIOMETRY

This unit is related to Key Idea 3 for the text and Performance Indicators 3.1, 3.2, and 3.3 for the assessments.

INTRODUCTION

A **compound** is a substance composed of two or more different elements that are chemically combined in a fixed proportion and can be broken down by chemical means. Chemical compounds are represented by a specific formula and assigned a name based on the IUPAC system. Examples are H_2O (water = dihydrogen oxide), CO_2 (carbon dioxide), CCl_4 (carbon tetrachloride).

A – FORMULA WRITING

A **symbol** may represent one atom or one mole of atoms of an element. One mole of atoms contains Avogadro's number (6.02×10^{23}) of atoms. A **formula** is a statement in chemical symbols that represents the composition of a substance.

CHEMICAL FORMULA

A **chemical formula** is both a qualitative and a quantitative expression of the composition of an element or a compound. For example, the formula for phosphoric acid is H_3PO_4. This formula describes a molecule of phosphoric acid composed of 3 atoms of hydrogen, 1 atom of phosphorus, and 4 atoms of oxygen. It also states that to make a mole of this compound, 3 moles of hydrogen atoms, 1 mole of phosphorus atoms, and 4 moles of oxygen atoms are needed.

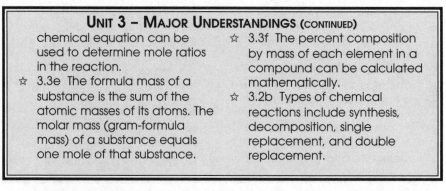

UNIT 3 – MAJOR UNDERSTANDINGS (CONTINUED)

chemical equation can be used to determine mole ratios in the reaction.

☆ 3.3e The formula mass of a substance is the sum of the atomic masses of its atoms. The molar mass (gram-formula mass) of a substance equals one mole of that substance.

☆ 3.3f The percent composition by mass of each element in a compound can be calculated mathematically.

☆ 3.2b Types of chemical reactions include synthesis, decomposition, single replacement, and double replacement.

There are three basic types of formulas:

- An **empirical formula** represents the simplest whole number ratio in which elements combine to form a compound. For example, the empirical formula for H_2O_2 is HO.

1 **Question**: What is the empirical formula of ethane (C_2H_6)?

$$CH_3$$

- The **molecular formula** is the whole number multiple of the empirical formula, and indicates the total number of atoms of each element needed to form the molecule, given the mole mass of substance. The formula mass of the empirical formula CH is $12 + 1 = 13$. The molecule with the same empirical formula but with a mass of 78 is C_6H_6.

Given the empirical formula and the molecular mass, it is possible to derive the molecular formula:

1) determine the formula mass of the empirical formula,
2) divide this formula mass into the molecular mass, and
3) multiply this result by the subscript of each atom in the compound.

- The **structural formula** demonstrates the connections between atoms of a molecule or ion in space.

Examples include: **CH₄**   **C₂H₆**

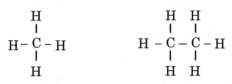

SKILLS 3.3VII *DETERMINE THE MOLECULAR FORMULA GIVEN THE EMPIRICAL FORMULA AND MOLECULAR MASS.*

2 A compound has an empirical formula of CH_2 and a molecular mass of 56. Its molecular formula is
(1) C_2H_4 (2) C_3H_6 (3) C_4H_8 (4) C_5H_{10}

3 The empirical formula of a compound is CH. Its molecular mass could be
(1) 21   (2) 40   (3) 51   (4) 78

4 The empirical formula of a compound is CH_2 and its molecular mass is 70. What is the molecular formula of the compound?
(1) C_2H_4 (2) C_2H_4 (3) C_4H_{10} (4) C_5H_{10}

5 What is the molecular formula of a compound whose empirical formula is CH_4 and molecular mass is 16?

   (1) CH_4 (2) C_3H_6 (3) C_4H_8 (4) C_8H_{18}

B – NAMING & WRITING CHEMICAL COMPOUND FORMULAS

The discussion of oxidation numbers and their rules will be covered in Unit 8 [☆ pg 221] in greater detail. However, the rules are included here in brief, because the student cannot write a valid formula without knowing the rules for applying oxidation numbers.

The common oxidation number (state) is found in the *Periodic Table of Elements* and is given for each of the elements. It represents the charge which an atom has, or appears to have, when the electrons are counted according to certain arbitrary rules. These rules result in the following operational rules for determining oxidation numbers.

- In the free element, each atom has an oxidation number of zero.

- In simple ions (ions containing one atom), the oxidation number is equal to the charge on the ion.

- The algebraic sum of all the oxidation numbers of the atoms of any molecule or compound is zero.

- The oxidation number of oxygen is -2, except in peroxides it is -1.

- Oxidation number of hydrogen is +1, except in hydrides it is -1.

- In nonmetal compounds, the less electronegative element is positive; the more electronegative element is negative.

- The algebraic sum of the charges of the atoms in a polyatomic ion is equal to the charge on the ion.

The chemical name of a compound generally indicates the chemical composition of the substance. The procedure used in naming and writing chemical formulas are as follows.

- In binary compounds composed of metals and nonmetals, the metallic element is usually named and written first. The name of the nonmetal ends in "**–ide**" (for example, sodium chloride, potassium bromide, lithium iodide).

- In compounds composed of two nonmetals, the less electro-negative element is usually named and written first. The name of the compound still ends in "–ide" (for example, hydrogen chloride, nitrogen bromide).

- Prefixes are used to indicate the number of atoms of each nonmetal in the compound. Examples include carbon dioxide (CO_2), sulfur trioxide (SO_3), carbon tetrachloride (CCl_4).

- In the naming of compounds, which include one or more poly-atomic ions, the metal is usually named first with polyatomic ions named last (for example, sodium hydroxide – NaOH, magnesium sulfate – $MgSO_4$).

The various **polyatomic ions** and their charges are listed in *Reference Table E*. There are two exceptions.

- The mercury ion is a polyatomic ion of a single element. Although it has a +2 charge, there are 2 atoms in the ion. Therefore, each of the atoms in the mercury ion has a +1 charge, and it is called the mercury (I) ion. For example, HgCl is called Mercury I Chloride and $HgCl_2$ is called Mercury II Chloride.

- The only polyatomic ion that has a positive charge and will be written first in compounds is the ammonium ion (NH_4^+). For example, ammonium nitrate is written NH_4NO_3 and ammonium chloride is written NH_4Cl.

In naming compounds of metals which may have more than one oxidation number, the **Stock System** should be used. In this system, Roman numerals indicate the oxidation number of the metal ion. For example, FeO is named iron (II) oxide, and Fe_2O_3 is named iron (III) oxide.

In naming compounds of two nonmetals with multiple oxidation states, the Stock system should be used to denote the oxidation state of the less electronegative member. For example, $N_2^{+1}O^{-2}$ is named nitrogen (I) oxide, $N^{+2}O^{-2}$ is named nitrogen (II) oxide, and $N^{+4}O_2^{-2}$ is named nitrogen (IV) oxide.

The following suggestions are used when naming acids. **Note**: Common Acids are found on *Reference Table K*.

- In **binary acids** (acids in which there are only two elements in the formula, hydrogen being one of them), hydrogen takes the place of a metal; therefore, the prefix for a binary acid will always be **Hydro–**. For example, Hydrochloric acid (HCl) and Hydrosulfuric acid (H_2S).

- In **ternary acids** (acids which combine hydrogen with a polyatomic ion and contain three elements in their formulas), the prefix Hydro– is dropped, and the acid is named after the polyatomic ion as follows:

  a) If the polyatomic ion ends with **–ate**, the name of the acid will end with **–ic**. (For example, SO_4^{2-} is called the sulfate ion. When it combines with hydrogen, its formula becomes H_2SO_4 and is called sulfuric acid.)

  b) If the polyatomic ion ends with **–ite**, the name of the acid will end with **–ous**. (For example, SO_3^{2-} is called the sulfite ion. When it combines with hydrogen, its formula becomes H_2SO_3 and is called sulfurous acid.)

6 **Question**: What are the names of the following acids?

HNO_3 _Nitric acid_ HNO_2 _nitrous acid_

H_3PO_4 _Phosphoric acid_ H_2CO_3 _carbonic acid_

When naming the common **bases**, follow the name of the metal with the word hydroxide. (Examples, KOH – potassium hydroxide, NaOH – sodium hydroxide, and $Ca(OH)_2$ – calcium hydroxide.) Salts are named as follows. **Note**: Common bases are found on *Reference Table L*.

- **Binary salts** always end with **–ide**. (Such as KBr – potassium bromide and $CaCl_2$ – calcium chloride.)

- When a metal is combined with a polyatomic ion, the name of the metal is followed with the name of the polyatomic ion. (Such as Na_2CO_3 – sodium carbonate and $K_2Cr_2O_7$ – potassium dichromate.)

C – CHEMICAL EQUATIONS

A chemical equation represents the type and the amount of changes in **bonding** and energy that take place in a chemical reaction. It is made up of **reactants** (those items that enter into the reaction and are usually found on the left side of the equation) and the **products** (those items produced and usually found on the right side of the equation). For example:

$$2H_2 + O_2 \rightarrow 2H_2O + heat$$

The addition of two molecules of hydrogen and one molecule of oxygen results in the production of two molecules of water and heat. Two moles of hydrogen plus one mole of oxygen results in 2 moles of water molecules. In all reactions there is a conservation of mass, energy, and change.

In an equation, it is often desirable to indicate the phase of reactants and products. This may be done by using the symbols: (s) = solid; (l) = liquid; (g) = gas; and (aq) = in an **aqueous solution**. The "written equation" is shown as:

$$2H_2\ (g)\ +\ O_2\ (g)\ \rightarrow\ 2H_2O\ (l)\ +\ \textbf{heat}$$

BALANCING EQUATIONS

The number of atoms of each element must be the same on both sides of the equation. This is done by placing numbers in front of the formulas (**coefficients**) in order to equalize the number of atoms.

1) Balancing equations by inspection:

$$\underline{3}\ H_2(g)\ +\ \underline{1}\ N_2\ (g)\ \rightarrow\ \underline{2}\ NH_3\ (g)$$

In order to balance the number of hydrogen atoms, the common multiple of 2 and 3 which is 6 is used. The coefficient 3 is placed in front of the H_2 on the left side of the equation and 2 in front of the product on the right side:

$$3H_2(g)\ +\ N_2\ (g)\ \rightarrow\ 2NH_3\ (g)$$

By coincidence, when the hydrogen atoms are balanced, nitrogen atoms are balanced out and the total equation is balanced.

2) Balancing equations with missing valid formulas. The word equation for the reaction of aluminum and sulfuric acid is

Note: Aluminum reacts with sulfuric acid to produce aluminum sulfate and hydrogen gas.

The *Periodic Table* provides the oxidation states which are used to write valid formulas. By writing the individual oxidation state above each atom or polyatomic ion and multiplying it by the number of atoms or polyatomic ions in the formula, the total oxidation state for each is obtained. When the oxidation states for each formula add up to 0, the formulas in the equation are valid.

$$
\begin{array}{llll}
0 & +2\ +6\ -8 & +6\quad -6 & 0 \;=\; 0 \text{ (total oxidation state)}\\
0 & +1\ +6\ -2 & +3\quad -2 & 0 \quad \text{(individual oxidation states)}
\end{array}
$$

$$Al(s)\ +\ H_2SO_4(aq)\ \rightarrow\ Al_2(SO_4)_3(aq)\ +\ H_2(g)$$

In order to balance the equation the coefficients are added:

$$2Al(s)\ +\ 3H_2SO_4(aq)\ \rightarrow\ Al_2(SO_4)_3(aq)\ +\ 3H_2(g)\ \text{(balanced equation)}$$

7. When the equation: $H_2 + Fe_3O_4 \rightarrow Fe + H_2O$ is completely balanced, using smallest whole numbers, the coefficient of H_2 would be:
   (1) 1   (2) 2   (3) 3   (4) 4

8. When the equation: $NH_3 + O_2 \rightarrow HNO_3 + H_2O$ is completely balanced, using smallest whole numbers, the coefficient of O_2 would be:
   (1) 1   (2) 2   (3) 3   (4) 4

9. Given the balanced equation: $2\,Na + 2\,H_2O \rightarrow 2\,X + H_2$ What is the correct formula for the product represented by the letter X?
   (1) NaO   (2) Na_2O (3) NaOH   (4) Na_2OH

10. When the equation: $1\,C_2H_4 + 3\,O_2 \rightarrow 2\,CO_2 + 2\,H_2O$ is correctly balanced, using smallest whole-numbered coefficients, the sum of all the coefficients is:
    (1) 16   (2) 12   (3) 8   (4) 4

11. When the above (question # 10) equation is balanced, using smallest whole numbers, what is the coefficient of the O_2?
    (1) 1   (2) 2   (3) 3   (4) 4

12. When the equation: $2\,Na(s) + 2\,H_2O(l) \rightarrow 2\,NaOH(aq) + 1\,H_2(g)$ is correctly balanced using smallest whole numbers, the coefficient of the water is
    (1) 1   (2) 2   (3) 3   (4) 4

13. When the equation: $4\,Al(s) + 3\,O_2(g) \rightarrow 2\,Al_2O_3(s)$ is correctly balanced using the smallest whole numbers, the coefficient of Al(s) is
    (1) 1   (2) 2   (3) 3   (4) 4

Directions: Balance each of the following equations.

14. $2\,Mg(s) + 1\,O_2(g) \rightarrow 2\,MgO(s)$

15. $2\,NaI(aq) + 1\,F_2(g) \rightarrow 2\,NaF(aq) + 1\,I_2(g)$

16. $2\,Al(s) + 3\,H_2SO_4(aq) \rightarrow 1\,Al_2(SO_4)_3(aq) + 3\,H_2(g)$

17. $1\,KNO_3(aq) + 1\,NaCl(aq) \rightarrow 1\,KCl(aq) + 1\,NaNO_3(aq)$

D – MOLE INTERPRETATION

A mole contains Avogadro's number (6.02×10^{23}) of particles and may be used in calculations involving the number of particles (atoms, molecules, ions, electrons, or other particles) involved in chemical reactions, the mass of elements or compounds, or the volume relationships in gases.

GRAM ATOMIC MASS (GRAM-ATOM)

The gram atomic mass (gram-atom) of an element represents the mass in grams of Avogadro's number (6.02×10^{23}) of atoms of the element. The gram-atomic mass is numerically equal to the atomic mass as shown in the *Periodic Table*. For example, the atomic mass of the element sulfur is 32.06 amu. A mole of this element weighs 32.06 grams.

GRAM FORMULA MASS (MOLAR-MASS)

The gram molecular mass (mass of 1 mole) is the sum of the gram atomic masses of the atoms that make up a particular molecule. The gram formula mass is the sum of the gram atomic masses of the atoms that make up a particular formula. The gram formula mass calculated from the empirical formula is used for ionic substances and network solids, since they are not molecular substances.

Sample Problem: What is the gram molecular mass of water (H_2O)?

Solution:

The gram atomic mass of 1 mole of hydrogen atoms is 1 g $\times$ 2 = 2 g

The gram atomic mass of 1 mole of oxygen atoms is 16 g $\times$ 1 = 16 g

The gram molar mass of water is therefore 16 + 2 = 18 g/mole

18 **Question**: What is the ratio by mass of hydrogen to oxygen in water?

H_2O

1:2 ratio

SKILLS 3.3VIII *CALCULATE THE FORMULA MASS AND THE GRAM FORMULA MASS.*

19 What is the mass in grams of 1.0 mole of $(NH_4)_2S$?
   (1) 50   (2) 54   (3) 64   (4) 68

20 The gram molecular mass of CO_2 is the same as the gram molecular mass of:
   (1) CO   (2) SO_2 (3) C_2H_6 (4) C_3H_8

21 Which quantity is equivalent to 39 grams of LiF?
   (1) 1.0 mole   (2) 2.0 moles   (3) 0.50 mole   (4) 1.5 moles

22 What is the gram molecular mass of fluorine?
    (1) 38   (2) 9   (3) 18   (4) 14

23 What is the gram formula mass of $CuSO_4 \cdot 5H_2O$?
    (1) 160. g   (2) 178 g   (3) 186 g   (4) 250. g

MOLAR VOLUME OF A GAS

A mole (6.02×10^{23}) of molecules of any gas occupies 22.4 liters at STP. It has a mass equal to the molecular mass expressed in grams.

E – STOICHIOMETRY

Stoichiometry is the study of the quantitative relationships implied by chemical formulas and by chemical equations. In stoichiometry, it is frequently convenient to use the mole interpretation and mole relationships in the solving of problems. In short, stoichiometry is the study of the molar proportions of:

- atoms in a chemical formula

- particles (molecules, ions, or compounds) in a chemical equation

SKILLS 3.3IV *CALCULATE SIMPLE MOLE-MOLE STOICHIOMETRY PROBLEMS - GIVEN A BALANCED EQUATION.*

24 Question: If 500 mL of a gas weighed 7.6 g, what is the molecular mass of the gas? (Note: One mole has a volume of 22.4 liters)

$$.5 L \times \frac{1 \text{ mol}}{22.4 L} = 0.022 \text{ mol}$$

25 Given the equation: $2C_2H_6 + 7O_2 \rightarrow 4CO_2 + 6H_2O$ When 30. grams of C_2H_6 (molecular mass = 30) are completely burned, the total number of moles of CO_2 produced is:
    (1) 1.0   (2) 2.0   (3) 8.0   (4) 4.0

26 Given the reaction: $2Na + 2H_2O \rightarrow 2NaOH + H_2$ What is the total number of moles of hydrogen produced when 4 moles of sodium react completely?
    (1) 1   (2) 2   (3) 3   (4) 4

27 Given the reaction: $2C_2H_6 + 7O_2 \rightarrow 4CO_2 + 6H_2O$ What is the total number of CO_2 molecules produced when one mole of C_2H_6 is consumed?
    (1) $1 \times 6.02 \times 10^{23}$ (3) $3 \times 6.02 \times 10^{23}$
    (2) $2 \times 6.02 \times 10^{23}$ (4) $4 \times 6.02 \times 10^{23}$

28 In the reaction: $Zn + 2HCl \rightarrow ZnCl_2 + H_2$ How many moles of hydrogen will be formed when 4 moles of HCl are consumed?
(1) 6   ((2)) 2   (3) 8   (4) 4

29 What is the total number of moles contained in 115 grams of C_2H_5OH?
(1) 1.00   (2) 1.50   ((3)) 3.00   (4) 2.5

30 What is the total number of moles of atoms represented by one mole of $(CH_3)_2NH$?
(1) 5   ((2)) 8   (3) 9   (4) 10

31 What is the mass of 2 moles of nitrogen gas?
(1) 14   (2) 56   (3) 24   ((4)) 28

32 Question: What does 22.4 liters of hydrogen gas weigh? (Note: a mole of hydrogen gas molecules occupies a volume of 22.4 liters.)

$$1 \; mol \; \frac{22.4}{22.4}$$

33 Question: What is the mass of 2.5 moles of carbon monoxide?

$$2.5 \; mol \times \frac{1 \, g}{}$$

34 Question: What is the mass of 2.5 moles of SiO_2?

$$2.5 \times \frac{35}{1 \; mol} = 87.5$$
$$mol$$

Directions: For question 35, follow the format below to show the conservation of matter and energy.

H_2	+	F_2	$\rightarrow$	$2HF$
(6.02×10^{23} H_2 molecules)		(6.02×10^{23} F_2 molecules)		$2(6.02 \times 10^{23}$ HF)
1 mole H_2 molecules		1 mole F_2 molecules		2 mole HF molecules
1 molar mass of H_2		1 molar mass of F_2		2 molar masses of HF
$2 \times 1.01g = 2.02g$		$2 \times 18.998g = 37.996g$		$2 \times 20.008g = 40.01g$
2.02g	+	37.996g	=	40.01g

35 Show the conservation of matter and energy for the following:

$$H_2 \qquad + \qquad Cl_2 \qquad \rightarrow \qquad 2HCl$$

PROBLEMS INVOLVING FORMULAS

Percent composition – The percent composition by mass of an element in a compound can be calculated by dividing the total mass of that element in the formula by the total **formula mass** of the compound.

Sample Problem: Calculate the percent composition by mass of H_2O.

First, calculate the formula mass by the following method.

Each hydrogen atom has a mass of … 1 amu = 1 amu × 2 = 2 amu

An oxygen atom has a mass of … 16 amu = 16 amu × 1 = 16 amu

Total formula mass … = 18 amu

Second, divide the total mass of each element by the formula mass, and multiply the resulting decimal by 100%.

$$\text{hydrogen} = \frac{2 \text{ amu}}{18 \text{ amu}} = 0.11 \times 100\% = 11\% \text{ (answer)}$$

$$\text{oxygen} = \frac{16 \text{ amu}}{18 \text{ amu}} = 0.89 \times 100\% = 89\% \text{ (answer)}$$

As noted in *Reference Table T*:

$$\% \text{ composition by mass} = \frac{\text{mass of part}}{\text{mass of whole}} \times 100\%$$

Sample Problem: Calculate the percent, by mass, of water of hydration in gypsum ($CaSO_4 \bullet 2H_2O$).

First, calculate the formula mass:

Ca = 40 × 1 = 40. amu
S = 32 × 1 = 32. amu
O = 16 × 6 = 96. amu
H = 1 × 4 = 04. amu
172. amu

Second, calculate the mass of water in the compound. As stated above, each water molecule has a mass of 18 amu. Since there are two (2) molecules in the formula, the mass of the water molecules is 36 amu. Divide the mass of the water molecules by the formula mass of the compound and multiple the decimal by 100%.

$$\frac{36 \text{ amu}}{172 \text{ amu}} = 0.21 \times 100\% = 21\% \text{ (answer)}$$

Problem: Determine the empirical formula from percent composition.

Step 1 – Divide the percent by the atomic weight.
Step 2 – Divide the result by the lowest number.
Step 3 – Change to the simplest whole number ratio and write formula.

Example: Find and write the empirical formula for 32..8% chromium and 67.2% chlorine.

Step 1 – $\dfrac{32.8}{52} = 0.63$ mole   and $\dfrac{67.2}{35.5} = 1.89$ moles

Step 2 – $\dfrac{.63 \text{ mole}}{.63 \text{ mole}} = 1$ (formula units)   and $\dfrac{1.89 \text{ moles}}{.63 \text{ mole}} = 3$ (formula units)

Step 3 – Result: $CrCl_3$

SKILLS 3.3V *DETERMINE THE EMPIRICAL FORMULA FROM A MOLECULAR FORMULA.*

Directions: Given the molecular formula, determine the empirical formula of the following:

36 Question: C_3H_{12}

37 Question: C_2H_6

Directions: Find and write the empirical formula for each of the following compounds:

38 Question: 32.8% chromium and 67.2% chlorine

39 Question: 71.4% calcium and 28.6% oxygen

40 Question: 94.1% oxygen and 5.9% hydrogen

☆ PROBLEMS INVOLVING EQUATIONS

The following three step procedure should be applied to equation problems.

Step One – Find the number of moles of the substance given.
If grams are given, divide the grams by the molecular mass of the substance. If liters are given, divide the number of liters by
22.4 liters/mole. If molecules are given, divide the number by
6.02×10^{23} molecules/mole. If moles are given, go directly to Step Two.

Step Two – Find the number of moles of the substance asked for.
Put the number of moles calculated in Step One above the substance calculated in the equation. Put an "X" above the substance asked for. Set up a proportion or use the mole-ratio method. Solve for X.

Step Three – Final calculation.
If asked for grams, multiply answer in Step Two by the molecular mass of X. If asked for liters, multiply answer in Step Two by
22.4 liters/mole. If asked for molecules, multiply answer in Step Two by 6.02×10^{23} molecules/mole. If asked for moles, skip Step Three.

NO PERMISSION HAS BEEN GRANTED BY N&N PUBLISHING COMPANY, INC TO REPRODUCE ANY PART OF THIS BOOK

N&N©   UNIT 3: MOLES/STOICHIOMETRY (KEY IDEA 3)   PAGE 73

Sample Problem: Mass – Mass

A balanced equation shows the mole proportions of reactants and products:

$$Mg(s) + 2\,HCl(aq) \rightarrow MgCl_2(aq) + H_2(g) \uparrow$$

How many grams of $MgCl_2$ are produced when 48 grams of $Mg(s)$ are used?

Step One – Find the number of moles given by dividing the mass of one mole into the amount given: mole of Mg = 24 g/mole

$$\frac{48\text{ g of }Mg(s)}{24\text{ g/mole of }Mg(s)} = 2\text{ moles }Mg(s)$$

Step Two –

$$\overset{\text{2 moles}}{Mg(s)} + 2\,HCl(aq) \rightarrow \overset{\text{X moles}}{MgCl_2(aq)} + H_2(g) \uparrow$$

1 mole   1 mole

Proportion Method:

$$\frac{2\text{ moles}}{1\text{ mole}} = \frac{X\text{ moles}}{1\text{ mole}} = 2\text{ moles }MgCl_2 \text{ (answer)}$$

Step Three –

$$2\text{ moles }MgCl_2 \times 96\text{ g/mole} = 192g \text{ (answer)}$$

Sample Problem: Mass – Volume

How many liters of carbon dioxide at STP are produced by the combustion of 684 grams of octane (C_8H_{18}) according to the equation:

$$2C_8H_{18} + 25O_2 \rightarrow 16CO_2(aq) + 18H_2O$$

Step One – Division

$$\text{mole of } C_8H_{18} = (8 \times 12) + (18 \times 1) = 114\text{ g/mole } C_8H_{18}$$

$$\frac{684\text{ g of }C_8H_{18}}{114\text{ g/mole }C_8H_{18}} = 6\text{ moles }C_8H_{18}$$

Step Two –

$$\overset{\text{6 moles}}{2C_8H_{18}} + 25O_2 \rightarrow \overset{\text{X moles}}{16CO_2} + 18H_2O$$

2 moles   16 moles

Proportion Method:

$$\frac{6\text{ moles}}{2\text{ mole}} = \frac{X\text{ moles}}{16\text{ mole}} = 48\text{ moles } \text{(answer)}$$

Mole-Ratio Method:
(Alternate Method)

$$^3 \cancel{6\text{-}C_8H_{18}} \times \frac{16\ CO_2}{\cancel{2\text{-}C_8H_{18}}} = 48 \text{ moles } CO_2 \text{ (answer)}$$

Step Three – Multiplication

48 moles CO_2 x 22.4 liters/mole = 1075.2 liters (answer)

Sample Problem: Volume – Volume

Since one mole of any gas occupies the same volume as one mole of any other gas at the same temperature, the volume of the gases involved in a reaction is proportional to the number of moles indicated by the numerical coefficients in a balanced equation. When reacting gases are at the same temperature and pressure, the volume ratio is equal to the mole ration.

In the reaction: $N_2 + 3H_2 \rightarrow 2NH_3$ at STP, calculate the volume of hydrogen gas required to form 100 liters of NH_3 at STP.

Solution:

Use same three step process.

$$\underset{X}{\overset{3 \text{ moles}}{N_2 + 3\ H_2}} \quad \rightarrow \quad \underset{100 \text{ liters}}{\overset{2 \text{ moles}}{2\ NH_3}}$$

X = 150 liters (answer)

The general types of chemical reactions include the following:

Composition or Synthesis – Two or more substances combine to form a compound.

$$X + Y \rightarrow XY$$

An example would be:

$$Mg + S \rightarrow MgS$$

Magnesium + Sulfur → Magnesium Sulfide

Decomposition or Analysis – The opposite of composition:

$$XY \rightarrow X + Y$$

Magnesium Sulfide → Magnesium + Sulfur

Single Replacement – The displacement of one substance in a compound by another substance:

$$X + YZ \rightarrow XZ + Y$$
or
$$A + YZ \rightarrow YA + Z$$

Examples:

$$K + NaCl \rightarrow KCl + Na$$
$$Cl_2 + 2NaI \rightarrow 2NaCl + I_2$$

Double Replacement or Ionic Reactions – In this reaction two compounds exchange in the following manner:

$$AB + CD \rightarrow AD + CB$$

In this reaction a product leaves the solution in the form of a precipitate or gas. One classic example is:

$$NaCl(aq) + AgNO_3(aq) \rightarrow NaNO_3 + AgCl(s) \downarrow \text{ (white precipitate)}$$

Precipitation reactions – As shown above, clear solutions of silver nitrate and sodium chloride are mixed and a white precipitate of silver nitrate forms.

SKILLS 3.2II *IDENTIFY TYPES OF CHEMICAL REACTIONS.*

Directions: Identify the following types of reactions as composition (synthesis), decomposition, single replacement, or double replacement (ionic).

41 __synthesis__ $2Mg(s) + O_2(g) \rightarrow 2 MgO(s)$

42 __single replacement__ $2NaI(aq) + F_2(g) \rightarrow NaF(aq) + I_2(g)$

43 __single replacement__ $2Al(s) + 3H_2SO_4(aq) \rightarrow Al_2(SO_4)_3(aq) + 3H_2(g)$

44 __double replacement__ $AgNO_3(aq) + NaCl(aq) \rightarrow AgCl(s) + NaNO_3(aq)$

🌎 REAL WORLD CONNECTIONS CHEMICAL WARNINGS

Dangers of mixing household chemicals together (e.g. bleach and ammonia) – The reaction of chlorine containing solutions such as bleach with which other cleansing agent that contain ammonium compounds causes a reaction releasing chlorine gas which is toxic.

Note: Always read the warning label on all products.

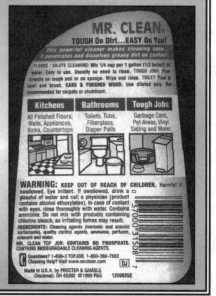

PERFORMANCE INDICATOR 3.3
ASSESSMENTS

PART A – MULTIPLE CHOICE

1. The empirical formula of a compound is CH_3. The molecular formula of this compound could be
   (1) CH_4 (2) C_2H_4 (3) C_2H_6 (4) C_3H_6

2. What is the empirical formula of a compound that contains 30.4% nitrogen and 69.6% oxygen by mass?
   (1) NO   (2) NO_2 (3) N_2O_3 (4) N_2O_5

3. Given the balanced equation:

$$Fe(s) + CuSO_4(aq) \rightarrow FeSO_4(aq) + Cu(s)$$

   What total mass of iron is necessary to produce 1.00 mole of copper?
   (1) 26.0 g   (2) 55.8 g   (3) 112 g   (4) 192 g

4. Which substance has the greatest molecular mass?
   (1) H_2O_2 (2) NO   (3) CF_4 (4) I_2

5. The gram atomic mass of oxygen is 16.0 grams per mole. How many atoms of oxygen does this mass represent?
   (1) 16.0   (2) 32.0   (3) 6.02×10^{23} (4) $2(6.02 \times 10^{23})$

6. Given the *unbalanced* equation: $N_2(g) + H_2(g) \rightarrow NH_3(g)$
   When the equation is balanced using smallest whole-number coefficients, the ratio of moles of hydrogen consumed to moles of ammonia produced is
   (1) 1:3   (2) 2:3   (3) 3:1   (4) 3:2

7. What is the gram formula mass of K_2CO_3?
   (1) 138 g   (2) 106 g   (3) 99 g   (4) 67 g

8. A compound is 86% carbon and 14% hydrogen by mass. What is the empirical formula for this compound?
   (1) CH   (2) CH_2 (3) CH_3 (4) CH_4

9. What is the total numer of nitrogen atoms in 0.25 mole of NO_2 gas?
   (1) 1.5×10^{23} (2) 6.0×10^{23} (3) 3.0×10^{23} (4) 1.2×10^{24}

10. A compound contains 46.7% nitrogen and 53.3% oxygen by mass. What is the empirical formula of the compound?
    (1) NO   (2) N_2O (3) N_2O_3 (4) N_2O_5

11. What is the volume, in liters, of 576 grams of SO_2 gas at STP?
    (1) 101   (2) 202   (3) 216   (4) 788

12. One mole of O_2 has approximately the same mass as one mole of?
    (1) CH_4 (2) S   (3) LiH   (4) Cl_2

13 What is the correct formula for iron (II) sulfide?
  (1) FeS   (2) $FeSO_3$ (3) Fe_2S_3 (4) $Fe_2(SO_4)_3$

14 An example of an empirical formula is
  (1) C_4H_{10} (2) $C_6H_{12}O_6$ (3) $HC_2H_3O_2$ (4) CH_2O

PART B – CONSTRUCTED-RESPONSE

1 **Question**: Given the following balanced equation:

$$CH_4(g) + 2O_2(g) \rightarrow CO_2(g) + 2H_2O(l)$$

How many moles of water will be produced when 1.5 moles of CH_4 reacts completely? 3 mols

2 **Question**: Given the following balanced equation:

$$C_3H_8(g) + 5O_2(g) \rightarrow 3CO_2(g) + 4H_2O(l)$$

How many moles of oxygen will be required to produce 5.0 moles of CO_2? 8.3 mols

3 **Question**: Given the following balanced equation:

$$2CH_3OH(l) + 3O_2(g) \rightarrow 2CO_2(g) + 4H_2O(l)$$

How many moles of oxygen will be needed to react with 2.5 moles of CH_3OH? 3.8 mols

4 **Question**: Given the following balanced equation:

$$C_2H_5OH(l) + 3O_2(g) \rightarrow 2CO_2(g) + 3H_2O(l)$$

How many moles of CO_2 will be produced when 5.0 moles of H_2O are produced?

5 **Question**: Given the following balanced equation:

$$2CO(g) + O_2(g) \rightarrow 2CO_2(g)$$

How many liters of $CO_2(g)$ will be produced when 4.5 liters of $O_2(g)$ react with excess $CO(g)$? 9 L

6 **Question**: Given the following balanced equation:

$$N_2(g) + 2O_2(g) \rightarrow 2NO_2(g)$$

How many liters of $O_2(g)$ will be required to react with 3.0 liters of $N_2(g)$?

7 **Question**: Given the following balanced equation:

$$4Al(s) + 3O_2(g) \rightarrow 2Al_2O_3(s)$$

How many grams of Al are needed to make 51.0 g of Al_2O_3?

8 **Question**: Given the following balanced equation:

$$4Al(s) + 3O_2(g) \rightarrow 2Al_2O_3(s)$$

How many grams of Al are needed to react with 32 grams of O_2?

9 **Question**: Given the following balanced equation:

$$2CH_3OH(l) + 3O_2(g) \rightarrow 2CO_2(g) + 4H_2O(l)$$

How many grams of water will be produced when 44.0 grams of CO_2 are produced?

10 **Question**: Given the following balanced equation taking place at STP:

$$2H_2(g) + O_2(g) \rightarrow 2H_2O(g)$$

How many liters of $H_2O(g)$ will be produced when 8.0 L of $O_2(g)$ react with excess $H_2(g)$?

11 **Question**: Given the following balanced equation taking place at STP:

$$C_3H_8(g) + 5O_2(g) \rightarrow 3CO_2(g) + 4H_2O(l)$$

How many grams of H_2O will be produced when 80.0 g of O_2 reacts with excess C_3H_8?

12 **Question**: Given the following balanced equation taking place at STP:

$$C_3H_8(g) + 5O_2(g) \rightarrow 3CO_2(g) + 4H_2O(l)$$

How many liters of $O_2(g)$ will be needed to produce 18.0 g of H_2O?

PART C – EXTENDED CONSTRUCTED-RESPONSE

Statement A: In his *Law of Definite Composition*, Proust stated that a compound consists of two or more different elements chemically combined in definite proportions by mass.

1 **Question**: Explain how this is illustrated in the formula for carbon dioxide, CO_2. [2]

Statement B: There are three different types of chemical formulas; empirical, molecular, and structural.

2 **Question**: Illustrate and describe in writing which formula(s) you would use if someone asked you to describe the composition and structure of an ethane molecule. [2]

Statement C: The empirical formula of a compound is the simplest whole number ratio of atoms of the elements in a compound. It may be the same or different from the molecular formula which is the actual ratio of the atoms in a molecule of that compound.

3 **Question**: Write the empirical formula of C_2H_6 and compare the masses of the molecular and empirical formulas to each other. [2]

Statement D: When water is decomposed into hydrogen and oxygen, the Law of Conservation of Matter is observed.

4 **Question**: Explain how this is illustrated in terms of both mole and mass values in the following equation: $2H_2O \rightarrow 2H_2 + O_2$ [3]

5   Question: Complete each of the following reactions by writing the correct formulas for the products, balance each equation, and identify the type of reaction synthesis, decomposition, single replacement, double replacement. [3]

a $Zn + O_2 \rightarrow$

b $H_2O \rightarrow$

c $Mg + HCl \rightarrow$

d $KI + PbCl_2 \rightarrow$

PART D – LABORATORY SKILLS

PERCENT BY MASS OF WATER IN A HYDRATED CRYSTAL

A hydrated crystal such as $CuSO_4 \cdot 5H_2O$ or $BaCl_2 \cdot 2H_2O$ is placed into a crucible, and the crucible and crystal are weighed. The crystal is then heated to constant mass. The mass which is "lost" during the heating is considered to be the water of hydration. The experimental result is used to find the percent of water of hydration in the original crystal and is found by using the following relationship:

$$\text{percent of water of hydration} = \frac{\text{mass of water}}{\text{mass of hydrated crystal}} \times 100\%$$

The end product after heating is a dry, anhydrous salt. Water is now added to the product in order to observe its transformation back into a hydrated crystal.

Directions: Find the percent (%) of hydration of each of the following hydrated crystals.

1   Question: _____ $Al(OH)_3 \bullet 3 H_2O$

2   Question: _____ $BaSO_4 \bullet 4 H_2O$

3   Question: _____ $CaCO_3 \bullet 2 H_2O$

UNIT 4
CHEMICAL BONDING

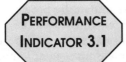

KEY IDEA **5**

ENERGY AND MATTER INTERACT
THROUGH FORCES THAT RESULT IN
CHANGES IN MOTION.

**PERFORMANCE
INDICATOR 3.1**

PERFORMANCE INDICATOR 5.2
*EXPLAIN CHEMICAL BONDING IN TERMS OF THE
BEHAVIOR OF ELECTRONS.*

UNIT 4 – MAJOR UNDERSTANDINGS

☆ 3.1dd Compounds can be differentiated by their physical and chemical properties.

☆ 5.2g Two major categories of compounds are ionic and molecular (covalent) compounds.

☆ 5.2a Chemical bonds are formed when valence electrons are:
• transferred from one atom to another (ionic)
• shared between atoms (covalent)
• mobile within a metal (metallic)

☆ 5.2e In a multiple covalent bond, more than one pair of electrons are shared between two atoms. Unsaturated organic compounds contain at least one double or triple bond.

☆ 5.2l Molecular polarity can be determined by the shape of the molecule and distribution of charge. Symmetrical (nonpolar) molecules include CO_2 , CH_4 , and diatomic elements. Asymmetrical (polar) molecules include HCl, NH_3, and H_2O.

☆ 5.2c When an atom gains one or more electrons, it becomes a negative ion and its radius increases. When an atom loses one or more electrons, it becomes a positive ion and its radius decreases.

☆ 5.2i When a bond is broken, energy is absorbed. When a bond is formed, energy is released.

Unit 4
Chemical Bonding

This unit is related to Key Idea 5 for the text and Performance Indicators 3.1 and 5.2 for the assessments.

Introduction

A **chemical bond** results from simultaneous attraction of electrons (either single or paired) to two or more nuclei. Two major categories of compounds are ionic or molecular (covalent) compounds.

A – The Nature of Chemical Bonding

Bonds Between Atoms

The electrons involved in bond formation may be transferred from one atom to another or may be shared equally or unequally between two atoms. When atoms of the elements enter into a chemical reaction, they do so in a manner that results in their becoming more like **inert** (noble gas) gas atoms. In this state, they contain their maximum complement of valence electrons, and they are in a condition of maximum stability.

UNIT 4 – MAJOR UNDERSTANDINGS (CONTINUED)

☆ 5.2b Atoms attain a stable valence electron configuration by bonding with other atoms. Noble gases have stable valence configurations and tend not to bond.

☆ 5.2n Physical properties of substances can be explained in terms of chemical bonds and intermolecular forces. These properties include conductivity, malleability, solubility, hardness, melting point, and boiling point.

☆ 5.2d Electron-dot diagrams (Lewis structures) can represent the valence electron arrangement in elements, compounds, and ions.

☆ 5.2j Electronegativity indicates how strongly an atom of an element attracts electrons in a chemical bond. Electronegativity values are assigned according to arbitrary scales.

☆ 5.2k The difference in electro-negativity between two bonded atoms is used to assess the degree of polarity in the bond.

☆ 5.2h Metals tend to react with nonmetals to form ionic compounds. Nonmetals tend to react with other nonmetals to form molecular (covalent) compounds. Ionic compounds containing polyatomic ions have both ionic and covalent bonding.

IONIC BONDS

An **ionic bond** is formed by the transfer of one or more electrons from metals to nonmetals. This transfer of electrons results in the formation of ions. The attraction between a positive ion and a negative ion is called an ionic bond.

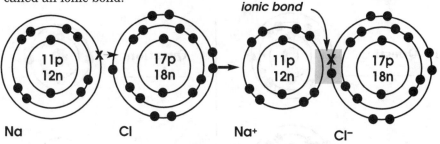

In ionic bonding, the number of electrons transferred is such that the atoms involved achieve an "inert" gas configuration, except for some transition elements. Since the ion has a different electron configuration than the atom, the properties of the ion differ from those of the atom. Also, ionic bonds may form between ions that were formed in a previous reaction as a result of a transfer of ions. For example:

$$\overset{+}{A}\overset{-}{g}NO_3(aq) \ + \ \overset{+}{N}\overset{-}{a}Cl(aq) \ \rightarrow \ \overset{+}{A}\overset{-}{g}Cl(s) \ + \ \overset{+}{N}\overset{-}{a}NO_3(aq)$$

Characteristics of Ionic Solids – Ionic solids have high melting points and do not conduct electricity. In the geometric structure of the solid ionic crystal, ions form the crystal lattice and are held in relatively fixed positions by electrostatic attraction. When melted or dissolved in water, the crystal lattice is destroyed and the ions move freely. This free movement of ions permits electrical conductivity. Examples of ionic solids are sodium chloride and magnesium oxide.

Crystal Lattice Energy – The structure at the right is an example of an ionic solid – sodium chloride (NaCl) (also, see crystals, pg. 108). Each ion is surrounded by an electric field of attraction to oppositely charged ions. The positions of the ions in a crystal of sodium chloride, determined by x-ray diffraction, are represented by lattice points which form a three-dimensional structure called a **lattice structure**. Its stability is measured experimentally and referred to as **crystal lattice energy**. The greater the energy released in the formation of the crystal, the more stable the crystal will be.

Key: ● sodium (Na⁺)
● chlorine (Cl⁻)

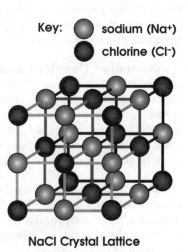

NaCl Crystal Lattice

Directions: Name each of the following elements and draw each ionic configuration with its positive or negative charge

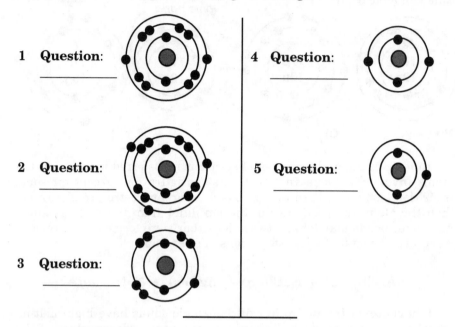

1 Question: _____

2 Question: _____

3 Question: _____

4 Question: _____

5 Question: _____

COVALENT BONDS

A **covalent bond** is a simultaneous attraction of two nuclei for the same electrons resulting in the sharing of those electrons. A covalent bond is formed when two atoms share electrons, instead of transferring them. In order to form this type of bond, the electronegativity difference between the two atoms forming the bond must be less than 1.7. Covalent bonds are classified as two types. Their structures can be demonstrated using Lewis dot structures.

Nonpolar Covalent Bond – When electrons are shared between atoms of the same element, they are shared equally, and the resulting bond is a **nonpolar bond**. An example of a nonpolar covalent bond is found in the fluorine molecule. Since the electronegativity of both fluorine atoms in the molecule is the same, the difference is zero, and the electron density of the molecule is symmetrical.

Polar Covalent Bonds – When electrons are shared between atoms of different elements, they are usually shared unequally. The resulting bond is polar. An example of a **polar covalent bond** is found in the hydrogen chloride molecule.

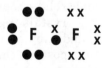

Chlorine, having an electronegativity value of 3.2 will attract the bonding electrons to a greater extent than hydrogen, which has an electronegativity value of 2.2. The difference of 1.0 denotes a covalent bond. Since the chlorine end of the molecule will show a greater electron density probability than the hydrogen end, the molecule will be asymmetrical and therefore polar.

In the illustration below, the hydrogen and fluoride molecules are both considered nonpolar, because both hydrogen atoms in the hydrogen molecule have the same electronegativity; therefore, the molecule is symmetrical. The same nonpolar symmetrical situation occurs in the fluorine molecule.

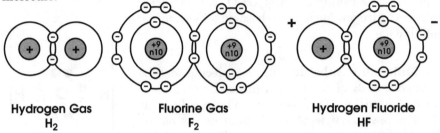

Hydrogen Gas
H_2

Fluorine Gas
F_2

Hydrogen Fluoride
HF

In the HF molecule, hydrogen has an electronegavity rating of 2.1 and fluorine 4.0; therefore, the fluorine atom attracts the shared electrons to a greater extent than hydrogen. The fluorine portion of the molecule becomes more negative, but unlike the hydrogen, it becomes positive. This arrangement makes for an unsymmetrical molecule called a **dipole**. The product of the charge and the distance of partial separation is called the **dipole moment**.

SKILLS 5.2V DISTINGUISH BETWEEN NONPOLAR COVALENT BONDS (TWO OF THE SAME NONMETALS) AND POLAR COVALENT BONDS.

Directions: Questions 6 through 13: : Identify the bond in each of the following molecules as either **polar** or **nonpolar**.

6 _____ HBr   10 _____ N_2

7 _____ Cl_2 11 _____ HCl

8 _____ HF   12 _____ O_2

9 _____ I_2 13 _____ F_2

Coordinate Covalent Bonds – When the two shared electrons forming a covalent bond are both donated by one of the atoms, this bond is called a coordinate covalent bond. A coordinate covalent bond, once formed, is not different from an ordinary covalent bond. The difference lies in the source of the electrons involved in the bond. This type of bond is frequently involved in the bonding within polyatomic ions and is very important in modern acid-base theories.

A classic example of a coordinate covalent bond is the ammonium ion. In the ammonium ion, the nitrogen atom has five valence electrons. Three electrons are unpaired but are shared with the electrons from three hydrogen atoms. The other two form a full pair and are not shared.

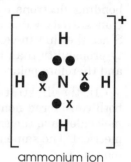

ammonium ion

It is at this unshared pair of electrons that the electron density is so great that the molecule may attract a hydrogen ion (proton). When that occurs, the ion is formed and takes on a charge of positive one (+1). For example, water (H_2O) can attract a proton (hydrogen nucleus) to become a hydromium ion (H_3O^+)

Molecular Substances – A molecule may be defined as a discrete particle formed by covalently bonded atoms. A molecule has also been defined as the smallest particle of an element or compound capable of independent existence. When a stable molecule is formed, a covalent bond is established. The atoms that form the bond usually assume electronic structures of inert gases by sharing electrons. Examples of molecules include:

hydromium ion

$$H_2 \quad NH_3 \quad H_2O \quad HCl \quad CCl_4 \quad S_8 \quad C_6H_{12}O_6$$

Characteristics of Molecular solids – Molecular substances may exist as gases, liquids, or solids, depending on the attraction that exists between the molecules. Generally, molecular solids are soft, good electrical insulators, poor heat conductors, and have low melting points.

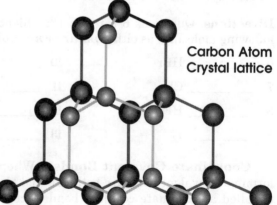

Carbon Atom Crystal lattice

Network Solids – Certain solids consist of covalently bonded atoms linked in a network that extends throughout the sample with an absence of simple discrete particles. Such a substance is said to be a network solid.

Generally, network solids are hard, are poor conductors of heat and electricity, and have high melting points. Examples of network solids are diamond (C), silicon carbide (SiC), and silicon dioxide (SiO_2).

METALLIC BONDING

Metallic bonding occurs between atoms of metals that have a small number of valence electrons leaving them with many vacant valence orbitals and low ionization energies.

A **metallic bond** consists of an arrangement of positive ions that are located at the crystal lattice sites and are immersed in a "sea" of mobile electrons. These mobile electrons can be considered as belonging to the whole crystal rather than to individual atoms.

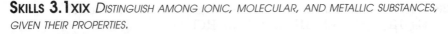

Metallic Bonding

Note: This mobility of electrons (previous page) distinguishes the metallic bond from an ionic or covalent bond and gives the metal the following characteristics:

- good conductors of electricity and heat
- great strength
- malleability and ductility
- luster

SKILLS 3.1XIX *DISTINGUISH AMONG IONIC, MOLECULAR, AND METALLIC SUBSTANCES, GIVEN THEIR PROPERTIES.*

Directions: Questions 14 through 23: Distinguish among *ionic*, *molecular*, and *metallic* substances according to their properties.

Ionic Properties	Molecular Properties	Metallic Properties
• poor conductor of electricity in solid state • high melting point • when melted or dissolved in water, become good conductors	• exists in gas, liquid, or solid state • soft • good insulators • poor heat conductor • low melting points	• good conductor of heat and electricity • great strength • good malleability and ductility • luster

14 _____ Al

15 _____ NaCl

16 _____ H$_2$O

17 _____ KF

(continued)

18 _____ HCl   21 _____ NH_3

19 _____ $C_{12}H_{22}O_{11}$ 22 _____ CaS

20 _____ Fe   23 _____ Cu

SKILLS 5.2I DEMONSTRATE BONDING CONCEPTS USING LEWIS DOT STRUCTURES
REPRESENTING VALANCE ELECTRONS; TRANSFERRED (IONIC BONDING; SHARED COVALENT
BONDING), IN A STABLE OCTET.

24 Which molecule contains a nonpolar covalent bond?

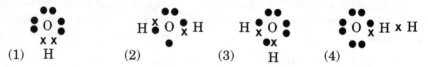

25 Which substance exists as a metallic crystal at STP (standard, temperature, pressure)?
(1) Ar   (2) Au   (3) SiO_2 (4) CO_2

26 Which of the following Lewis dot structures best represents water?

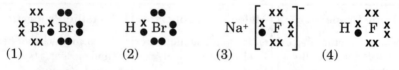

27 The bonds present in silicon carbide, SiC, are
(1) covalent   (3) metallic
(2) ionic   (4) van der Waals

28 Which compound has the greatest degree of ionic character?
(1) HF   (2) HI   (3) HCl   (4) HBr

29 Which electron dot formula represents a molecule that contains a
nonpolar covalent bond?

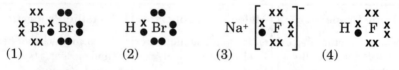

SATURATED & UNSATURATED COMPOUNDS

A bond formed between carbon atoms by the sharing of one pair of
electrons is referred to as a **single bond**. Organic compounds, where carbon atoms are bonded by the sharing of a single pair of electrons, are said
to be **saturated compounds**.

Organic compounds, containing two adjacent carbon atoms bonded by the sharing of more than one pair of electrons, are said to be **unsaturated compounds**. A bond between carbon atoms by the sharing of two pairs of electrons is referred to as a **double bond**. A bond formed between carbon atoms by the sharing of three pairs of electrons is referred to as a **triple bond**. Examples include

$$H-\underset{\underset{\displaystyle H}{|}}{\overset{\overset{\displaystyle H}{|}}{C}}-\underset{\underset{\displaystyle H}{|}}{\overset{\overset{\displaystyle H}{|}}{C}}-H \qquad H-\underset{\underset{\displaystyle H}{|}}{C}=\underset{\underset{\displaystyle H}{|}}{C}-H \qquad H-C\equiv C-H$$

Single Bonds   Double Bonds   Triple Bonds
(Saturated)

B – DIRECTIONAL NATURE
OF COVALENT BONDS

NON POLAR MOLECULES

Because of the directional nature of the covalent bonds which form them, some molecules composed of more than two atoms may be nonpolar – even though the individual bonds are polar if the shape of the molecule is such that symmetric distribution of charge results (i.e., carbon dioxide – CO_2 is a nonpolar molecule). **CO_2** molecule can be shown in many ways. Examples follow:

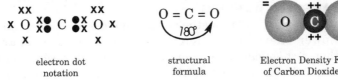

electron dot notation   structural formula   Electron Density Formula of Carbon Dioxide – CO_2

Because of the greater electronegativity of oxygen, the electron density is greater around the oxygen atoms. The bond with an electronegativity difference of 0.9 is polar, but because the bond angle is 180° and the molecule is symmetrical, it is considered a nonpolar molecule.

Carbon tetrafluoride molecule can be shown to be a nonpolar molecule with polar bonds (other examples include: CH_4, CCl_4, CBr_4, CI_4):

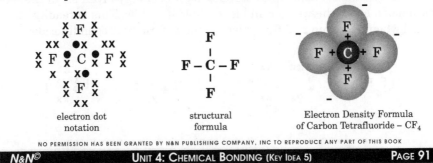

electron dot notation   structural formula   Electron Density Formula of Carbon Tetrafluoride – CF_4

Fluorine has an electronegativity of 4.0, and Carbon has an electronegativity of 2.6. The difference, 1.4, indicates a polar covalent bond. However, because the tetrahedral molecule is symmetrical, the molecule is nonpolar.

When two hydrogen atoms bond to form a hydrogen molecule (H_2) they form a nonpolar bond with an electronegativity difference of 0. The molecule they form is a nonpolar, symmetrical molecule. This is true of other diatomic molecules such as oxygen, chlorine, and fluorine.

Because of its molecular structure, carbon tetrafluoride, called Freon-14 (CF_4) gas is used in refrigeration. Freon is symmetrical. It forms bonds between two Freon molecules with weak van der Waals forces which are easily affected by temperature and pressure. This causes the gas to condense and evaporate readily, making it a good refrigerant. Note: recent government restrictions have banned its use because of its negative effect on global warming.

CHEMICAL ENERGY

Potential energy is stored in molecules, and the transfer or release of some of this energy manifests itself in the form of chemical energy. Substances possess energy because of their composition and structure. Factors such as mass, types of bonding, and types of motion influence the absorption and storage of energy by molecules.

ENERGY CHANGES IN BONDING

When two atoms are held together by a chemical bond, they are generally at a lower energy condition than when they are separated. Therefore, when a chemical bond is formed, energy is released, and when a chemical bond is broken, energy is absorbed.

BONDING & STABILITY

Because there is a release of energy when bonds are formed, systems at lower energy levels are more stable than systems at higher energy levels. So, it follows that bonding will more often occur among atoms if the changes lead to a lower energy condition and, therefore, a more stable structure. The more energy given off when a bond is formed, the stronger and more stable the bond will be. Also, the less energy given off in the formation of a bond, the weaker and less stable it will be. This is readily illustrated when hydrogen and fluorine combine to form hydrogen fluoride:

$$\text{H} \overset{\bullet}{\underset{\times}{}} \text{H} \ + \ \overset{\bullet\bullet}{\underset{\bullet\bullet}{}} \text{F} \overset{\times\times}{\underset{\times\times}{}} \text{F} \overset{\times}{\underset{\times}{}} \ \rightarrow \ \text{H} \overset{\times\times}{\underset{\times\times}{}} \text{F} \overset{\times}{\underset{\times}{}} \ + \ \text{H} \overset{\times\times}{\underset{\times\times}{}} \text{F} \overset{\times}{\underset{\times}{}}$$

In order for the bonds of the reactants (ex.: hydrogen and fluoride molecules) to break and form the products, energy must be added:

$$436.8 \text{ kJ/mole} + 155.4 \text{ kJ/mole} \rightarrow 567 \text{ kJ/mole} + 567 \text{ kJ/mole}$$

total energy in = 592.3 kJ   *total energy given off* = 1,134 kJ

Note 1: As bonds are formed, energy is given off. It is easily seen that more energy is given off in the formation of the products, than is required to break the bonds in the reactants. Therefore, the products are more stable than the reactants.

Note 2: Review from Unit 1 the definition of valence electrons. Note that valence electrons may be represented by electron dot symbols in which the kernel of the atom is represented by the letter symbol for the element and the valence electrons are represented by dots.

Note 3: Metals tend to react with nonmetals to form ionic compounds (i.e. NaCl, MgBr, KI). Nonmetals tend to react with nonmetals to form covalent (molecular) compounds; i.e. CO, NF_3, SCl_2. Compounds containing polyatomic ions have both ionic and covalent bonding. By definition these compounds are charged ionic substances; but, within the molecule they have covalent bonds; i.e. SO_4^{2-}, PO_4^{3-}, CN^-.

POLAR MOLECULES

Generally, the geometric structure of covalent substances, which result from the directional nature of the covalent bond, helps to explain properties of the resulting molecule. The polarity of a water molecule is explained by the asymmetrical shape of the molecule. The water molecule (H_2O) is shown as follows:

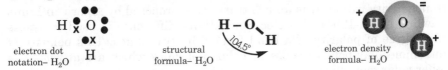

electron dot notation– H_2O structural formula– H_2O electron density formula– H_2O

Oxygen's electronegativity is 3.4, and hydrogen's electronegativity is 2.1. The difference, 1.3, indicates a polar covalent bond. The bond angle is such that there exists an unsymmetrical distribution of electron density. Therefore, a polar molecule results. Other examples of polar molecules include the following (see *Reference Table S*):

Hydrogen Chloride – electronegativity = hydrogen 2.1, chlorine = 3.2, difference = 1.1

Ammonia – electronegativity = hydrogen 2.1, nitrogen = 3.0, difference = 0.9

The electrons involved in bond formation may be transferred from one atom to another or may be shared equally or unequally between two atoms. When the atoms of these elements enter into a chemical reaction, they do so in a manner that results in their becoming more like "inert" gas atoms. In this state, they contain their maximum complement of valance electrons, and they are in a condition of maximum stability.

IONIC RADIUS

A loss or gain of electrons by an atom causes a corresponding change in size. Metal atoms lose one or more electrons when they form ions. Ionic radii of metals are smaller than the corresponding atomic radii. Nonmetal atoms gain one or more electrons when they form ions. Ionic radii of nonmetals are larger than the corresponding atomic radii. Atomic and ionic radii are usually measured in Angstrom (Å) units ($1Å = 1 \times 10^{-10}$ meter).

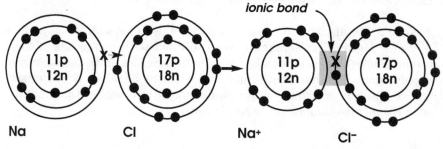

C – INTERMOLECULAR FORCES

Physical properties of substances such as conductivity, malleability, solubility, hardness, melting point, and boiling point can be explained in terms of chemical bonds and intermolecular forces. The strength of attraction that an atom has for another atom is a measure of its electronegativity rating. It is an arbitrary scale proposed by American Linus Pawling (1901-1994). The electronegativity difference is used to assess the degree of polarity of a bond formed by two atoms. This polarity of intramolecular bonds results in polar molecules which are attracted to other polar molecules.

DIPOLES

The asymmetric distribution of an electrical charge in a molecule causes a molecule that is polar in nature and is referred to as a **dipole**. That is, the uneven electron cloud density will cause one end of a molecule to be more negative than the other end. A molecule composed of only two atoms will be a dipole if the bond between the atoms is polar. For example, the hydrogen chloride molecule is a dipole because

- the chlorine atom is larger than the hydrogen atom, and
- the difference in electronegativity of hydrogen (2.1) and chlorine (3.2).

These factors allow chlorine to share electrons closer to itself than to hydrogen. When the bond is formed, the electron density around the chlorine atom is greater than around the hydrogen atom, leading to a polar molecule (a dipole). The bond between two hydrogen chloride molecules is a result of dipole—dipole attraction (at right)

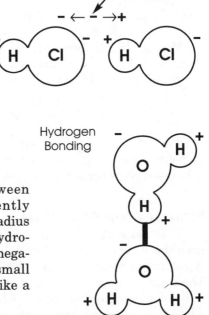

HYDROGEN BONDING

Hydrogen bonds are formed between molecules when hydrogen is covalently bonded to an element of small atomic radius and high electronegativity. When a hydrogen atom is bonded to a highly electronegative atom, the hydrogen has such a small share of the electron pair that it acts like a bare proton.

As such it can be attracted to the more electronegative atom of an adjacent molecule. The sulfur atom is larger in radius and has an electronegativity of 2.6, compared to the smaller radius of the oxygen atom and its higher electronegativity of 3.4. The greater polarity of the water molecules results in stronger electrostatic bonds between them. This accounts for the lower vapor pressure and the higher boiling point of H_2O, as compared with the boiling point of H_2S.

Hydrogen bonding (shown in a quantity of water) is important in compounds of hydrogen with fluorine, oxygen, or nitrogen. These compounds represent special cases of dipole to dipole attraction.

These forces also account for the meniscus when water or any other liquid is poured into a measuring instrument.

VAN DER WAALS FORCES

In the absence of dipole attraction and hydrogen bonding, as in nonpolar molecules, weak attractive forces exist between molecules. These forces are called **van der Waals forces**.

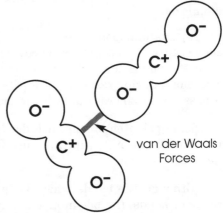

Van der Waals forces make it possible for species of small nonpolar molecules, such as hydrogen, helium, oxygen, etc., to exist in the liquid and solid phases under conditions of low temperature and high pressure.

Van der Waals forces appear to be due to chance distribution of electrons resulting in momentary dipole attractions. Therefore, these forces are momentary electrostatic forces that increase as the distance between molecules decreases. Also, as the size of the molecules increases, the greater the Van der Waals forces.

The effect of molecular size on the magnitude of the van der Waals forces accounts for the increasing boiling points of a series of similar compounds (such as the alkane series of hydrocarbons).

MOLECULE ION ATTRACTION

Polar solvents, when interacting with ionic compounds, attract ions from these compounds and form a solution. Ionic compounds are generally soluble in polar solvents such as water, alcohol, and liquid ammonia. The negative ion of the substance being dissolved is attracted to the positive end of the adjacent polar molecules, while the positive ion is attracted to the negative end of the polar molecules. Water is the polar substance most commonly used to dissolve these ionic compounds. When an ionic compound is dissolved in water, its crystal lattice is destroyed, and water molecules surround each ion, forming hydrated ions. It is because water is a dipole that this attraction between the water molecules and the positive or negative ion exists. The orienting of water molecules around ions is called the hydration of the ions. This process is important in aqueous chemistry.

POLYATOMIC IONS

A single atom with a charge is called a **monatomic ion**. A compound of two or more covalently bonded atoms with a charge is called a polyatomic ion.

A polyatomic ion is very stable and behaves like a monatomic particle, because it contains strong covalent bonds. These bonds are stronger than the bonds that hold it to the rest of the atoms in the compound. Therefore, during reactions, the polyatomic ion usually remains intact as it passes from the reactants to the products.

Some polyatomic ions include: NH_4^+ (ammonium ion), PO_4^{-3} (phosphate ion), and NO_3^- (nitrate ion). Other examples can be found in the *Reference Table E*.

Although the bonds which keep the atoms in a polyatomic ion are covalent bonds, the polyatomic ions possess a charge. When they attach themselves to a metal ion or another polyatomic ion, they do so by forming an ionic bond. The final compound contains both ionic and covalent bonds. Some examples include: $Na^+NO_3^-$ and $NH_4^+OH^-$. In general,

- metals tend to react with nonmetals to form ionic compounds;

- nonmetals tend to react with other nonmetals to form covalent (molecular compounds; and,

- ionic compounds containing polyatomic ions have both ionic and covalent bonding.

REAL WORLD CONNECTIONS

Free radicals are molecules which have one open bond and, as a result, have become charged. When these highly reactive molecules are present in great numbers in living organisms, they often react with other molecules, exchanging electrons and disrupting their normal molecular structure. This is particularly damaging in the case of large functioning macromolecules, such as carbohydrates, proteins, and nucleic acids.

Photosynthesis is the process during which light energy is converted into the chemical energy of organic molecules. Most of the chemical energy available to organisms results from photosynthetic activity. In addition to food production, photosynthesis releases most of the oxygen that is in the air.

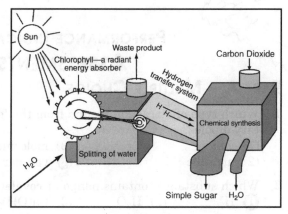

Most cells which carry on photosynthesis contain chloroplasts. These chloroplasts contain pigments which include chlorophylls ("green leaf"). Chlorophyll absorbs light energy. In the chloroplasts, carbon dioxide (CO_2) and water (H_2O) are used in the formation of simple sugar ($C_6H_{12}O_6$) molecules and oxygen (O_2). During photosynthesis, light energy is trapped by chlorophyll and converted into the chemical energy of simple sugar molecules. Simplified summary statements for photosynthesis are:

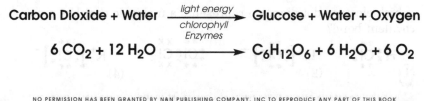

DNA bonding. In 1953, James Watson (1928-), an American biologist, and Francis Crick (1916-), a British biophysicist, developed a model of the DNA molecule. This most important scientific breakthrough won them the Nobel Prize in 1962 and opened the door to modern genetics. In this model, the DNA molecule consists of two complementary chains of nucleotides.

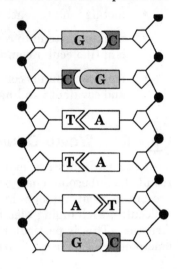

The DNA molecule has a "ladder" type organization. This "ladder" is thought to be twisted around a protein "framework" in the form of a double helix. The uprights of the "ladder" are composed of alternating phosphate and deoxyribose molecules. Each rung of the "ladder" is composed of bases held together by relatively weak hydrogen bonds: adenine (A) - thymine (T) and guanine (G) - cytosine (C); thus the combinations: A—T and C—G.

PERFORMANCE INDICATOR 3.1
ASSESSMENTS
PART A - MULTIPLE CHOICE

1   Which type of attraction results from the formation of weak momentary dipoles?
   (1) ionic
   (2) metallic
   (3) molecule-ion
   (4) van der Waals forces

2   Which substance contains nonpolar covalent bonds?
   (1) H_2 (2) H_2O (3) $Ca(OH)_2$ (4) CaO

3   Which substance contains a bond with the greatest ionic character?
   (1) KCl (2) HCl (3) Cl_2 (4) F_2

4   Compared to an atom of potassium, an atom of calcium has a
   (1) larger radius and lower reactivity
   (2) larger radius and higher reactivity
   (3) smaller radius and lower reactivity
   (4) smaller radius and higher reactivity

5   Which electron dot diagram represents a molecule that has a polar covalent bond?

   H ×Cl: Li⁺ [:Cl:]⁻   :Cl×Clx   K⁺ [:Cl:]⁻
   (1)   (2)   (3)   (4)

6 Which type of bond is formed when an atom of potassium transfers an electron to a bromine atom?
(1) metallic (3) nonpolar covalent
(2) ionic (4) polar covalent

7 Which molecule is polar and contains polar bonds?
(1) CCl_4 (2) CO_2 (3) N_2 (4) NH_3

8 The *strongest* van der Waals forces of attraction exists between molecules of
(1) I_2 (2) Br_2 (3) Cl_2 (4) F_2

9 Which molecule has an asymmetrical shape?
(1) N_2 (2) NH_3 (3) Cl_2 (4) CCl_4

10 The elements Li and F combine to form an ionic compound. The electron configurations in this compound are the same as the electron configurations of atoms in Group
(1) 1 (2) 14 (3) 17 (4) 18

11 Which electron dot formula represents a substance that contains a nonpolar covalent bond?

[Na]$^+$[ːC̤Iˣ]$^-$ ˣC̤Iˣ ˣ C̤Iː   HˣC̤Iˣ   ːO̤ˣH
(1) (2) (3) (4) H

12 The bond between hydrogen and oxygen in a water molecule is classified as
(1) ionic and nonpolar (3) covalent and nonpolar
(2) ionic and polar (4) covalent and polar

13 In which system do molecule-ion attractions exist?
(1) $NaCl(aq)$ (3) $C_6H_{12}O_6(aq)$
(2) $NaCl(s)$ (4) $C_6H_{12}O_6(s)$

14 Which sequence of Group 18 elements demonstrates a gradual *decrease* in the strength of the van der Waals forces?
(1) $Ar(l)$, $Kr(l)$, $Ne(l)$, $Xe(l)$ (3) $Ne(l)$, $Ar(l)$, $Kr(l)$, $Xe(l)$
(2) $Kr(l)$, $Xe(l)$, $Ar(l)$, $Ne(l)$ (4) $Xe(l)$, $Kr(l)$, $Ar(l)$, $Ne(l)$

15 Which substance is an example of a network solid?
(1) nitrogen dioxide (3) carbon dioxide
(2) sulfur dioxide (4) silicon dioxide

16 Which combination of atoms can form a polar covalent bond?
(1) H and H (2) H and Br (3) N and N (4) Na and Br

17 Which pair of atoms is held together by a covalent bond?
(1) HCl (2) LiCl (3) NaCl (4) KCl
hydrogen is an exception

PART B – CONSTRUCTED-RESPONSE

Directions: Use the following chemical equation for questions 1 through 3:

$$N_2 + 3H_2 \rightarrow 2NH_3 + 92.4 \text{ kJ}$$

1   **Question**: Explain how the combined bond strengths of the reactants compares to the bond strengths found in the products of the accompanying reaction. [1]

2   **Question**: Describe the type of bond that exists between the atoms making up the NH_3 molecule. [1]

3   **Question**: The NH_3 molecule produced is capable of combining chemically with a H^+ ion to form a coordinate covalent bond as it produces the ammonium ion, NH^{4+}. Explain how this coordinate covalent bond is formed. [1]

Directions: Using the representative chemical species illustrated below, answer questions 4 through 7:

$$H_2, N_2, O_2, H_2O, NH_3, NH_4^+, CO_2, CCl_4, NaCl, CuSO_4, Fe, Al$$

4   **Question**: Identify and write the formula(s) of the molecule(s) that could form a coordinate covalent bond with an H^+ ion. [1]

5   **Question**: Identify and write the formula(s) for the compound(s) that contain both ionic and covalent bonds. [1]

6   **Question**: Identify and write the formula(s) for the compound(s) that contain a coordinate covalent bond. [1]

7   **Question**: Identify and write the formula(s) for the metals that are illustrated. [2]

Directions: Using the representative chemical species illustrated below, answer questions 8 through 14:

$$H_2, N_2, O_2, H_2O, NH_3, NH_4^+, CO_2, CCl_4, NaCl, CuSO_4, Fe, Al$$

8 **Question**: Identify and write the formula(s) of the nonpolar molecule(s) illustrated. [5]

9 **Question**: Identify and write the formula(s) of the polar molecule(s) illustrated. [1]

10 **Question**: Identify and write the formula(s) for the ionic compound(s) illustrated. [2]

11 **Question**: Identify and write the formula(s) for the molecule(s) that are nonpolar and held together by nonpolar covalent bonds. [4]

12 **Question**: Identify and write the formula(s) for the moleclules that are nonpolar and held together by polar covalent bonds. [2]

13 **Question**: Identify and write the formula(s) of those elements that are good conductors of heat and electricity, and are malleable and ductile. [2]

14 **Question**: Identify and write the formula(s) of the substance(s) that contain both ionic and covalent bonds. [2]

PART C – EXTENDED CONSTRUCTED-RESPONSE

Article A: The many different organic molecules produced by carbon are made possible by the fact that carbon atoms are tetravalent. Carbon needs to form four bonds in order to complete its outer principle energy level. The electron configuration in the ground state only produces two half-filled orbitals in the *p* sublevel. However, due to *sp³* hybridization, carbon mixes the orbitals in its outer principal energy level and produces four half-filled orbitals, each with only one electron in it. These four half-filled orbitals are what make it possible for carbon to always form four bonds.

1   **Question**: Using the information supplied by the *Periodic Table*, state which outer principal energy level contains the valence electrons of carbon. [1]

2   **Question**: Based on the article and based upon the electron configuration of carbon in the ground state, state how many bonds it would form if it did not undergo hybridization. [1]

Statement B: The polarity of molecules is based upon the distribution of the electrons within the molecule. If the electrons are evenly distributed within the molecule, the molecule will be nonpolar. However, if the electrons are unevenly distributed within the molecule, then the molecule will be polar.

3   **Question**: Using the electron distribution within the molecule and bond type between the atoms explain why water is a polar molecule. [1]

4   **Question**: Explain in terms of bond type and electron distribution why CH_4 is a nonpolar molecule. [1]

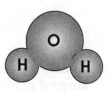

Statement C: Physical properties of substances can be explained in terms of chemical bonds and intermolecular forces. These properties include conductivity, malleability, solubility, hardness, melting point, and boiling point. Metals tend to react with nonmetals to form ionic compounds, and nonmetals tend to react with other nonmetals to form molecular compounds.

5   **Question**: In terms of the forces of attraction holding them together, explain why a NaCl crystal has a melting point of 800°C while an ice cube of pure water has a melting pint of 0°C. [3]

(ionic)NaCl has a stronger bond than (covalent)H2O so it takes more energy to break the bonds.

Statement D: Electronegativity indicates how strongly an atom of an element attracts electrons in a chemical bond. The difference in electronegativity between the bonding atoms determines the type of bond that exists between them.

6   **Question**: Arrange the following compounds in order of increasing electronegativity difference between the bonding atoms, and identify the type of bond that forms between the bonding atoms in each formula: $NaCl$, $AlCl_3$, PCl_5 [3]

Part D - Laboratory Skills

Identify Differences Between Inorganic and Organic Substances

Differences in solubility, melting point, stability, and electrical conductivity may be qualitatively demonstrated using sodium chloride and sucrose.

These differences are due, in the most part, to types of bonds in organic and inorganic compounds in solvents. Organic compounds dissolve in nonpolar solvents and are generally insoluble in polar compounds except organic acids and alcohol. Because of the weak van der Waals forces between the molecules, the molecules dissociate easily, giving them low melting points. Also as a result, they do not conduct electricity. Whereas, inorganic compounds usually have ionic bonds that will dissolve in polar solvents but not in nonpolar solvents. They have high melting points, making them very stable, and will conduct electricity in solution.

There are exceptions to these general observations. For instance, although plastics are organic substances, some conduct electricity and have high melting points.

Directions: For questions 1 through 4, indicate whether the characteristics listed below refer to inorganic or organic compounds.

1   **Question**: High melting point   _____

2   **Question**: Dissolves in nonpolar solvents.   _____

3   **Question**: When melted, conducts electricity.   _____

4   **Question**: Readily conducts electricity in solution. _____

5   **Question**: Why does a solution of NaCl conduct electricity and a solution of sucrose does not?

6   **Question**: Why does NaCl and sucrose dissolve in water?

7   **Question**: Which compound is more soluble in water? Explain.

UNIT 5
PHYSICAL BEHAVIOR
OF MATTER

KEY IDEA **4** ENERGY EXISTS IN MANY FORMS, AND WHEN THESE FORMS CHANGE ENERGY IS CONSERVED.

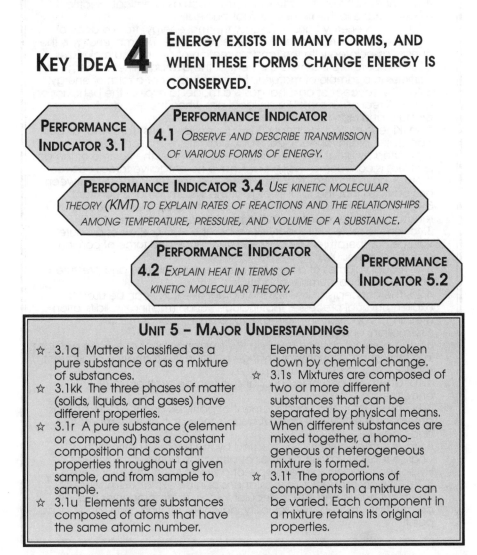

PERFORMANCE INDICATOR 3.1

PERFORMANCE INDICATOR
4.1 *OBSERVE AND DESCRIBE TRANSMISSION OF VARIOUS FORMS OF ENERGY.*

PERFORMANCE INDICATOR **3.4** *USE KINETIC MOLECULAR THEORY (KMT) TO EXPLAIN RATES OF REACTIONS AND THE RELATIONSHIPS AMONG TEMPERATURE, PRESSURE, AND VOLUME OF A SUBSTANCE.*

PERFORMANCE INDICATOR
4.2 *EXPLAIN HEAT IN TERMS OF KINETIC MOLECULAR THEORY.*

PERFORMANCE INDICATOR 5.2

UNIT 5 – MAJOR UNDERSTANDINGS

☆ 3.1q Matter is classified as a pure substance or as a mixture of substances.

☆ 3.1kk The three phases of matter (solids, liquids, and gases) have different properties.

☆ 3.1r A pure substance (element or compound) has a constant composition and constant properties throughout a given sample, and from sample to sample.

☆ 3.1u Elements are substances composed of atoms that have the same atomic number.

Elements cannot be broken down by chemical change.

☆ 3.1s Mixtures are composed of two or more different substances that can be separated by physical means. When different substances are mixed together, a homogeneous or heterogeneous mixture is formed.

☆ 3.1t The proportions of components in a mixture can be varied. Each component in a mixture retains its original properties.

☆ 3.1nn Differences in properties such as density, particle size, molecular polarity, boiling and freezing points, and solubility permit physical separation of the components of the mixture.

☆ 3.1oo A solution is a homogeneous mixture of a solute dissolved in a solvent. The solubility of a solute in a given amount of solvent is dependent on the temperature, the pressure, and the chemical natures of the solute and solvent.

☆ 3.1pp The concentration of a solution may be expressed in molarity (M), percent by volume, percent by mass, or parts per million (ppm).

☆ 3.1qq The addition of a nonvolatile solute to a solvent causes the boiling point of the solvent to increase and the freezing point of the solvent to decrease. The greater the concentration of solute particles, the greater the effect.

☆ 4.1a Energy can exist in different forms, such as chemical, electrical, electromagnetic, heat, mechanical, nuclear.

☆ 4.2a Heat is energy transfer (usually thermal energy) from a body of higher temperature to one of lower temperature. Thermal energy is the energy associated with the random motion of atoms and molecules.

☆ 4.2b Temperature is a measurement of the average kinetic energy of particles in a sample of material. Temperature is not a form of energy.

☆ 3.4a The concept of an ideal gas is a model to explain the behavior of gases. A real gas is most like an ideal gas when the real gas is at low pressure and high temperature.

☆ 3.4b Kinetic molecular theory (KMT) for an ideal gas states that all gas particles: • are in random, constant, straight-line motion. • are separated by great distances relative to their size; the volume of the gas particles is considered negligible. • have no attractive forces between them. • have collisions that may result in a transfer of energy between gas particles, but the total energy of the system remains constant.

☆ 3.4d Collision theory states that a reaction is most likely to occur if reactant particles collide with the proper energy and orientation.

☆ 3.4c Kinetic molecular theory describes the relationships of pressure, volume, temperature, velocity, and frequency and force of collisions among gas modules.

☆ 3.4e Equal volumes of gases at the same temperature and pressure contain an equal number of particles.

☆ 4.2c The concepts of kinetic and potential energy can be used to explain physical processes that include: fusion (melting), solidification (freezing), vaporization (boiling, evaporation), condensation, sublimation, and deposition.

☆ 3.2a A physical change results in the rearrangement of existing particles in a substance. A chemical change results in the formation of different substances with changed properties.

☆ 4.1b Chemical and physical changes can be exothermic or endothermic.

☆ 3.1jj The structure and arrangement of particles and their interactions determine the physical state of a substance at a given temperature and pressure.

☆ 5.2m Intermolecular forces created by the unequal distribution of charge result in varying degrees of attraction between molecules. Hydrogen bonding is an example of a strong intermolecular force.

☆ 5.2n Physical properties of substances can be explained in terms of chemical bonds and intermolecular forces. These properties include conductivity, malleability, solubility, hardness, melting point, and boiling point.

UNIT 5
PHYSICAL BEHAVIOR OF MATTER

This unit is related to Key Idea 4 for the text and Performance Indicators 3.1, 3.4, 4.1, 4.2, and 5.2 for the assessments.

INTRODUCTION

Matter is something that occupies space, has mass, and exists as a solid, liquid, or gas. Matter is classified as a substance or a mixture of substances.

SKILLS 3.1XXII *USE A SIMPLE **PARTICLE MODEL** TO DIFFERENTIATE AMONG PROPERTIES OF A SOLID, A LIQUID, AND A GAS,*

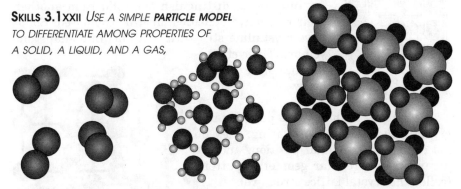

Gas - particles are random and at greater distances.   Liquid - particles are less random, closer, and better organized.   Solid - particles are arranged in a specific pattern making it rigid.

Compounds can be differentiated by their chemical and physical properties. **Properties of matter** are those characteristics that distinguish one kind of matter from another. There are two types of properties: physical and chemical.

PHYSICAL PROPERTIES

Physical properties are those characteristics that can be described without changing the identity of the material. Physical properties are described as

- **Extensive Properties** – These are dependent on the amount of material in a system and include volume, mass, length, width, and height (i.e. the energy content in a pot of tea is greater than a cup of tea).

- **Intensive Properties** – these are *not* dependent on the quantity of material present in a system. They include melting and boiling point, color, and density (also refracture index, crystalline shape ductility and malleability).

CHEMICAL PROPERTIES

Chemical Properties describe the behavior of a substance when it reacts with other substances. In gases, oxygen supports combustion but does not itself burn. Hydrogen burns but does not support combustion.

A – PHASES OF MATTER

The term "**phase**" is used to refer to the gas (g), liquid (l), or solid (s) form of matter. Note that the word "phase" is now used instead of "state" to avoid confusion with other conditions, such as the "state of equilibrium."

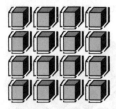

Solid - particles vibrate "in place".

SOLID PHASE (s)

In order to distinguish one solid from another, their respective densities must be compared. Solids have crystalline structures with definite shape and volume. Their characteristics are explained below.

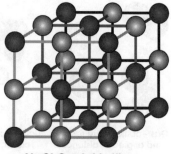

NaCl Crystal Lattice

Crystals – Although the particles in a crystal are constantly vibrating, they do not change their regular positions and are arranged in a regular geometric pattern (called the crystal lattice structure).

The particles in glass and certain plastics are not arranged in a regular geometric pattern and behave as highly viscous liquids. Since all true solids have crystalline structures, these materials are often considered solids, but are really **super-cooled liquids**. Therefore, they are not considered true solids.

©PhotoDisk

🌐 REAL WORLD CONNECTIONS

Metallic Solids have unique properties:

*   **Strength** (as in iron and its alloys) makes metals useful in the manufacturing of cars, buildings, bridges, and machinery.

*   **Malleability** (as in copper and aluminum) allows the metal to be drawn into wires. Also, since these

metals have dislocated electrons, they can carry an electric current or heat energy.

Crystalline Solids (such as copper II sulfate) is used to clear ponds and lakes of algae along with common table salts which provide us with essential nutrients.

Amorphous Solids, such as glass and opal, are unique since their atoms do not exist in the normal ridged crystalline structure. Instead, they are fixed in a completely random manner throughout the material. Often, these metals are said to have the properties of liquids with very high viscosity. If broken, they shatter into irregular sized pieces.

LIQUID PHASE (*L*)

In the liquid phase, the particles are character-ized as having acquired two types of motion, vibrat-ing and rotating. However, this phase is also considered an intermediate state having all three types of motion found in the gaseous state, but to a much more limited degree of motion with limited space between the particles. Liquid water is a good example of this phase. Liquids exhibit certain char-acteristics which include:

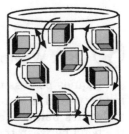

Liquid - particles
vibrate and rotate.

Vapor Pressure – As a result of the free movement of particles in a liquid, a certain quantity of collision occurs among them, releasing ener-gy in the process. This energy, absorbed by individual particles, allows them to acquire the translational energy with which they break those intermolecular bonds holding them to one another, and they become gaseous particles. When a liquid substance changes to a gas, the process is called **evaporation**. Evaporation tends to take place at the surface of a liquid and at all temperatures.

The term "vapor" is frequently used to refer to the gas phase of a sub-stance that is normally a liquid or solid at room temperature. The vapor (gas) produced exerts a pressure, known as vapor pressure, which increas-es as the temperature of the liquid is raised and is specific for each sub-stance and temperature.

Boiling Point – A liquid will boil at the temperature at which the vapor pressure equals the pressure on the liquid. The "normal boiling point" is the temperature at which the vapor pressure of the liquid equals one atmosphere (example: H_2O: 100°C or 373 K). Usually when reference is made to the "boiling point" of a substance, it is the normal boiling point that is indicated.

SKILLS 5.2III *EXPLAIN VAPOR PRESSURE, EVAPORATION RATE, AND PHASE CHANGES IN TERMS OF INTERMOLECULAR FORCES.*

1 As the temperature of liquid water decreases, its vapor pressure
   (1) decreases (2) increases (3) remains the same

2 A sample of pure water is boiling at 90.0°C. The vapor pressure of the water is closest to [may refer to *Reference Table H*]
   (1) 12.0 kPa (2) 48.4 kPa (3) 69.9 kPa (4) 101.3 kPa

3 The normal boiling point of water is equal to
   (1) 173 K (2) 273 K (3) 373 K (4) 473 K

4 When the vapor pressure of a liquid in an open container equals the atmospheric pressure, the liquid will
   (1) freeze (2) melt (3) boil (4) crystallize

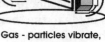 REAL WORLD CONNECTIONS

Liquids possess the following properties: Surface tension – the bonding between the water molecules on the surface of a liquid and the water molecules below them is stronger than the bond between the surface water molecules and the air molecules above them. This sets up a tight tension between the water molecules on the surface of the liquid.

Capillary action is the strength between the hydrogen bonds between the water molecules allows them to remain

©PhotoDisc

together while being absorbed by some blotting material so much so as to defy gravity. Viscosity of some liquids is made up of larger molecules with multiple hydrogen bonds among them which causes them to be more viscous (resistance to flow) than others.

GASEOUS PHASE

In a gaseous phase, the molecules are all translating, as well as rotating and vibrating. When translating in the gaseous state, the molecules have broken the intermolecular bonds between themselves and other molecules, and the distance between molecules is great. In this state, the molecules have attained a greater amount of randomness. The degree of the randomness of a substance is defined as **entropy** (see [☆ pg 16] for additional material on gases).

Gas - particles vibrate, rotate, and translate.

REAL WORLD CONNECTIONS

Phase Change in Water – The nature of water in our environment is to change from a solid to a liquid and then to a gas and vice versa.

In the spring, as the snow and ice melt, the molecules which were vibrating in a solid state begin also to rotate around each other. The structure begins to liquefy. This liquid water then proceeds to flow toward the lakes and seas where the Sun and the surrounding sea water warm it further. This causes an increase in the movement of the molecules to such a degree that many of the molecules break their intermolecular bonds and acquire a third motion, a straight line motion called translational motion, allowing vaporization. The vapor accumulates to form clouds, which produce precipitation, beginning the cycle all over again.

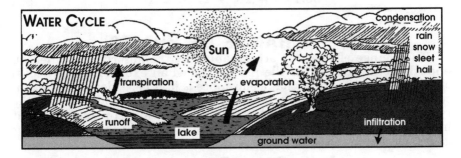

PHYSICAL & CHEMICAL CHANGE

Physical Change occurs when the property of matter changes but its identity does not. **Chemical Change** occurs when the identity and composition of matter is altered. For example, burning wood in air produces gases and ash which are altogether different in appearance than the wood.

As energy is supplied in a system, the atoms become more active and their movements increase to break the ridged lattice structure from just vibrations to vibration and rotational movements and become a liquid. The atomsthen proceed to transform into a vapor or gas phase where they add the movement of translation to the movements of vibration and rotation and break their inter molecular bonds and move further away from each other.

ENERGY & CHEMICAL CHANGE

Energy is absorbed by molecules when chemical bonds are broken and liberated when bonds are formed. Usually, this energy occurs in the form of heat. During a chemical reaction, when the bonds of molecules are broken and new ones are formed, the net energy absorbed or given off depends on the strength of the bonds broken, as compared to the strength of the bonds formed. Reactions involving heat energy are classified as:

- **Exothermic reactions** – When the energy required to break the existing bonds is less than the energy given off as new bonds are formed, the excess heat energy is given off. This reaction is called an exothermic reaction, and the container in which the exothermic reaction is taking place becomes warm. For example:

$$C + O_2 \rightarrow CO_2 + 418\,kJ$$

- **Endothermic reactions** – When the energy required to break the existing bonds is greater than the energy given off in the formation of new ones, heat energy is absorbed into the reaction. This reaction is called an endothermic reaction, and the container in which the reaction is taking place becomes cool. For example:

$$50.4\,kJ + H_2 + I_2 \rightarrow 2\,HI$$

B - CHANGE OF PHASES

The change of phase is accompanied by the absorption (called an **endothermic process**) or the release (called an **exothermic process**) of heat energy. The phase that a substance is in is dependent on temperature and pressure. Also, the phases of matter are characterized by the type of motion that the particles are undergo. **Note**: In equations that include heat, the phase of each species should be specified, such as (**g**) for gas, (**l**) for liquid, and (**s**) for solid.

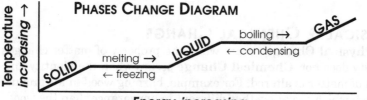

Reading from left to right, the diagram shows the phase change of a solid as heat energy is added. As the temperature of the substance increases, it reaches its melting point. While a phase change takes place, the temperature remains the same (horizontal lines) until all of the sample has melted. The temperature begins to rise until the boiling point is reached. During this second phase change, the temperature remains constant until all of the sample has changed from a liquid phase to a gaseous phase.

SKILLS 4.2II *EXPLAIN PHASE CHANGES IN TERMS OF THE CHANGES IN ENERGY AND INTERMOLECULAR DISTANCE.*

5 When the average kinetic energy of a gaseous system is increased, the average molecular velocity of the system
   (1) increases and the molecular mass increases
   (2) decreases and the molecular mass increases
   (3) increases and the molecular mass remains the same
   (4) decreases and the molecular mass remains the same

6 As a substance goes from a solid to a liquid, the particles
  (1) move closer
  (2) remain in position
  (3) move further apart
  (4) slow their motion down

SKILLS 4.2III *QUALITATIVELY INTERPRET HEATING AND COOLING CURVES IN TERMS OF CHANGES IN KINETIC AND POTENTIAL ENERGY, HEAT OF VAPORIZATION, HEAT OF FUSION, AND PHASE CHANGES.*

7 The graph at the right represents the relationship between temperature and time as heat is added uniformly to a substance, starting when the substance is a solid below its melting point.

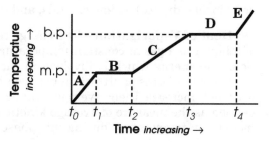

Which portions of the graph represent times when heat is absorbed and potential energy increases while kinetic remains constant?
  (1) *A* and *B*
  (2) *B* and *D*
  (3) *A* and *C*
  (4) *C* and *D*

8 The graph at the right represents the uniform cooling of a substance, starting with the substance as a gas above its boiling point. During which interval is the substance completely in the liquid phase?
  (1) *AB*
  (2) *BC*
  (3) *CD*
  (4) *DE*

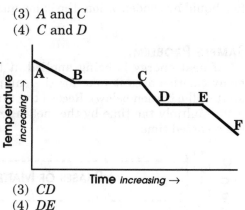

Melting point – The "normal melting point" is the temperature at which a solid substance will change to a liquid at 1 atmosphere pressure. Melting point may also be defined as the temperature at which the solid and liquid phases can exist in equilibrium. At the melting point temperature, all of the particles once in a definite geometric pattern have acquired rotational energy and are no longer a part of a lattice structure. Melting points can be determined from cooling curves which are obtained experimentally.

Heat of fusion – The energy required to change a unit mass of a solid to a liquid at constant temperature is called its heat of fusion. Keep in mind that fusion is another word for melting. As found in *Reference*

Table B – Physical Constants for Water, the heat of fusion of water is 334 J/g (joules per gram) of water. **Note**: When a gram of water is frozen into ice, the same amount of heat is given off.

Sublimation – Sublimation is a change from the solid phase directly to the gas phase without passing through an apparent liquid phase. (**Note**: The opposite is **deposition**, moving from a gas to a solid.) Solids which sublime have high vapor pressures and low intermolecular attractions. Examples of solids that sublime at room temperature are solid carbon dioxide (dry ice), iodine crystals, and naphthalene.

Heat of Vaporization – The energy required to vaporize a unit mass of a liquid to a gas at constant temperature is called its heat of vaporization. The energy which is involved in the change of phase is needed to overcome the forces of attraction between particles (potential energy) and does not increase their average kinetic energy. Since temperature is defined as the measure of average kinetic energy in a system, there is no increase in temperature during this phase change.

As found in *Reference Table B*, the heat of vaporization of water is 2260 Joules/gram of water to be vaporized. **Note**: When a gas is changed to a liquid by condensation, the same quantity of heat is given off.

SAMPLE PROBLEM:
If heat energy is being applied at the rate of 210 kJ/minute, how many calories does it take for the sample to melt? (Refer to Phases of Matter illustration below). Record the time that it takes for the sample to melt. Multiply the time by the melting rate, which is 210 kJ/minute, by the recorded time.

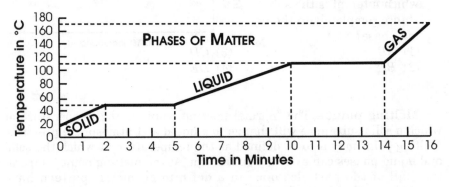

Solution: 3 min x 210 kJ/min = 630 kJ

Note: Both plateaus on the *Phases of Matter* graph above indicate a change of phase is taking place, and the temperature does not change during a phase change. The energy added is being used to change the potential energy of the molecules; therefore, the kinetic energy (temperature) remains constant.

Multiplying the time factor by the constant or average rate of heat energy supplied determines the joules of heat energy used during any portion of the graph. **Note**: The *Phases of Matter* graph could read from right to left as a cooling curve.

SKILLS 4.2IV *CALCULATE THE HEAT INVOLVED IN A PHASE OR TEMPERATURE CHANGE FROM A GIVEN SAMPLE OF MATTER.*

9 The graph at the right represents changes of state for an unknown substance. What is the boiling temperature of the substance?

(1) 0°C   (3) 70°C
(2) 20°C   (4) 40°C

Base your answers to questions 10 and 11 on the diagram at the right which represents a substance being heated from a solid to a gas, the pressure remaining constant.

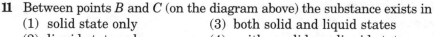

10 The substance begins to boil at point

(1) *E*   (3) *C*
(2) *B*   (4) *D*

11 Between points *B* and *C* (on the diagram above) the substance exists in

(1) solid state only   (3) both solid and liquid states
(2) liquid state only   (4) neither solid nor liquid state

12 The graph at the right represents the uniform cooling of a substance, starting with the substance as a gas above its boiling point. How much time passes between the first appearance of the liquid phase of the substance and the presence of the substance completely in its solid phase?

(1) 5 minutes
(2) 2 minutes
(3) 7 minutes
(4) 4 minutes

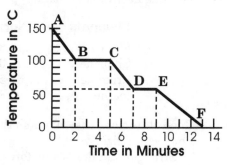

13 Which change of phase is exothermic?

(1) gas to liquid   (3) solid to gas
(2) solid to liquid   (4) liquid to gas

14 The diagram at the right represents the uniform heating of a substance that is a solid at t_0. What is the freezing point of the substance?
(1) 1°C
(2) 12°C
(3) 60°C
(4) 100°C

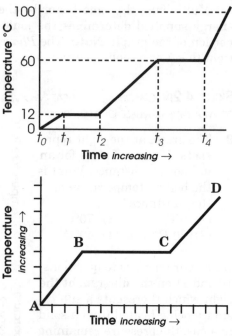

15 The graph at the right represents the relationship between temperature and time as heat was added uniformly to a substance, starting as a solid below its melting point. During the B–C portion of the curve, the average kinetic energy of the molecules of the substance
(1) increases and the potential energy increases
(2) decreases and the potential energy increases
(3) remains the same and the potential energy increases
(4) remains the same and the potential energy decreases

SKILLS 5.2II *COMPARE THE PHYSICAL PROPERTIES OF SUBSTANCES BASED UPON CHEMICAL BONDS AND INTERMOLECULAR FORCES.*

16 Which type of solid does pure water form when it freezes?
(1) ionic   (2) network   (3) metallic   (4) molecular

17 The table below shows boiling points for the elements listed.

Elements	Normal Boiling Points	
Fluorine	-188.1 °C	85 K
Chlorine	-34.6 °C	239 K
Bromine	+58.8 °C	332 K
Iodine	+184.4 °C	458 K

Which statement best explains the pattern of boiling points relative to molecular size?
(1) Stronger van der Waals forces occur in larger molecules.
(2) Weaker van der Waals forces occur in larger molecules.
(3) Stronger hydrogen bonds occur in larger molecules.
(4) Weaker hydrogen bonds occur in larger molecules.

C – SUBSTANCES

A **substance** is defined as homogeneous matter when it has identical properties and composition. For example, all samples of a particular substance have the same heat of vaporization, melting point, boiling point, and other properties related to composition. These properties can be used for the identification of the substance.

18 Question: Which of the following is not classified as a substance?
(1) oxygen   (2) water   (3) concrete   (4) an iron slab

Substances include:

Elements – All samples of an element are composed of atoms of the same atomic number and are considered substances that cannot be decomposed by chemical means. Although the periodic table of elements names just one hundred and nine elements, more have recently been discovered or made.

19 Question: Give the symbols for some elements which are metals.

20 Question: Give the symbols for some nonmetallic elements.

Compounds – Compounds are two or more different elements chemically combined in a definite ratio by weight. Therefore, all samples of a compound have identical composition and can only be decomposed by chemical change. Those compounds, which are made up of just two elements, are called binary compounds. In addition, those compounds that are made up of three elements are called ternary compounds.

The properties of a compound are quite different from the separate elements which make them up. For example, sodium is a soft, very active, metal that must be stored under benzene so that it does not react with air. Chlorine is a green, deadly gas. They combine in a definite weight ratio of 23g of sodium to 35.5g of chlorine. When combined, they form the compound sodium chloride (common table salt) which is stable in air and is required, to a limited extent, for the body to function normally.

21 Question: A compound with two elements is called a binary compound, what is a compound with three elements in its formula called?

22 Question: Name a compound with three elements in it.

D – MIXTURES

Mixtures are combinations of varying amounts of two or more distinct substances (either elements or compounds) that differ in properties and composition. Mixtures may be homogeneous or heterogeneous.

Homogeneous mixtures have a **uniform** intermixture of particles and are called solutions. A **solution** is produced when one substance dissolves or dissociates in another. Examples include:

- gas in gas – such as air
- solid in liquid – such as salt dissolved in water [$NaCl(aq)$]
- solid in solid – an alloy, such as brass, a combination of copper and zinc
- liquid in liquid – such as alcohol and water, in which the components are considered miscible [$C_3H_5OH(aq)$]

Heterogeneous mixtures have uniformly dispersed ingredients. Examples include:

- iron and sulfur
- oil and water
- concrete
- sand and water

Mixtures differ from compounds in that the amounts of the different substances which make up mixtures are not in a fixed ratio by weight, whereas, in compounds they are. For example, a sand and water mixture can contain various quantities of sand and water and still be considered a mixture of sand and water. Also, the components of a mixture can be separated by physical means and do not lose their identity. The sand and water mixture would be separated by either boiling off the water or by filtering out the sand. These are both physical means of separation.

Finally, compounds are made up of elements, but mixtures can be made up of either elements or compounds.

SKILLS 3.1XXIV *DESCRIBE THE PROCESS AND USE OF FILTRATION, DISTILLATION, AND CHROMATOGRAPHY IN THE SEPARATION OF A MIXTURE.*

- **Filtration** – Soluble substances can be separated from insoluble substances by passing the mixture through a filter.

- **Distillation** – A liquid is vaporized and re-condensed. Using this procedure can find the percent of water in vinegar.

- **Density** – A lead shot and water mixture can be separated by filtration or by decanting the water off the top of the lead shot.

- **Particle Size** – Sight and hand can be used to separate objects.

- **Magnetic separation** – A magnet can be used separate iron ore from sulfur.

REAL WORLD CONNECTIONS
CHROMATOGRAPHY

Chromatography is a process which uses a moving phase to separate the fixed or stationary phase components of a mixture. The two phases are:

- **Fixed phase** or adsorbent, can be a column of finely powdered solids, a strip of porous paper, or a liquid held in a firm support.

- **Moving phase** is a solvent, either a gas or liquid. Other terms for the moving phase include eluant, solvent, or solvent system. The moving phase may contain more than one substance.

  There is no way to predict the best choice of phases for a particular separation. It is something that must be worked out by trial and error in experiments.

Ratio: The ratio (R_f) can be used to identify substances.

$$R_f = \frac{\text{Distance Traveled by the Component}}{\text{Distance Traveled by the Solvent Front}}$$

- **Boiling Point** – A salt and water mixture can be separated by boiling off the water, leaving the salt behind.

- **Freezing Point** – Cooling a salt water solution below 0°C will cause the water to freeze into ice, separating it from the salt.

- **Solubility** – A salt and sand mixture can be placed in water, allowing the salt to dissolve and the sand to settle to the bottom to be filtered off.

REAL WORLD CONNECTIONS

Separation of mixtures includes filtration, distillation, chromatography, and desalination – removing salts from sea water through boiling off the water and condensing it and leaving the crystalline salts behind. **Reverse osmosis** involves forcing water through a fine membrane which allows the water through and leaves the salt behind. **Electrodialysis**, as the name implies, an electric current and a membrane is used. The current separates the components of the salts into its positive and negative poles and the water is drawn off. With windmills to capture the sea/land breeze and produce the direct current needed, this may well be the cheapest way to desalinate water. **Crystallization** occurs when you have a supersaturated solution of sugar or some other solid and you add a sugar crystal or some other foreign matter to the solution. The excess dissolved sugar will crystallize out into rock candy.

23 Question: Describe the process of separating an aqueous solution of a salt and sand mixture.

Alloys – Alloys are industrial metals which contain significant amounts of other elements. Natural impurities (metals) are found in combined form with oxides, sulfides, or carbonates. Artificial impurities (as found in alloys) are produced by melting the metal together with others, then cooling the mixture. The resulting alloys often have properties unlike those of the separate elements. An alloy

- tends to be harder than its component parts (silver-copper alloy is used to make sterling silver);
- tends to have a lower melting point than its component parts (Woods' metal composed of tin, cadmium, and lead melts in hot water but none of its components do);
- tends to be a poor conductor of electricity (Nichrom, a nickel-chromium alloy has such a great resistance to electric current flow, it is used as a heating element in toasters);
- tends to be less active than its separate elements (stainless steel is very slow to act with most chemicals). Some examples of alloys with their component parts include bronze w/ copper and tin; brass w/ copper and zinc; stainless steel w/ iron, chromium, carbon, manganese, and nickel; gold coins w/ copper and gold.

Water quality testing – *E. coli* level and pH are two tests performed by state registered laboratories.

Colloids – Colloids are 1 to 1,000 nanometers size particles, suspended in a media which are not detected by the naked eye and appear to be homogeneous, but the dispersions are readily detected when a light is scattered by it. This scattering of light by colloidal dispersion is called the **Tyndall Effect** (e.g., fog is a liquid in gas; smoke is a solid in a gas; aerosol foam is a gas in a liquid; liquid emulsion is a liquid dispersed in a liquid).

Emulsifiers – An **emulsion** is a heterogeneous suspension of a liquid in a liquid such as vinegar in oil as in mayonnaise or water in cream as in ice cream. The agent that allows them to bind together is called an **emulsifier**. In mayonnaise and ice cream the emulsifier is eggs added to the liquids and mixed vigorously until it has a creamy consistency.

Sewage – Sewage a suspension of water carrying human, animal, or organic wastes along with inorganic matter from homes, industrial establishments, or other places. Aerobic bacterial action causes the decomposition of organic matter. Settling filtration and aeration is also used to treat sewage before it is released into streams.

E – SOLUTIONS

A **solution** is a homogeneous mixture of two or more substances, the composition of which may vary within limits. The component of a solution which is usually a liquid and is present in excess is called the **solvent**, while the other component which is dissociated (dissolved) in the solvent is called the **solute**. The dissociation of ionic solute particles by a solvent is called **solvation**.

Most solutions dealt with in beginning courses in chemistry are aqueous solutions. When water is the solvent, the dissociation of solute particles is called **hydration**.

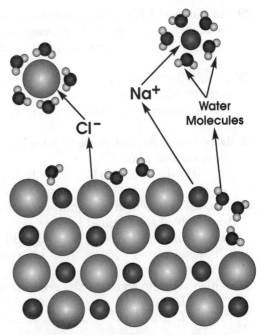

Na$^+$

Cl$^-$

Water Molecules

Solvation – When NaCl (ionic crystal) is added to water, the Na$^+$ ions attract the negative end of the water dipole and the Cl$^-$ ions attract the positive end. This results in dissociation.

SKILLS 3.1XXV *INTERPRET AND CONSTRUCT SOLUBILITY CURVES (USE REFERENCE TABLE G).*

24 According to *Reference Table G*, which of the following substances is *least* soluble in 100 grams of water at 50°C?
(1) NaCl   (2) KCl   (3) NH$_4$Cl   (4) HCl

25 According to *Reference Table G*, which compound's solubility decreases most rapidly when the temperature increases from 50°C to 70°C?
(1) NH$_3$ (2) HCl   (3) SO$_2$ (4) KNO$_3$

26 A solution in which the crystallizing rate of the solute equals the dissolving rate of the solute must be
(1) saturated   (3) concentrated
(2) unsaturated   (4) dilute

27 According to *Reference Table G*, which compound is most soluble at 20° C?
(1) SO$_2$ (2) NaCl   (3) KI   (4) KCl

28 How many grams of KNO$_3$ are needed to saturate 50.0 grams of water at 70°C?
(1) 30. g   (2) 65 g   (3) 130. g   (4) 160. g

29 As additional $KNO_3(s)$ is added to a saturated solution of KNO_3 at constant temperature, the concentration of the solution
(1) decreases (2) increases (3) remains the same

30 As additional solid KCl is added to a saturated solution of KCl, the conductivity of the solution
(1) decreases (2) increases (3) remains the same

31 Based on *Reference Table G*, which of the following substances is most soluble at 60°C?
(1) NH_4Cl (2) KCl   (3) NaCl   (4) NH_3

32 A solution in which an equilibrium exists between dissolved and undissolved solute must be
(1) saturated   (3) dilute
(2) unsaturated   (4) concentrated

33 Which solution contains the greatest number of moles of solute?
(1) 0.5 L of 0.5 M   (3) 2 L of 0.5 M
(2) 0.5 L of 2 M   (4) 2 L of 2 M

REAL WORLD CONNECTIONS

POLAR SOLUTES DISSOLVE IN POLAR SOLVENTS

When an ionic substance dissociates in water, the water molecules surround the ions and insulate them from regrouping again. The greater the insulation effect, the better will be the process of dissociation. This insulating of ionic solutes in a solvent is called the ***dielectric effect*** and is described in terms of a dielectric constant. For example, water has a dielectric constant of 80 and benzene is 2.3. Benzene's low dielectric constant (a nonpolar solvent) does not reduce the force of attraction of the ions for each other and does not allow them to dissociate.

NONPOLAR SOLUTES GENERALLY DISSOLVE IN NONPOLAR SOLVENTS

Naphthalene (moth balls – $C_{10}H_8$) is a solid made up of nonpolar molecules which does not dissolve in water, but does dissolve in benzene C_6H_6, because the attractive forces between the naphthalene molecules and the benzene molecules are about the same as those between the benzene molecules, themselves. In this case, it is the entropy factor (a randomizing effect) which causes the dissolution of the naphthalene molecules in the benzene. This entropy factor is important in the painting (both water base and oil base paints) and dry cleaning business where stains must be treated without ruining the clothes. It is also important in the manufacturing of ceramics, cosmetics, and pharmaceuticals.

DISSOLUTION

Generally, a polar solvent (water) will dissolve polar and ionic substances (salt and sugar) and a non-polar solvent (carbon tetrachloride) will dissolve a non-polar solute (oils and greases). This concept is especially useful in the dry cleaning business.

SKILLS 3.1XXVI *APPLY THE ADAGE "LIKE DISSOLVES LIKE" TO REAL WORLD SITUATIONS.*

34 **Question**: The dielectric constant of some common substances are

water: 80   liquid ammonia: 18   grain alcohol: 25
ether: 4   carbon tetrachloride: 2

Which of these might be good solvents for

a   ionic solutes ___   *b*   nonpolar solutes ___

35 **Question**: What property of water is responsible for preventing the oppositely charged ions in a solution from recombining?

36 **Question**: What are the characteristics of the water molecule that make it a good solvent for ionic substances?

37 **Question**: For the following questions, refer to *Reference Table G - Solubility Curves*.

a   Which substance is the most soluble at 20°C?

b   Which substance is the least soluble at 20°C?

c   How many grams of NaCl will dissolve in 100 grams of water at 100°C?

d   How many grams of NaCl will dissolve in 400 grams of water at 50°C?

REAL WORLD CONNECTIONS

From *Reference Table G - Solubility Curves* it is observed that as the temperature rises, gaseous substances (i.e., NH_3, SO_2, and HCl) become less soluble. This is also true in Earth's environment. In cold polar areas, the waters contain greater quantities of oxygen gas than the warm waters near the equator. This allows the colder waters to support great quantities of living things. Some fish, such as freshwater trout, require a great amount of dissolved oxygen in order to flourish. That is why fishing for trout in warm southern waters is a waste of energy. Another indication of the solubility of gases concerns pressure. Pressure is used when soda water containing CO_2 (gas) is bottled. When a can or bottle of soda is opened, the decrease in the pressure on the solution causes the "hissing" sound, produced by the CO_2 (gas) escaping from the liquid.

©PhotoDisc

METHODS OF INDICATING CONCENTRATIONS

The main way of measuring and describing the concentration of solutions is through **molarity**. The molarity (M) of a solution is the number of moles of solute contained in a liter (1000 mL) of solution. The formula is:

$$\text{molarity (M)} = \frac{\text{number of moles of solute}}{\text{1 liter of solution}}$$

Therefore, a two molar (2M) solution contains 2 moles of solute per liter of solution and 0.1 molar solution, (0.1M) contains 0.1 mole of solute per liter of solution. By rearranging the above formula, it can also be state that the concentration in moles per liter multiplied by the volume in liters equals the number of moles of solute in the solution, or

moles of solute = molarity x volume in liters

The mass in grams of solute can be determined by multiplying the number of moles of solute by the mass of 1 mole.

grams (of solute) = **number of moles** (of solute) **x mass of 1 mole** (of solute)

To determine the number of moles of a solute used, use the following gram formula mass equation:

$$\textbf{number of moles} \text{ (of solute)} = \frac{\textbf{given mass in grams (of solute)}}{\textbf{gram formulas mass (of solute)}}$$

Sample Problem 1: How many moles of NaOH are contained in 200 mL of 0.1M solution of NaOH?

Solution:

$$\text{Moles of solute} = \text{molarity} \times \text{volume in liters}$$

$$\text{Moles of NaOH} = 0.1 \text{ M} \times 0.2 \text{ liters}$$

$$= 0.02 \text{ moles}$$

Sample Problem 2: How many grams of NaOH are contained in a 500 mL of 0.5 M solution of NaOH?

Solution: In order to find the mass of NaOH, first find the moles of NaOH used by substituting in the same equation.

$$\text{Moles of solute} = \text{molarity} \times \text{volume of solution}$$

$$\text{Moles of NaOH} = 0.5 \text{ M} \times 0.5 \text{ liters}$$

$$= 0.25 \text{ moles}$$

Now find the grams of NaOH used by using the formula:

$$\text{Grams of solute} = \text{no. of moles} \times \text{mass of one mole}$$

$$= 0.25 \times 40\text{g}$$

$$= 10\text{g}$$

Sample Problem 3: What is the molarity of a solution of KOH if a 500 mL of the solution contains 5.6 grams of KOH?

Solution: First, find the moles of KOH by substituting in the equation:

$$\text{Grams of solute} = \text{no. of moles} \times \text{mass of one mole}$$
$$5.6 \text{ g} = X \times 56 \text{ g/mole}$$

$$\frac{5.6 \text{ g}}{5.6 \text{ g/mole}} = X$$
$$0.1 \text{ mole} = X$$

Now, find the molarity by substituting in the formula:

$$\text{Molarity (M)} = \frac{\text{moles of solute}}{\text{liter of solution}}$$

$$X = \frac{0.1 \text{ mole}}{0.5 \text{ liter}} = 0.2 \text{ M}$$

OTHER DESCRIPTOR FOR CONCENTRATION OF SOLUTIONS

- A **miscible solution** is a solution of liquid solutes that are soluble in liquid solvents, such as alcohol in water; whereas an **immiscible solution** is a solution of liquid solutes that are insoluble in liquid solvents, such as oil in water.

- A **dilute solution** is a solution in which a large amount of solvent is required to dissolve a small amount of solute. For example, at 30°C, only about 12 grams of Cesium Sulfate will dissolve in 100 grams of water. However, a **concentrated solution** is a solution in which a large amount of solute can be dissolved in a small amount of solvent. For example, at 30°C, about 97 grams of Sodium Nitrate will dissolve in 100 grams of water.

- **Percent by volume** refers to the percentage of solute per volume of solution or percentage of solute per volume of solvent, and **percent by mass** refers to the number of grams of solute in 100 grams of solvent, usually water. It is represented by a solubility curve whose vertical axis is grams of solute/100 grams of solvent and horizontal axis is temperature change.

Table G   Solubility Curves

- **Saturated solution** is a solution, which under specific conditions, holds all of the solute that it is capable of holding in a dissolved state. At this point, the liquid and solid phase are in a state of equilibrium. For example, according to *Reference Table G*, any points on the line graphs represent saturated solutions at that temperature.

- **Unsaturated Solution** is a solution in which less solute is dissolved than is capable of being dissolved under specific conditions. For example, at a specific temperature, a point below any line in *Reference Table G* indicates that the solution is not in equilibrium and, therefore, unsaturated at that temperature.

- **Supersaturated Solution** is a solution in which more solute is dissolved than can be dissolved under specific conditions. For example, at a specific temperature, a point above any line graph on *Reference Table G* indicates that the amount of solute dissolved in solution is greater than is normally dissolved and is called supersaturated.

Note: **Parts per million (ppm)** refers to the amount of solute per million parts of solution.

🌐 REAL WORLD CONNECTIONS
DEGREE OF SATURATION OF SOLUTIONS – MAKING ROCK CANDY
In a 200 mL beaker, add 100 mL of water and 50. g of sugar. Stir until all of the sugar goes into solution. At this stage, it is a **concentrated solution**. Continue to add sugar, stirring until the point that no more sugar will dissolve. At this point, it is a **saturated solution**. Filter, then heat the solution to 75°C, and add 25 g of sugar to the **heated solution**. Drop one end of a 15 cm string into the hot solution. Turn off the heat and allow the solution to cool slowly (overnight). The cool clear solution is a supersaturated solution. Add a few crystals of sugar to the solution and the excess sugar will collect around the string into a typical rock candy crystalline structure.

SKILLS 3.1xxx *DESCRIBE THE PREPARATION OF A SOLUTION GIVEN THE MOLARITY.*

38 Question: How many milliliters of 0.50 M NaCl would contain 10. g of pure NaCl?

39 Question: How many moles of KOH are contained in 200. mL of a 2M solution of KOH in water? Also, how many grams of KOH does this represent?

40 Question: How many milliliters of 10. M NaOH would be required to prepare 600. mL of a 0.5 M solution?

41 A 20.-milliliter sample of 0.60 M HCl is diluted with water to a volume of 40. milliliters. What is the new concentration of the solution?
(1) 0.15 M   (2) 0.60 M   (3) 0.30 M   (4) 1.2 M

42 What is the concentration of a solution of 10. moles of copper (II) nitrate in 5.0 liters of solution?
(1) 0.50 M   (2) 2.0 M   (3) 5.0 M   (4) 10. M

SKILLS 3.1xxvii *INTERPRET SOLUTION CONCENTRATION DATA.*

43 Refer to *Reference Table G*. A solution contains 50 grams of solute per 100 grams of water at 80°C. This solution could be a saturated solution of
(1) NaCl   (2) $NaNO_3$ (3) KCl   (4) $KClO_3$

44 If 0.50 liter of a 12-molar solution is diluted to 1.0 liter, the molarity of the new solution is
(1) 2.4   (2) 6.0   (3) 12   (4) 24

F – EFFECT OF SOLUTE ON SOLVENT

The presence of dissolved particles affects some properties of the solvent. Properties which depend on the relative number of particles rather than on the nature of the particles are called **colligative properties**. Colligative properties, as related to solutions, include changes in boiling point, freezing point, vapor pressure, and osmotic pressure.

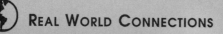

REAL WORLD CONNECTIONS

WINTERIZING FOR SAFETY
When salt is applied to an icy surface, the freezing point of the water is decreased, and the ice turns to liquid. Ice cream manufacture in the home is accomplished by the addition of salt to the ice surrounding the bowl which holds the cream, milk, sugar, and flavoring. This causes the ice to melt the water and reach temperatures colder than the ice. In the process, this causes the bowl to become cold enough to allow the ice cream to form. this principle is also used to antifreeze/engine coolant and airplane deicing solutions containing ethylene glycol as a solute instead of salt.

N&N's Ed Stich: "Softening" Water
By decreasing the freezing point of water, ice is phase changed into liquid.
©Stich

The effect on the boiling point and the freezing point on a solvent by the addition of a solute is measured by knowing the **molality** of the solution. The molality of a solution is an expression of the solution's concentration and is defined as the number of moles of a solute dissolved in 1,000 grams (1kg) of solvent. It is arrived at by using the following formula:

$$\text{molality (m)} = \frac{\text{moles of solute}}{\text{kg of solvent}}$$

Boiling Point Elevation – The presence of a nonvolatile solute raises the boiling point of the solvent. The amount of increase is proportional to the concentration of dissolved solute particles.

One mole of particles per 1000 grams of water raises the boiling point of water 0.52°C. The relationship between moles of solute and grams of solvent is expressed in the concentration unit, molality.

Freezing Point Depression – The presence of a solute lowers the freezing point of the solvent by an amount that is proportional to the concentration of dissolved solute particles. One mole of particles per 1,000 grams of water lowers the freezing point of water 1.86°C.

Abnormal Behavior of Electrolytes – Non-electrolytes dissolve in solution to form molecules which are not charged and will not conduct an electric current.

Electrolytes dissolve in solution and dissociate into ions that carry an ionic charge and, therefore, they do conduct an electric current.

REAL WORLD CONNECTIONS

FIRE BURN & CAULDRON BUBBLE
One application of adding salt to water and bringing it to a boil is in the cooking of pasta or potatoes. The water boils at a higher temperature and cooks the pasta or potatoes at a higher temperature, therefore they will cook faster.
©Stich

A mole of sugar ($C_{12}H_{22}O_{11}$), which is a non-electrolyte, will dissolve in 1 kg of water to give a mole of sugar molecules. A mole of salt (NaCl), which is an electrolyte, will dissolve in the same amount of water and also dissociate to give two moles of ions (1 mole of Na^+ plus 1 mole of Cl). Therefore, a 1 mole solution of NaCl will increase the boiling point of the solvent by +1.04°C. Whereas, a 1 mole solution of sugar will increase the boiling point of the solvent by +0.52°C. The same solution of NaCl will lower the freezing point of the solvent by -3.72°C. Also, a 1 mole solution of sugar will lower the freezing point of the solvent by -1.86°C. This behavior of electrolytes in solution gives evidence of the existence of ions.

G – ENERGY

The *Law of the Conservation of Energy* states:

Energy May Be Converted From One Form To Another
But Is Never Created Or Destroyed.

FORMS OF ENERGY

Mechanical energy, heat energy, radiant energy (such as light, radio waves, and all other forms of electromagnetic radiation), chemical energy (derived from movements of electrons in forming bonds), and nuclear energy (as in fission or fusion reactions) are examples of energy. Energy is broken down into two types: Potential and kinetic.

Potential energy is the energy of position (such as, dammed up water). **Kinetic energy** is the energy of motion (such as, a moving truck).

The classical example is the process of starting up a car. In this process, energy is converted from electrical energy from the battery, to chemical energy from combustion, and then to mechanical energy.

Heat is the result of a transfer of thermal energy (which is associated with the random collisions of atoms or molecules) between two systems and always flows from a body of higher temperature to a body of lower temperature.

Temperature is a measure of the heat intensity of a body and defined as the average kinetic energy of the particles of a system.

Thermometers are instruments used to measure temperature. Most contain liquid mercury, which has the advantage of remaining liquid over a wide range of temperatures, and also has the advantage of expanding and contracting evenly. There are two measurement scales frequently used by scientists in calibrating thermometers.

The **celsius** (°C) temperature scale has fixed points. They are: 0°C at the ice-water equilibrium temperature and 1 atmosphere pressure, and 100°C at the steam—water equilibrium temperature and 1 atmosphere pressure.

The **Kelvin (K)** or **absolute temperature scale** also has fixed points. They are: 273 K at the ice-water equilibrium temperature and 1 atmosphere pressure, and 373 K at the steam—water equilibrium temperature and 1 atmosphere pressure. **Absolute zero or zero K (kelvin) is equivalent to -273°C.**

When the temperature is given in degrees celsius, but one needs to find the temperature in kelvin, one should use the following equation:

Kelvin = 273 + degrees Celsius

Fahrenheit	Celsius	Kelvin
Water boils ---- 220	110	380
200	100	370
180	90	360
160	80	350
140	70	340
120	60	330
Human body temperature ---- 100	50	320
80	40	310
Room temperature 60	30	300
40	20	290
Ice melts ---- 20	10	280
0	0	270
-20	-10	260
-40	-20	250
-60	-30	240
	-40	230
	-50	220

Note: All measurements on the Kelvin scale are positive, but the difference between one kelvin (1 K) and one celsius degree (1°C) is the same.

A rise on the Celsius scale from 100°C to 101°C would be stated in the Kelvin scale as 373 to 374. The kelvin (absolute) temperature scale has its zero point at -273°C, with the size of the degrees the same as on the celsius scale, as illustrated above. **Note**: All gases liquefy before they reach absolute zero, and this point of absolute zero has not been reached yet.

SKILLS 3.4III *CONVERT TEMPERATURES IN CELSIUS DEGREES (°C) TO KELVIN (K), AND KELVIN TO CELSIUS DEGREES.*

45 Which kelvin temperature is equal to -33°C?
   (1) -33 K   (2) 33 K   (3) 240 K   (4) 306 K

46 Which temperature is the same as 260 K?
   (1) -333°C   (2) -13°C   (3) 286°C   (4) 533°C

47 Which kelvin temperature is equal to -73°C?
   (1) 100 K   (2) 173 K   (3) 200 K   (4) 346 K

SPECIFIC HEAT

The **specific heat** of a material is the amount of heat energy required to raise the temperature of 1 gram of the material one degree Celsius.

For determining reaction heats in calories, the value of the specific heat of water is considered a standard. It is 1 calorie per gram of water, per degree Celsius or cal/g°C. One calorie is equivalent in energy to 4.18 joules. When determining the reaction heat in joules, the value of the specific heat of water is 4.18 joules per gram of water, per degree Celsius or 4.2 J/g°C (rounded).

Sample Problem:
A 3.0×10^3 gram mass of water in a calorimeter has its temperature raised 5.0°C. How much heat energy was transferred to the water in calories and in joules?

Solution in Calories: Heat transferred to the water is the product of three factors:

$$\text{Heat} = \left(\begin{array}{c}\textbf{mass}\\ \textbf{of water}\end{array}\right) \times \left(\begin{array}{c}\textbf{change in temp.}\\ \textbf{of water}\end{array}\right) \times \left(\begin{array}{c}\textbf{specific heat}\\ \textbf{of water}\end{array}\right)$$

$$= \quad \textbf{3.0} \times \textbf{10}^3\,\textbf{g} \quad \textbf{x 5.0°C x 1.0 cal/g°C}$$

$$= \quad \textbf{15,000 calories or 15 kilocalories}$$

Answer: **1.5 x 10⁴ calories** (to the correct number of significant digits)

Solution in Joules: To calculate the heat energy in joules, use the specific heat of water as 4.18 J/g°C.

$$\textbf{Heat} = \textbf{3.0} \times \textbf{10}^3\,\textbf{g x 5.0°C x 4.18 J/g°C}$$

$$= \quad \textbf{6.27 x 10}^4\,\textbf{joules}$$

Answer: **6.3 x 10⁴ joules** (to the correct number of significant digits)

48 How many joules of heat are absorbed when 50 grams of water at 100°C are completely vaporized? [See *Reference Table B.*]
  (1) 2.478 kJ   (2) 22.68 kJ   (3) 113.0 kJ   (4) 226.8 KJ

49 When 20 Joules of heat are added to 2.0 grams of water at 15°C, the temperature of the water increases to
  (1) 5°C   (2) 17.39°C   (3) 25°C   (4) 50°C

H – KINETIC MOLECULAR THEORY FOR IDEAL GASES

SKILLS 3.4I *EXPLAIN THE GAS LAWS IN TERMS OF KINETIC MOLECULAR THEORY*

Studies of gas behavior have led to a model referred to as the "Ideal Gas Model." It is based on several assumptions.

- A gas is composed of individual particles which are in continuous, random straight line motion.

- Gas particles are separated by great distances relative to their size. Therefore, the volume of gas particles is considered negligible.

- Gas particles are considered as having no attraction to each other.

- The *Collisions Theory* states that a reaction is most likely to occur if the reactant particles collide with the proper energy and orientation.

🌎 REAL WORLD CONNECTIONS
EARTH'S PRIMITIVE ATMOSPHERE

Models are often used to explain something that cannot be seen. There have been many theories as to what made up Earth's atmosphere in the beginning. However, it is widely accepted that Earth's primitive atmosphere was composed primarily of methane (CH_4), ammonia (NH_3), carbon dioxide (CO_2), and water vapor (H_2O). Because these molecules can not be observed by the human senses, models (molecular and structural formulas) have been developed to represent the formulas and shapes of these molecules. These models are used to visualize what the molecules look like and how they behave in chemical reactions that alter their identity.

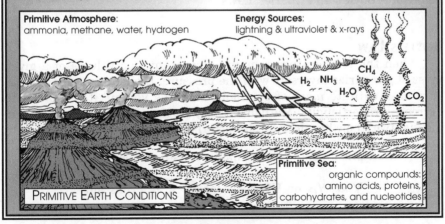

Primitive Atmosphere: ammonia, methane, water, hydrogen

Energy Sources: lightning & ultraviolet & x-rays

CH_4 H_2 NH_3 H_2O CO_2

PRIMITIVE EARTH CONDITIONS

Primitive Sea: organic compounds: amino acids, proteins, carbohydrates, and nucleotides

---

Ideal Gas Models can be useful in the study of the behavior of gases. It should be emphasized that a model is only an approximation and is only as good as its ability to predict behavior under new conditions.

DEVIATIONS FROM THE GAS LAWS

The **Ideal Gas Model** does not exactly represent real gases under all conditions. Hydrogen (H_2) and Helium (He) are the two most ideal gases. No real gas follows the ideal model under all conditions of temperature and pressure. Deviations from the gas laws occur because the model is not perfect. That is, gas particles have volume and exert some attraction for each other.

Note: These factors become significant under conditions of relatively high pressure, low temperature, and decreased velocity due to increased molecular mass.

GASES

The space between molecules in a gaseous phase is about 1,000 times greater than in a liquid or solid phase. Molecules possess greater kinetic energy and have overcome the attractive forces that hold them together. At 0°C and 1 atmosphere they independently travel in random directions at a speed of about 10^3m/sec. At this speed, it is estimated that they travel about 10^{-7}m before they collide with each other or the walls of their container. the frequency at which they collide has been estimated to be 5×10^9 per second. Therefore, the density of a gas is lower as compared to a liquid or solid.

In the gas phase, molecules possess vibrational, rotational, and translational movements. This allows them to fill the volume of the container in which they are located. There are two laws that describe their behavior – Boyle's and Charles' Laws.

BOYLE'S LAW

When the temperature remains a constant, the volume of a given mass of gas varies inversely with the pressure. If one increases the pressure on a definite mass of gas molecules, the volume it occupies will decrease proportionally. Mathematically, an inverse proportion concerning just two items has definite characteristics:

- Multiplied together they equal a constant. For example:

$$\mathbf{V} \; \alpha \; \mathbf{^1/_P} \; \text{ or } \; \mathbf{VP = k,} \quad \text{where } \mathbf{k} \text{ is a constant}$$

- Using the two values as graphing coordinates, the graph should represent a hyperbola.

Boyle's Law can also be represented in a mathematical formula: $V/V' = P'/P$

Where **V** and **P** represent the initial volume and pressure, and **V'** and **P'** represent a new volume and pressure.

Sample Problem: A storage container holds 400 liters of a gas at 2 atm. If the pressure is increased to 5 atmospheres at constant temperature, what will the volume of the gas be?

Solution: Since the temperature is a constant, the two variables will be volume and pressure. Since they are inversely proportional, the volume will increase or decrease when compared to the second pressure of the gas with the first pressure. Since the second pressure is higher than the first pressure, the volume will decrease.

Simply write the amounts for each of the values and key them into the formula:

$$\frac{V}{V'} = \frac{P'}{P}$$

Where: **V** = 400 L
P = 2 atm
P' = 5 atm

Solve for **V'**

$$\frac{400 \text{ L}}{V'} = \frac{5 \text{ atm}}{2 \text{ atm}}$$

$$\frac{\overset{80}{\cancel{400} \text{ L} \times 2 \text{ atm}}}{\cancel{5 \text{ atm}}} = V'$$

$$160 \text{ L} = V'$$

CHARLES' LAW

At constant pressure, the volume of a given mass of gas varies directly with the kelvin (absolute) temperature.

Charles' Law can be illustrated by the difference in the size of two hot air balloons. Both are at the same altitude (constant pressure), but the air in the second balloon is heated to double the temperature (in Kelvin) of the first balloon. The volume of the higher air temperature balloon increases to double that of the first balloon.

Mathematically, Charles' Law can be represented by the formula: $V/V' = T/T'$

V and **T** represent the initial volume and temperature, and **V'** and **T'** represent the new volume and temperature. Graphically, it is represented by a straight line. Starting at 0°C, with each decrease of 1°C, the volume of a gas decreases by $1/273$ of its original volume.

Sample Problem: At constant pressure and 27°C, a gas has a volume of 150 mL. If the temperature is increased to 327°C, what will be the new volume?

Solution: *First,* since the pressure is constant, the only two variables are temperature and volume.

Since there is a direct relationship between volume and temperature, the following can be estimated: since the temperature is rising, the volume will increase.

Second, the next step is to convert the temperature from degrees celsius to kelvin; then, list the known items along with the unknown and key them into the formula and solve for **V'**.

$$\frac{V}{V'} = \frac{T}{T'}$$

Where: **V** = 150 L
T = 300 K
T' = 600 K

$$\frac{150 \text{ mL}}{V'} = \frac{300 \text{ K}}{600 \text{ K}}$$

Solve for **V'**

$$\frac{150 \text{ mL} \times \overset{2}{\cancel{600}} \text{ K}}{\underset{1}{\cancel{300}} \text{ K}} = V'$$

$$300 \text{ mL} = V'$$

RELATIONSHIP BETWEEN TEMPERATURE & PRESSURE

In a rigid container at constant volume as the Kelvin temperature is increased, the pressure exerted by a given mass of a gas is also increased.

This relationship is a direct proportion and can be shown mathematically as:

$$P/P' = T/T'$$

Sample problem: In a rigid container, a gas exerts a pressure of 66.64 kPa at 77°C. What would the pressure be at -98°C?

Solution: Convert the temperature values from celsius to kelvin degrees, then place these temperatures in the the above equation and solve:

$$\frac{350 \text{ K}}{175 \text{ K}} = \frac{66.64 \text{ kPa}}{P'}$$

$$P' = \frac{66.64 \text{ kPa} \times 175 \text{ K}}{350 \text{ K}}$$

$$P' = 33.32 \text{ kPa}$$

STANDARD TEMPERATURE & PRESSURE (STP)

As noted above, there are three variables which we must consider when we study gases. They are volume, temperature, and pressure. Since the volume of a given mass of gas varies with changes in temperature and pressure, cannot be given the volume of a gas without specifying its temperature and pressure. Therefore, gas volumes are usually calculated to an arbitrary standard, which are abbreviated as STP. Standard temperature and pressure (STP) of a gas are defined as 0°C (273 K) and 101.3 kPa or 1 atmosphere pressure. Standard temperature for those phases other than a gas is 25°C (298 K).

COMBINED GAS LAWS

In studying the gases, three variables are concerned: volume, pressure, and temperature. Boyle's Law is concerned with the relationship of volume and pressure, when temperature is a constant. Charles' Law is concerned with the relationship of volume and absolute temperature, when pressure is a constant. Since changes in volume, pressure, and temperature often occur simultaneously, it is convenient to combine the two equations of Boyle and Charles into a single equation.

The combined gas law equation may be written:

$$\frac{P_1 V_1}{T_1} = \frac{P_2 V_2}{T_2}$$

P_1, V_1, and T_1 are the original conditions of pressure, volume and kelvin temperature. P_2, V_2, and T_2 are the corresponding values of the final conditions. **Note**: The definitive units given for both pressures must be the same, and both temperatures must be in kelvin degrees.

Sample Problem: A gas that behaves ideally at STP occupies 1000 milliliters. What volume will it occupy at 546 K and 0.5 atmospheres?

Solution: First, make up a list of the known items (the facts):

$$P_1 = 1 \text{ atm} \qquad P_2 = 0.5 \text{ atm}$$
$$V_1 = 1000 \text{ mL} \qquad V_2 = X$$
$$T_1 = 273 \text{ K} \qquad T_2 = 546 \text{ K}$$

Next, use the Combined Gas Law equation as noted in *Reference Table T*:

$$\frac{P_1 V_1}{T_1} = \frac{P_2 V_2}{T_2}$$

Finally, put the known values into the equation and solve for X.

$$\frac{1 \text{ atm} \times 1000 \text{ mL}}{273 \text{ K}} = \frac{0.5 \text{ atm} \times X}{546 \text{ K}}$$

$$\frac{1 \text{ atm} \times 1000 \text{ mL} \times 546 \text{ K}}{273 \text{ K} \times 0.5 \text{ atm}} = X$$

$$4{,}000 \text{ mL} = X \text{ (answer)}$$

50 Question: 200 mL of a gas is collected at STP. What will the volume be of the gas at 273°C (note: temperature must be changed to kelvin degrees) and 3 atm pressure?

$$\frac{200mL (1)}{273k} = \frac{V(3)}{546} \qquad 819V = 1092000$$
$$V = 1333.333$$

51 Question: Calculate the pressure required to reduce the volume of a gas from 800 mL at 2 atm pressure to 400 mL with the temperature — at a constant 273 K.

$$\frac{800(2)}{1} = \frac{400(x)}{1}$$
$$P_2 = 4$$

52 Question: 600 mL of a gas are collected at 2 atm pressure and 30°C. If the pressure is increased to 6 atm and the temperature is reduced to 20°C, what is the new volume?

Question: 48 liters of a gas are collected at 0.5 atm and standard temperature. Calculate the volume of the gas at STP.

$$\frac{48L(.5)}{273} = \frac{V(1)}{273} \qquad \frac{273V}{273} = \frac{6552}{273}$$
$$V = 24 L$$

Question: Calculate the pressure required to reduce the volume of a gas from 800 mL at 6 atm to 400 mL with the temperature remaining constant at 543 K.

$$\frac{800(6)}{543} = \frac{400mL(x)}{543}$$

$$X = 12$$

DALTON'S LAW OF PARTIAL PRESSURES

$$48 \quad 2600.400 = 217200x$$

The pressure exerted by each of the gases in a gas mixture is called the partial pressure of that gas. Therefore, the total pressure of a gas mixture is equal to the sum of the individual partial pressures of each of the gases comprising the mixture. The partial pressure of each gas is determined by its molecular ratio (or mole ratio).

Sample Problem: A container holds three gases, each of which exert pressure on the side of the container. Gas **A** exerts a pressure of 1.0 atm, gas **B** exerts a pressure of 1.5 atm, and gas **C** exerts a pressure of 2.5 atm. What is the total pressure of the gases on the sides of the container?

Solution:

$$\text{Total pressure} = \frac{\text{Pressure}}{\text{of gas } A} + \frac{\text{Pressure}}{\text{of gas } B} + \frac{\text{Pressure}}{\text{of gas } C}$$

$$= 1.0 \text{ atm} + 1.5 \text{ atm} + 2.5 \text{ atm}$$

$$= 5.0 \text{ atm}$$

REAL WORLD CONNECTIONS

Graham's Law – Because gases possess translational movement as well as vibrational and rotational movement, they will eventually spread out and fill their container. The "spreading out" of a substance is called diffusion. As we have stated before, temperature is a measure of the kinetic energy in a system. Therefore, all the molecules in a system at a specific temperature will have the same amount of kinetic energy, regardless of their size.

The equation that is concerned with kinetic energy (**K.E.**), mass (**m**), and velocity (**v**), is:

$$\textbf{K.E.} = \tfrac{1}{2}\,\textbf{mv}^2$$

If the kinetic energy for all the molecules in a system is equal, whether large or small, the value for **K.E.** = $\frac{1}{2}mv^2$ is the same for all of them. Therefore, it follows that if a gas has less mass than another, the value of its velocity must be greater. Since different particles have different masses, each particle will move at a different rate. This relationship between mass and velocity (which is called the rate of diffusion) was studied by Thomas Graham, a Scottish chemist, who concluded:

"Under the same conditions of temperature and pressure, gases diffuse at a rate inversely proportional to the square roots of their molecular masses."

Therefore, H_2 $\left(\frac{1}{\sqrt{2}}\right)$ *diffuses faster than* O_2 $\left(\frac{1}{\sqrt{16}}\right)$.

AVOGADRO'S HYPOTHESIS

Avogadro's hypothesis states that equal volumes of all gases under the same conditions of temperature and pressure contain equal numbers of particles. For example, at the same temperature and pressure, the number of particles in 1 liter of hydrogen is the same as the number of particles in 1 liter of oxygen although the individual particles of oxygen are heavier (by a ratio of 16 to 1) and larger than the individual particles of hydrogen.

The amount of matter than contains 6.02×10^{23} (Avogadro's number) particles is called a **mole of matter**. One mole of any substance contains as many particles (molecules, atoms, ions, etc.) as there are atoms of carbon-12 in 12.000g of carbon-12 isotope.

Since it is inconvenient to work with individual particles, chemists have chosen a unit containing many particles for comparing amounts of different materials. The mole is a unit which contains 6.02×10^{23} particles. A mole of particles of any gas occupies a volume of 22.4 liters at STP and is called a **molar volume**.

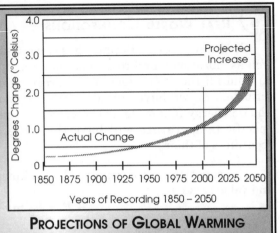
SKILLS 4.2III *QUALITATIVELY INTERPRET HEATING AND COOLING CURVES IN TERMS OF CHANGES IN KINETIC AND POTENTIAL ENERGY, HEAT OF VAPORIZATION, HEAT OF FUSION, AND PHASE CHANGES.*

55 Under the same conditions of temperature and pressure, which of the following gases would behave most like an ideal gas?
(1) $He(g)$ (2) $NH_3(g)$ (3) $Cl_2(g)$ (4) $CO_2(g)$

56 Which gas under high pressure and low temperature has a behavior closest to that of an ideal gas?
(1) $H_2(g)$ (2) $O_2(g)$ (3) $NH_3(g)$ (4) $CO_2(g)$

57 Which temperature represents absolute zero?
(1) 0 K   (2) 0°C   (3) 273 K   (4) 273°C

58 One reason that a real gas deviates from an ideal gas is that the molecules of the real gas have
(1) a straight-line motion
(2) no net loss of energy on collision
(3) a negligible volume
(4) forces of attraction for each other

59 A sample of $H_2(g)$ and a sample of $N_2(g)$ at STP contain the same number of molecules. Each sample must have
(1) the same volume, but a different mass
(2) the same mass, but a different volume
(3) both the same volume and the same mass
(4) neither the same volume nor the same mass

60 At STP, equal volumes of $N_2(g)$ and $CO_2(g)$ contain equal numbers of
(1) atoms   (2) electrons   (3) molecules   (4) protons

61 What is the volume of 4.40 grams of CO_2 at STP?
(1) 2.24 L   (2) 4.48 L   (3) 22.4 L   (4) 44.8 L

62 What is the total number of molecules in 11.2 liters of N_2 gas at STP?
(1) 3.01×10^{23} (3) 14.0
(2) 6.02×10^{23} (4) 28.0

63 Which gas has properties that are most similar to those of an ideal gas?
(1) N_2 (2) O_2 (3) He   (4) Xe

64 When the vapor pressure of a liquid in an open container equals the atmospheric pressure, the liquid will
(1) freeze   (3) melt
(2) crystallize   (4) boil

65 In a closed system, as the temperature of a liquid increases, the vapor pressure of the liquid
(1) decreases (2) increases (3) remains the same

66 As the temperature of a liquid increases, its vapor pressure
(1) decreases (2) increases (3) remains the same

67 As the temperature of liquid water decreases, its vapor pressure
(1) decreases (2) increases (3) remains the same

68 The boiling point of water at standard pressure is
(1) 0.000 K   (2) 100. K   (3) 273 K   (4) 373 K

69 Which sample of water has the greatest vapor pressure?
(1) 100 mL at 20°C   (3) 20 mL at 30°C
(2) 200 mL at 25°C   (4) 40 mL at 35°C

70 The melting of sodium is accompanied by the
(1) destruction of energy   (3) absorption of energy
(2) creation of energy   (4) release of energy

71 Which process occurs when dry ice, $CO_2(s)$ is changed into $CO_2(g)$?
(1) crystallization   (3) sublimation
(2) condensation   (4) solidification

Calorimetry – People who are interested in eating the proper amount of food often read the labels on food containers in the grocery store in order to determine the number of calories supplied by each service of the product. However, the calories listed on food labels refer to kilocalories and not the calories used in chemistry class experiments.

The energy changes involved in chemical reactions are measured in calorimeters. These reactions do not normally use external forms of energy, except in cases of combustion reactions, when electrical energy is used to spark the reaction forward.

The construction of a calorimeter is very simple. It consists of a reaction chamber constructed of a metal, which is a good conductor of heat energy. Surrounding the reaction chamber is a known mass of water, which is held in an insulated container. The reaction takes place in the reaction chamber and raises the temperature of the water. Knowing the mass of the water and the temperature difference, the formula used is

Calories gained or lost	=	mass of water in grams	x	change in temperature in grams	x	specific heat or water

In using a calorimeter, the heat gained or lost by the container is disregarded. Also the heat capacity (specific heat) of the water (in the liquid phase) is assumed to be one calorie per gram, per Celsius degree.

Although calories are used for measuring heat energy, the basic SI unit of energy is the **Joule**. Since one calorie = 4.18 Joules, it is easy to convert the heat energy to joules by simply multiplying the number of calories by 4.18 Joules/1 calorie. Note: *Reference Table B* rounds off this figure to two (2) decimal places and uses 4.2 Joules/g as specific heat capacity.

Refrigeration – The usual manner of refrigeration is to use a compressor to compress a gas into a liquid. Then it directs the liquid into a series of tubes. As the liquid absorbs the heat energy in the refrigerator generated by the food, it turns back into a gas, cooling the food in the process. This series is repeated constantly to maintain the food at a constant temperature.

Editor's Note: our cool, award-winning instructor of high school chemistry, Nick Romano.

PERFORMANCE INDICATORS 3.1, 3.4, 4.1, 4.2, & 5.2
ASSESSMENTS

PART A – MULTIPLE CHOICE

1 Which graph best shows the relationship between kelvin temperature and average kinetic energy?

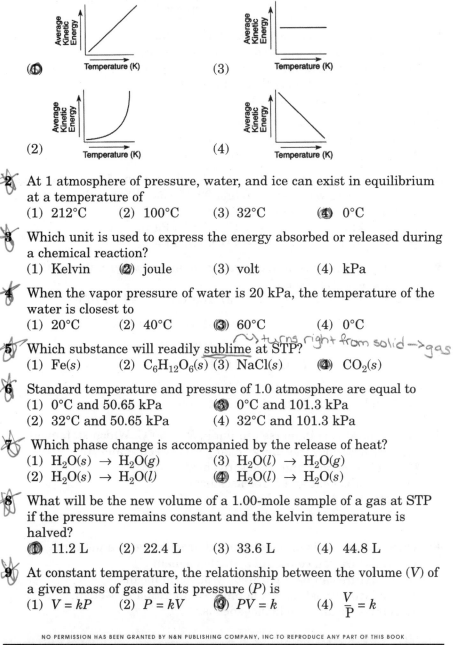

2 At 1 atmosphere of pressure, water, and ice can exist in equilibrium at a temperature of
(1) 212°C   (2) 100°C   (3) 32°C   (4) 0°C

3 Which unit is used to express the energy absorbed or released during a chemical reaction?
(1) Kelvin   (2) joule   (3) volt   (4) kPa

4 When the vapor pressure of water is 20 kPa, the temperature of the water is closest to
(1) 20°C   (2) 40°C   (3) 60°C   (4) 0°C

5 Which substance will readily sublime at STP? ⟿ turns right from solid→gas
(1) $Fe(s)$ (2) $C_6H_{12}O_6(s)$ (3) $NaCl(s)$ (4) $CO_2(s)$

6 Standard temperature and pressure of 1.0 atmosphere are equal to
(1) 0°C and 50.65 kPa   (3) 0°C and 101.3 kPa
(2) 32°C and 50.65 kPa   (4) 32°C and 101.3 kPa

7 Which phase change is accompanied by the release of heat?
(1) $H_2O(s) \rightarrow H_2O(g)$ (3) $H_2O(l) \rightarrow H_2O(g)$
(2) $H_2O(s) \rightarrow H_2O(l)$ (4) $H_2O(l) \rightarrow H_2O(s)$

8 What will be the new volume of a 1.00-mole sample of a gas at STP if the pressure remains constant and the kelvin temperature is halved?
(1) 11.2 L   (2) 22.4 L   (3) 33.6 L   (4) 44.8 L

9 At constant temperature, the relationship between the volume (V) of a given mass of gas and its pressure (P) is
(1) $V = kP$ (2) $P = kV$ (3) $PV = k$ (4) $\dfrac{V}{P} = k$

10 The formula Al_2S_3 represents   3 elements
   (1) an element   (3) a ternary compound
   (2) a binary compound   (4) a mixture   1 element /mixed 1 element
                   2 elements
11 As the temperature of a gas is increased from 0°C to 10°C at constant pressure, the volume of the gas will

   (1) increase by $\dfrac{1}{273}$ (3) decrease by $\dfrac{1}{273}$

   (2) increase by $\dfrac{10}{273}$ (4) decrease by $\dfrac{10}{273}$

12 Which statement best describes all compounds?
   (1) They can be decomposed by chemical change.
   (2) They can be decomposed by physical means.
   (3) They contain at least three elements.
   (4) They contain ionic bonds.

13 Which change of phase is exothermic?
   (1) solid to liquid   (3) solid to gas
   (2) gas to liquid   (4) liquid to gas

14 A gas sample consisting of 2 moles of hydrogen and 1 mole of oxygen is collected over water at 29°C and 99.97 kPa. What is the partial pressure of the hydrogen in the sample?
   (1) 31.99 kPa $99.97 \begin{smallmatrix} 33H \\ 33H \end{smallmatrix}$ (3) 95.97 kPa
   (2) 66.65 kPa $\dfrac{}{3} \quad 330$ (4) 99.97 kPa
                        33 + 33 = 66

15 What is the equilibrium temperature of an ice-water mixture at a pressure of 1 atmosphere?
   (1) 0°C   (2) 32°C   (3) 100°C   (4) 273°C

16 The list below shows four samples: A, B, C, and D.

   aq = in water   (A) HCl(aq)   (C) HCl(g)
                    (B) NaCl(aq)   (D) NaCl(s)

   Which samples are substances?
   (1) A and B   (2) A and C   (3) C and B   (4) C and D

17 Solid A at 80°C is immersed in liquid B at 60°C. Which statement correctly describes the energy changes between A and B?
   (1) A releases heat and B absorbs heat.
   (2) A absorbs heat and B releases heat.
   (3) Both A and B absorb heat.
   (4) Both A and B release heat.

18 Which statement is an identifying characteristic of a mixture?
   (1) A mixture can consist of a single element.
   (2) A mixture can be separated by physical means.
   (3) A mixture must have a definite composition by weight.
   (4) A mixture must be homogeneous.

19 What volume will a 300.-milliliter sample of a gas at STP occupy when the pressure is doubled at constant temperature?
(1) 150. mL   (2) 450. mL   (3) 300. mL   (4) 600. mL

$$\frac{P_1 V_1}{} = \frac{P_2 V_2}{} \qquad 1(300) = 2(x) \qquad x =$$

20 Which substance can be decomposed by a chemical change?
(1) ammonia   (3) magnesium
(2) aluminum   (4) manganese

21 The heat required to change 1 gram of a solid at its normal melting point to a liquid at the same temperature is called the heat of
(1) vaporization   (3) reaction
(2) fusion   (4) formation

22 A real gas would behave most like an ideal gas under conditions of
(1) low pressure and low temperature
(2) low pressure and high temperature
(3) high pressure and low temperature
(4) high pressure and high temperature

23 The volume of a sample of a gas at 273°C is 200. liters. If the volume is decreased to 100. liters at constant pressure, what will be the new temperature of the gas?
(1) 0 K   (2) 100. K   (3) 273 K   (4) 546 K

24 The graph at the right represents the relationship between pressure and volume of a given mass of a gas at constant temperature.

The product of pressure and volume is constant. According to the graph, what is the product in atm × mL?
(1) 20.   (3) 60.
(2) 40.   (4) 80.

25 The diagrams at the right represent two solids and the temperature of each. What occurs when the two solids are placed in contact with each other?

Solid A   Temperature 50°C
Solid B   Temperature 80°C

(1) Heat energy flows from solid A to solid B. Solid A decreases in temperature.
(2) Heat energy flows from solid A to solid B. Solid A increases in temperature.
(3) Heat energy flows from solid B to solid A. Solid B decreases in temperature.
(4) Heat energy flows from solid B to solid A. Solid B increases in temperature.

26 *Definition of solid* The particles of a substance are arranged in a definite geometric pattern and are constantly vibrating. This substance can be in
(1) the solid phase, only   (3) either the liquid or the solid phase
(2) the liquid phase, only   (4) neither the liquid nor the solid phase

27 What is the pressure of a mixture of CO_2, SO_2, and H_2O gases, if each gas has a partial pressure of 33.32 kPa?
(1) 33.32 kPa (2) 66.65 kPa (3) 99.97 kPa   (4) 133.29 kPa

28 Which substances can be decomposed chemically?
(1) CaO and Ca   (3) CO and Na
(2) MgO and Mg   (4) CaO and MgO

29 A gas sample has a volume of 25.0 milliliters at a pressure of 1.00 atmosphere. If the volume increases to 50.0 milliliters and the temperature remains constant, the new pressure will be
(1) 1.00 atm   (2) 2.00 atm   (3) 0.250 atm   (4) 0.500 atm

30 The table at the right shows the temperature, pressure, and volume of five samples. Which sample contains the same number of molecules as sample A?
(1) E (3) C
(2) B (4) D

Sample	Substance	Temperature (K)	Pressure (atm)	Volume (L)
A	He	273	1	22.4
B	O_2	273	1	22.4
C	Ne	273	2	22.4
D	N_2	546	2	44.8
E	Ar	546	2	44.8

31 The energy absorbed when ammonium chloride dissolves in water can be measured in
(1) degrees   (3) moles per liter
(2) kilojoules   (4) liters per mole

32 At 1 atmosphere of pressure, the steam-water equilibrium occurs at a temperature of
(1) 0 K   (2) 100 K   (3) 273 K   (4) 373 K

33 Which kelvin temperature is equal to -73°C?
(1) 100 K   (2) 173 K   (3) 200 K   (4) 346 K

34 A substance that is composed only of atoms having the same atomic number is classified as *Definition of element*
(1) a compound   (3) a homogeneous mixture
(2) an element   (4) a heterogeneous mixture

35 At which temperature will water boil when the external pressure is 101.3 kPa? [Use *Reference Table H.*]
(1) 14.5°C   (2) 65°C   (3) 20°C   (4) 100°C

36 At which point do a liquid and a solid exist at equilibrium?
(1) sublimation point   (3) boiling point
(2) vaporization point   (4) melting point

37 The phase change represented by the equation $I_2(s) \rightarrow I_2(g)$ is called
    (①) sublimation   (3) melting
    (2) condensation   (4) boiling

38 The graph at the *look for where Y stays the same* right represents the relationship between temperature and time as heat is added uniformly to a substance, starting when the substance

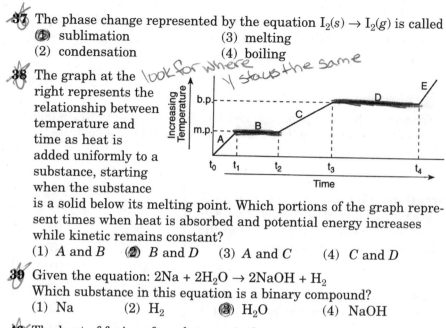

is a solid below its melting point. Which portions of the graph represent times when heat is absorbed and potential energy increases while kinetic remains constant?
    (1) *A* and *B*   (②) *B* and *D*   (3) *A* and *C*   (4) *C* and *D*

39 Given the equation: $2Na + 2H_2O \rightarrow 2NaOH + H_2$
Which substance in this equation is a binary compound?
    (1) Na   (2) H_2 (③) H_2O (4) NaOH

40 The heat of fusion of a substance is the energy measured during a
    (①) phase change   (3) chemical change
    (2) temperature change   (4) pressure change

PART B – CONSTRUCTED-RESPONSE

Directions: The accompanying table represents the data obtained by a student who measured different volumes of a liquid using a graduated cylinder and then determined the mass of each volume by weighing it on a scale.

Mass	Volume
1 g	3 mL
2 g	6 mL
3 g	9 mL
4 g	12 mL
5 g	15 mL

1 Question: Plot the data points on the accompanying graph. Label the axes of your graph correctly placing the independent variable on the x-axis. Using the information provided by your graph, determine the density of the liquid. [2]

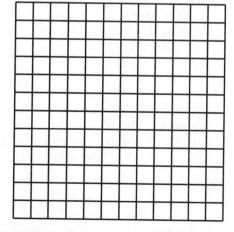

2 **Question**: Using the information provided by your graph, determine the mass of 18.0 mL of the liquid. [1]

3 **Question**: If this liquid is immiscible with water, state which liquid would be found on top if you mixed them together in a beaker. [1]

Directions: Use the accompanying data table with g solute/100 g of solvent vs. saturation temperature values (°C) and the blank grid for the resulting graph.

g Solute per 100g Solvent	Saturation Temperature °C
15	0°
30	10°
45	20°
60	30°
75	40°
90	50°
108	60°

4 **Question**: Graph the following data points on the accompanying graph. [1]

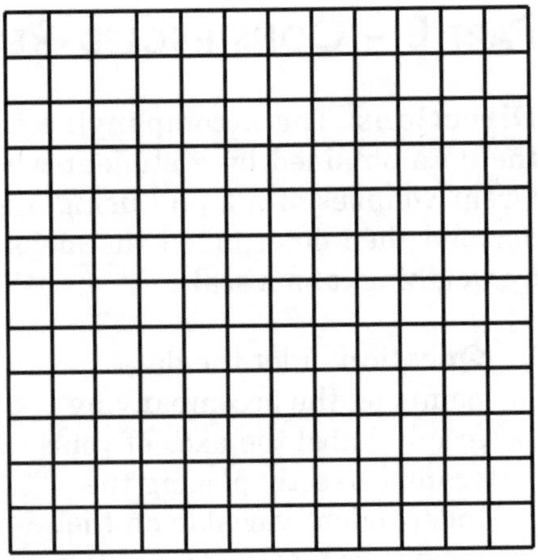

5 **Question**: Identify the dissolving process as either endothermic or exothermic. [1]

6 **Question**: State whether more or less solute will dissolve with a decrease in temperature. [1]

7 **Question**: If 100.0 g of the solvent is saturated with the compound at 60°C, determine the number of grams of the compound that will precipitate out if the solution is cooled to 15°C. [1]

Directions: Use *Reference Table H: Vapor Pressure of Four Liquids* to answer questions 8 through 10.

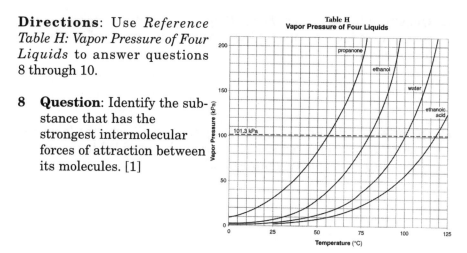

8 **Question**: Identify the substance that has the strongest intermolecular forces of attraction between its molecules. [1]

9 **Question**: Explain how the boiling point temperature is affected as the vapor pressure of a substance increases. [1]

10 **Question**: Describe how the vapor pressure of a liquid changes with an increase in temperature. [1]

Directions: Use the *Change of Phase Diagram* below to answer questions 11 through 14.

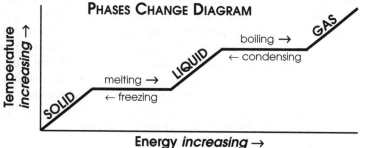

11 **Question**: Looking at the *Phase Change Diagram*, describe the change in potential energy that is taking place as the substance cools from the vapor phase to the liquid phase. [1]

12 **Question**: In the *Phase Change Diagram*, identify the portion of the curve where the molecules of the substance are arranged in a regular geometric pattern. [1]

13 **Question**: In the *Phase Change Diagram*, explain why the temperature stays the same even though energy is being added to the substance during the melting process. [2]

14 **Question**: In the *Phase Change Diagram*, describe the difference between the energy possessed by the particles in the vapor phase compared to that of the particles in the liquid phase. [2]

PART C – EXTENDED CONSTRUCTED-RESPONSE

Statement A: Matter can be classified as pure substance or as a mixture of substances. A pure substance (element or compound) has a constant composition and constant properties throughout a given sample and from sample to sample. Mixtures are composed of two or more different substances that can be separated by physical means. When different substances are mixed together, a homogeneous or heterogeneous mixture is formed. A student separated a sample of sodium chloride solution by distillation. When she was done, she had pure water in one flask and a residue of $NaCl(s)$ in the bottom of the original flask.

1 **Question**: Explain what the words homogeneous and heterogeneous mean. [1]

2 Question: Explain why the salt water is considered to be a homogeneous mixture instead of a heterogeneous mixture. [1]

3 Question: Identify the following as an element, compound, pure substance, or mixture by placing an "x" in the column(s) that applies. [2]

	Element	Compound	Pure Substance	Mixture
a NaCl(s)	___	___	___	___
b $H_2O(l)$	___	___	___	___
c NaCl(aq)	___	___	___	___
d $N_2(g)$	___	___	___	___
e Mg(s)	___	___	___	___
f $H_2SO_4(aq)$	___	___	___	___
g $HgNO_3(aq)$	___	___	___	___

Statement B: Mixtures are composed of two or more different substances that can be separated by physical means. Differences in properties such as density, particle size, molecular polarity, boiling point, solubility, and freezing point, permit physical separation of the components of a mixture.

4 Question: Describe the procedure you would use to separate the three components of a solution of sodium chloride NaCl(aq) and insoluble sand (SiO_2). [3]

5   **Question**: Explain in terms of molecular polarity and intermolecular forces of attraction, why water by itself cannot be used to dissolve nonpolar grease molecules. [2]

Statement C: A solution is a homogeneous mixture of a solute dissolved in a solvent. The solubility of a solute in a given amount of solvent is dependent on the temperature, the pressure (for gases), and the chemical natures of the solute and solvent.

6   **Question**: Explain how you would adjust the temperature and pressure in order to get more oxygen gas dissolved into a sample of water. [1]

7   **Question**: Using your *Table of Solubility Curves* located in your *Chemistry Reference Tables* and your understanding of the solution process, determine what you could do to get more NaCl dissolved into a fixed amount of waterr. [1]

8   **Question**: State two ways for increasing the rate of solution into a beaker of water of a spoonful of sodium chloride. [2]

Statement D: Thermal energy is the energy associated with the random motion of atoms and molecules. Temperature is a measurement of the average kinetic energy of the particles in a sample of a material.

9   **Question**: As the temperature of a sample of water increases, explain what is happening to the average kinetic energy of the water molecules and how the thermal energy of the water is changing. [2]

Statement E: The concept of an ideal gas is a model to explain the behavior of gases. A real gas behaves most like an ideal gas under conditions of high temperature and low pressure.

10 **Question**: Explain how heating the air inside a hot air balloon will cause it to behave more closely to that of an ideal gas. [3]

The heat increases the pressure in a hot air balloon & this helps the pressure & temperature in the No attraction which helps become an ideal gas

Statement F: A student recorded the rates of different chemical reactions as he varied the concentration and temperature. He first held the temperature constant and varied the concentration of the reactants. He observed that as the concentration of the reactants increased, the rate of the reaction also increased. Next, he held the concentration of the reactants constant and varied the temperature at which the reaction was run. He observed that as the temperature increased, the rate of the reaction also increased. The student concluded that the rates of chemical reactions are affected by both temperature and concentration.

11 **Question**: Explain why an increase in the concentration of the reactants and an increase in the temperature will increase the rate of a chemical reaction. [2]

Directions: Use the general *Change of Phase Diagram* below to answer questions 12 through 14

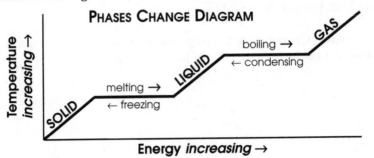

PHASES CHANGE DIAGRAM

12 **Question**: Identify each of the following changes on the *Change of Phase Diagram* as being either endothermic or exothermic and explain how the potential energy of the molecules changes as the change of phase takes place. [3]

   a   solid to liquid

   b   liquid to vapor

   c   vapor to solid

13 **Question**: Using the information supplied by the *Change of Phase Diagram* for water, explain how the atmosphere is warmed when water vapor condenses and clouds are formed. [1]

14 **Question**: Using the information supplied by the *Change of Phase Diagram* for water, explain why someone will be cooled by the evaporation of perspiration. [1]

Statement H: The structure and arrangement of particles and their interactions determine the physical state of a substance at a given temperature and pressure.

15 Question: Explain what intermolecular forces make it possible for butter to melt at room temperature. [2]

16 Question: Explain how the forces holding a molecular solid together differ from those forces holding a crystal of sodium chloride (NaCl) together? [1]

Statement I: The same amount of energy was applied to two different liquids contained in two different beakers. The first beaker contained water that boiled at a higher temperature than the liquid in the second beaker that contained a nonpolar liquid.

17 Question: Explain this difference in boiling point in terms of the intermolecular forces and vapor pressure that exists in the two liquids. [1]

18 Question: In terms of molecular polarity and intermolecular forces of attraction, explain why oil and water do not mix. [1]

PART D –
LABORATORY SKILLS

**CARRY OUT AN ACTIVITY
INVOLVING PHASE CHANGE
AND INTERPRET A SIMPLE
HEATING OR COOLING
CURVE BASED ON THIS
ACTIVITY.**

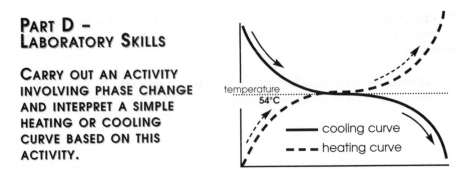

Ice or paradichlorobenzene or naphthalene may be used to determine some portions of a heating and/or cooling curve. The illustration above represents the heating and cooling curves of paradichlorobenzene (mp. 54°C) superimposed on the same graph. This allows a vivid demonstration of how the temperature remains constant during a phase change.

Directions: Use the phase change diagram at the right. Select the correct letter (*A* through *E*) to answer questions 1 through 4.

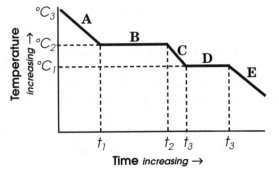

1 **Question**: Identify the pure liquid phase.   _____

2 **Question**: Identify the solid to liquid phase change.   _____

3 **Question**: Identify the gas to liquid phase change.   _____

4 **Question**: Identify the liquid to solid phase change. _____

UNIT 6
KINETICS
& EQUILIBRIUM

KEY IDEA **3** MATTER IS MADE UP OF PARTICLES WHOSE PROPERTIES DETERMINE THE OBSERVABLE CHARACTERISTICS OF MATTER AND ITS REACTIVITY

PERFORMANCE INDICATOR 3.1

PERFORMANCE INDICATOR 4.1

PERFORMANCE INDICATOR **3.4** *USE KINETIC MOLECULAR THEORY (KMT) TO EXPLAIN RATES OF REACTIONS AND THE RELATIONSHIPS AMONG TEMPERATURE, PRESSURE, AND VOLUME OF A SUBSTANCE.*

UNIT 6 - MAJOR UNDERSTANDINGS

☆ 3.4d Collision Theory states that a reaction is most likely to occur if reactant particles collide with the proper energy and orientation.

☆ 3.4f The rate of a chemical reaction depends on several factors: temperature, concentration, nature of the reactants, surface area, and the presence of a catalyst.

☆ 3.4h Some chemical and physical changes can reach equilibrium.

☆ 3.4i At equilibrium the rate of the forward reaction equals the rate of the reverse reaction. The measurable quantities of reactants and products remain constant at equilibrium.

☆ 3.4j LeChatelier's principle can be used to predict the effect of stress (change in pressure, volume, concentration, and temperature) on a system at equilibrium.

☆ 4.1c Energy released or absorbed during a chemical reaction can be represented by a potential energy diagram.

UNIT 6
KINETICS/EQUILIBRIUM

This unit is related to Key Idea 3 for the text and Performance Indicators 3.4 and 4.1 for the assessments.

INTRODUCTION

A – KINETICS

Chemical kinetics is the branch of chemistry concerned with the rate of chemical reactions and the mechanisms by which chemical reactions occur. The **rate** of a chemical reaction is measured in terms of the number of moles of reactant consumed (or moles of product formed) per unit volume in a unit of time.

The **mechanism** of a chemical reaction is a sequence of stepwise reactions by which the overall change occurs. Though many reactions take place because of a series of steps, only the net reaction is often observable. The net reaction represents a summation of all the changes that occur.

BONDING & STABILITY

Because there is a release of energy when bonds are formed, systems at lower energy levels are more stable than systems at higher energy levels. So, it follows that bonding will more often occur among atoms if the changes lead to a lower energy condition and, therefore, a more stable structure. The more energy given off when a bond is formed, the stronger and more stable the bond will be. Also, the less energy given off in the formation of a bond, the weaker and less stable it will be.

UNIT 6 – MAJOR UNDERSTANDINGS (CONTINUED)

☆ 4.1d Energy released or absorbed during a chemical reaction (heat of reaction) is equal to the difference between the potential energy of the products and potential energy of the reactants.

☆ 3.4g A catalyst provides an alternate reaction pathway, which has a lower activation energy than an un-catalyzed reaction.

☆ 3.1ll Entropy is a measure of the randomness or disorder of a system. A system with greater disorder has greater entropy.

☆ 3.1mm Systems in nature tend to undergo changes toward lower energy and higher entropy.

COLLISION THEORY

Experiments and observation show that in order for chemical reactions to occur, reacting particles must collide with enough energy and proper orientation so that old bonds are broken and new bonds are formed. This is called an **effective collision**.

SKILLS 3.4VI *USE COLLISION THEORY TO EXPLAIN HOW VARIOUS FACTORS SUCH AS TEMPERATURE, SURFACE AREA, AND CONCENTRATION, INFLUENCE THE RATE OF REACTION.*

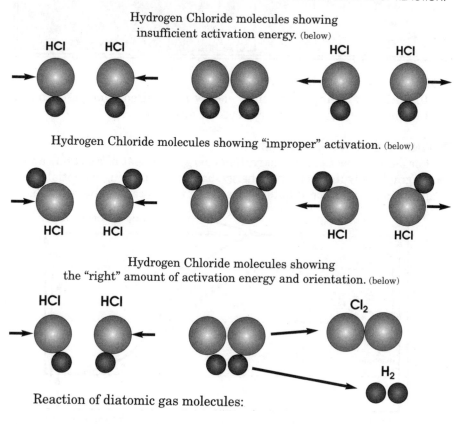

Hydrogen Chloride molecules showing insufficient activation energy. (below)

Hydrogen Chloride molecules showing "improper" activation. (below)

Hydrogen Chloride molecules showing the "right" amount of activation energy and orientation. (below)

Reaction of diatomic gas molecules:

$$2HCl(g) \rightarrow H_2(g) + Cl_2(g)$$

In order for the above reaction to take place, two conditions must be present:

- Particles must collide with enough **activating energy** to form an **activated complex**.

- Particles must collide with the proper geometric orientation so that when the activated complex is formed it can break up to form the new products.

REAL WORLD CONNECTIONS

HOT AIR BALLOON
The collision of heated gas molecules against the side of balloons cause the balloon to expand and displace the air outside the balloon and rise. ©PhotoDisc 1993

ROLE OF ENERGY IN REACTIONS
To initiate a chemical reaction, energy is required. Once a chemical reaction begins, energy may be released or absorbed.

POTENTIAL ENERGY DIAGRAM
For a given reaction, the activation energy and heat of reaction can be shown graphically in a potential energy diagram by plotting potential energy against a reaction coordinate representing the process of the reaction.

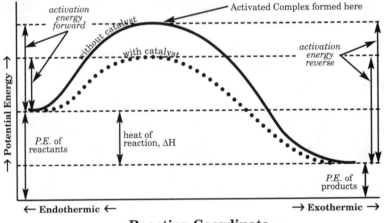

Reaction Coordinate

- If the potential energy of the products is higher than the potential energy of the reactants, energy has been absorbed (endothermic reaction).

- If the potential energy of the products is lower than the potential energy of the reactants, energy has been liberated (exothermic reaction).

The graph above, when read from left to right, represents an exothermic reaction with the products at a lower potential energy than the reactants. If the graph is reversed, or read from right to left, it would represent an endothermic reaction. The highest point in the curve represents the potential energy of the activated complex. The difference between this point and the initial potential energy of the reactants represents the activation energy of the reaction. **Note**: A catalyst provides an alternative reaction mechanism which has a lower activation energy than the un-catalyzed reaction.

🌐 REAL WORLD CONNECTIONS

ENZYMES: "ORGANIC CATALYSTS"

Enzymes may be referred to as organic catalysts (modify and increase the rate of a reaction) since they are the principal regulators of most chemical activity in living systems. Each chemical reaction requires a specific enzyme which modifies the rate of the reaction. Enzymes are not changed during the reaction and therefore can be reused. However, they eventually are destroyed and new ones must be synthesized.

Enzymes are large complex proteins consisting of one or more polypeptide chains whose names end in "–ase." Enzymes are named for the substrate (chemical being acted upon). For example, Maltose is hydrolyzed by Maltase.

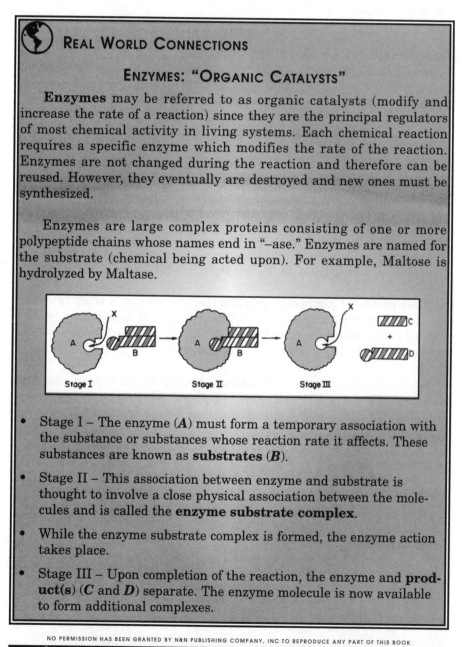

- Stage I – The enzyme (**A**) must form a temporary association with the substance or substances whose reaction rate it affects. These substances are known as **substrates (B)**.

- Stage II – This association between enzyme and substrate is thought to involve a close physical association between the molecules and is called the **enzyme substrate complex**.

- While the enzyme substrate complex is formed, the enzyme action takes place.

- Stage III – Upon completion of the reaction, the enzyme and **product(s) (C and D)** separate. The enzyme molecule is now available to form additional complexes.

ENERGY OF CHEMICAL REACTION

By graphing the potential energy of the reactants, the activation energy, and the potential energy of the products against a time sequence, one may describe the energies involved in a chemical reaction.

ACTIVATION ENERGY

Activation energy is the minimum energy required to initiate a reaction by forming an activated complex.

HEAT (ENTHALPY) OF REACTION

Heat (enthalpy) of reaction (ΔH) is the heat energy released or absorbed in the formation of the products. It represents the difference in heat content between the products and reactants.

$$\Delta H = H \text{ products} - H \text{ reactants}$$

In an exothermic reaction, energy is released. The products have a lower potential energy than the reactants, and the sign of ΔH is negative. The sign that may be used when energy is included in a chemical equation should not be confused with the sign for ΔH. For example, the equation for the reaction of hydrogen and oxygen to form water may be written:

$$H_2(g) + \tfrac{1}{2}O_2(g) \rightarrow H_2O(l) + 285.8 \text{ kJ}$$

Since this is an exothermic reaction (because energy is being produced and is written with the products), the sign of ΔH is negative (value: –285.5 J.) In equations that include heat, the phase of each species should be specified, such as (g) for gas, (l) for liquid, and (s) for solid.

When water is formed from gaseous hydrogen and oxygen, the first product that is formed is water vapor [$H_2O(g)$], which condenses into liquid water [$H_2O(l)$]. One possible mechanism for the reaction is:

$$H_2(g) + O_2(g) \rightarrow HOH(g) + O(g) + 241.8 \text{ kJ}$$

$$O(g) + H_2(g) \rightarrow HOH(g) + 241.8 \text{ kJ}$$

$$2H_2O(g) \rightarrow 2H_2O(l) + 87.78 \text{ kJ}$$

Summarizing:

$$2 H_2(g) + O_2(g) \rightarrow 2H_2O(l) + 571.6 \text{ kJ}$$

The above reaction shows that when two moles of $H_2O(l)$ are formed, the heat energy produced is 571.6 kJ. *Reference Table I* lists the standard heats of reaction of one mole of various compounds under "standard condition" (1 atm pressure and 298 K) as:

- energy of formation for one mole of $H_2O(g)$ is 241.8 kJ

- energy of formation for one mole of $H_2O(l)$ is 285.8 kJ

In an endothermic reaction, energy is absorbed, the products have a higher potential energy than the reactants, and the sign of ΔH is positive.

A good example of this type of reaction is the reverse of the above reaction. If 285.8 kJ is released when one mole of water molecules is formed, when a mole of water molecules is broken down so as to form 1 mole of hydrogen gas and $1/2$ mole of oxygen gas, the reaction requires 285.8 kJ of energy. For an endothermic reaction, the energy is written with the reactant. For example:

$$H_2O(l) + 285.8 \text{ kJ} \rightarrow H_2(g) + 1/2O_2(g)$$

FACTORS AFFECTING RATE OF REACTION

Chemical reactions depend on collisions between the reacting particles, atoms, molecules, or ions. It is these collisions that will produce an activated complex so the reaction will take place. The rate of reaction is affected by the number of collisions occurring and the fraction of these collisions that are effective. These effective collisions depend on factors such as the nature of the reactants, concentration, temperature, surface area, and any catalysts involved.

NATURE OF THE REACTANTS

Since bonds may be broken or formed in a reaction, the nature of the bond is an important fact for affecting reaction rates. Reactions that involve **negligible bond re-arrangements** are usually rapid at room temperature, such as the reactions of ionic substances in aqueous solutions. Reactions that involve the breaking of bonds tend to be slow at room temperature, such as the reaction between hydrogen and oxygen.

CONCENTRATION AFFECTS THE RATES OF REACTION

- An increase in the concentration of one or more reactants generally increases the rate of reaction.

- An increase in the concentration of a reactant increases the frequency of collisions by increasing the number of collisions per unit time.

- In a gaseous system, an increase in pressure will result in an increase in concentration and thus an increase in the rate of reaction.

TEMPERATURE AFFECTS THE RATES OF REACTION
An increase in temperature increases the rate of all chemical reactions. An increase in temperature increases the speed (and thus the kinetic energy) of the particles and increases not only the number of collisions per unit time, but also of greater importance, the effectiveness of the collisions.

SURFACE AREA
Increasing the **surface area of reactants** increases their rate of reaction. By increasing the concentration of the reactants, the number of collisions increases. In heterogeneous reactions, surface area plays an important role. For example, a given amount of zinc will react more readily with dilute hydrochloric acid if the surface area of zinc is increased by using smaller pieces.

CATALYSTS
Catalysts change the activation energy required and thus change the rate of reaction. Also, a catalyst changes the mechanism of a reaction to one involving less activation energy, but does not change the overall process. A catalyst does not initiate a chemical reaction.

SKILLS 4.1 II *READ AND INTERPRET POTENTIAL ENERGY DIAGRAMS. PE OF REACTANTS AND PRODUCTS, ACTIVATION ENERGY (WITH OR WITHOUT A CATALYST), HEAT OF REACTION.*

1. The diagram at the right represents the energy changes that occur during the formation of a certain compound under standard conditions.

   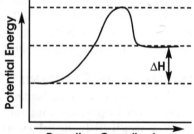

   According to *Reference Table I*, the compound could be
   (1) $C_2H_6(g)$ (3) $NO(g)$
   (2) $CO_2(g)$ (4) $NH_3(g)$

2. An increase in the surface area of reactants in a heterogeneous reaction will result in
   (1) a decrease in the rate of the reaction
   (2) an increase in the rate of the reaction
   (3) a decrease in the heat of reaction
   (4) an increase in the heat of reaction

3. The potential energy diagram of a chemical reaction is shown at the right. Which arrow represents the part of the reaction most likely to be affected by the addition of a catalyst?
   (1) A   (3) C
   (2) B   (4) D

   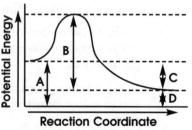

4 In a gaseous system, temperature remaining constant, an increase in pressure will
 (1) increase reaction rate   (3) increase activation energy
 (2) decrease reaction rate   (4) decrease activation energy

5 In a reversible reaction, the difference between the activation energy of the forward reaction and that of the reverse reaction is equal to the
 (1) activation complex   (3) potential energy of reactants
 (2) heat of reaction   (4) potential energy of products

6 Which statement explains why the speed of some chemical reactions is increased when the surface area of the reactant is increased?
 (1) This change increases the density of the reactant particles.
 (2) This change increases the concentration of the reactant.
 (3) This change exposes more reactant particles to a possible collision.
 (4) This change alters the electrical conductivity of the reactant particles.

7 According to *Reference Table I*, which compound forms exothermically?
 (1) ammonia – $NH_3(g)$ (3) ethene – $C_2H_4(g)$
 (2) hydrogen iodide – $HI(g)$ (4) ethyne – $C_2H_2(g)$

8 The potential energy diagram shown at the right represents the reaction $A + B \rightarrow AB$. Which statement correctly describes this reaction?
 (1) It is endothermic and energy is absorbed.
 (2) It is endothermic and energy is released.
 (3) It is exothermic and energy is absorbed.
 (4) It is exothermic and energy is released.

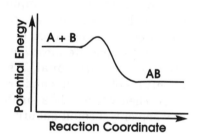

9 The reverse reaction in question 8, is best described as an
 (1) exothermic reaction in which energy is released
 (2) exothermic reaction in which energy is absorbed
 (3) endothermic reaction in which energy is released
 (4) endothermic reaction in which energy is absorbed

10 A potential energy diagram of a chemical reaction is shown at the right. What is the difference between the potential energy of the reactants and the potential energy of the products?
 (1) 84 kJ   (3) 252 kJ
 (2) 168 kJ   (4) 336 kJ

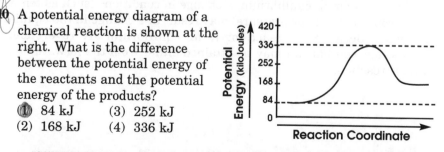

B - EQUILIBRIUM

When a quantity of water is placed in a closed container, it is not long before evaporation begins. The result is small beads of water collecting on the bottom of the cap of the container, and eventually dropping back down to the bottom of the container. This indicates that some of the water vaporized, and because of its added translational movement, hit the bottom of the cap, lost some of its kinetic energy, and condensed.

When the condensed water droplet becomes heavy enough, it drops back into the bottom of the container, where it will start once again on the odyssey of evaporation and condensation. This change of phase from liquid to vapor to liquid is called **phase equilibrium**. If the temperature remains constant, it will continue indefinitely as long as the container is closed.

Equilibrium is a state of balance between two opposing reactions (physical or chemical) occurring at the same rate. Most reactions in closed systems are reversible. Equilibrium is dynamic and only describes the overall appearance of the system. It does not describe the activity of individual particles.

The word dynamic implies motion, and **dynamic equilibrium** is that condition where the interaction of the particles of the reactants in one direction, is balanced by the interaction of the particles of the products in the opposite direction. Although the reaction rates for the opposing reactions are equal, a state of equilibrium may exist where the quantities of reactants and products are not equal. Thus equilibrium may be reached when only a small quantity of the products has been formed or when only a small quantity of reactant remains.

Note: The quantity of water on the bottom of the cap may not be as great as the quantity of water in the bottom container. However, the rates of evaporation and condensation will be equal.

Note: At equilibrium the quantity of water on the bottom of the cap may not be as great as the quantity of water in the bottom container. However, the rates of evaporation and condensation will be equal.

For a system in equilibrium, a change in conditions (such as temperature, concentration, or pressure) may result in a change in the equilibrium point. Because the reactions in an equilibrium are reversible, it follows that equilibrium may be attained either from the forward or the reverse reaction.

PHASE EQUILIBRIUM

In general, phase changes (solid to liquid or liquid to gas) are reversible, and, in a closed system, equilibrium may be attained.

Normally, if a solid or a liquid is confined in a closed container, eventually there will be enough particles in the vapor phase so that rate of return is equal to the rate of escape. Therefore, a dynamic equilibrium results where there is an equilibrium vapor pressure, characteristic of the solid or the liquid. The word dynamic refers to the fact that every molecule in the system is participating in a phase change. The basic example is the one stated above, as water changes to a vapor and then returns to its liquid form.

SKILLS 3.4VII *IDENTIFY EXAMPLES OF PHYSICAL EQUILIBRIA AS SOLUTION EQUILIBRIUM AND PHASE EQUILIBRIUM INCLUDING THE CONCEPT THAT A SATURATED SOLUTION IS AT EQUILIBRIUM.*

11 Solution equilibrium always exists in a solution that is
(1) unsaturated
(2) saturated
(3) dilute
(4) concentrated

12 The diagram at the right shows a bottle containing $NH_3(g)$ dissolved in water. How can the equilibrium $NH_3(g) \leftrightarrow NH_3(aq)$ be reached?
(1) Add more water.
(2) Add more $NH_3(g)$.
(3) Cool the contents.
(4) Stopper the bottle.

SOLUTION EQUILIBRIUM
GASES IN LIQUIDS

In a closed system, equilibrium may exist between a gas dissolved in a liquid and the undissolved gas above the liquid. The equilibrium between dissolved and undissolved gas is affected by temperature and pressure in the following ways:

• increased temperature decreases the solubility of gases in liquids

• increased pressure increases the solubility of gases in liquids

An example that points out this type of equilibrium is a bottle of soda. As you decrease the pressure on the top of the soda, by removing the cap, the gas becomes less soluble. You hear the resulting "swoosh..." as the gas escapes.

SOLIDS IN LIQUIDS

A solution equilibrium exists when the opposing processes of dissolving and crystallizing a solute occur at equal rates. Such a solution exhibiting equilibrium between the dissolved and recrystallized solute must be a saturated solution.

For example, if salt is added to water in a beaker, the salt would dissolve. If more salt is added, the solution will become so saturated with the compound that for every sodium chloride particle going into solution, one would recrystallize out of solution. At this point, solution equilibrium exists, and a **saturated solution** results.

SOLUBILITY

Solubility is an expression of concentration of a solute in a solvent and can be given under two conditions. The solubility of a solute is defined as the maximum mass of the solute dissolved in a given volume of solvent under specified conditions, not necessarily a saturated solution. And, solubility may also be defined as the concentration of solute in a saturated solution.

REACTIONS WHICH GO TO COMPLETION

Continuous removal of the product in a closed system may destroy the equilibrium system by removing all of that substance necessary for the reverse reaction. Removal of a product usually causes the reactants to exhaust themselves and the forward reaction to go nearer to completion or to an end.

In an open system, products may be removed from a reaction, wholly or in part by the formation of a gas, formation of an insoluble product (precipitate), or by the formation of an essentially un-ionized product, such as water in an ionic reaction. Such reactions are said to go to "completion."

CHEMICAL EQUILIBRIUM

Chemical equilibrium is attained when the concentration of the reactants and products remains constant. When observable changes (such as color, pressure, and temperature) no longer occur in a reacting chemical system, the system has reached a state of equilibrium. At this point the forward reaction and the reverse reaction are occurring at equal rates.

REAL WORLD CONNECTIONS

HABER PROCESS (ALSO CALLED HABER-BOSCH PROCESS)

In the Haber process, $N_2(g) + 3H_2(g) \leftrightarrow 2 NH_3(g)$, four moles (volume) of reactants form two moles (volume) of product. The forward reaction thus results in a decrease in the total number of moles (lower volume). Therefore, an increase in pressure will result in an increased production of ammonia, which relieves the effect of increased pressure.

However, in the reaction: $H_2(g) + Cl_2(g) \leftrightarrow 2HCl(g)$ a change in pressure does not affect the equilibrium, since there is an equal volume of gases on either side. **Note**: Solids and liquids are not affected by a pressure change to any appreciable amount.

Le Chatelier's Principle

If a stress, such as a change in concentration, pressure, or temperature, is applied to a system at equilibrium, the equilibrium is shifted in a way that usually relieves the effects of the stress. When a chemical system at equilibrium is disturbed, chemical reaction occurs and equilibrium is re-established at a different point (such as with new concentrations of reactants and products).

- **Effect of Concentration** – Increasing the concentration of one substance in a reaction at equilibrium will cause the reaction to go in such a direction as to consume the increase. Eventually, a new equilibrium will be established. For example, in the equilibrium reac-

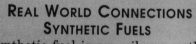

REAL WORLD CONNECTIONS
SYNTHETIC FUELS

Synthetic fuel is any oil or gas that is made from bitumen, coal, oil shale, or tar sand. Synthetic fuel is very important as the world supply of petroleum (crude oil and natural gas) is estimated to run out in the next 25 to 50 years. Since there is a great amount of bitumen, coal, oil shale and tar sand reserves in the world, synthetic fuel is being made and will be made from them.

Are Synthetics Better? The molecules in synthetic oil are much more consistent in size and shape than the base stocks produced from crude petroleum. Mobil 1 has a minimum of short chain molecules that burn off or volatilize during high engine temperatures. Unlike conventional motor oil, there is no wax present in the synthetic stocks which contributes to excellent low-temperature flow characteristics.

Source: http://www.mobil1.com/index.jsp

tion, $N_2(g) + 3H_2(g) \leftrightarrow 2NH_3(g)$, increasing the concentration of either nitrogen or hydrogen will increase the rate of ammonia formation. If the system remains closed, the increased concentration of ammonia that results will increase the rate of decomposition of ammonia, and a new equilibrium point will be established.

Removal of one product of a reaction results in a decrease in its concentration. This will cause the reaction to go in such a direction as to increase the concentration of the products.

- **Effect of Pressure** – A change in pressure affects chemical equilibria in which gases are involved. An increase in pressure will displace the point of equilibrium in the direction that favors the formation of a lesser number of moles (lower volume). If no change in the number of moles is involved (equal volumes of reactants and products), a change in pressure has no effect on the equilibrium.

- **Effect of Temperature** – When the temperature of a system in an equilibrium is raised, the equilibrium is displaced in such a way that heat is absorbed. Chemical changes involve either the evolution or the absorption of energy. In every system in equilibrium, an endothermic and exothermic reaction are taking place simultaneously. The endothermic reaction is favored by an increase in temperature, the exothermic reaction by a decrease in temperature. Keep in mind that the rates of all reactions, both endothermic and exothermic, are increased by a rise in temperature.

However, the opposing reactions are increased unequally, resulting in a displacement of the equilibrium. For example, in the Haber process, $N_2(g) + 3H_2(g) \leftrightarrow 2NH_3(g) + 91.8 \text{ kJ}$, raising the temperature favors the decomposition of ammonia.

- **Effect of Catalyst** – In a system in equilibrium, a catalyst increases the rate of both the forward and reverse reactions equally, and produces no net change in the equilibrium concentrations. A catalyst may cause equilibrium to be reached more quickly, but does not affect the point of equilibrium.

SKILLS 3.4IV *DESCRIBE THE CONCENTRATION OF PARTICLES AND RATES OF OPPOSING REACTIONS IN AN EQUILIBRIUM SYSTEM.*

13 Given the system at chemical equilibrium:

$$2O_3(g) \leftrightarrow 3O_2(g)$$

The concentration of O_3 and O_2 must be
(1) constant   (2) equal   (3) increasing   (4) decreasing

14 The addition of concentrated hydrochloric acid to the system

$$AgCl(s) \leftrightarrow Ag^+(aq) + Cl^-(aq)$$

at equilibrium will result in
(1) a decrease in the amount of $AgCl(s)$
(2) a decrease in the concentration of $H_3O^+(aq)$
(3) an increase in the concentration of $Ag^+(aq)$
(4) an increase in the concentration of $Cl^-(aq)$

15 Given the reaction at equilibrium:

$$A(g) + B(g) \leftrightarrow C(g) + D(g) + heat$$

As additional $A(g)$ is added to the system at constant temperature, the concentration of $B(g)$
(1) decreases (2) increases (3) remains the same

16 Given the reaction at equilibrium:

$$AgCl(s) \leftrightarrow Ag^+(aq) + Cl^-(aq)$$

The addition of Cl^- ions will shift the equilibrium to the
(1) right, decreasing the solubility of $AgCl(s)$
(2) right, increasing the solubility of $AgCl(s)$
(3) left, increasing the amount of $AgCl(s)$
(4) left, increasing the solubility of $AgCl(s)$

SKILLS 3.4V *QUALITATIVELY DESCRIBE THE EFFECT OF STRESS ON EQUILIBRIUM USING LECHATELEIR'S PRINCIPLE.*

17 Given the reaction at equilibrium:

$$N_2(g) + 3H_2(g) \leftrightarrow 2NH_3(g) + 91.8 \text{ kJ}$$

Which stress would cause the equilibrium to shift to the left?
(1) increasing the temperature
(2) increasing the pressure
(3) adding $N_2(g)$ to the system
(4) adding $H_2(g)$ to the system

18 Given the reaction at equilibrium:

$$N_2(g) + 3H_2(g) \leftrightarrow 2NH_3(g)$$

Increasing the concentration of $N_2(g)$ will increase the forward reaction rate due to
(1) a decrease in the number of effective collisions
(2) an increase in the number of effective collisions
(3) a decrease in the activation energy
(4) an increase in the activation energy

REAL WORLD CONNECTIONS

Catalysts and inhibitors – Thrombokinase is an enzyme released into the human bloodstream by damaged platelet cells when a wound is incurred. This enzyme catalyzes the conversion of a plasma protein called prothrombin into thrombin, which, in turn, catalyzes fibrinogin into fibrin. Both of these enzymes require Calcium (Ca^{++}) ions, located in the blood to proceed. Cross linkages between the fibrin molecules in turn produce a clot. If the blood is low in calcium, the clot will take a longer time to form.

☆ LAW OF CHEMICAL EQUILIBRIUM

When a reversible reaction has attained equilibrium at a given temperature, a mathematical relationship occurs. The product of the molar concentrations of the substances on the right side of the equation (products), divided by the product of the molar concentrations of the substances on the left side of the equation (reactants), is a **constant**. **Note**: Each concentration is raised to the power equal to the coefficients in the balanced equation.

For the reaction: $aM(g) + bN(g) \leftrightarrow cP(g) + dQ(g)$

The equilibrium expression is written:

$$\frac{[P]^c\,[Q]^d}{[M]^a\,[N]^b} = K \text{ a constant at constant temperature}$$

This constant is called the **equilibrium constant**. In the mathematical expression of this law

- the equation must be balanced;

- square brackets " [ ] " are used to indicate "concentrations measured in moles per liter;"

- the concentrations of the products on the right of the chemical equation form the numerator, and the concentrations of reactants on the left form the denominator;

- the power of each concentration is derived from its coefficient;

- finally, the mathematical proportion obtained in the first four steps, at a specific temperature, is equal to a constant which is designated as follows:

    K_{eq} for all forms of chemical reactions,
    K_a for acids,
    K_b for bases,
    K_{sp} for solubility of solids, and
    K_w for the ionization of water.

Also, note the following:

- The concentration of a solid or a liquid is essentially constant. In the expression of the equilibrium constant for any reaction involving a solid or a liquid, the concentration of the solid or liquid can be included in the constant; therefore, it does not appear in the equation.

- The magnitude of **K** is used by chemists to predict the extent of chemical reactions. A large value for **K** indicates the products are favored; that is, the equilibrium mixture consists largely of products. A small value for **K** indicates that reactants are favored.

- The equilibrium constant has a numerical value for any given chemical reaction at a particular temperature. This value remains constant even though the concentrations of the substances involved may increase or decrease. In general, in the reaction given (on page 172), an increase in the concentration of P would cause the reaction to go to the left. This decreases the concentration of Q and increases the concentrations of M and N. The value of K would remain constant.

- The equilibrium constant changes with a change of temperature. In a reversible reaction, the reaction rates of the forward and reverse reactions are not affected equally by change in temperature.

C – Spontaneous Reactions

Under specific conditions, ice melts into water; other conditions turn water back to ice. The initiating ingredient here is temperature; the rest occurs spontaneously. Once the activation energy is applied, in the form of a match, paper will combust rapidly under specific conditions. These are forms of physical and chemical spontaneous reactions. After studying these phenomena for many years, it has been discovered that spontaneous reactions depend on the balance between the two fundamental tendencies in nature:

- toward a lower energy state $\Delta H^* = (-)$

- toward randomness $\Delta S^* = (+)$(**greater entropy**)

*see page 175

Energy Changes

As learned earlier, the activation energy required for an exothermic reaction is less than that required for an endothermic reaction. That difference is the energy of the reaction (ΔH). Therefore, when particles collide, they require less energy to go in the exothermic direction than in the endothermic direction.

This tendency in nature favors the exothermic reaction, in which ΔH is negative. Generally, at constant temperature and pressure, a system tends to change from one of high energy to one of low energy.

ENTROPY CHANGES

Entropy is a measure of the disorder, randomness, or lack of organization of a system. The solid phase is in regular crystalline arrangement and is more organized than the liquid phase. The liquid phase is more organized than the gaseous phase. Entropy is so defined that the more random a system is, the higher the entropy.

An increase in entropy during a change in the state of a system means that in its final state, the system is more disordered (random) than in its initial state. High entropy (randomness) is favored by high temperatures. High temperatures increase the rate of motion of the particles and, therefore, increases randomness.

At constant temperature, a system tends to undergo a reaction so that in its final state, it has higher entropy (greater randomness) than in its initial state. Therefore, **note**: A system tends to change from a state of great order to a state of less order. For chemical systems, this change in entropy is represented mathematically as ΔS.

REAL WORLD CONNECTIONS

Chaos Theory, **randomness vs. order** – The third law of thermodynamics, formulated by Walther Nernst in 1906, indicates that no matter how cold an object becomes, it can be made still colder without quite attaining absolute zero. Absolute Zero is the absence of heat. At this temperature matter would possess zero entropy and maximum molecular order, the volume of an ideal gas would vanish, and a thermodynamic heat engine would operate at 100 percent efficiency. Absolute zero cannot actually be reached.

The Law states, "The entropy of a pure perfect crystal at absolute zero temperature is zero." At this temperature, a state of perfect order has been achieved. First, it should be noted that we have not been able to reach absolute zero or O kelvin. Second, as the temperature is raised from near O kelvin the entropy increases. Therefore, there are those who state that systems tend to go toward greater chaos rather than toward a state of order.

The American physical chemist William Giauque (1895-1982) did significant work in chemical thermodynamics, particularly on the behavior of substances at very low temperatures, for which he was awarded the 1949 Nobel Prize for chemistry. Giauque determined accurately the entropy of a large number of substances near absolute zero. He also proved that the third law of thermodynamics is correct.

Substances that are solids have ridged bonds with just vibrational movement. As energy is applied, the atoms acquire vibrational and rotational motion which increases the randomness (entropy) of the atoms in the substance, causing it to become a liquid. Finally, as more energy is applied to the substance, the atoms along with the vibrational and rotational motion that they already possess, acquire translational motion. This motion causes the rigid bonds between the atoms to break and it becomes a gas in this phase, and is at its highest state of randomness (or entropy).

19 Identify the substances that are in the highest state of entropy.

__Na(s) __Hg(l) __F$_2$(g) __KCl(s) __Br$_2$(l) __Ca(OH)$_2$(s) __He(g)

FREE ENERGY CHANGE

The difference between energy change and entropy change is the free energy change (ΔG). It is expressed by the following equation:

$$\Delta G = \Delta H - T\Delta S$$

Where,

ΔG is the free energy change and represents the net energy of the reaction that can perform work.

ΔH represents the energy factor, or the total heat energy, given off or taken on during the reaction.

T is the temperature in degrees Kelvin.

ΔS is the measurement of entropy and represents the change in randomness of the reactants to the products.

Since ΔS is multiplied by the temperature, the whole expression TΔS is considered the entropy factor. For a spontaneous change to occur in a system, the free energy change (ΔG) must be negative.

Mathematically, in order for ΔG to be negative, the ideal condition occurs when ΔH is negative and ΔS is positive (as in combustion reactions). However, other conditions can occur and also result in a negative ΔG. These cases depend on the value of the temperature. If the temperature is high enough, the significance of ΔH diminishes, and the TΔS term dominates. If instead, the temperature is very low, the TΔS term is small, and the influence it has on the value of ΔG is diminished. It is overbalanced by a large negative value for ΔH.

PREDICTING SPONTANEOUS REACTIONS

As stated above, for a spontaneous change to occur in a system, the free energy change (ΔG) must be negative. In a system at equilibrium, the free energy change is zero. When the two factors (tendency toward lower energy content, and tendency toward higher entropy in a system) cannot be satisfied simultaneously, the spontaneous change that may take place will be determined by the factor that is dominant at the temperature of the system. From energy changes alone, exothermic reactions would always be expected to occur spontaneously, and endothermic reactions would never be expected to occur spontaneously. Exceptions to both of these predictions may occur when a change in entropy opposes an exothermic reaction or favors an endothermic reaction. The following two passages illustrate this condition.

• The change in phase from water to ice is an exothermic reaction and, from the consideration of energy only, water might be expected to freeze spontaneously at any temperature. However, the tendency toward higher entropy favors the reaction from ice to water. At temperatures below the freezing point, the energy change is dominant and water will freeze spontaneously. At temperatures above the freezing point, the entropy change becomes the dominant factor, and ice melts.

• The reaction, $2KClO_3(s) \rightarrow 2KCl(s) + 3O_2(g)$, is an endothermic reaction. The energy change would oppose a spontaneous reaction. However, the reaction results in an increase in entropy due to the formation of a gas and a solid. At high temperatures, the effect of the entropy changes becomes sufficient to overcome the effect of the energy change, and the reaction takes place. If the temperature is not high enough, the reaction will not take place spontaneously.

🌎 REAL WORLD CONNECTIONS

Exothermic reaction (burning of fossil fuels) – The burning of wood and carbon-based substances occurs when ignition of the reactants takes place in the presence of oxygen. Once ignition occurs, the reaction proceeds and the potential energy in the fuels is transferred into kinetic energy with the production of light and heat. The reaction for the complete combustion of fossil fuels is:

$$2C_8H_{18}(l) + 25O_2(g) \rightarrow 16CO_2(g) + 18H_2O(l) + \text{energy}$$

☆ SOLUBILITY PRODUCT CONSTANT (K_{SP})

The solubility product constant, K_{sp}, is a measure of the concentration of slightly soluble salts in water. In a saturated solution of an ionic solid, an equilibrium is established between the ions in the saturated solution and the excess solid phase. The value of the K_{sp} changes with a change of temperature. For the reaction:

$$AB(s) \leftrightarrow A^+(aq) + B^-(aq)$$

$$K_{sp} = [A^+][B^-]$$

The concentration (mass/unit volume) of a solid is essentially constant. In the expression of the equilibrium constant for any reaction involving a solid, the concentration of the solid can be included in the constant. It does not appear in the equation. Therefore, in the case of the solubility equilibrium (below), application of the law of chemical equilibrium would give:

$$K = \frac{[A^+]\,[B^-]}{[AB]}$$

Since (**AB**) itself is constant, then

$$[A^+]\,[B^-] = K\,[AB] = K_{sp}$$

The magnitude of K_{sp} is used in comparing the solubilities of slightly soluble salts. For example, at room temperature

$$K_{sp}\ CaSO_4 = 2.4 \times 10^{-5}$$
$$K_{sp}\ BaSO_4 = 1.6 \times 10^{-9}$$

Since the K_{sp} of $BaSO_4$ is less than that of $CaSO_4$, $BaSO_4$ must be less soluble than $CaSO_4$ and would be precipitated at a lower concentration.

COMMON ION EFFECT

The addition of a common ion to the solution of a slightly soluble salt results in a decrease in the solubility of the salt. Consider the equilibrium:

$$AgCl(s) \leftrightarrow Ag^+(aq) + Cl^-(aq)$$

Addition of NaCl, or any other soluble chloride salt, to this equilibrium system increases the $Cl^-(aq)$ concentration and, according to LeChatelier's Principle shifts the equilibrium to the left. This results in a decrease in the solubility of AgCl.

REAL WORLD CONNECTIONS

Photosynthesis (endothermic reaction) is a process during which light energy is converted into chemical energy. Photochemical smog is the high temperature combustion of fuels producing the following reaction:

$$N_2(g) + O_2(g) \rightarrow 2NO(g) \qquad \Delta H = +182.6\ kJ\ \text{(endothermic reaction)}$$

Urban smog occurs in steps; the first requires the conversion of NO to NO_2. Then, on bright sunny mornings when the concentration of NO_2 is high, the nitrogen dioxide is dissociated.

$$NO_2(g) \rightarrow NO(g) + O(g)$$

The oxygen atoms produced react with oxygen molecules in the air to produce O_3 (ozone), a major component of photochemical smog. Ozone attacks organic molecules, especially unsaturated molecules with double and triple bonds.

PERFORMANCE INDICATOR 3.1, 3.4, & 4.1
ASSESSMENTS

PART A - MULTIPLE CHOICE

1 A solute is added to water and a portion of the solute remains undissolved. When equilibrium between the dissolved and undissolved solute is reached, the solution must be
   (1) dilute   (3) unsaturated
   (2) saturated   (4) supersaturated

2 Adding a catalyst to a chemical reaction changes the rate of reaction by causing
   (1) a decrease in the activation energy
   (2) an increase in the activation energy
   (3) a decrease in the heat of reaction
   (4) an increase in the heat of reaction

3 Which factors must be *equal* when a reversible chemical process reaches equilibrium?
   (1) mass of the reactants and mass of the products
   (2) rate of the forward reaction and rate of the reverse reaction
   (3) concentration of the reactants and concentration of the products
   (4) activation energy of the forward reaction and activation energy of the reverse reaction

4 Given the reaction at equilibrium: $H_2(g) + I_2(g) \rightarrow 2HI(g)$ Which expression correctly represents the K_{eq} for this reaction?

   (1) $K_{eq} = \dfrac{[2HI]}{[H_2][I_2]}$ (3) $K_{eq} = \dfrac{[HI]^2}{[H_2][I_2]}$

   (2) $K_{eq} = \dfrac{[H_2][I_2]}{[HI]^2}$ (4) $K_{eq} = \dfrac{[H][I]}{[HI]^2}$

5 Given the reaction at equilibrium:

   $$BaCrO_4(s) \leftrightarrow Ba^{2+}(aq) + CrO_4^{2-}(aq)$$

   Which substance, when added to the mixture, will cause an increase in the amount of $BaCrO_4(s)$?
   (1) K_2CO_3 (2) $CaCO_3$ (3) $BaCl_2$ (4) $CaCl_2$

6 Which equation is used to determine the free energy change during a chemical reaction?
   (1) $\Delta G = \Delta H - \Delta S$ (3) $\Delta G = \Delta H - T\Delta S$
   (2) $\Delta G = \Delta H + \Delta S$ (4) $\Delta G = \Delta H + T\Delta S$

7 What is the K_{sp} expression for the salt PbI_2?
   (1) $[Pb^{2+}][I^-]^2$ (3) $[Pb^{2+}][I_2]^2$
   (2) $[Pb^{2+}][2I^-]$ (4) $[Pb^{2+}][2I^-]^2$

8 Which is the correct equilibrium expression for the reaction $2A(g) + 3B(g) \leftrightarrow C(g) + 3D(g)$?

(1) $K = \dfrac{[2A] + [3B]}{[C] + [3D]}$

(2) $K = \dfrac{[C] + [3D]}{[2A] + [3B]}$

(3) $K = \dfrac{[A]^2 [B]^3}{[C] [D]^3}$

(4) $K = \dfrac{[C] [D]^3}{[A]^2 [B]^3}$

9 Which statement describes characteristics of an endothermic reaction?
(1) The sign of ΔH is positive, and the products have less potential energy than the reactants.
(2) The sign of ΔH is positive, and the products have more potential energy than the reactants.
(3) The sign of ΔH is negative, and the products have less potential energy than the reactants.
(4) The sign of ΔH is negative, and the products have more potential energy than the reactants.

10 Given the equilibrium system: $PbCO_3(s) \leftrightarrow Pb^{2+}(aq) + CO_3^{2-}(aq)$
Which changes occur as $Pb(NO_3)_2(s)$ is added to the system at equilibrium?
(1) The amount of $PbCO_3(s)$ decreases, and the concentration of $CO_3^{2-}(aq)$ decreases.
(2) The amount of $PbCO_3(s)$ decreases, and the concentration of $CO_3^{2-}(aq)$ increases.
(3) The amount of $PbCO_3(s)$ increases, and the concentration of $CO_3^{2-}(aq)$ decreases.
(4) The amount of $PbCO_3(s)$ increases, and the concentration of $CO_3^{2-}(aq)$ increases.

11 Which statement best describes a chemical reaction in which energy is released?
(1) It is exothermic and has a negative ΔH.
(2) It is exothermic and has a positive ΔH.
(3) It is endothermic and has a negative ΔH.
(4) It is endothermic and has a positive ΔH.

12 The potential energy diagram of a chemical reaction is shown at the right. Which arrow represents the heat of the reaction, ΔH?
(1) *A, only*
(2) *B, only*
(3) *C*
(4) *D*

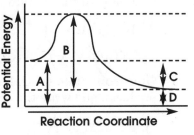

13 Given the reaction at equilibrium: $N_2(g) + O_2(g) \leftrightarrow 2NO(g)$ As the concentration of $N_2(g)$ increases, the concentration of $O_2(g)$ will
(1) decrease   (2) increase   (3) remain the same

PART B - CONSTRUCTED-RESPONSE

Directions: To answer questions 1 through 5, use the *Potential Energy Diagram*, showing an exothermic reaction, with the accompanying equation:

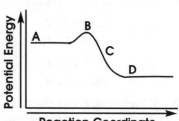

$$N_2(g) + 3H_2(g) \rightleftharpoons 2NH_3(g) + 91.8 \text{ kJ}$$

1 Question: State whether the *Potential Energy Diagram* illustrates an exothermic or endothermic reaction. [1]

> exothermic

2 Question: Describe what will happen to the rate of the forward reaction if the temperature is increased. [1]

> The rate will increase
> Kinetic energy increases, molecules move faster

3 Question: Describe what will happen to the value of the activated complex if a catalyst is added to the reaction vessel. [1]

> The activation will decrease.
> (B)

4 Question: Describe how the addition of a catalyst will alter the rates of both the forward and reverse reactions. [1]

> The catalyst will decrease the amount of activation energy needed   increase in both directions

5 Question: State which has greater enthalpy, the reactants or the products, and write the value of ΔHr for the reaction. [2]

> reactants
> ΔH -91.8

Directions: Cube **A** respresents a single cube of a particular volume. **B** represents 8 cubes with the *same* total volume as Cube **A**.

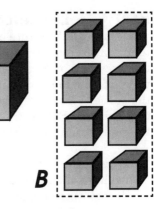

6   **Question**: If the particles of Cube **A** were oxidized, describe how the reaction rate of the particles making up Cube **B** would compare to the reaction rate of the particles making up Cube **A**. [1]

Cube B has more
SA / concentration & will react quicker

Illustration C: Answer the following questions based upon the accompanying equilibrium reaction which is taking place in a closed flask at 298 K:

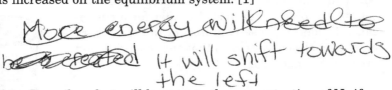

$$N_2(g) + 3H_2(g) \rightleftharpoons 2NH_3(g) + 91.8 \text{ kJ}$$

7   **Question**: Describe how the equilibrium will shift when the temperature is increased on the equilibrium system. [1]

~~More energy will need to be created~~ It will shift towards the left

8   **Question**: Describe what will happen to the concentration of N_2 if more H_2 is injected into the flask. [1]

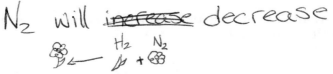

N_2 will ~~increase~~ decrease

9   **Question**: Describe how the temperature and pressure on the system could be altered in order to make the equilibrium shift to the right. [2]

increase pressure & decrease temp

10   **Question**: Describe what will happen to the equilibrium system if the flask is opened. [1]

↓ pressure equilibrium will be lost

PART C – EXTENDED CONSTRUCTED-RESPONSE

Statement A: The rate of a chemical reaction depends on several factors: temperature, concentration, nature of the reactants, surface area, and the presence of a catalyst. Grain elevators in the Midwest have found ways of keeping large amounts of dust out of the air and making sure that all electrical switches are grounded so that no electrical spark will be produced. Before this was done, devastating explosions produced by the rapid oxidation of the dust particles sometimes occurred.

1 **Question**: In terms of the kinetic molecular theory of reaction rates, explain what factors are being controlled in order to prevent these devastating chemical reactions from taking place. [2]

Statement B: Some chemical and physical changes reach equilibrium. Equilibrium exists when the rate of the forward reaction equals the rate of the reverse reaction. In order for a chemical, solution or phase equilibrium to exist, there must be a closed system so that the reactants and products cannot escape.

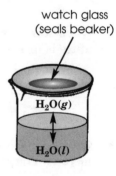

watch glass
(seals beaker)

$H_2O(g)$

$H_2O(l)$

$$H_2O(l) + heat = H_2O(g)$$

2 **Question**: Explain what kind of equilibrium exists in the accompanying illustration. [1]

3 **Question**: Explain what would have to be done in order to increase the equilibrium vapor pressure. [1]

4 **Question**: Explain why the equilibrium will be disrupted if the cover on the beaker is removed. [1]

Statement C: LeChatelier's Principle states that when a stress is brought to bear upon a system at equilibrium, the system will react so as to relieve the stress.

The Haber Process reaction is used in the manufacture of ammonia using the following reaction:

$$3H_2(g) + N_2(g) = 2NH_3(g) + 91.8 \text{ kJ}$$

During this reaction, hydrogen gas and nitrogen gas combine to form ammonia gas. At a specific point in the reaction, the reverse reaction rate becomes equal to the forward reaction rate bringing about a system in equilibrium.

5 **Question**: Explain how the stresses of temperature and pressure can be manipulated in order to make the equilibrium shift to the left. [1]

6 **Question**: Name one factor that could be manipulated in order to get the reverse reaction to occur at a faster rate. [1]

Statement D: A *Potential Energy Diagram* can be used to illustrate the change in potential energy that is taking place within a chemical reaction.

Illustration: A potential energy diagram showing an endothermic reaction, with an enthalpy change = **66.4 kJ** accompanied by the following chemical reaction:
$N_2 + 2O_2 + 66.4 \text{ kJ} = 2NO_2$

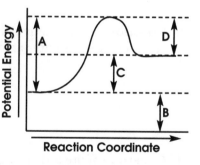

7 **Question**: Using the *Potential Energy Diagram* and equation, discuss how the potential energy of the products compares to that of the reactants. [1]

8   **Question**: Using the accompanying potential energy diagram and equation, explain how the bond energies of the reactants compare to the bond energies of the products. [1]

9   **Question**: Using the graph on page 183, compare the energy of activation (A) for the forward reaction to the energy of activation (D) for the reverse reaction. What can you conclude about the bond strengths of the reactants of the forward reaction compared to the bond strengths of the reactants of the reverse reaction? [1]

Statement E: The energy released or absorbed during a chemical reaction is called the heat of reaction. It is equal to the difference between the potential energy of the products and the potential energy of the reactants. (**Hint**: Use the Haber Process reaction to answer this question.)

$$3H_2(g) + N_2(g) = 2NH_3(g) \qquad\qquad \Delta H = \text{-91.8 kJ}$$

10 **Question**: State whether the products or reactants of the forward reaction have a greater amount of potential energy. [1]

11 **Question**: Write a thermochemical equation placing the heat term on the correct side of the equation (Statement E) to illustrate the enthalpy change taking place during the reaction. [1]

Statement F: When bonds are formed, energy is released and, when bonds are broken, energy is absorbed. A thermochemical equation illustrates the overall energy balance within a chemical reaction. When the equation is endothermic, then more energy had to be put in to break the bonds than was released when the bonds were formed and the heat term is added to the reactant side. If the equation is exothermic, the heat term is added to the product side.

12 **Question**: In terms of bond energies, explain why the following reaction is exothermic: $N_2 + 3H_2 = 2NH_3 + 91.8$ kJ [1]

13 **Question**: For the reaction in question 12, explain which has the greater amount of energy, the reactants or the products? [1]

PART D – LABORATORY SKILLS

MEASURE HEATS OF SIMPLE REACTIONS

A simple activity in calorimetry may be done using water as a calorimetric liquid and a burning candle to determine the heat of combustion of the candle. First take the mass of the candle and the water, along with the temperature of the water before heating takes place. The amount of heat rise of the water can be determined, using the standard apparatus. Then, by reweighing the used candle, determine the amount of calories required to combust a quantity of the candle. Use the formula:

calories = mass of H_2O x ΔT x specific heat of H_2O

Then, divide the formula answer by the weight of the wax used up to obtain the answer in calories per gram of wax. Finally, multiply your answer by 4.18 Joules/calorie to obtain your answer in Joules.

1 **Question**: Name three (3) possible variables that could bring about errors in your calculations.

2   **Question**: How are the Calories used in diet regimes related to the calories used in this lab investigation?

3   **Question**: Scented candles contain smelly volatile oils (oils that evaporate readily at normal temperatures and pressures). Based on the experiment and your knowledge of chemistry, which will burn faster: scented or unscented candles? Explain.

UNIT 7
ORGANIC CHEMISTRY

KEY IDEA 3

MATTER IS MADE UP OF PARTICLES WHOSE PROPERTIES DETERMINE THE OBSERVABLE CHARACTERISTICS OF MATTER AND ITS REACTIVITY

PERFORMANCE INDICATOR 3.1 *EXPLAIN THE PROPERTIES OF MATERIALS IN TERMS OF THE ARRANGEMENT AND PROPERTIES OF THE ATOMS THAT COMPOSE THEM.*

PERFORMANCE INDICATOR 3.2

PERFORMANCE INDICATOR 5.2

UNIT 7 – MAJOR UNDERSTANDINGS

☆ 3.1ff Organic compounds contain carbon atoms which bond to one another in chains, rings, and networks to form a variety of structures. Organic compounds can be named using the IUPAC system.

☆ 3.1gg Hydrocarbons are compounds that contain only carbon and hydrogen. Saturated hydrocarbons contain only single carbon-carbon bonds. Unsaturated hydrocarbons contain at least one multiple carbon-carbon bond.

☆ 3.1hh Organic acids, alcohols, esters, aldehydes, ketones, ethers, halides, amines, amides, and amino acids are categories of organic molecules that differ in their structures. Functional groups impart distinctive physical and chemical properties to organic compounds.

☆ 3.1ii Isomers of organic compounds have the same molecular formula but different structures and properties.

UNIT 7
ORGANIC CHEMISTRY

This unit is related to Key Idea 3 for the text and Performance Indicators 3.1, 3.2, and 5.2 for the assessments.

INTRODUCTION

Organic chemistry is the chemistry of the compounds of carbon. Organic compounds occur extensively in nature. All living things are composed predominantly of organic compounds.

Carbon is able to form four covalent bonds not only with other kinds of atoms, but also with other carbon atoms. This makes possible a very large number of compounds. Consequently, organic compounds are much more numerous than **inorganic compounds**.

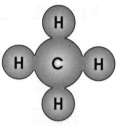

Carbon atoms bond to one another in chains, rings, and networks to form a variety of structures. The major sources of raw materials from which organic chemicals are obtained are petroleum, coal, wood, and other plant products and animal sources.

 REAL WORLD CONNECTIONS

Types, varieties, uses of organic compounds – Organic (carbon) compounds exist in all life forms. Their uses range from fuels to construction material; however, most importantly, organic compounds are used in the field of medicine to diagnose and treat diseases.

UNIT 7 – MAJOR UNDERSTANDINGS (CONTINUED)

☆ 5.2e In a multiple covalent bond, more than one pair of electrons are shared between two atoms. Unsaturated organic compounds contain at least one double or triple bond.

☆ 3.2c Types of organic reactions include: addition, substitution, polymerization, esterification, fermentation, saponification, and combustion.

A – CHARACTERISTICS
OF ORGANIC COMPOUNDS

Solubility – Organic compounds are generally nonpolar and tend to dissolve in nonpolar solvents.

Question: Can you name a few nonpolar solvents?

Those organic compounds that are somewhat polar, such as acetic acid, are soluble in water. Generally organic compounds are insoluble in water and soluble in nonaqueous solvents.

Conductivity – Organic compounds are generally nonelectrolytes. These organic acids that are electrolytes are very weak.

Melting Points – Organic compounds generally have low melting points. Since most organic compounds are essentially nonpolar, the intermolecular forces are weak. Therefore, the compounds have relatively low melting points (under 300°C).

Organic Compound Reactions – Most reactions involving organic compounds are slower than those involving inorganic compounds. Because of strong covalent bonding within the molecule, organic compounds do not readily form activated complexes (intermediates), and thus, reactions take place slowly. The activation energy required for organic reactions is generally high.

B – BONDING

Carbon atoms bond with the following characteristics:

- the four valence electrons of the carbon allow it to form four covalent bonds;
- these four single bonds of the carbon atom are spatially directed toward the corners of a regular tetrahedron;
- the carbon atom can share electrons with other carbon atoms;
- two adjacent carbon atoms can share one to three pairs of electrons; and,
- the covalent bonding results in compounds that have molecular characteristics.

Below are two ball and stick models (Carbon Tetrahedral Model - left) showing the spatial arrangement of the tetrahedral model of the carbon atom. Spatial arrangement (Methane - right) showing bond angles and overlap covalent bonds of methane.

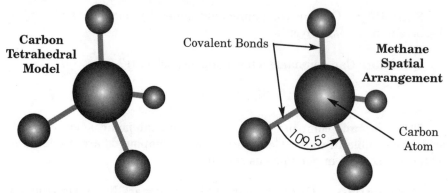

STRUCTURAL FORMULAS

The covalent bond is usually represented by a short lien (or dash) representing one pair of shared electrons. A formula showing the bonding in this manner is known as a structural formula.

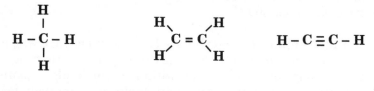

REAL WORLD CONNECTIONS

Organic isomers – These are compounds that have the same molecular formula but different structures are called **isomers**. The compounds CH_3CH_2CHO (propanal – used in the manufacture of aromatic compounds) and CH_3COCH_3 (acetone – used as solvents) are isomers, both having the molecular formula C_3H_6O.

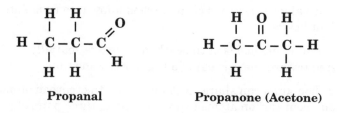

Note: you are expected to identify isomers both in molecular formulas and structural formulas. As the number of atoms in the molecule increases, the possibilities of more spatial arrangements (therefore, the number of isomers) increase.

The illustrations (page 190) show molecular formulas and structural formulas of a single, double, and triple bonded organic molecule. It is important to remember that molecules or organic compounds are three-dimensional in nature. Note: Hydrocarbons are compounds that contain only carbon and hydrogen.

SATURATED & UNSATURATED COMPOUNDS

A bond, formed between carbon atoms by the sharing of one pair of electrons, is referred to as a **single bond**. Organic compounds, where carbon atoms are bonded by the sharing of a single pair of electrons, are said to be **saturated** compounds.

Organic compounds, containing two adjacent carbon atoms bonded by the sharing of **more than one pair** of electrons, are said to be **unsaturated** compounds. A bond between carbon atoms by the sharing of two pairs of electrons is referred to as a **double bond**. A bond formed between carbon atoms by the sharing of three pairs of electrons is referred to as a **triple bond**.

 REAL WORLD CONNECTIONS

Saturated v. unsaturated compounds Health Connections – Saturated organic compounds have just one bond between the carbon atoms. This is called a **sigma (Σ) bond**. Unsaturated compounds have more than one bond. The first is called a sigma bond which is a strong overlap bond. The second is a **pi (π) bond** which can be broken easier than the sigma bond. Since the pi bond is weaker, it is more reactive. Because of this reactivity of the bond, unsaturated organic compounds react more than saturated organic compounds. Fats are made up of fatty acids plus glycerol. Those fats made up of saturated fatty acids like butter and palm oil and lard are not thought to be as healthful as those made up of unsaturated fatty acids like oleic acid such as olive oil.

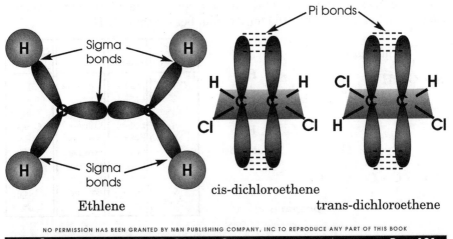

Ethlene

cis-dichloroethene

trans-dichloroethene

C – HOMOLOGOUS SERIES OF HYDROCARBONS

Compounds containing only carbon and hydrogen are known as **hydrocarbons**. The study of organic chemistry is simplified by the fact that organic compounds can be classified into groups having related structures and properties. Such groups are called **homologous series**. Each member of a homologous series differs from the one before it by a common increment. The increment CH_2 is what distinguishes one member of a series from another in each of the homologous series.

Most carbon compounds are named from, and can be considered as related to, corresponding hydrocarbons. As the members of a series increase in molecular size, the boiling points and freezing points increase due to the increased number of van der Waals forces between molecules. (Refer to *Reference Table Q – Homologous Series of Hydrocarbons*.)

ALKANES

The series of saturated hydrocarbons having the general formula C_nH_{2n+2} is called the alkane series. This general formula allows scientists to deduce the molecular formula, once they know what **n** (number of carbon atoms) equals. Therefore, if they know that a molecule contains 16 carbon atoms, they simply substitute 16 for **n** and find the molecular formula to be $C_{16}H_{34}$. The alkane series is also called the **methane series** or the **paraffin series**.

In naming organic compounds the IUPAC rules of nomenclature are followed. For the hydrocarbon series these rules are based on the number of carbon atoms in the molecule. The number of carbon atoms is indicated in the prefix of the name of each molecule, followed by the suffix, which for the **alkanes** is "**–ane**."

The data table (below right) and *Reference Table P* describe the naming of the first ten members of the alkane series. The alkane series shows isomerism beginning with the fourth member (butane, C_4H_{10}).

Number of Carbon Atoms	Prefix	Full Name	Molecular Formula
1	meth–	methane	CH_4
2	eth–	ethane	C_2H_6
3	prop–	propane	C_3H_8
4	but–	butane	C_4H_{10}
5	pent–	pentane	C_5H_{12}
6	hex–	hexane	C_6H_{14}
7	hept–	heptane	C_7H_{16}
8	oct–	octane	C_8H_{18}
9	non–	nonane	C_9H_{20}
10	dec–	decane	$C_{10}H_{22}$

Isomers of Butane C_4H_{10}

In alkanes, when adding a side chain or group, number the parent carbon chain by starting at whichever end results in the use of the lowest number.

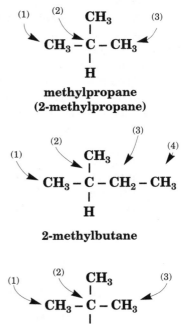

methylpropane
(2-methylpropane)

Isomers of Pentane C_5H_{12}

Numbering the carbon atoms left to right, this molecule is called 3 - methylbutane. Numbering from right to left, this molecule is called 2 - methylbutane

2-methylbutane

If the same group occurs more than once as a side chain, indicate this by the prefix di–, tri–, tetra– to show how many of these groups there are. Indicate by various numbers the positions of each group as illustrated by the second isomer of pentane: 2,2 dimethylpropane.

2,2-dimethylpropane

ALKENES

This series of unsaturated hydrocarbons containing one double bond and having the general formula C_nH_{2n} is called the alkene series. In the IUPAC system of nomenclature, the **alkenes** are named from the corresponding alkane by changing the ending "**-ane**" to "**-ene**." The alkene series is also called the ethylene series or the olefin series.

First member:	ethene — C_2H_4
Second member:	propene — C_3H_6
Third member:	butene — C_4H_8
Fourth member:	pentene — C_5H_{10}

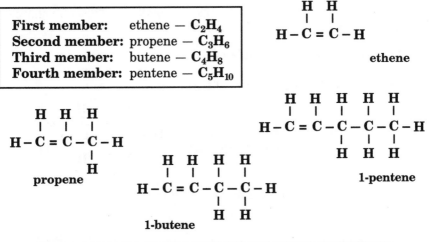

ethene

propene

1-butene

1-pentene

ALKYNES

The series of unsaturated hydrocarbons containing one triple bond and having the general formula C_nH_{2n-2} is called the alkyne series. In the IUPAC system of nomenclature the alkynes are named from the corresponding alkane by changing the ending "**-ane**" to "**-yne**." The common name of the first member of this series C_2H_2, is "acetylene," and the common name of the series is the **acetylene series**. **Note**: In naming alkyne compounds, the prefix is the same as the alkanes; however, the suffix is "yne" instead of "ane."

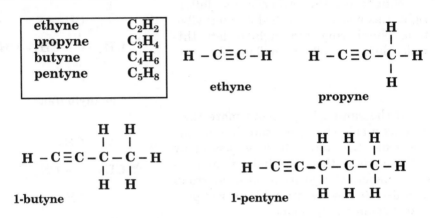

ethyne	C_2H_2
propyne	C_3H_4
butyne	C_4H_6
pentyne	C_5H_8

H – C ≡ C – H
ethyne

H – C ≡ C – C – H
propyne

H – C ≡ C – C – C – H
1-butyne

H – C ≡ C – C – C – C – H
1-pentyne

ALKADIENES

There is an homologous series of hydrocarbons containing more than one double bond, such as the **dienes**. They have the same general formula as the alkynes C_nH_{2n-2}. They are not members of the alkene series. An example of an alkadiene is butadiene, $CH_2CHCHCH_2$.

H – C = C – C = C – H
1,3-butadiene

SKILLS 3.1XXI *DRAW STRUCTURAL FORMULAS FOR ALKANES, ALKENES, AND ALKYNES CONTAINING A MAXIMUM OF TEN CARBON ATOMS.*

1   Draw the structural formula of CH_4.

2   Draw the structural formula of C_6H_6.

3   Draw a structural formula of an isomer for the compound at the right).

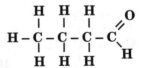

4   Draw the structural formula for Propene.

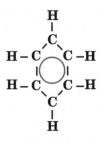

benzene

BENZENE SERIES

Cyclic hydrocarbons differ from **open chain** hydrocarbons (includes the alkane, alkene, and alkyne series), in that they are arranged in a ring structure. The most important **cyclic series** is called the **benzene series**. The benzene series is a group of aromatic hydro-carbons having the general formula C_nH_{2n-6}. Members of the **aromatic** hydrocarbons can be easily detected by their odors.

The simplest member of the benzene series is **benzene**, C_6H_6. The second member is toluene; its molecular formula is C_7H_8 (toluene is also called methylbenzene and is represented by the formula ($C_6H_5CH_3$).

benzene

toluene (methylbenzene)

All of the carbon-carbon bonds in the benzene ring are the same, and they have structure and properties intermediate between single bonds and double bonds. Benzene is rather unreactive and in many of its reactions, it behaves like a saturated hydrocarbon rather than unsaturated hydrocarbon.

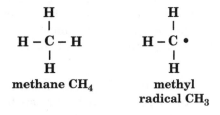

benzene   **toluene (methylbenzene)**

This represents a "super position," an average of single and double bonds. For simplicity, the chemist often uses either one of the structures shown (above right).

ALKYL RADICALS

When an alkane molecule loses a hydrogen atom, it has an open bond and is called an **alkyl radical**. Its formula will be the same as the alkane molecule except that it will have one less hydrogen in the formula, for example (Methyl at right):

methane CH$_4$ **methyl radical CH$_3$**

A **functional group** is a particular arrangement of a few atoms that gives characteristic properties to an organic molecule. Organic compounds can often be considered as being composed of one or more functional groups attached to a hydrocarbon group. The functional groups include alcohol and organic acid.

ALCOHOLS

In alcohols, one or more hydrogens of a hydrocarbon have been replaced by an -**OH** group. No more than one -**OH** group can be attached to one carbon atom under ordinary conditions. The alcohols are not bases. The -**OH** group of an alcohol does not form a hydroxide ion in aqueous solution.

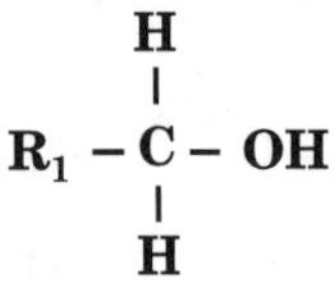

$$\begin{array}{c} H \\ | \\ R_1 - C - OH \\ | \\ H \end{array}$$

Primary alcohols. In primary alcohols, one -**OH** group is attached to the end carbon of a hydrocarbon. Since the functional group can be the end group of any hydrocarbon, the typical alcohol is frequently represented as **R-OH**, where "**R**" represents the rest of the molecule. The end group of a primary alcohol has the structure seen at the left.

The primary alcohol is frequently written as -**CH$_2$OH**. Primary alcohols contain the functional group -**CH$_2$OH**. In the IUPAC system, primary alcohols are named from the corresponding hydrocarbon by replacing the final "-e" with the ending "-**ol**."

The common names of the alcohols were formerly derived from the name of the corresponding hydrocarbon by changing the ending "-ane" to "-**yl**" and adding the name "alcohol." Thus, **CH$_3$OH**, methanol, is called methyl alcohol.

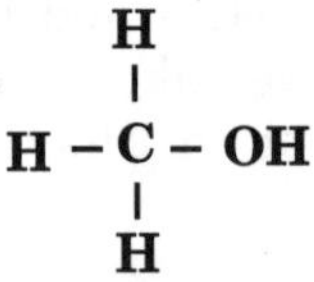

$$\begin{array}{c} H \\ | \\ H - C - OH \\ | \\ H \end{array}$$

methanol
CH$_3$OH

$$\begin{array}{c} H \quad H \\ | \quad | \\ H - C - C - OH \\ | \quad | \\ H \quad H \end{array}$$

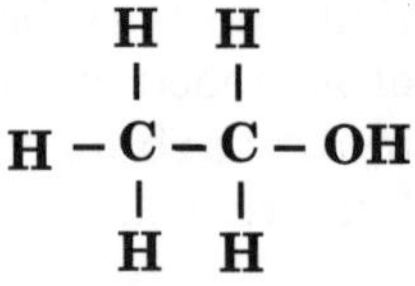

ethanol
C$_2$H$_5$OH

ORGANIC ACIDS

Organic acids contain the functional group -**COOH**. Acids are represented by the general formula **R-COOH**, except for the first member. The structural formula of the acid group is shown at the right.

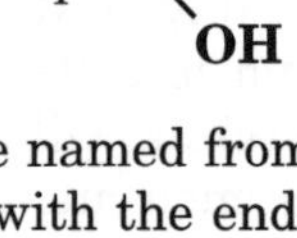

$$R_1 - C \begin{array}{c} {}^{\diagup\diagup O} \\ {}_{\diagdown OH} \end{array}$$

In the IUPAC system of nomenclature, organic acids are named from the corresponding hydrocarbons by replacing the final "-e" with the ending "-**oic**" and adding the name "**acid**."

The first two members of this series, methanoic acid, **HCOOH**, and ethanoic acid, **CH$_3$COOH**, are more familiarly known as their common names, **formic acid** and **acetic acid**.

ADDITIONAL MATERIALS IN ORGANIC CHEMISTRY

ALCOHOLS

Alcohols contain the functional group of **-OH**. Alcohols can be classified according to the number of **-OH** groups in the molecule. They may also be classified according to the number of carbon chains attached to the carbon having the **-OH** group. "**R**" is an abbreviation and represents any hydro-carbon group.

MONOHYDROXY ALCOHOLS

Monohydroxy alcohols have one **-OH** group.

$$H - \underset{\underset{H}{|}}{\overset{\overset{H}{|}}{C}} - OH$$

Primary Alcohols – A primary alcohol is represented by a hydroxyl group attached to a primary carbon.

methanol CH_3OH

Methanol (above right) and ethanol (right) are common primary alcohols.

$$H - \underset{\underset{H}{|}}{\overset{\overset{H}{|}}{C}} - \underset{\underset{H}{|}}{\overset{\overset{H}{|}}{C}} - OH$$

ethanol

Secondary Alcohols – The secondary alcohol group is:

$$R_1 - \underset{\underset{OH}{|}}{\overset{\overset{H}{|}}{C}} - R_2$$

An example is 2-propanol (isopropanol). In this molecule, the carbon atom, to which the hydroxyl group is attached, is bonded to the other two carbon atoms.

$$H - \underset{\underset{H}{|}}{\overset{\overset{H}{|}}{C}} - \underset{\underset{OH}{|}}{\overset{\overset{H}{|}}{C}} - \underset{\underset{H}{|}}{\overset{\overset{H}{|}}{C}} - H$$

2-propanol

Tertiary Alcohols – The tertiary alcohol group is:

$$R_1 - \underset{\underset{OH}{|}}{\overset{\overset{R_2}{|}}{C}} - R_3$$

An example is 2-methyl-2-propanol (tertiary butanol). In this molecule, the carbon atom, to which the hydroxyl group is attached, is bonded to three other carbon atoms.

$$H - \underset{\underset{H}{|}}{\overset{\overset{H}{|}}{C}} - \underset{\underset{OH}{|}}{\overset{\overset{\overset{H}{|}}{\overset{H-C-H}{|}}}{C}} - \underset{\underset{H}{|}}{\overset{\overset{H}{|}}{C}} - H$$

2-methyl,
2-propanol

DIHYDROXY ALCOHOLS

Compounds containing two -OH groups are known as dihydroxy (dihydric) alcohols, or glycols. The most important glycol is 1,2-ethanediol, commonly called ethylene glycol. It has the structural formula at the right.

$$H-\overset{\overset{\displaystyle H}{|}}{C}-\overset{\overset{\displaystyle H}{|}}{C}-H$$
$$\;\;OH\;\;OH$$

ethylene glycol

TRIHYDROXY ALCOHOLS

Compounds containing three -OH groups are known as trihydroxy (trihydric) alcohols. The most important trihydroxy alcohol is 1,2,3 - propanetriol (glycerol), having the structural formula at the right.

$$H-\overset{\overset{\displaystyle H}{|}}{C}-\overset{\overset{\displaystyle H}{|}}{C}-\overset{\overset{\displaystyle H}{|}}{C}-H$$
$$\;\;OH\;\;\;OH\;\;\;OH$$

glycerol (glycerine)

ALDEHYDES

Aldehydes contain the functional group:

$$\overset{\overset{\displaystyle H}{|}}{-C}=O$$

In the IUPAC system of nomenclature, aldehydes are named from the corresponding hydrocarbons by replacing the final "-e" with the ending "**al**." The first member of the aldehydes is called methanal and is commonly called **formaldehyde**. Its molecular formula is **HCHO**, and its structural formula is represented at the right.

$$H-C=O$$
$$\;\;\;\;\;|$$
$$\;\;\;\;\;H$$

All other aldehydes are represented by the general formula **R-CHO** where "**R**" is any hydrocarbon group. Primary alcohols can be oxidized to aldehydes.

$$R-\overset{\overset{\displaystyle H}{|}}{\underset{\underset{\displaystyle H}{|}}{C}}-OH + \textbf{oxidizing agent} \rightarrow R-\overset{\overset{\displaystyle H}{|}}{C}=O + H_2O$$

Aldehyde groups are easily oxidized to acids.

$$R-\overset{\overset{\displaystyle H}{|}}{C}=O + \text{oxidizing agent} \rightarrow R-C\overset{\nearrow O}{\searrow_H}$$

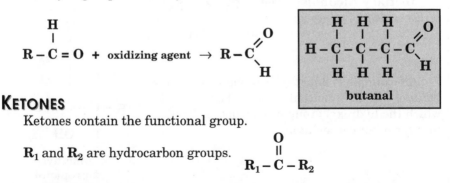

butanal

KETONES

Ketones contain the functional group.

R₁ and **R₂** are hydrocarbon groups.

$$R_1-\overset{\overset{\displaystyle O}{\|}}{C}-R_2$$

An important ketone, widely used as a solvent, is propanone. It is generally referred to by its common name, acetone. Secondary alcohols can be oxidized to ketones.

$$\begin{array}{ccccc} & H & O & H & \\ & | & || & | & \\ H & - C & - C & - C & - H \\ & | & & | & \\ & H & & H & \end{array}$$

acetone (propanone)

$$\begin{array}{c} OH \\ | \\ R_1 - C - R_2 \\ | \\ H \end{array} + \text{ oxidizing agent } \rightarrow \begin{array}{c} O \\ || \\ R_1 - C - R_2 \end{array} + H_2O$$

ETHERS

The functional group of an ether is $R_1 - O - R_2$

Diethyl ether, $C_2H_5OC_2H_5$, is used as an anesthetic. Primary alcohols can be dehydrated to give ethers.

$$R_1 - OH + R_2 - OH \rightarrow R_1 - O - R_2 + H_2O$$

$$\begin{array}{ccccc} H & H & & H & H \\ | & | & & | & | \\ H - C & - C & - O - C & - C & - H \\ | & | & & | & | \\ H & H & & H & H \end{array}$$

diethyl ether

ESTERS

These have the following general formula where R' is always an alkyl group and R is either an alkyl group or a hydrogen atom. Oils and fats are esters of long carbon chain acids and glycerol. This is done by the hydrolysis of an ester in a basic solution. $C_3H_7COOC_2H_5$ represents the ester ethyl butyrate which imparts the flavor and taste to pineapples. All esters have names which end with "**ate**" such as methyl salicylate and octyl acetate (see page 204).

$$\begin{array}{ccccc} H & O & & H & H \\ | & || & & | & | \\ H - C & - C & - O - C & - C & - H \\ | & & & | & | \\ H & & & H & H \end{array}$$

ethyl acetate

AMINES

These are derivatives of ammonia NH_3 in which the hydrogen atoms are replaced with organic radicals.

CH_3NH_2 – primary amine called methylamine

$(CH_3)_2NH$ – secondary amine called ethylamine

$(CH_3)_3N$ – tertiary amine called propylamine

$$\begin{array}{c} H \\ | \quad \diagup H \\ H - C - N \\ | \quad \diagdown H \\ H \end{array}$$

methylamine

The above are simple amines. More complex ones are used in the manufacture of plastics, drugs, and cleansing compounds.

AMIDES

The general formula for a primary amide is:

$$\begin{array}{c} O \\ || \\ R - C - NH_2 \end{array}$$

They are a combination of ammonia and an amine or a carboxylic acid. Their names are derived by replacing the suffix **-oic** of the carboxylic acid with **-amide**. For example, CH_3CONH_2 is called ethanamide. Amides have wide usage in drug manufacture.

AMINO ACIDS

The building blocks of proteins with a general formula of amine group:

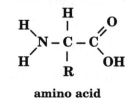

amino acid

IUPAC uses what it describes as "trivial" names to these acids. The first two are glycine and alanine. Their symbols are Gly and Ala. Their formulas are NH_2CH_2COOH and $NH_2C_2H_4COOH$ respectively. They join together at their amino (NH_2) group, making a peptide linkage and eliminating a water molecule at each link as they form proteins. Found both in animal and plant tissue, they link together in large numbers to form long chain proteins.

SKILLS 3.1XVII *CLASSIFY AN ORGANIC COMPOUND BASED ON ITS STRUCTURAL OR CONDENSED STRUCTURAL FORMULA.*

5   Which organic compound will dissolve in water to produce a solution that will turn blue litmus red?

(1)
```
    H  H
    |  |
H - C -C - H
    |  |
    H  H
```

(3)
```
    H  O
    |  ||
H - C -C - O - H
    |
    H
```

(2)
```
    H      H
    |      |
H - C - O -C - H
    |      |
    H      H
```

(4)
```
    H  O  H
    |  || |
H - C -C -C - H
    |     |
    H     H
```

6   Which structural formula represents a primary alcohol?

(1)
```
    H  H  H  H
    |  |  |  |
H - C -C -C -C - H
    |  |  |  |
    H  H  H  OH
```

(3)
```
    H  H  H  H
    |  |  |  |
H - C -C -C -C - H
    |  |  |  |
    H  OH H  H
```

(2)
```
    H  H  H  H
    |  |  |  |
H - C -C -C -C - H
    |  |  |  |
    H  OH OH H
```

(4)
```
    H  H  OH OH
    |  |  |  |
H - C -C -C -C - H
    |  |  |  |
    H  H  H  OH
```

7 Given the compound (at the right): Which structural formula represents an isomer?

$$\begin{array}{cccc} H & H & H & \\ | & | & | & \diagup O \\ H-C-C-C-C & \\ | & | & | & \diagdown H \\ H & H & H & \end{array}$$

(1)
$$\begin{array}{cccc} H & H & H & H \\ | & | & | & | \\ H-C-C-C-C-OH \\ | & | & | & | \\ H & H & H & H \end{array}$$

(3)
$$\begin{array}{ccccc} H & H & & H & H \\ | & | & & | & | \\ H-C-C-O-C-C-H \\ | & | & & | & | \\ H & H & & H & H \end{array}$$

(2)
$$\begin{array}{cccc} H & H & H & \\ | & | & | & \diagup O \\ H-C-C-C-C & \\ | & | & | & \diagdown OH \\ H & H & H & \end{array}$$

(4)
$$\begin{array}{cccc} H & O & H & H \\ | & || & | & | \\ H-C-C-C-C-H \\ | & & | & | \\ H & & H & H \end{array}$$

8 What is the structural formula for 1,2-ethanediol?

(1)
$$\begin{array}{cc} H & OH \\ | & | \\ H-C-C-OH \\ | & | \\ H & H \end{array}$$

(3)
$$\begin{array}{cc} OH & OH \\ | & | \\ H-C-C-H \\ | & | \\ H & H \end{array}$$

(2)
$$\begin{array}{ccc} H & H & OH \\ | & | & | \\ H-C-C-C-OH \\ | & | & | \\ H & H & H \end{array}$$

(4)
$$\begin{array}{ccc} H & OH & OH \\ | & | & | \\ H-C-C-C-OH \\ | & | & | \\ H & H & H \end{array}$$

9 Which structural formula represents an organic acid?

(1)
$$\begin{array}{ccc} H & H & H \\ | & | & | \\ H-C-C-C-OH \\ | & | & | \\ H & H & H \end{array}$$

(3)
$$\begin{array}{ccc} H & H & \\ | & | & \diagup O \\ H-C-C-C & \\ | & | & \diagdown OH \\ H & H & \end{array}$$

(2)
$$\begin{array}{ccc} H & OH & H \\ | & | & | \\ H-C-C-C-H \\ | & | & | \\ H & H & H \end{array}$$

(4)
$$\begin{array}{ccc} H & H & H \\ | & | & | \\ HO-C-C-C-OH \\ | & | & | \\ H & H & H \end{array}$$

10 Which structural formula represents a primary alcohol?

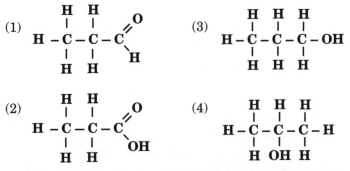

(1)
$$\begin{array}{cc} H & H & \\ | & | & \diagup O \\ H-C-C-C & \\ | & | & \diagdown H \\ H & H & \end{array}$$

(3)
$$\begin{array}{ccc} H & H & H \\ | & | & | \\ H-C-C-C-OH \\ | & | & | \\ H & H & H \end{array}$$

(2)
$$\begin{array}{cc} H & H & \\ | & | & \diagup O \\ H-C-C-C & \\ | & | & \diagdown OH \\ H & H & \end{array}$$

(4)
$$\begin{array}{ccc} H & H & H \\ | & | & | \\ H-C-C-C-H \\ | & | & | \\ H & OH & H \end{array}$$

11   **Question**: Draw the structural formula of **methylamine**.

12   **Question**: Draw the structural formula of C_3H_7COOH.

13   **Question**: Draw a structural formula for any amino acid and name it.

14   **Question**: Draw the structural formula for 2-propanol (isopropanol).

15   **Question**: Draw the structural formula for 1,2-ethanediol (ethylene glycol).

D – ORGANIC REACTIONS

Organic reactions generally take place more slowly than inorganic reactions. These reactions frequently involve only the functional groups of the reacting species, leaving the greater part of the reacting molecules relatively unchanged during the course of the reaction.

SUBSTITUTION

Substitution means replacement of one kind of atom or group by another kind of atom or group. For saturated hydrocarbons, reactions (except for combustion and thermal decomposition) necessarily involve replacement of one or more hydrogen atoms. The hydrogen atoms of saturated hydrocarbons can be replaced by active halogen family atoms. The general term for these reactions is **halogen substitution** (or halogenation) and the products are called **halogen derivatives**. For example:

$$CH_4 + Cl_2 \rightarrow CH_3Cl + HCl$$

ADDITION

Addition usually involves adding one or more atoms at a double or triple bond of a unsaturated molecule, resulting in saturation of the compound. Addition is characteristic of unsaturated compounds.

The addition of chlorine and bromine (iodine usually cannot be added) takes place at room temperature. The compounds formed are also called halogen derivatives, and the reaction is referred to as halogenation. For example:

$$\begin{array}{c} \quad\; H \quad H \\ \quad\; | \quad\;\; | \\ H-C=C-H \; + \; Cl_2 \;\rightarrow\; H-C-C-H \\ \qquad\qquad\qquad\qquad\quad\;\; | \quad\;\; | \\ \qquad\qquad\qquad\qquad\quad Cl \quad Cl \end{array}$$

Because addition reactions take place more easily than substitution reactions, unsaturated compounds tend to be more reactive than saturated compounds. Some addition reactions are about as fast as the reactions between ions. Alkynes are more reactive than alkenes. The addition of hydrogen to an unsaturated substance is called **hydrogenation**. This reaction usually requires the presence of a catalyst and a raised temperature.

FERMENTATION

In the fermentation process, enzymes produced by living organisms act as catalysts. A common fermentation product, ethanol, results from the fermentation of sugar. For example:

$$C_6H_{12}O_6 \xrightarrow{\text{zymase}} 2C_2H_5OH \; + \; 2CO_2$$

REAL WORLD CONNECTIONS

FERMENTATION – ANTIBIOTIC PRODUCTION

In addition to the manufacturing of ethanol to supplement gasoline usage in internal combustion engines, fermentation has become an important manufacturing process in the production of antibiotic and other medicines. In the schematic below, all production takes place in the fermenting tanks. The other procedures are used for recovery, extraction, purification, and crystallization of the product.

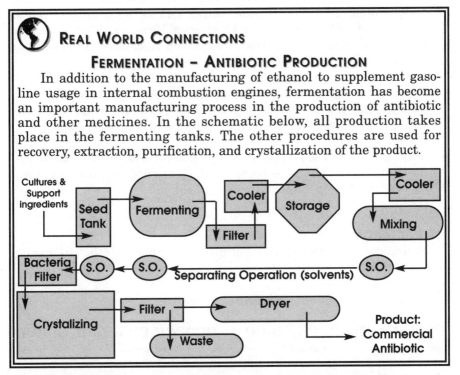

COMBUSTION OF FUELS

In order for combustion to take place, two items must be present. They are 1) two or more reactants which are unstable and, 2) energy to activate or start the reaction.

Oxygen, because of its high electronegativity, will have a tendency of drawing electrons to it. When the correct amount of activation energy is supplied, it will react with an unstable element or compound to form more stable products.

An example would be the combustion of this book. The paper in this book is made up of hydrocarbons. If a lighted match was put to a sheet of this book, the flame would supply the activation energy to cause the atmospheric oxygen to oxidize the hydrocarbons giving off energy in the form of heat and light which acts as the activation energy used to ignite the rest of the book in a chain reaction, and in the process forming new products.

Rapid combustion occurs when fuels are oxidized. An example would be a spark which would cause the combustion of acetylene gas.

$$2C_2H_2(g) + 5O_2(g) \rightarrow 4CO_2(g) + 2H_2O(l) + 2508 \text{ kJ}$$

The products formed are more stable than the reactants. Note that this is an exothermic redox reaction with oxygen as the agent that causes the oxidation of both the carbon and hydrogen. However, oxygen reacts in slow relentless form when it reacts with food to cause it to spoil. Two major causes are related to food spoilage.

* The continual maturation of food once collected. (i.e. sprouting of potatoes and grains and the ongoing changes caused by electrochemical reactions using catalysts called enzymes in meats and eggs).

* Microorganisms such as yeast, molds, and bacteria. Of the three, by far the most dangerous, is bacteria which are not discernable nor can they be eliminated without very high heat.

ESTERIFICATION

Esterification is the reaction of an acid with an alcohol to give an ester and water:

$$\text{acid} + \text{alcohol} \rightarrow \text{ester} + \text{water}$$

$$\text{HCOOH} + \text{CH}_3\text{CH}_2\text{CH}_2\text{CH}_2\text{OH} \rightarrow \text{HCOOCH}_2\text{CH}_2\text{CH}_2\text{CH}_3 + \text{HOH}$$

| acetic acid + | butanol | → | butyl acetate | + | water |

Esterification is not an ionic reaction. It proceeds slowly and is reversible. To increase the yield of the ester, concentrated sulfuric acid is added decreasing the concentration of the water and favoring the forward reaction. Esters have certain characteristics. They are 1) covalent compounds, and 2) esters usually have pleasant odors. The aromas of many fruits, flowers, and perfumes are due to esters. (**Fats** are esters derived from glycerol and long-chain organic acids.)

SAPONIFICATION

The hydrolysis of fats by bases is called **saponification**. To make soap, fat (a glycerol ester) is saponified by hot alkali (base). The products are soap (a salt of an organic fatty acid) and glycerol.

REAL WORLD CONNECTIONS

MAKING SOAP

Wear protective glasses. Dissolve 2.5 gm. of solid sodium hydroxide in 15 mL of 50% supercool alcohol (prepared with distilled water) in a 150-mL beaker. Add 6 mL of cottonseed oil and heat the mixture, with constant stirring, for about 30 minutes. Use a hot plate and avoid vigorous boiling. Add 50% alcohol as needed to maintain a constant volume of liquid in the beaker.

After heating, pour the mixture in to a 250-mL beaker containing 150-mL of saturated sodium chloride solution. Filter the mixture to obtain the soap which separates into this "salting out" process. Wash the soap with 10-mL of ice-cold distilled water. Test the soap which remains on the filter paper for sudsing action by mixing a small amount of the soap with 5 mL of distilled water in a test tube and shaking the mixture thoroughly. The appearance of suds indicates a successful saponification reaction.

OXIDATION (COMBUSTION)

Saturated hydrocarbons react readily with oxygen under conditions of combustion. In an excess of oxygen, hydrocarbons burn completely to form carbon dioxide and water.

$$CH_4 + 2O_2 \rightarrow CO_2 + 2H_2O$$

Burning in a limited supply of oxygen may produce carbon monoxide and carbon as well.

$$2CH_4 + 3O_2 \rightarrow 2CO + 4H_2O$$

$$CH_4 + O_2 \rightarrow C + 2H_2O$$

POLYMERIZATION

Polymerization involves the formation of a large molecule from smaller molecules called **monomers**. Synthetic rubbers, plastics such as polyethylene, and other chain molecules synthesized by humans are polymers. In nature polymerization occurs in the production of proteins, starches, and other chemicals by living organisms.

POLYMERS

A polymer is composed of many repeating units called monomers. Starch, cellulose, and proteins are natural polymers. Nylon and polyethylene are synthetic polymers. Polymerization is the process of joining monomers. Polymers may be formed by condensation or by additional polymerization.

CONDENSATION POLYMERS

Condensation polymerization results from the bonding of monomers by a dehydration reaction. Water is the usual by-product. A condensation process may be illustrated by:

$$\underset{\text{monomer}}{HO-\overset{\displaystyle H}{\underset{\displaystyle H}{C}}-\overset{\displaystyle H}{\underset{\displaystyle H}{C}}-OH} + \underset{\text{monomer}}{HO-\overset{\displaystyle H}{\underset{\displaystyle H}{C}}-\overset{\displaystyle H}{\underset{\displaystyle H}{C}}-OH} \rightarrow \underset{\text{dimer}}{HO-\overset{\displaystyle H}{\underset{\displaystyle H}{C}}-\overset{\displaystyle H}{\underset{\displaystyle H}{C}}-O-\overset{\displaystyle H}{\underset{\displaystyle H}{C}}-\overset{\displaystyle H}{\underset{\displaystyle H}{C}}-OH} + H_2O$$

This process may be repeated to give a long-chain polymer. The prerequisite for this is that the starting material (monomer) has at least two functional groups, one at each end, so that an attachment can be accomplished. Silicone, polyester, polyamides, phenolic plastics, and nylons are all examples of condensation polymers.

$$\underset{\text{Adipic Acid} + \text{Hexamethylamine} \rightarrow}{C_6H_{10}O_4 \qquad + \qquad C_6H_{16}N_2} \rightarrow \underset{\text{Nylon} \qquad + \quad \text{Water}}{(C_{12}H_{22}O_2N_2)_n + nH_2O}$$

ADDITION POLYMERS

An addition polymerization results from the joining of monomers of unsaturated compounds by "opening" double or triple bonds in the carbon chain. An addition process may be illustrated as:

$$nC_2H_4 \rightarrow (-C_2H_4-)_n \qquad \text{or} \qquad n(C_2H_{2n-2}) \rightarrow (C_2H_{2n})_n$$

Vinyl plastics such as polyethylene and polystyrene are examples of addition polymers.

$$n\Big(CH_2 \ = \ CH_2 \Big) \rightarrow \underset{\text{polyethylene}}{\Big(-CH_2 - CH_2 - \Big)_n}$$

$$\Big(\overset{\displaystyle H}{\underset{\bigcirc}{C}} = CH_2 \Big) \rightarrow \underset{\text{polystyrene}}{\Big(-\overset{\displaystyle H}{\underset{\bigcirc}{C}} - CH_2 - \Big)_n}$$

Synthetic polymers and their usage –

    polyethylene - plastic bags and toys
    polystyrene - cups, insulation
    polypropylene - carpets, bottles
    polytetrafluoro ethylene - teflon, nonstick surfaces
    polyacrilonitrile - yarns, fabric, wigs

Polymerization – formation of starches

Polysaccharides – including starch, cellulose, and glycogen (animal starch) have a general formula of $(CH_2O)_n$. Made up of many monosaccarides, the polysaccharide molecule is large and tends to be insoluble or only slightly soluble in water. This gives it colloidal properties.

SKILLS 3.2IV *IDENTIFY TYPES OF ORGANIC REACTIONS*

16 Proteins are produced through the process of
  (1) addition
  (2) substitution
  (3) polymerization
  (4) combustion

17 What are the products of a fermentation reaction?
  (1) an alcohol and carbon monoxide
  (2) an alcohol and carbon dioxide
  (3) a salt and water
  (4) a salt and an acid

18 Which reaction best represents the complete combustion of ethene?
  (1) $C_2H_4 + HCl \rightarrow C_2H_5Cl$
  (3) $C_2H_4 + 3O_2 \rightarrow 2CO_2 + 2H_2O$
  (2) $C_2H_4 + Cl_2 \rightarrow C_2H_4Cl_2$
  (4) $C_2H_4 + H_2O \rightarrow C_2H_5OH$

19 The reaction $CH_2CH_2 + H_2 \rightarrow CH_3CH_3$ is an example of
  (1) substitution
  (2) addition
  (3) esterification
  (4) fermentation

20 A condensation polymerization reaction produces a polymer and
  (1) H_2
  (2) O_2
  (3) CO_2
  (4) H_2O

21 Which equation represents a fermentation reaction?
  (1) $C_2H_4 + CH_2 \rightarrow C_2H_6$
  (2) $CH_4 + 2Cl_2 \rightarrow CH_2Cl_2 + 2HCl$
  (3) $HCOOH + CH_3OH \rightarrow HCOOCH_3 + HOH$
  (4) $C_6H_{12}O_6 \rightarrow 2C_2H_5OH + 2CO_2$

22 The reaction $CH_2CH_2 + Cl_2 \rightarrow CH_2ClCH_2Cl$ is an example of
  (1) substitution
  (2) addition
  (3) esterification
  (4) fermentation

23 In the reaction:

$$H-\underset{\underset{H}{|}}{\overset{\overset{H}{|}}{C}}-\underset{}{\overset{\overset{H}{|}}{C}}=\underset{}{\overset{\overset{H}{|}}{C}}-\underset{\underset{H}{|}}{\overset{\overset{H}{|}}{C}}-H + Cl_2 \rightarrow X$$

Which structural formula correctly represents X?

(1)
$$H-\underset{\underset{H}{|}}{\overset{\overset{H}{|}}{C}}-\underset{\underset{Cl}{|}}{\overset{\overset{H}{|}}{C}}=\underset{\underset{Cl}{|}}{\overset{\overset{H}{|}}{C}}-\underset{\underset{H}{|}}{\overset{\overset{H}{|}}{C}}-H$$

(3)
$$H-\underset{\underset{Cl}{|}}{\overset{\overset{H}{|}}{C}}-\underset{\underset{H}{|}}{\overset{\overset{H}{|}}{C}}-\underset{\underset{Cl}{|}}{\overset{\overset{H}{|}}{C}}-\underset{\underset{H}{|}}{\overset{\overset{H}{|}}{C}}-H$$

(2)
$$H-\underset{\underset{Cl}{|}}{\overset{\overset{H}{|}}{C}}-\underset{\underset{H}{|}}{\overset{\overset{H}{|}}{C}}-\underset{\underset{H}{|}}{\overset{\overset{H}{|}}{C}}-\underset{\underset{Cl}{|}}{\overset{\overset{H}{|}}{C}}-H$$

(4)
$$H-\underset{\underset{H}{|}}{\overset{\overset{H}{|}}{C}}-\underset{\underset{Cl}{|}}{\overset{\overset{H}{|}}{C}}-\underset{\underset{Cl}{|}}{\overset{\overset{H}{|}}{C}}-\underset{\underset{H}{|}}{\overset{\overset{H}{|}}{C}}-H$$

24 Question: What is the missing product X?

$$C_6H_6 + Br_2 \rightarrow C_6H_5Br + X$$

25 Question: What is the missing product X?

$$CH_4 + O_2 \rightarrow CO_2 + X$$

26 Question: What is the missing reactant X?

$$CH_4 + X \rightarrow CO_2 + 2H_2O$$

🌎 REAL WORLD CONNECTIONS

BIOCHEMICAL MOLECULES FORMATION

Carbohydrates (hydrates of carbon) are products of photosynthesis, carbohydrates include sugars, starches, wood, paper and various fibers such as cotton and cellulose products such as rayon.

Proteins are basically a combination of carbon, hydrogen, oxygen, and nitrogen with other elements and are connected by a peptide link which bonds the amino group of one amino acid to the carboxyl group of another. Proteins account for about 70% of the dry weight of all living cells. They make up muscle tissue, skin, hair, nails, blood plasma, and cell components, along with hormones and enzymes.

Fats (lipids) chemically are long carbon-chain atoms with a glycerol molecule attached. They are lipids, therefore they are classed as esters, having the same molecular structure as oils which are liquids at room temperature and contain unsaturated fatty acids, fats however are solids at room temperature and contain saturated fatty acids.

Nucleic acids are a group of large complex molecules found in all plant and animal cells and viruses. They are of great importance since they control the formation of proteins in the cells and also take part in the transmission of genetic information. They fall into two chemically distinct classes: ribonucleic acid (RNA), sugar pentose attached to amino acid bases, and deoxyribonucleic acid (DNA), sugar deoxypentose which is attached to amino acid bases.

Disposal problems of synthetic polymers exist – In the past, synthetic polymers were made that did not biodegrade and were piling up in sanitary landfills at a high rate. Newer forms of polymers are presently being produced which do break down easily and can be remelted and reused.

The first class of commercially important synthetic dyes were the azo dyes which are intensely colorful derivatives of **azobenzene** $C_{12}H_{10}N_2$.

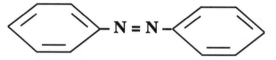

PERFORMANCE INDICATOR 3.1
ASSESSMENTS
PART A – MULTIPLE CHOICE

1 Which compound is an isomer of CH_3CH_2OH?
   (1) CH_3COOH (3) CH_3OCH_3
   (2) $CH_3CH_2CH_3$ (4) CH_3COOH_3

2 Given the organic reaction:

$$
\begin{array}{ccc}
\text{H} & \text{H} & \text{H} \\
| & | & | \\
\text{H} - \text{C} - \text{C} = \text{C} - \text{H} \\
| \\
\text{H}
\end{array}
+ \text{Br}_2 \rightarrow
\begin{array}{ccc}
\text{H} & \text{H} & \text{H} \\
| & | & | \\
\text{H} - \text{C} - \text{C} - \text{C} - \text{H} \\
| & | & | \\
\text{H} & \text{Br} & \text{Br}
\end{array}
$$

The reaction is an example of

   (1) fermentation   (3) substitution
   (2) addition   (4) saponification

3 Which structural formula represents a saturated hydrocarbon?

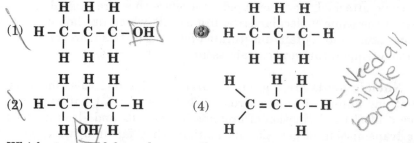

(1)
$$H-\underset{\underset{H}{|}}{\overset{\overset{H}{|}}{C}}-\underset{\underset{H}{|}}{\overset{\overset{H}{|}}{C}}-\underset{\underset{H}{|}}{\overset{\overset{H}{|}}{C}}-OH$$

(3)
$$H-\underset{\underset{H}{|}}{\overset{\overset{H}{|}}{C}}-\underset{\underset{H}{|}}{\overset{\overset{H}{|}}{C}}-\underset{\underset{H}{|}}{\overset{\overset{H}{|}}{C}}-H$$

(2)
$$H-\underset{\underset{H}{|}}{\overset{\overset{H}{|}}{C}}-\underset{\underset{OH}{|}}{\overset{\overset{H}{|}}{C}}-\underset{\underset{H}{|}}{\overset{\overset{H}{|}}{C}}-H$$

(4) C = C – C – H

Need all single bonds

4 Which structural formula correctly represents an organic compound?

(1) C = C = C – C – H

(3)
$$H-\underset{\underset{H}{|}}{\overset{\overset{H}{|}}{C}}-\underset{\underset{H}{|}}{\overset{\overset{H}{|}}{C}}=C=\underset{\underset{H}{|}}{\overset{\overset{H}{|}}{C}}-\underset{\underset{H}{|}}{\overset{\overset{H}{|}}{C}}-H$$

(2)
$$H-\underset{\underset{H}{|}}{\overset{\overset{H}{|}}{C}}-\overset{\overset{H}{|}}{C}=C\equiv C-H$$

(4) $H-C\equiv C-C=C-H$

5 Which formula represents a saturated compound?
(1) C_2H_4 (2) C_2H_2 (3) C_3H_6 (4) C_3H_8

6 Which materials are naturally occurring polymers?
(1) nylon and cellulose   (3) starch and cellulose
(2) nylon and polyethylene   (4) starch and polyethylene

7 The reaction: $CH_2CH_2 + Br_2 \rightarrow CH_2BrCH_2Br$ is an example of
(1) substitution   (3) esterification
(2) addition   (4) fermentation

8 Which compound belongs to the alkene series?
(1) C_2H_2 (2) C_2H_4 (3) C_6H_6 (4) C_6H_{14}

9 What is the name of the compound with the formula at the right?
(1) propanone   (3) propanal
(2) propanol   (4) propanoic acid

$$H-\underset{\underset{H}{|}}{\overset{\overset{H}{|}}{C}}-\underset{\underset{H}{|}}{\overset{\overset{H}{|}}{C}}-\overset{\overset{O}{\|}}{C}-OH$$

10 The fermentation of $C_6H_{12}O_6$ will produce CO_2 and
(1) $C_3H_5(OH)_3$ (3) $Ca(OH)_2$
(2) C_2H_5OH (4) $Cr(OH)_3$

11 Which statement explains why the element carbon forms so many compounds?
(1) Carbon atoms combine readily with oxygen.
(2) Carbon atoms have very high electronegativity.
(3) Carbon readily forms ionic bonds with other carbon atoms.
(4) Carbon readily forms covalent bonds with other carbon atoms.

12 Which structural formula represents an organic acid?

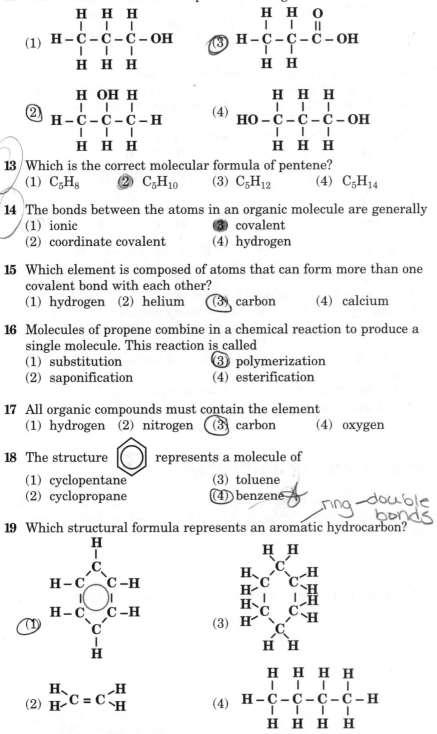

(1)
$$H - \overset{\overset{\displaystyle H}{|}}{\underset{\underset{\displaystyle H}{|}}{C}} - \overset{\overset{\displaystyle H}{|}}{\underset{\underset{\displaystyle H}{|}}{C}} - \overset{\overset{\displaystyle H}{|}}{\underset{\underset{\displaystyle H}{|}}{C}} - OH$$

(3)
$$H - \overset{\overset{\displaystyle H}{|}}{\underset{\underset{\displaystyle H}{|}}{C}} - \overset{\overset{\displaystyle H}{|}}{\underset{\underset{\displaystyle H}{|}}{C}} - \overset{\overset{\displaystyle O}{||}}{C} - OH$$

(2)
$$H - \overset{\overset{\displaystyle H}{|}}{\underset{\underset{\displaystyle H}{|}}{C}} - \overset{\overset{\displaystyle OH}{|}}{\underset{\underset{\displaystyle H}{|}}{C}} - \overset{\overset{\displaystyle H}{|}}{\underset{\underset{\displaystyle H}{|}}{C}} - H$$

(4)
$$HO - \overset{\overset{\displaystyle H}{|}}{\underset{\underset{\displaystyle H}{|}}{C}} - \overset{\overset{\displaystyle H}{|}}{\underset{\underset{\displaystyle H}{|}}{C}} - \overset{\overset{\displaystyle H}{|}}{\underset{\underset{\displaystyle H}{|}}{C}} - OH$$

13 Which is the correct molecular formula of pentene?
(1) C_5H_8 (2) C_5H_{10} (3) C_5H_{12} (4) C_5H_{14}

14 The bonds between the atoms in an organic molecule are generally
(1) ionic   (3) covalent
(2) coordinate covalent   (4) hydrogen

15 Which element is composed of atoms that can form more than one covalent bond with each other?
(1) hydrogen   (2) helium   (3) carbon   (4) calcium

16 Molecules of propene combine in a chemical reaction to produce a single molecule. This reaction is called
(1) substitution   (3) polymerization
(2) saponification   (4) esterification

17 All organic compounds must contain the element
(1) hydrogen   (2) nitrogen   (3) carbon   (4) oxygen

18 The structure ⬡ represents a molecule of
(1) cyclopentane   (3) toluene
(2) cyclopropane   (4) benzene

ring — double bonds

19 Which structural formula represents an aromatic hydrocarbon?

(1)
$$H - C \overset{\overset{\displaystyle H}{|}}{\underset{}{\overset{C}{\bigcirc}}} C - H$$

(2) $\overset{H}{\underset{H}{}} C = C \overset{H}{\underset{H}{}}$

(3)

(4)
$$H - \overset{\overset{\displaystyle H}{|}}{\underset{\underset{\displaystyle H}{|}}{C}} - \overset{\overset{\displaystyle H}{|}}{\underset{\underset{\displaystyle H}{|}}{C}} - \overset{\overset{\displaystyle H}{|}}{\underset{\underset{\displaystyle H}{|}}{C}} - \overset{\overset{\displaystyle H}{|}}{\underset{\underset{\displaystyle H}{|}}{C}} - H$$

20 In a condensation polymerization, the two products formed are a polymer and
(1) water
(2) carbon dioxide
(3) an acid
(4) a base

21 Which are products of a fermentation reaction?
(1) an ester and water
(2) a salt and water
(3) an alcohol and carbon dioxide
(4) a soap and glycerol

22 Which structural formula represents a ketone?

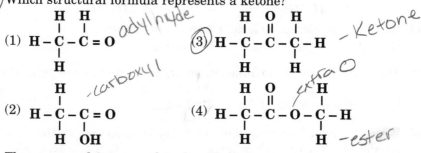

23 The compound 2-propanol is classified as a
(1) primary alcohol
(2) secondary alcohol
(3) tertiary alcohol
(4) dihydroxy alcohol

24 What is the name of the process that begins with the joining of monomer molecules?
(1) fermentation
(2) polymerization
(3) esterification
(4) hydrogenation

PART B – CONSTRUCTED-RESPONSE

1 Question: In terms of the number of carbon and hydrogen atoms in the formula, explain how each member of the alkane homologous series differs from the one before it. [1]

2 Question: Draw the structural formula for methane in the space provided. [1]

H – C – H
with H above and H below the C

3 Question: Explain how carbon always forms four bonds in spite of the fact that its electronic configuration in the ground state is: $1s^2 2s^2 2p^2$ [1]

4 Question: Draw the formula for 2-methylpentane in the space provided. [1]

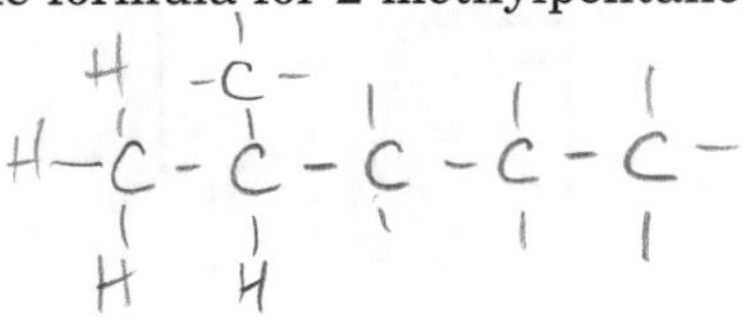

5 Question: Identify each of the following reactions by placing the letter of the reaction next to its name. [3]

A Substitution   D Polymerization
C Combustion   F Esterification
B Addition   E Fermentation

a $2CH_4 + Cl_2 \rightarrow 2CH_3Cl + H_2$

b $2C_2H_4 + Cl_2 \rightarrow CH_2Cl\text{-}CH_2Cl$

c $C_4H_{10} + O_2 \rightarrow CO_2 + H_2O + heat$

d $nC_2H_4 \rightarrow (C_2H_4)_n$

e $C_6H_{12}O_6 + enzymes \rightarrow 2C_2H_5OH + 2CO_2$

f $CH_3COOH + C_2H_5OH \rightarrow CH_3COOC_2H_5$

6 Question: Draw an isomer of $CH_3\text{-}CH_2\text{-}CH_2OH$. [1]

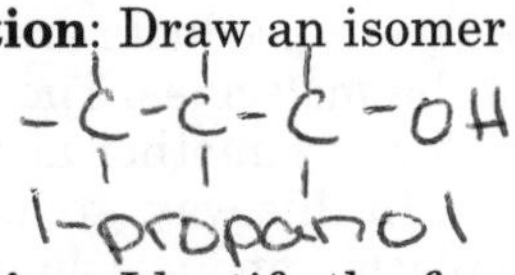

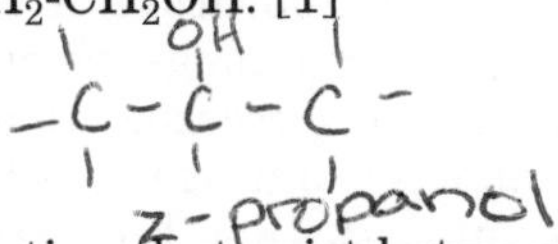

1-propanol   2-propanol

7 Question: Identify the forces of attraction that exist between nonpolar organic compounds. [1]

8 Question: Explain the difference between a primary, secondary, and tertiary alcohol. [1]

9 Question: Draw the structural formula for 2-methyl, 3-chloropentane. [1]

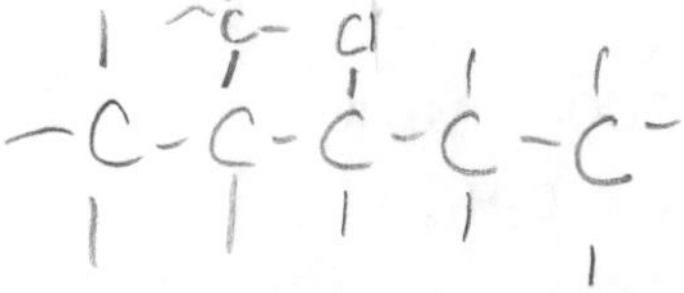

PART C – EXTENDED CONSTRUCTED-RESPONSE

ARTICLE A: FRACTIONAL DISTILLATION

Directions: Use the information below and the illustration at the right of fractional distillation to answer questions 1 through 4.

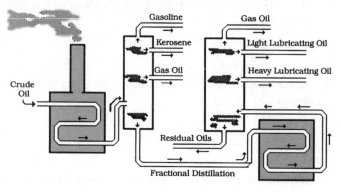

Fractional Distillation

Petroleum products are used as fuels, and they are the important starting material for many chemical products like plastics, textiles, rubber, and detergents. Natural gas (mostly methane), a common fuel, is often found with petroleum. Common bottled gases such as propane and butane are obtained from petroleum. Many products that are derived from petroleum are obtained by the following processes:

- **Fractional distillation** – Because hydrocarbons differ in boiling points, petroleum (called crude oil) can be separated into many different components by fractional distillation which is based upon the different boiling points and condensation temperatures of the products. The products with the higher boiling points and condensation temperatures are collected near the bottom and products with lower boiling points and condensation temperatures continue to rise in the tower. The temperature at which the different products are collected depends in large measure on the size of the molecules. The larger molecules have greater attractive forces for one another and, therefore, condense out at lower temperatures. In this way, greases condense out first, then lubricating oils, kerosene, and gasoline. The gasoline fraction is also added to by the process of cracking which breaks long chain hydrocarbon in smaller molecules.

1 **Question**: What is the process called in which large molecules are broken down into smaller molecules and used commercially to increase the yield of gasoline from petroleum? [1]

2 **Question**: Which equation represents a simple example of cracking?

(1) $N_2 + 3H_2 \rightarrow 2NH_3$

(2) $S + O_2 \rightarrow SO_2$

(3) $C_3H_8 + 5O_2 \rightarrow 3CO_2 + 4H_2O$

(4) $C_{14}H_{30} \rightarrow C_7H_{16} + C_7H_{14}$

3 **Question**: What is the process that increases the yield of gasoline from crude oil? [1]

4 **Question**: The components of petroleum are separated from each other by fractional distillation. On what component differences does this process depend? [1]

5 **Question**: What determines the temperature at which the different products are collected? [1]

6 **Question**: Name two bottled gases that are obtained from petroleum. [1]

Article B:

Chlorinated hydrocarbons are organic molecules to which one or more chlorine atoms have been attached. Many of these chlorinated hydrocarbons were used extensively in industry until relatively recently when it was discovered that they are harmful to living organisms and to the environment. Tetrachloromethane (carbon tetrachloride) is a molecule composed of one carbon atom to which four chlorine atoms have been attached in a tetrahedral shape. Due to the nonpolar nature of this molecule, tetrachloromethane was used frequently by dry cleaners for dissolving grease, oil and fat. It was found to be carcinogenic however and its use has been discontinued. Dichlorodiphenyltrichloroethane (known as DDT) was used for many years as a pesticide. It was found to be poisonous, however, to fish and other living organisms as well, and also interfered with bird reproduction. Polychloronated biphenols (PCBs) are chlorinated hydrocarbons that were used as coolants and insulators for electrical equipment. These, and the very toxic dioxins (composed of chloronated aromatic hydrocarbons) have been shown to be carcinogenic and are related to a wide variety of health problems.

Chlorofluorocarbons (CFCs) are hydrocarbons in which both chlorine and fluorine have been substituted for hydrogen atoms. CFCs were, at one time, used as propellants in aerosol cans and as coolants in refrigerators and air conditioners. It was discovered, however, that the CFCs that escaped into the atmosphere were responsible for destroying part of the ozone layer in the stratosphere. This layer is important for filtering out harmful ultraviolet radiation that leads to skin cancer and the formation of cataracts. Less harmful substances are now used as propellants and coolants in refrigeration units.

7   **Question**: Explain what a chlorinated hydrocarbon is. [1]

8   **Question**: Give the name of two different chlorinated hydrocarbons and identify how each one is harmful to living organisms or the environment. [2]

9   **Question**: Using the rule of thumb that "like dissolves like," explain how you know that grease, oil and fat are nonpolar molecules. [1]

10 **Question**: State one reason why DDT is no longer used as a pesticide. [1]

11 **Question**: Identify one chlorinated hydrocarbon that is known to be carcinogenic. [1]

12 **Question**: Explain what chlorofluorocarbons (CFCs) are. [1]

13 **Question**: State one way CFCs were used in commercial products. [1]

14 **Question**: Explain why chlorofluorocarbons are no longer used by industry. [1]

15 Question: Identify the location of the ozone layer in the atmosphere. [1]

16 Question: State one reason why it is important not to destroy the ozone layer. [1]

17 Question: Identify one disease that can be caused by harmful exposure to ultraviolet radiation. [1]

PART D - LABORATORY SKILLS

PREPARATION OF ETHYL ALCOHOL BY FERMENTATION

Purpose: The process of fermentation should be familiar to all chemistry students and can best be understood by actually preparing a fermentable mixture. Various carbohydrates may be used for this purpose, but either sucrose or molasses is usually readily available.

Materials: 2 liter glass bottle, one hole rubber stopper, delivery tubing, cardboard, wide mouth collecting bottle, ring stand, bunsen burner, test tube, buret clamp, thermometer, funnel, filter paper, dropper, one liter of distilled water, 500 cc molasses, $\frac{1}{2}$ packet of yeast, 200 cc lime water, one iodine crystal, 10 cc olive oil, 2M sodium hydroxide

Procedure:
1 Place the molasses, water, and yeast in the bottle.

2 Mix thoroughly and run the delivery tube through the cardboard into the wide mouth bottle and into the limewater which is covered with a thin layer of kerosene in order to exclude air from contact with the lime water, as shown.

3 After the fermentation reaction has taken place for a short time, examine the limewater for evidence of the evolution of carbon dioxide gas.

4 Allow the fermentation to continue for five to six days. At the end of this period of time, remove a small amount of the fermented mixture, filter it, and test for the presence of ethyl alcohol.

5   To test for ethyl alcohol, dissolve a crystal of iodine in about 5 ml of the filtrate in a test tube. Add 2M sodium hydroxide drop-wise until a yellow color appears. Heat the test tube to a temperature of approximately 60°C and allow to stand for a few minutes until a precipitate appears.

REVIEW QUESTIONS

1   **Question**: Write a word equation to show the total reaction.

2   **Question**: Explain what caused the yellow color to occur.

3   **Question**: What is the color of the end precipitate?

4   **Question**: Identify the end precipitate.

SUBSTITUTION REACTION

CAUTION: PENTANE IS HIGHLY flammable. Make sure that no flames or electrical sparks are present.

Procedure: Place two drops of pentane or petroleum ether in each of two test tubes in which four drops of bromine water has been added. Stopper each test tube and shake them. Place one in a dark place and the other in sunlight or direct artificial light.

Observations: Compare the contents of the test tubes over a period of 10 to 15 minutes. List your observations as to color change and write the chemical reaction that caused it.

Directions: Complete and balance the following reactions:

5   **Question**: $C_2H_6 + Cl_2 \rightarrow$

6   **Question**: $C_5H_{12} + Br_2 \rightarrow$

UNIT 8
OXIDATION –
REDUCTION

KEY IDEA 3 MATTER IS MADE UP OF PARTICLES WHOSE PROPERTIES DETERMINE THE OBSERVABLE CHARACTERISTICS OF MATTER AND ITS REACTIVITY

PERFORMANCE INDICATOR 3.2
USE ATOMIC AND MOLECULAR MODELS TO EXPLAIN COMMON CHEMICAL REACTIONS.

PERFORMANCE INDICATOR 3.3

UNIT 8 – MAJOR UNDERSTANDINGS

☆ 3.2d An oxidation-reduction (redox) reaction involves the transfer of electrons (e -).

☆ 3.2e Reduction is the gain of electrons.

☆ 3.2f A half-reaction can be written to represent reduction.

☆ 3.2g Oxidation is the loss of electrons.

☆ 3.2h A half-reaction can be written to represent oxidation.

☆ 3.3b In a redox reaction the number of electrons lost is equal to the number of electrons gained.

☆ 3.2i Oxidation numbers (states) can be assigned to atoms and ions. Changes in oxidation numbers indicate that oxidation and reduction have occurred.

☆ 3.2j An electrochemical cell can be either voltaic or electrolytic. In an electrochemical cell, oxidation occurs at the anode and reduction at the cathode.

☆ 3.2k A voltaic cell spontaneously converts chemical energy to electrical energy.

☆ 3.2l An electrolytic cell requires electrical energy to produce a chemical change. This process is known as electrolysis.

UNIT 8

OXIDATION–REDUCTION

This unit is related to Key Idea 3 for the text and Performance Indicators 3.2 and 3.3 for the assessments.

INTRODUCTION

Many reactions result from the transfer of electrons between atoms, and the term used for this oxidation-reduction transfer is **redox**.

A - REDUCTION

Reduction represents a gain, or apparent gain, of electrons. Any chemical change in which there is a decrease of the oxidation number is called reduction.

The particle that decreases in oxidation number is said to be reduced. Since it is the agent that causes the oxidation of another atom, it is referred to as the **oxidizing agent**.

B - OXIDATION

Oxygen, having the second highest electronegativity rating of 3.4, after fluorine (4.0), was isolated over 100 years before fluorine, and its properties have become well known. Chemists found that whenever an element combined with oxygen, it had a tendency to lose electrons. This tendency of losing electrons was associated with the element oxygen and was called **oxidation**.

Oxidation represents a loss or an apparent loss of electrons. Any chemical change in which there is an increase in oxidation number – due to a loss of negative charge (electrons) – is called oxidation.

The particle that increases in oxidation number is said to be oxidized. Since it is the agent that causes the reduction of another, it is referred to as the **reducing agent**.

In other words, when attempting to identify the oxidizing or reducing agents, a simple rule could be applied. The item oxidized is the reducing agent, and the item reduced is the **oxidizing agent**.

Oxidation Numbers (States)

The oxidation number (oxidation state) of an atom is the charge which an atom has, or appears to have, when electrons are counted according to certain arbitrary rules. This oxidation number, although arbitrary, is a convenient notation for keeping track of the number of electrons involved in a chemical reaction. In assigning oxidation numbers, electrons shared between two unlike atoms are counted as belonging to the more electronegative atom. The electrons shared between two like atoms are divided equally between the sharing atoms.

Operational Rules for Determining Oxidation Number

Applying the general rules above, has resulted in the following operational rules.

- In the free elements, each atom has an oxidation number of zero (**0**). For example, hydrogen in H_2, sodium in Na, and sulfur in S_8; all have oxidation numbers of zero (**0**).

- In simple ions (ions containing one atom) the oxidation number is equal to the charge on the ion. These common ionic charges (oxidation states) can be found in the *Reference Tables* and the *Periodic Table of Elements*; for example, Na^+, Zn^{++}, Cl^-.

- When monatomic ions make up an ionic compound, the oxidation number of each ion is equal to its ionic charge. The algebraic sum of these charges is equal to zero (**0**). For example, in $CaCl_2$, calcium has an oxidation number of **+2** and each chlorine **-1**, giving chlorine a total charge of **-2**; therefore, the total charge of the compound adds up to zero (**0**). Iron in $FeCl_2$ has an oxidation number of **+2**, and each chlorine **-1**, which gives chlorine a total oxidation state of **-2**, so that the total sum of the positive and negative charges is again zero (**0**). In $FeCl_3$, iron has an oxidation number of **+3**, and each chlorine a **-1**, giving chlorine a total negative charge of **-3**, and the compound a total charge of zero (**0**).

- All metals in **Group 1** form only **1+** ions and their oxidation number is **+1** in all compounds.

- All metals in **Group 2** form only **2+** ions and their oxidation number is **+2** in all compounds.

- Oxygen has an oxidation number of **-2** in all its compounds except in peroxides (such as H_2O_2) when it is **-1** and in compounds with fluorine (OF and OF_2) when it may be **+1** or **+2**. For example, in H_2SO_4, oxygen has an oxidation number of **-2**.

- Hydrogen has an oxidation number of **+1** in all its compounds (such as HCl and H_2SO_4) except in the metal hydrides (such as LiH and CaH_2) when it is **-1**.

- For **polyatomic ions** (charged particles that contain more than one atom) the oxidation numbers of all the atoms must add up to the charge on the ion. For example, in SO_4^{2-} the four oxygen atoms contribute a total oxidation number of **-8**. Therefore, the sulfur must contribute an oxidation number of **+6** to give the ion a charge of **2-**.

All oxidation numbers must be consistent with the conservation of charge. For neutral molecules, the algebraic sum of the oxidation number of all the atoms must add up to zero. For example, in H_2SO_4, the two hydrogens contribute a total of **+2**, and the four oxygens contribute a total of **-8**. Therefore, the sulfur must contribute an oxidation number of **+6**.

SKILLS 3.2III *DETERMINE THE MISSING REACTANT OR PRODUCT IN A BALANCED EQUATION.*

1   Identify X in the following balanced equation:
$$X + CuSO_4 \rightarrow ZnSO_4 + Cu$$

2   Given the redox reaction:
$$2Cr(s) + 3Sn^{2+}(aq) \rightarrow 2Cr^{3+}(aq) + 3X$$
Identify the species (X).

3   Which half-reaction correctly represents oxidation?
(1) $Fe(s) \rightarrow Fe^{2+}(aq) + 2e^-$ (3) $Fe(s) + 2e^- \rightarrow Fe^{2+}(aq)$
(2) $Fe^{2+}(aq) \rightarrow Fe(s) + 2e^-$ (4) $Fe^{2+}(aq) + 2e^- \rightarrow Fe(s)$

Directions: For questions 4 and 5, identify and name the missing part, **X**.

4   **Question**: $2\,Ag^+ + Cu^0 \rightarrow 2Ag^0 + X$ _____

5   **Question**: $Zn^0 + Cu^{2+} \rightarrow Zn^{2+} + X$ _____

C – REDOX REACTIONS

Oxidation and reduction occur simultaneously – one cannot occur without the other. In oxidation and reduction, the increase and decrease of oxidation number results from a shift of electrons. The only way by which electrons can be shifted away from an atom (oxidation) is for them to be pulled toward another atom or ion (reduction). There is a conservation of charge as well as a conservation of mass in a redox reaction. Redox reactions fall into three categories: composition, decomposition or analysis, and single replacement reactions.

COMPOSITION REACTIONS

$$\overset{0}{2Na} + \overset{0}{Cl_2} \rightarrow \overset{1+ \; 1-}{2NaCl}$$

In this reaction (above):

• Sodium's oxidation state changes from 0 to +1, and it is oxidized.

• Chlorine's oxidation state changes from 0 to -1, and it is reduced.

DECOMPOSITION OR ANALYSIS REACTIONS

$$\overset{1+ \; 1-}{2HCl} \rightarrow \overset{0}{H_2} + \overset{0}{Cl_2}$$

In this reaction:

• Hydrogen's oxidation state changes from +1 to 0, and it is reduced.

• Chlorine's oxidation state changes from -1 to 0, and it is oxidized.

SINGLE REPLACEMENT REACTIONS

$$\overset{0}{Mg} + \overset{1+ \; 1-}{2HCl} \rightarrow \overset{2+ \; 1-}{MgCl_2} + \overset{0}{H_2}$$

In this reaction:

• Magnesium's oxidation state changes from 0 to +2, and it is oxidized.

• Hydrogen's oxidation state changes from +1 to 0, and it is reduced.

Note: Ionic or double replacement reactions are not usually redox reactions.

BALANCING SIMPLE REDOX EQUATIONS

In any reaction, the loss of electrons by the species oxidized must be equal to the gain of electrons by the species reduced. As stated previously, there is a conservation of charge as well as a conservation of mass in a redox reaction. For example:

$$Cu^0 + 2Ag^+ \rightarrow Cu^{2+} + 2Ag^0$$

In the above reaction, the oxidation state of copper has changed from 0 to 2^+. This means that the copper atom has lost two of its electrons and has become a positive 2 ion. Meanwhile, two silver ions have each picked up one electron and have changed their oxidation state from positive one (+1) to zero (0). Another example includes the following reaction:

$$2Al^0 + 6H^+ \rightarrow 2Al^{3+} + 3H_2^0$$

In the above reaction two aluminum atoms give up 3 electrons each to become 2 aluminum ions with a charge of positive 3. The six hydrogen ions have picked up the 6 electrons given up by the 2 aluminum atoms and have become 3 molecules of hydrogen.

BALANCING REDOX REACTIONS

In any reaction, the loss of electrons by the species oxidized must be equal to the gain of electrons by the species reduced. There is a conservation of charge as well as a conservation of mass in a redox reaction.

One method for balancing the reaction between aqueous nitric acid and solid iodine follows. Given the unbalanced equation:

$$HNO_3 + I_2 \rightarrow HIO_3 + NO_2 + H_2O$$

Proceed with the following steps:

1) Assign oxidation numbers to each element.

$$\overset{+1 \, +5 \, -2}{HNO_3} + \overset{0}{I_2} \rightarrow \overset{+1 \, +5 \, -2}{HIO_3} + \overset{+4 \, -2}{NO_2} + \overset{+1 \, -2}{H_2O}$$

2) Determine the change in oxidation number (transfer of electrons) of the elements.

For nitrogen, $+5 \rightarrow +4$ (this shows a gain of 1 electron)
For iodine, $0 \rightarrow +5$ (this shows a loss of 5 electrons)

3) Write partial electronic equations for the materials oxidized and reduced.

$$N^{+5} + 1e^- \rightarrow N^{+4}$$

$$I_2^0 \rightarrow 2I^{+5} + 10e^-$$

4) Balance the electrons gained and lost by writing appropriate coefficients for the two half-reactions and cancel out the electrons gained and lost.

$$10N^{+5} + 10e^- \rightarrow 10N^{+4}$$

$$2I^0 \rightarrow 2I^{+5} + 10e^-$$

$$10N^{+5} + I_2^0 \rightarrow 10N^{+4} + 2I^{+5}$$

This equation is the net equation and does not include any spectator ions or atoms that are not involved in the redox reaction.

5) Insert the coefficients from the net equation into the skeletal equation.

$$10HNO_3 + I_2 \rightarrow 2HIO_3 + 10NO_2 + H_2O$$

6) Insert other coefficients consistent with the conservation of matter, and balance by inspection.

$$10HNO_3 + I_2 \rightarrow 2HIO_3 + 10NO_2 + 4H_2O$$

PRACTICE

6 Given the reaction:

$$\_Cu(s) + \_HNO_3(aq) \rightarrow \_Cu(NO_3)_2(aq) + \_NO_2(g) + \_H_2O(l)$$

When the reaction is completely balanced using smallest whole numbers, the coefficient of $HNO_3(aq)$ will be
(1) 1   (2) 2   (3) 3   (4) 4

7 What is the coefficient of the Cl_2 when the equation below is correctly balanced?

$$MnO_2 + 4H^+ + 4\ Cl^- \rightarrow 2H_2O + Mn^{2+} + 2Cl^- + Cl_2:$$

(1) 1   (2) 2   (3) 3   (4) 4

8 Given the unbalanced equation: $\_Ca^0 + 2Al^{3+} \rightarrow 3Ca^{2+} + 2Al^0$, when the equation is completely balanced with the smallest whole-number coefficients, what is the coefficient of Ca^0?
(1) 1   (2) 2   (3) 3   (4) 4

9 When the equation $4NH_3 + \_O_2 \rightarrow 2N_2 + 6H_2O$ is completely balanced using the smallest whole numbers, the coefficient of the O_2 will be
(1) 1   (2) 2   (3) 3   (4) 4

D - CORROSION

Corrosion is a gradual attack on a metal by its surroundings. When the metal returns to its ionic form, the usefulness of the metal may be destroyed. Corrosion is a redox reaction. Moisture, some gases in the air, and some chemicals contribute to corrosion.

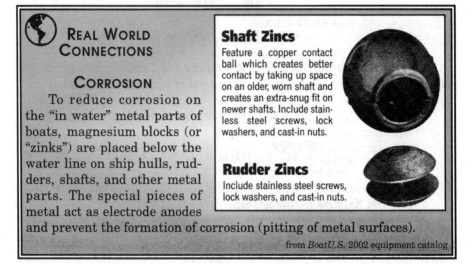

🌎 **REAL WORLD CONNECTIONS**

CORROSION

To reduce corrosion on the "in water" metal parts of boats, magnesium blocks (or "zinks") are placed below the water line on ship hulls, rudders, shafts, and other metal parts. The special pieces of metal act as electrode anodes and prevent the formation of corrosion (pitting of metal surfaces).

Shaft Zincs

Feature a copper contact ball which creates better contact by taking up space on an older, worn shaft and creates an extra-snug fit on newer shafts. Include stainless steel screws, lock washers, and cast-in nuts.

Rudder Zincs

Include stainless steel screws, lock washers, and cast-in nuts.

from *BoatU.S.* 2002 equipment catalog

Some metals, such as aluminum and zinc, form self-protective coatings. Aluminum is more susceptible to corrosion than iron. However, the corrosion of aluminum is not a serious problem, since the aluminum oxide formed can adhere tightly to the uncorroded aluminum beneath it and provide a protective layer that prevents further corrosion.

In the case of iron, the oxide formed from corrosion lacks the ability to adhere to the metal. It constantly flakes off, exposing fresh iron to corrosion.

Metals that corrode easily, like iron, may be protected by a variety of methods. Some methods include:

- Plating with self-protective metals like aluminum and zinc, or plating with corrosion-resistant metals like chromium and nickel.

- Sometimes, a more active metal like magnesium corrodes preferentially when it is connected to iron. This is called **cathode protection**. Magnesium plates are added to the hulls of sea going ships so that the magnesium corrodes and not the hull.

- The alloying of iron with corrosion resistant metals like nickel and chromium has produced stainless steel.

- Coating iron with paints, oils, or glass (porcelain) has proven effective against corrosion.

CORROSION OF METALS (RUSTING)

Oxygen, moisture, and impurities combine to react with metallic surfaces resulting in corrosion, which is an electrochemical reaction. A prime example of this reaction is the rusting of iron.

- Anode iron is oxidized

$$Fe(s) \rightarrow Fe^{\pm 2} + 2e^-$$

- Cathode oxygen is reduced

$$\tfrac{1}{2}O_2(g) + H_2O + 2e\text{-} \rightarrow 2(OH)^-(aq)$$

Adding the above half-reactions gives

$$Fe(s) + \tfrac{1}{2}O_2(g) + H_2O \rightarrow Fe(OH)_2 (s)$$

Further oxidation gives

$$2Fe(OH)_2(s) + \tfrac{1}{2}O_2 + H_2O \rightarrow 2Fe(OH)_3(s)$$

This reddish, flaky product [$Fe(OH)_3$] is called **rust**. Ferrous corrosion is so widespread, that it is estimated to cost over 12 billion dollars a year in the United States alone.

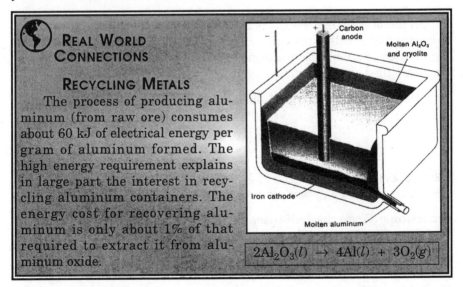

REAL WORLD CONNECTIONS

RECYCLING METALS

The process of producing aluminum (from raw ore) consumes about 60 kJ of electrical energy per gram of aluminum formed. The high energy requirement explains in large part the interest in recycling aluminum containers. The energy cost for recovering aluminum is only about 1% of that required to extract it from aluminum oxide.

+ Carbon anode
−
Molten Al_4O_3 and cryolite
Iron cathode
Molten aluminum

$$2Al_2O_3(l) \rightarrow 4Al(l) + 3O_2(g)$$

PHOTOGRAPHY

The sensitiveness of silver compounds to light has brought about an industry with both artistic and scientific accomplishments. If silver bromide, dispersed in a gelatin medium is exposed to light, then treated with a developer (a solution with reducing properties), metallic silver forms an image and the bromine is removed by a solvent in order to get a permanent (fixed) negative.

E – HALF-REACTIONS

A redox reaction may be considered in two parts, one representing a loss of electrons (oxidation) and the other representing a gain of electrons (reduction). Each reaction is known as a half-reaction. A separate equation showing gain or loss of electrons (electronic equation) can be written for each half-reaction. For example:

$$\overset{0}{Mg} + \overset{0}{Cl} \rightarrow \overset{2+\ 1-}{MgCl_2}$$

It can be represented as:

$$Mg^0 \rightarrow Mg^{2+} + 2e\text{-} \quad \text{(oxidation)}$$

$$Cl_2 + 2e\text{-} \rightarrow 2Cl\text{-} \quad \text{(reduction)}$$

In the above reaction, Mg^0 is supplying the electrons and is considered the agent that causes the chlorine to be reduced. It is called the reducing agent. Substances with low ionization energies and low electronegativities are easily oxidized so they are called strong reducing agents.

10 Question: Which group of elements are strong reducing agents?

On the other hand the Cl_2 is considered the agent that causes Mg to be oxidized. It is called the **oxidizing agent**. Elements with high electronegativities and ionization energies are more easily reduced and, therefore, are called strong oxidizing agents.

11 Question: Which group of elements include strong oxidizing agents?

SKILLS 3.2VI *WRITE AND BALANCE THE HALF-REACTIONS FOR OXIDATION AND REDUCTION OF FREE ELEMENTS AND THEIR MONATOMIC IONS.*

Directions: Write the half-reactions for each of the following balanced equations. Show both oxidation and reduction half reactions.

12 $Mg(s) + Cl_2 \rightarrow MgCl_2(s)$

13 $Cu(s) + 2Ag^+(aq) \rightarrow Cu^{2+}(aq) + 2Ag(s)$

14 $3Cu(s) + 2NO_3^-(aq) + 8H^+(aq) \rightarrow 3Cu^{2+}(aq) + 2NO + 4H_2O$

15 $Al^0 + Cr^{3+} \rightarrow Al^{3+} + Cr^0$

16 $Pb^0 + Cu^{2+} \rightarrow Pb^{2+} + Cu^0$

17 $Mg(s) + 2H^+ \rightarrow Mg^{2+}(aq) + H_2(g)$

18 $2Fe^{2+}(aq) + Cl_2^0(g) \rightarrow Fe^{3+}(aq) + 2Cl^-(aq)$

19 $Mg^0(s) + 2Ag^+(aq) \rightarrow Mg^{2+}(aq) + 2Ag^0(s)$

F – ELECTROCHEMICAL (VOLTAIC) CELLS
STANDARD ELECTRODE POTENTIALS

In order to ascertain if a reaction will occur spontaneously in an electrochemical cell or if it would require an outside power source to drive it forward as in an electrolytic cell, a ***Table of Electrode Potentials*** was devised. [Note, this table is a more complete table than *Reference Table J* because *Table J* does not list the standard reduction potentials for the half-reactions. The standard reduction potential (E^0) represents the potential difference between the specified half-reaction and the hydrogen half-reaction.

Using hydrogen as an arbitrary standard, the ***Standard Electrode Potentials Table*** demonstrates a number of reduction half-cell reactions. In each instance in the forward reaction, electrons are being added to a substance. The reactions take place in water at 298 K and 1 atm in a 1 M ionic concentration. The difference is measured in volts.

In the electrochemical cell, a reduction half-cell reaction must be accompanied by an oxidation half-cell reaction. Therefore, the half-cell reduction potential cannot be directly measured without comparing it to another half-cell reaction. So, hydrogen is used as the standard, and assigned an E^0 value of 0.00. Having done this, it can now be compared to the other reactions on the Table.

All of the reactions which show a positive E^0 value will accept electrons from hydrogen. In fact, any substance in the Table will reduce those above it and will oxidize those below it. In order for an electrochemical cell to exist, it must be spontaneous. It becomes spontaneous only when the algebraic sum of

STANDARD ELECTRODE POTENTIALS	
Ionic Concentrations 1 M Water At 298 K, 1 atm	
Half-Reaction	E^0 (volts)
$F_2(g) + 2e^- \rightarrow 2F^-$	+2.87
$8H^+ + MnO_4^- + 5e^- \rightarrow Mn^{2+} + 4H_2O$	+1.51
$Au^{3+} + 3e^- \rightarrow Au(s)$	+1.50
$Cl_2(g) + 2e^- \rightarrow 2Cl^-$	+1.36
$14H^+ + Cr_2O_7^{2-} + 6e^- \rightarrow 2Cr^{3+} + 7H_2O$	+1.23
$4H^+ + O_2(g) + 4e^- \rightarrow 2H_2O$	+1.23
$4H^+ + MnO_2(s) + 2e^- \rightarrow Mn^{2+} + 2H_2O$	+1.22
$Br_2(\ell) + 2e^- \rightarrow 2Br^-$	+1.09
$Hg^{2+} + 2e^- \rightarrow Hg(\ell)$	+0.85
$Ag^+ + e^- \rightarrow Ag(s)$	+0.80
$Hg_2^{2+} + 2e^- \rightarrow 2Hg(\ell)$	+0.80
$Fe^{3+} + e^- \rightarrow Fe^{2+}$	+0.77
$I_2(s) + 2e^- \rightarrow 2I^-$	+0.54
$Cu^+ + e^- \rightarrow Cu(s)$	+0.52
$Cu^{2+} + 2e^- \rightarrow Cu(s)$	+0.34
$4H^+ + SO_4^{2-} + 2e^- \rightarrow SO_2(aq) + 2H_2O$	+0.17
$Sn^{4+} + 2e^- \rightarrow Sn^{2+}$	+0.15
$2H^+ + 2e^- \rightarrow H_2(g)$	0.00
$Pb^{2+} + 2e^- \rightarrow Pb(s)$	-0.13
$Sn^{2+} + 2e^- \rightarrow Sn(s)$	-0.14
$Ni^{2+} + 2e^- \rightarrow Ni(s)$	-0.26
$Co^{2+} + 2e^- \rightarrow Co(s)$	-0.28
$Fe^{2+} + 2e^- \rightarrow Fe(s)$	-0.45
$Cr^{3+} + 3e^- \rightarrow Cr(s)$	-0.74
$Zn^{2+} + 2e^- \rightarrow Zn(s)$	-0.76
$2H_2O + 2e^- \rightarrow 2OH^- + H_2(g)$	-0.83
$Mn^{2+} + 2e^- \rightarrow Mn(s)$	-1.19
$Al^{3+} + 3e^- \rightarrow Al(s)$	-1.66
$Mg^{2+} + 2e^- \rightarrow Mg(s)$	-2.37
$Na^+ + e^- \rightarrow Na(s)$	-2.71
$Ca^{2+} + 2e^- \rightarrow Ca(s)$	-2.87
$Sr^{2+} + 2e^- \rightarrow Sr(s)$	-2.89
$Ba^{2+} + 2e^- \rightarrow Ba(s)$	-2.91
$Cs^+ + e^- \rightarrow Cs(s)$	-2.92
$K^+ + e^- \rightarrow K(s)$	-2.93
$Rb^+ + e^- \rightarrow Rb(s)$	-2.98
$Li^+ + e^- \rightarrow Li(s)$	-3.04

the E^0 values is positive. Since this Table represents a list of reduction potentials only and since the other half-cell reaction is an oxidation reaction, in order to evaluate it correctly, the arrow must be reversed in the reaction, and the sign changed in front of the E^0 value. That is: if hydrogen and aluminum were compared, the aluminum being below (in the Table), the hydrogen would be oxidized in order to reduce the hydrogen.

Therefore, reversing the arrow of the aluminum half-cell would give you an E^0 value of +1.66. Since the E^0 value of hydrogen is 0.00, the sum of the two half-cells will be +1.66, indicating that the reaction is spontaneous.

HALF-CELLS
It is possible to set up reactions so that each half of a redox reaction takes place in a separate vessel. This occurs if the vessels are connected by an external conductor and a salt bridge or porous partition. This permits the migration of ions but does not allow the solutions to mix (see page 232 for figure).

SKILLS 3.2x *USE THE TABLE OF REDUCTION POTENTIALS TO DETERMINE WHETHER A REDOX REACTION IS SPONTANEOUS.*

Directions: Use the *Standard Electrode Potentials Table* on ☆ pg 229 or where indicated, use *Reference Table J*.

20 Given the reaction: $2Fe^{3+} + 2I^- \rightarrow 2Fe^{2+} + I_2$ The net potential $[E^0]$ for the overall reaction is
   (1) 1.00 V   (2) 1.31 V   (3) 2.08 V   (4) 0.23 V

21 What is the E^0 for the half-reaction $Cu^+ + e^- \rightarrow Cu(s)$?
   (1) -0.52 V   (2) -0.34 V   (3) +0.34 V   (4) +0.52 V

22 According to *Standard Electrode Potentials Table*, which redox reaction occurs spontaneously?
   (1) $Cu(s) + 2H^+ \rightarrow Cu^{2+} + H_2(g)$
   (2) $Mg(s) + 2H^+ \rightarrow Mg^{2+} + H_2(g)$
   (3) $2Ag(s) + 2H^+ \rightarrow 2Ag^+ + H_2(g)$
   (4) $Hg(l) + 2H^+ \rightarrow Hg^{2+} + H_2(g)$

23 Which reduction half-reaction has a standard electrode potential (E^0) of 1.50 volts?
   (1) $Au^{3+} + 3e^- \rightarrow Au(s)$ (3) $Co^{2+} + 2e^- \rightarrow Co(s)$
   (2) $Al^{3+} + 3e^- \rightarrow Al(s)$ (4) $Ca^{2+} + 2e^- \rightarrow Ca(s)$

24 According to *Reference Table J*, which metal will react spontaneously with Ag^+ ions, but not with Zn^{2+} ions?
   (1) Cu   (2) Au   (3) Al   (4) Mg

25 In order for a redox reaction to be spontaneous, the potential (E^0) for the overall reaction must be
(1) greater than zero   (3) between zero and -1
(2) zero   (4) less than -1

26 According to *Standard Electrode Potentials Table*, what is the standard electrode potential (E^0) for the oxidation of $Cu(s)$ to Cu^{2+}?
(1) +0.52   (2) +0.34   (3) -0.52   (4) -0.34

27 Given the equation: $Cu^{2+} + 2e^- \rightarrow Cu$, the reduction potential (E^0) for this half-reaction is
(1) +0.52 V   (2) +0.34 V   (3) -0.54 V   (4) -0.34 V

28 What is the oxidation potential (E^0) of the half-reaction: $Cu(s) \rightarrow Cu^+ + e$?
(1) +0.34 volt   (3) -0.34 volt
(2) +0.52 volt   (4) -0.52 volt

29 According to *Reference Table J*, which metal will react spontaneously with $Cr^{3+}(aq)$ but not with $Ca^{2+}(aq)$?
(1) Mg   (2) Co   (3) Ba   (4) Pb

30 Given the reaction: $Mg^0 + Pb^{2+} \rightarrow Mg^{2+} + Pb^0$, what is the cell potential (E^0) for the overall reaction?
(1) -2.24 volts   (3) -2.50 volts
(2) +2.24 volts   (4) +2.50 volts

31 Based on *Reference Table J*, which of the following elements will replace Pb from $Pb(NO_3)_2(aq)$?
(1) Mg(*s*)   (2) Au(*s*)   (3) Cu(*s*)   (4) Ag(*s*)

32 According to *Standard Electrode Potentials Table*, which pair will react spontaneously
(1) $I_2 + 2Br^-$ (2) $I_2 + 2Cl^-$ (3) $F_2 + 2Cl^-$ (4) $Cl_2 + 2F^-$

ELECTRODES

The **electrode** at which reduction occurs in a cell is called a **cathode**. The cathode is identified as follows:

- In an electrochemical (voltaic) cell, the cathode is the positive electrode.

- In an electrolytic cell, the cathode is the negative electrode.

The electrode at which oxidation occurs in a cell is called the **anode**. The anode is identified as follows:

- In an electrochemical (voltaic) cell, the anode is the negative electrode.

- In an electrolytic cell, the anode is the positive electrode.

⭐ CHEMICAL CELLS – ELECTROCHEMICAL (VOLTAIC CELLS)

Redox reactions that occur spontaneously may be employed to provide a source of electrical energy.

When the two half-cells of a redox reaction are connected by an external conductor and a salt bridge or a porous cup that allows the migration of ions, a flow of electrons (electric current) is produced. In a voltaic cell, a chemical reaction is used to produce a spontaneous electric current by converting chemical energy to electrical energy.

$$Al \xrightarrow[\text{(at anode)}]{\text{oxidation}} \overset{3+}{Al} + 3e^- \qquad \overset{2+}{Zn} + 2e^- \xrightarrow[\text{(at cathode)}]{\text{reduction}} \overset{0}{Zn}$$

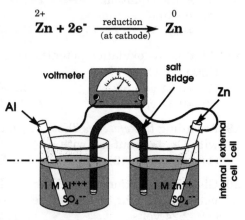

In the figure at the right, when the voltmeter is connected to allow the flow of electrons, the aluminum metal strip which is immersed in a solution of $Al_2(SO_4)_3$ which contains both Al^{+++} and SO_4^{--} ions will supply the electrons which flow through the voltmeter to the zinc electrode. The excess of electrons allows the zinc ions in the solution of $Zn^{++}SO_4^{--}$ to pick up electrons at the zinc electrode and become zinc metal atoms Zn^0. In an electrochemical cell, oxidation occurs at the anode and reduction at the cathode.

The aluminum metal atoms Al^0 each lost three electrons to become Al^{3+} ions. Since the loss of electrons takes place at the aluminum electrode it is called the anode, and the zinc electrode, where reduction takes place, is called the cathode. The E^0 values are established after setting up the two half-cell reactions

Reaction	E^0 Value
$\overset{0}{Al} \rightarrow \overset{3+}{Al} + 3e^-$	+ 1.66
$\overset{2+}{Zn} + 2e^- \rightarrow \overset{0}{Zn}$	– 0.76
	+ 0.90

The +0.90 E^0 value indicated:

*   The reaction is spontaneous.
*   The maximum voltage that can be registered on the voltmeter at 1 M concentration.

As the current continues, the flow of electrons diminishes until the cell reaches a state of equilibrium when the voltmeter will read zero.

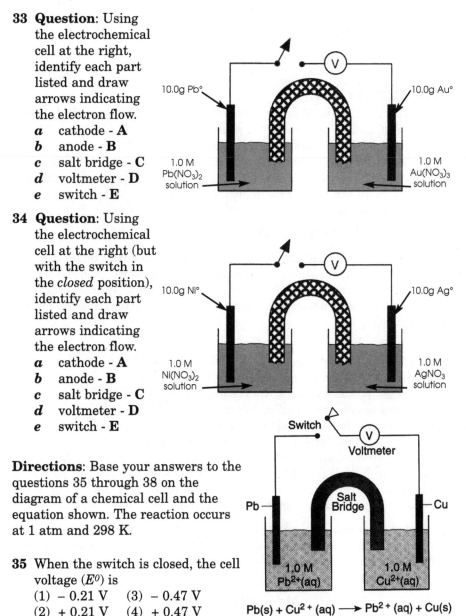

33 Question: Using the electrochemical cell at the right, identify each part listed and draw arrows indicating the electron flow.
  a cathode - **A**
  b anode - **B**
  c salt bridge - **C**
  d voltmeter - **D**
  e switch - **E**

10.0g Pb°

10.0g Au°

1.0 M Pb(NO$_3$)$_2$ solution

1.0 M Au(NO$_3$)$_3$ solution

34 Question: Using the electrochemical cell at the right (but with the switch in the *closed* position), identify each part listed and draw arrows indicating the electron flow.
  a cathode - **A**
  b anode - **B**
  c salt bridge - **C**
  d voltmeter - **D**
  e switch - **E**

10.0g Ni°

10.0g Ag°

1.0 M Ni(NO$_3$)$_2$ solution

1.0 M AgNO$_3$ solution

Switch

Voltmeter

Directions: Base your answers to the questions 35 through 38 on the diagram of a chemical cell and the equation shown. The reaction occurs at 1 atm and 298 K.

Pb

Salt Bridge

Cu

1.0 M Pb^{2+}(aq)

1.0 M Cu^{2+}(aq)

$$Pb(s) + Cu^{2+}(aq) \longrightarrow Pb^{2+}(aq) + Cu(s)$$

35 When the switch is closed, the cell voltage (E^0) is
  (1) − 0.21 V   (3) − 0.47 V
  (2) + 0.21 V   (4) + 0.47 V

36 Which change occurs when the switch is closed?
  (1) Pb is oxidized, and the electrons flow to the Cu electrode.
  (2) Pb is reduced, and the electrons flow to the Cu electrode.
  (3) Cu is oxidized, and the electrons flow to the Pb electrode.
  (4) Cu is reduced, and the electrons flow to the Pb electrode.

37 Question: When the switch is closed, identify on the diagram (on the previous page) the **ANODE** and the **CATHODE** electrodes.

38 Question: What is the species being oxidized?

HALF-CELL POTENTIAL

Comparison of the driving force of a half-reaction with that of the hydrogen standard establishes a scale of voltages. It is impossible to measure the **absolute reducing tendency** of a half-reaction except by comparison with an another half-reaction. For purposes of measuring the **relative reducing tendency** of a half-reaction, it has been found convenient to adopt the half reaction for the reduction of the hydrogen ion as an arbitrary standard:

$$2H^+ + 2e^- \rightarrow H_2 \qquad E^0 = 0.00$$

When each half-reaction is compared to the standard under specified conditions of concentration, temperature, and pressure, standard electrode potentials can be obtained. The standard electrode potential (E^0) gives the potential difference in the specified half-reaction and the hydrogen half-reaction.

☆ USE OF STANDARD ELECTRODE POTENTIALS

Standard electrode potentials are useful in determining whether or not a specific redox reaction will take place. Any pair of half-reactions can be combined to give the complete reaction for a cell whose potential difference can be calculated by adding the appropriate half-cell potentials. In combining half-reactions, it must be remembered that, in any redox reaction there must be an oxidation half-reaction and a reduction half-reaction. In the *Standard Electrode Potentials Table* (on ☆ pg 229), half-reactions are written as reductions. If read from left to right, all half-reactions result in the gaining of electrons.

To write the equation and the potential for the oxidation half-reaction correctly, the equation as written in the table must be reversed, and the sign (–,+) of E^0 also reversed. For example, in the reaction:

$$\overset{0}{Mg} + \overset{0}{Cl_2} \rightarrow \overset{2+}{Mg}\overset{1-}{Cl_2}$$

The magnesium is oxidized. Therefore, to obtain the equation and the potential for this oxidation half-reaction, the equation for magnesium as written in the table must be reversed, and the sign of E^0 changed. Chlorine is reduced in this reaction, and, therefore, its reduction potential is obtained directly from *Standard Electrode Potentials Table*. The two half-reactions may now be combined (top of page 235):

$$\begin{array}{ll} Mg \rightarrow Mg^{2+} + 2e^- & E^0 = +2.37 \\ \underline{Cl_2 + 2e^- \rightarrow 2Cl^-} & \underline{E^0 = +1.36} \\ Mg + Cl_2 \rightarrow Mg^{2+} + Cl^- & E^0 = +3.73 \end{array}$$

In combining half-reactions, if the potential (E^0) for the overall reaction is positive, the reaction is spontaneous. Such a reaction is called an **electrochemical cell reaction**. When combining half-reactions, the electron transfer must be balanced. For example, in the reaction:

$$2Na + Cl_2 \rightarrow 2NaCl$$

The two half-reactions would be combined as follows:

$$\begin{array}{ll} 2(Na \rightarrow Na^+ + 2e^-) & E^0 = +2.71 \\ \underline{Cl_2 + 2e^- \rightarrow 2Cl^-} & \underline{E^0 = +1.36} \\ 2Na + Cl_2 \rightarrow Na^+ + 2Cl^- & E^0 = +4.07 \end{array}$$

Metals with negative reduction potentials will produce hydrogen upon reaction with an acid. For example, if magnesium metal is added to a solution of an acid, the net reaction, if one occurs, could be represented by the equation:

$$Mg + 2H^+ \rightarrow Mg^{2+} + H_2$$

Combining the half-reactions:

$$\begin{array}{ll} Mg \rightarrow Mg^{2+} + 2e^- & E^0 = +2.37 \\ \underline{2H^+ + 2e^- \rightarrow H_2} & \underline{E^0 = +0.00} \\ Mg + 2H^+ \rightarrow Mg^{2+} + H_2 & E^0 = +2.37 \end{array}$$

Since this value is positive, the reaction will take place spontaneously. **Note**: The Standard Electrode Potentials (E^0) are not multiplied by the coefficients in calculating the E_0 for the reaction.

G – ELECTROLYTIC CELLS

In combining half-reactions, if the potential (E^0) for the overall reaction is negative, a reaction will not take place spontaneously. For example, metals with positive reduction potentials will not produce hydrogen on reaction with an acid. If copper metal is added to a solution of an acid, the reaction would not occur spontaneously. For example:

$$Cu + 2H^+ \rightarrow Cu^{2+} + H_2$$

or combining the half-reactions

$$\begin{array}{ll} Cu^- \rightarrow Cu^{2+} + 2e^- & E^0 = -0.34 \\ \underline{2H^+ + 2e^- \rightarrow H_2} & \underline{E^0 = -0.00} \\ Cu + 2H^+ \rightarrow Cu^{2+} + H_2 & E^0 = -0.34 \end{array}$$

Note: Since the resulting E^0 is negative, the reaction cannot take place spontaneously.

Equilibrium is attained in chemical cells when the voltage measured is equal to zero. The E^0 values given in the *Standard Electrode Potentials Table* are for definite concentrations. As a reaction proceeds, these concentrations change, and the measured value falls off until at equilibrium, the measured voltage is equal to zero.

ELECTROLYSIS

Redox reactions that do not occur spontaneously can be forced to take place by supplying energy with an externally applied electric current. The use of an electric current to bring about a chemical reaction is called **electrolysis**. In an electrolytic cell, an electric current is used to produce a chemical reaction. Water is decomposed into hydrogen gas and oxygen gas by electrolysis. In electrolysis, positive ions are reduced at the cathode and negative are oxidized at the anode.

The overall reaction is

$$2H_2O(l) + 571.6 \text{ kJ} \rightarrow 2H_2(g) + O_2(g)$$

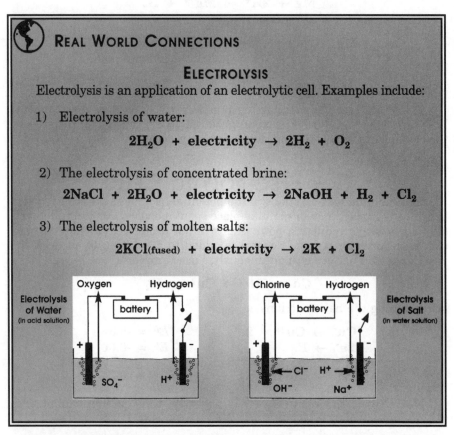

REAL WORLD CONNECTIONS

ELECTROLYSIS

Electrolysis is an application of an electrolytic cell. Examples include:

1) Electrolysis of water:

$$2H_2O + \text{electricity} \rightarrow 2H_2 + O_2$$

2) The electrolysis of concentrated brine:

$$2NaCl + 2H_2O + \text{electricity} \rightarrow 2NaOH + H_2 + Cl_2$$

3) The electrolysis of molten salts:

$$2KCl_{(fused)} + \text{electricity} \rightarrow 2K + Cl_2$$

The half-cell reactions are as follows:

$$2H_2O(l) + 2e^- \rightarrow 2OH^-(aq) + H_2(g)$$

$$6H_2O(l) \rightarrow 4H_3O(aq) + O_2(g) + 4e^-$$

SKILLS 3.2IX *COMPARE AND CONTRAST VOLTAIC AND ELECTROLYTIC CELLS.*

39 The diagram at the right represents an electrochemical cell.

What occurs when the switch is closed?

(1) Zn is reduced.
(2) Cu is oxidized.
(3) Electrons flow from Cu to Zn.
(4) Electrons flow from Zn to Cu.

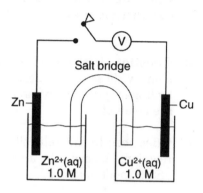

40 In an electrolytic cell, a negative ion will migrate to and undergo oxidation at the
(1) anode, which is negatively charged
(2) anode, which is positively charged
(3) cathode, which is negatively charged
(4) cathode, which is positively charged

41 The diagram at the right shows the electrolysis of fused KCl. What occurs when the switch is closed?
(1) Positive ions migrate toward the anode, where they lose electrons.
(2) Positive ions migrate toward the anode, where they gain electrons.
(3) Positive ions migrate toward the cathode, where they lose electrons.
(4) Positive ions migrate toward the cathode, where they gain electrons.

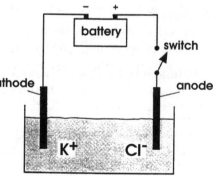

Directions: Refer to the illustration at the right and the reaction below to answer the following questions.

$$2H_2O(l) + 571.6\ kJ \rightarrow 2H_2(g) + O_2(g)$$

42 Question: Is the reaction endothermic or exothermic?

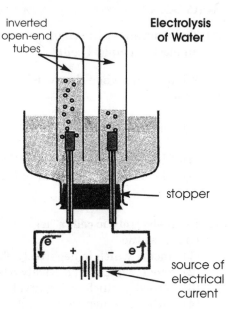

43 Question: In the illustration, identify those sides where the hydrogen gas and oxygen gas are given off.

44 Question: In the half-cell reactions, identify the anode and cathode reactions.

45 Question: At which electrode is oxidation occurring?

46 Question: At which electrode is reduction occurring?

BATTERIES

Batteries produce an electrical current and fall into two distinct categories: non-rechargeable primary batteries, and secondary, chargeable ones.

Primary batteries can supply energy but cannot be recharged. The best example of a primary battery is the Leclanche (common flashlight battery) cell.

Anode reaction takes place at the zinc wall:

$$Zn^0(s) \rightarrow Zn^{2+}(aq) + 2e^-$$

Cathode reaction takes place at the carbon rod:

$$Mn^{4+} + 2e^- \rightarrow 2Mn^{3+}$$

The ammonia produced collects around the carbon to insulate it and drop the voltage. The electrolyte is a paste of MH_4Cl, $ZnCl_2$, NH_4Cl, and H_2O. The overall energy producing reaction is

$$Zn + 2MnO_2 \rightarrow ZnO + Mn_2O_3$$

Secondary batteries, once discharged can be recharged. The most widely used secondary battery is the alkaline rechargeable cell which can be recharged several times. This battery uses KOH rather than NH_4Cl in the electrolytic paste, which

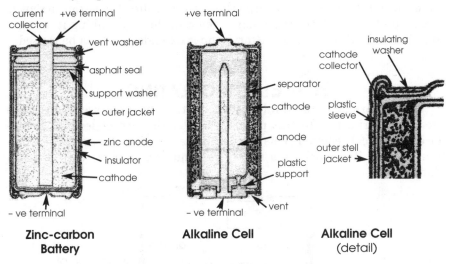

Zinc-carbon Battery

Alkaline Cell

Alkaline Cell (detail)

Another secondary battery is the **lead storage battery**. This 12-volt storage battery is used in automobiles and is made up of six voltaic cells. Each voltaic cell has a lead plate with a grid that contains a gray spongy form of lead which is the anode. Alternating with these anode plates is another set of six lead plates filled with lead (IV) oxide (PbO_2) which is the cathode portion of the cell. Both sets of plates are immersed in an aqueous solution of sulfuric acid (H_2SO_4) which is the electrolyte.

When an auto's ignition key is turned to initiate a current, the lead in the anode plates is oxidized to Pb^{2+} ions which immediately react with SO_4^{2-} ions in the electrolyte, forming $PbSO_4$ (lead sulfate) which precipitates on the anode plates. Meanwhile, lead dioxide at the cathode is reduced to Pb^{2+} which also combines with sulfate ions to form more $PbSO_4$.

Anode reaction:
$$Pb(s) + SO_4^{2-}(aq) \rightarrow PbSO_4(s) + 2e^-$$

At cathode:
$$PbO_2(s) + 4H^+(aq) + SO_4^{2-}(aq) + 2e^- \rightarrow PbSO_4(s) + 2H_2O$$

Net reaction:
$$Pb(s) + PbO_2(s) + 4H^-(aq) + 2SO^{2-}(aq) \rightarrow 2PbSO_4(s) + 2H_2O$$

As seen in the above equations, when the cell discharges, the product in each case is a solid deposit of lead sulfate. This material collects on both plates and replaces some of the lead (anode) and the lead oxide (cathode). As part of the result, the concentration of the sulfuric acid decreases. These items contribute to limit a battery's life and usefulness.

While it is discharging, the lead storage battery acts as an electrochemical cell. In order to recharge the battery, a direct electric current is hooked up to reverse the direction of the cell, thereby making it an electrolytic cell. In this way, the battery's life is extended and can be reused.

H – ELECTROPLATING

Silver, chrome, and stainless steel plating are processes that make use of this principle. In this process, an electric current is used to produce a chemical reaction. This results in the covering of a surface (usually a metallic item such as a spoon, car bumper, or trim) with a metal plating.

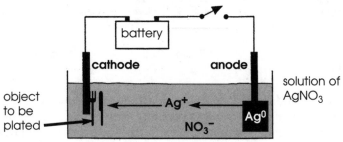

In the illustration above, the passage of one mole of electrons (6.02 x 10^{23} electrons) through the cathode will allow one mole of Ag^+ ions to be plated onto the object to be coated.

The procedure used is to make a solution of the salt that contains the plating metal ions and immerse the object to be plated (which is attached to the negative pole of a power pack) into the solution. Then, the flow of electric current is switched on. The concentration of the solution and the amount of time that the current is allowed to continue determines how thick the layer of plated material will be. In this process, reduction takes place at the cathode, which is negative in charge. The object to be plated is placed touching the cathode. Oxidation takes place at the anode, which is composed of the metal to be plated.

CALCULATIONS TO PERFORM CONCERNING CHEMICAL CELLS
- **Predict the direction of electron flow** – By referring to the *Standard Electrode Potential Table* [☆ pg 229], it can be determined which item will be oxidized and which will be reduced. The element closest to the top of the table will be reduced, and that which is closest to the bottom will be oxidized.

- **Predict the direction of ion movement** – By first identifying the anode and cathode and then determining the charge on the ion, the direction of ion movement can easily be predicted.

- **Calculate the net potential for the redox reaction** – This is done by writing the two half-cell reactions, along with their E^0 values. The algebraic sum of the E^0 values will give the net potential of the reaction.

Note: Do not forget to change the value of the species which is oxidized.

I – REDUCTION OF METALS

The ores of most metals contain the metal in an oxidized state (with a positive ionic charge). The form in which a metal occurs is related to the chemical activity of the metal and the stability of its compounds. In general, compounds of metals that occur in nature have high stability and low solubility in water.

Reduction (the taking on of electrons by the positively charged metal ion so that it may become a metal atom with a zero charge of the ore) is necessary to obtain the metal. The method of reduction depends on the activity of the metal and the type of ore.

The most active metals are obtained from their fused compounds by electrolytic reduction. These include Groups 1 and 2 metals, which are obtained by the electrolysis of their fused (melted) salts:

$$2NaCl \text{ (fused)} + electricity \rightarrow 2Na + Cl_2$$

Metals that form relatively stable compounds can be liberated from their compounds by stronger reducing agents. For example, in the production of chromium, aluminum reduces the chromium oxide:

$$2Al + Cr_2O_3 \rightarrow Al_2O_3 + 2Cr$$

Many metals are found as sulfides and carbonates (ZnS, CuS). These ores are converted to the oxide form by reacting the ore with oxygen through a process called "roasting." After that, the oxide ores are reduced by carbon (coke) or carbon monoxide:

$$ZnO + C + heat \rightarrow Zn + CO$$

$$Fe_2O_3 + 3CO + heat \rightarrow 3CO_2 + 2Fe$$

REAL WORLD CONNECTIONS

Smelting is the **melting** (fusing) of metallic ores in order to separate metal from other items in the ore; e.g. heating the oxide of iron with carbon which combines with the oxygen to free the iron metal.

Leaching (in the refining of gold) – Normally, a metal such as gold exists in an ore with other metallic salts such as salts of copper or silver. The ore is combined with a leaching agent such as dilute sulfuric acid. The salts are dissolved, leaving the gold metal to be separated and retrieved.

Thermite reaction – A mixture, called thermite, is made up of a less-active metal such as iron III oxide and a more-active metal such as powdered aluminum. When thermite is ignited, it burns with a very hot flame (3,000°C to 3,500°C). The aluminum reduces the oxide to a free metal. The following is a typical thermite reaction:

$$2Al + Fe_2O_3 \rightarrow 2Fe + Al_2O_3 \qquad \Delta H = -849 \text{ kJ}$$

In cases where carbon does not readily reduce metallic oxides, the thermite reaction can be used to recover metals such as titanium, molybdenum, and tungsten, used to manufacture of steel alloys. This reaction is also used to produce the high temperatures in welding torches needed for the repair of machinery and ship building.

Recovery of active nonmetals – Silver Nitrate is added to brine solution of the iodine salts forming silver iodide which is precipitated out. The presence of ferric hydroxide plus the addition of scrap iron causes the silver to precipitate out and ferrous iodide to form. Chlorine is added to decompose the ferrous iodide and the iodine is precipitated out. Examples include: salts of iodine found in seawater, seaweed, and in nitrate salt deposits in Chile.

Patina protection – (e.g., copper as on the Statue of Liberty) is the green colored carbonate salt that forms on copper and bronze after long exposure to air. Although unsightly, the formation of this salt on its surface protects the metal underneath it.

Metallurgy of iron and steel – The most common iron ore is hematite (Fe_2O_3), to which is added coke (reducing agent) and limestone ($CaCO_3$) that is used to react with impurities. These are heated together in a huge bottle-like structure called a blast furnace in which a hot blast (about 500°C) of oxygen is fed into the mix and reacts with the coke. This results in the formation of pig iron (which is used to make steel) and the impurities called slag. Steel is an alloy of

©Garnsey, 2001

iron and other metals such as Cr, Ni, Mo, Mn, V, Cu, and Si. Pig iron must be oxidized in order to decrease its impurities (e.g. phosphorus and sulfur). This is usually accomplished by either the open hearth or electric furnace processes.

- **Open hearth process** – Pig iron charge (containing iron ore and limestone which react with the impurities to form slag) is heated in large oven-like structure by the addition of burning gases, hot air, and oxygen. Alloying metals are added to form the steel mix and the slag is drained off.

Small Open-Hearth Process
©PhotoDisc

- **Electric furnace process** – The procedure is essentially the same as the open hearth. The exception is that the heating is provided by an electric arc which forms between large graphite electrodes when the current is turned on. This process can be more accurately controlled to give a higher quality product.

PERFORMANCE INDICATOR 3.1
ASSESSMENTS

PART A – MULTIPLE CHOICE

1   A student wishes to set up an electrochemical cell. The following list of materials and equipment will be used:

- two 250-mL beakers
- wire
- one piece of Zn metal
- 125 mL of 0.10 M $Zn(NO_3)_2$

- voltmeter
- switch
- one piece of Pb metal
- 125 mL of 0.10 M $Pb(NO_3)_2$

For the cell to operate properly, the student will also need
(1) an anode
(2) a cathode
(3) an external path for electrons
(4) a salt bridge

2   Given the cell reaction:

$$Sn(s) + Pb^{2+}(aq) \rightarrow Sn^{2+}(aq) + Pb(s)$$

The reduction half-reaction for this cell is
(1) $Pb^{2+}(aq) + 2e^- \rightarrow Pb(s)$
(2) $Pb(s) \rightarrow Pb^{2+}(aq) + 2e^-$
(3) $Sn^{2+}(aq) + 2e^- \rightarrow Sn(s)$
(4) $Sn(s) \rightarrow Sn^{2+}(aq) + 2e^-$

3 Based on *Standard Electrode Potentials Table* [☆ pg 229] the standard electrode potential for the reduction of gold (III) ions is
(1) +1.50 V   (2) +0.80 V   (3) -0.80V   (4) -1.50 V

4 The oxidation number of nitrogen in N_2 is
(1) +1   (2) 0   (3) +3   (4) -3

5 Given the reaction:

$$2Al(s) + 6H^+(aq) \rightarrow 2Al^{3+}(aq) + 3H_2(g)$$

What is the total number of moles of electrons gained by $H^+(aq)$ when 2 moles of Al(s) is completely reacted?
(1) 6   (2) 2   (3) 3   (4) 12

6 Given the redox reaction:

$$Mg(s) + CuSO_4(aq) \rightarrow MgSO_4(aq) + Cu(s)$$

Which species acts as the oxidizing agent?
(1) Cu(s)   (2) $Cu^{2+}(aq)$ (3) Mg(s)   (4) $Mg^{2+}(aq)$

7 In an electrolytic cell, the negative electrode is called the
(1) anode, at which oxidation occurs
(2) anode, at which reduction occurs
(3) cathode, at which oxidation occurs
(4) cathode, at which reduction occurs

8 What is the oxidation number of chlorine in $HClO_4$?
(1) +1   (2) +5   (3) +3   (4) +7

9 The diagram at the right shows the electrolysis of fused NaCl. What occurs when the switch is closed?
(1) Positive ions migrate toward the anode, where they lose electrons.
(2) Positive ions migrate toward the anode, where they gain electrons.
(3) Positive ions migrate toward the cathode, where they lose electrons.
(4) Positive ions migrate toward the cathode, where they gain electrons.

10 Given the balanced equation:

$$2Al(s) + 6H^+(aq) \rightarrow 2Al^{3+}(aq) + 3H_2(g)$$

When 2 moles of Al(s) completely reacts, what is the total number of moles of electrons transferred from Al(s) to $H^+(aq)$?
(1) 5   (2) 6   (3) 3   (4) 4

11 Which half-reaction correctly represents reduction?
(1) $Cr^{3+} + 3e^- \rightarrow Cr(s)$ (3) $Cr(s) \rightarrow Cr^{3+} + 3e^-$
(2) $Cr^{3+} \rightarrow Cr(s) + 3e^-$ (4) $Cr(s) + 3e^- \rightarrow Cr^{3+}$

12 Which statement best describes how a salt bridge maintains electrical neutrality in the half-cells of an electrochemical cell?
(1) It prevents the migration of electrons.
(2) It permits the migration of ions.
(3) It permits the two solutions to mix completely.
(4) It prevents the reaction from occurring spontaneously.

13 Which atom forms an ion that would migrate toward the cathode in an electrolytic cell?
(1) F   (2) I   (3) Na   (4) Cl

14 Given the equations A, B, C, and D:

(A) $AgNO_3 + NaCl \rightarrow AgCl + NaNO_3$
(B) $Cl_2 + H_2O \rightarrow HClO + HCl$
(C) $CuO + CO \rightarrow CO_2 + Cu$
(D) $NaOH + HCl \rightarrow NaCl + H_2O$

Which two equations represent redox reactions?
(1) A and B (2) B and C (3) C and A (4) D and B

PART B – CONSTRUCTED-RESPONSE

voltaic = saltbridge
2 - beakers
-anode (- ox.)
- cathode (+ red)

Directions: For questions 1 through 7, use the diagram at the right and your knowledge of the electrochemical cell.

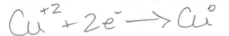

V

Al   Cu

1.0 M   1.0 M
$Al(NO_3)_3$ $Cu(NO_3)_2$

electrolytic
-1 container
-no bridge
- anode + cathode -

1   **Question**: Write the half-reaction that represents the oxidation that is taking place in the electrochemical cell. [1] Al^{+3} Cu^{+2}

table

$Al^0 \longrightarrow Al^{+3} + 3e^-$

2   **Question**: Write the half-reaction that represents the reduction that is taking place. [1]

$$Cu^{+2} + 2e^- \longrightarrow Cu^0$$

3   **Question**: Write the balanced, net redox reaction that is taking place in the electrochemical cell. [1]

$$2Al^0 + 3Cu^{+2} \longrightarrow 2Al^{+3} + 3Cu^0$$

4   Question: Identify the chemical species that is acting as the anode. [1]

Al

5   Question: Identify the chemical species that is acting as the cathode. [1]

Cu

6   Question: Using an arrow, indicate the direction in which the electrons flow on the diagram of the electrochemical cell (pg 245). [1]

left to right
ox to red.

7   Question: State the purpose of the salt bridge. [1]

To transfer energy back
through the cell current
continue to flow

Directions: For questions 8 through 10, use the diagram at the right and your knowledge of the electrolytic cell.

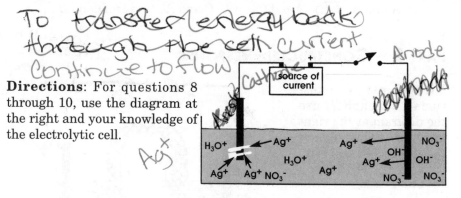

Ag^x

8   Question: Label the anode and cathode. [1]

9   Question: Write the half-reaction that is taking place at the cathode. [1]

Ag + 1e$^-$ → Ag^o

10   Question: Identify the electrode to which an object being electroplated should be attached. [1]

source of current   cathode

PART C – EXTENDED CONSTRUCTED-RESPONSE

Statement A: An oxidation-reduction (redox) reaction is one in which a change in oxidation number occurs. The species undergoing oxidation looses electrons and the species undergoing reduction gains electrons. Because oxidation-reduction occurs simultaneously, the chemical species that is undergoing oxidation is called the reducing agent, and the species that is undergoing reduction is called the oxidizing agent.

1 **Question**: Assign oxidation numbers to the chemical species in the accompanying reaction, and explain why the reaction illustrated below is considered to be a redox reaction. [2]

(oxidation numbers)$\rightarrow$

$$Ca + 2HCl \rightarrow 2CaCl_2 + H_2$$

2 **Question**: Identify the species undergoing reduction in the reaction shown above and write the half reaction for the reduction that is taking place. [2]

3 **Question**: In the reaction shown above, identify the reducing agent. [1]

Statement B: In oxidation-reduction reactions, there is a conservation of charge as well as a conservation of mass. This means that the number of electrons lost by one reactant must be gained by another reactant.

4 **Question**: Assign the oxidation numbers to the chemical species in the following reaction. [1]

(oxidation numbers)$\rightarrow$
$$2Al + 3ZnCl_2 \rightarrow 2AlCl_3 + 3Zn$$

5 **Question**: Using half-reactions, illustrate how the number of electrons gained equals the number of electrons lost in the above reaction. [2]

Statement C: A voltaic electro-chemical cell is one that produces electricity as the result of separating the two halves of a redox reaction. A metal wire that conducts electricity and a salt bridge that allows for the transfer of ions connects the two half-cells. As long as there is a positive difference in electromotive potential between one half-cell and the other half-cell, the electrons will flow from the

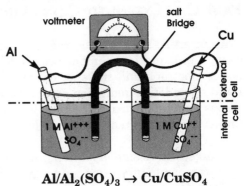

$$Al/Al_2(SO_4)_3 \rightarrow Cu/CuSO_4$$

half-cell where the oxidation half-reaction is taking place to the half-cell where reduction is taking place. Electrons will flow from the anode that is labeled with a negative sign to the cathode that is labeled with a positive sign until equilibrium is reached, at which time the voltage will be zero.

6 **Question**: Write the half-reaction that is taking place at the anode in the above electrochemical cell. [1]

7 **Question**: Write the half-reaction that is taking place at the cathode in the above electrochemical cell. [1]

8 **Question**: Write the balanced, net ionic reaction that takes place in the above electrochemical cell. [1]

9 **Question**: Identify both the anode and the cathode and label with the appropriate signs. [2]

10 **Question**: Using arrows, indicate the direction that the electrons will flow from one half-cell to the other. [1]

11 Question: Using the table [☆ pg 229] , calculate the voltage produced by the cell when it is new. [1]

12 Question: Explain why the voltage of the electrochemical cell will eventually become zero. [1]

Statement D: Electrolytic cells can be used for electroly- sis or electroplating. Electro lytic cells use an external source of electricity to allow a redox reaction to take place that would not normally occur spontaneously. Oxidation takes place at the anode and reduc-

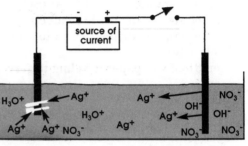

tion takes place at the cathode. However, the signs of the terminals are different than those found in an electrochemical cell. This is due to the fact that an external source of electricity is being used. In this case, the terminal receiving the electrons from the external source is labeled with a negative sign and the other terminal is labeled with a positive sign. When an individual wants to electroplate an object, the object is always attached to the negative terminal so that it can be plated. The metallic ions of the solution gain electrons and are reduced to metal in the ground state on the surface of the object being electroplated.

13 Question: A student wants to electroplate a piece of metal with sil- ver. To which electrode (+ or -) should the object being electroplated be attached? [1]

14 Question: Label the electrodes as either the anode or cathode. [1]

15 Question: Write the half-reaction that takes place at the cathode in this cell. [1]

PART D – LABORATORY SKILLS

LEVEL TWO LAB: CONSTRUCTING AN ELECTROCHEMICAL CELL

Purpose:
To construct an electrochemical cell and determine its voltage

Materials:
Two 250 mL beakers
100 mL solutions of 0.1 M $ZnSO_4$ solution
100 mL solutions of 0.1 M $Al_2(SO_4)_3$ solution
a zinc strip attached to conducting wire
an aluminum strip attached to conducting wire
voltmeter
length of wet paper toweling to serve as a salt bridge

Procedure:
Directions: Use your text, library references, and your knowledge of chemistry to construct an electrochemical cell and answer the following questions.

1   Complete the circuit by touching the contacts of the voltmeter to the metal electrodes, and record the voltage produced.

2   Make a diagram of your electrochemical cell and label the following parts:

> anode
> cathode
> positive electrode
> negative electrode
> salt bridge
> voltmeter with wires attached to the metal electrodes.

Diagram of electrochemical cell:

Conclusion and Review Questions:

3 Write the two half-reactions for this electrochemical cell, one that represents oxidation and one that represents reduction.

4 Write the balanced, net ionic reaction that takes place in this electro-chemical cell.

5 Calculate the theoretical voltage of the cell when it is new.

6 Identify which electrode will increase in mass and which electrode will decrease in mass as the reaction proceeds.

7 What is the voltage of the cell after equilibrium is reached?

8 What is the purpose of the salt bridge?

9 Into which half-cell will the positive ions from the salt bridge flow?

UNIT 9
ACIDS, BASES, & SALTS

KEY IDEA **3** MATTER IS MADE UP OF PARTICLES WHOSE PROPERTIES DETERMINE THE OBSERVABLE CHARACTERISTICS OF MATTER AND ITS REACTIVITY

PERFORMANCE INDICATOR 3.1 *EXPLAIN THE PROPERTIES OF MATERIALS IN TERMS OF THE ARRANGEMENT AND PROPERTIES OF THE ATOMS THAT COMPOSE THEM.*

UNIT 9 – MAJOR UNDERSTANDINGS

☆ 3.1uu Behavior of many acids and bases can be explained by the Arrhenius theory. Arrhenius acids and bases are electrolytes.

☆ 3.1rr An electrolyte is a substance which, when dissolved in water, forms a solution capable of conducting an electric current. The ability of a solution to conduct an electric current depends on the concentration of ions.

☆ 3.1vv Arrhenius acids yield $H^+(aq)$ (hydrogen ion) as the only positive ion in an aqueous solution. The hydrogen ion may also be written as $H_3O^+(aq)$, hydronium ion.

☆ 3.1ww Arrhenius bases yield $OH^-(aq)$, hydroxide ion as the only negative ion in an aqueous solution.

☆ 3.1xx In the process of neutralization, an Arrhenius acid and an Arrhenius base react to form a salt and water.

☆ 3.1zz Titration is a laboratory process in which a volume of a solution of known concentration is used to determine the concentration of another solution.

☆ 3.1yy There are alternate acid-base theories. One theory states that an acid is an H^+ donor and a base is an H^+ acceptor.

UNIT 9
ACIDS, BASES, & SALTS

This unit is related to Key Idea 3 for the text and Performance Indicator 3.1 for the assessments.

INTRODUCTION

An **electrolyte** (i.e., various ions, such as sodium, potassium, or chloride) will dissolve in water to form a solution that will conduct an electric current. The ability of a solution to conduct an electric current is due to the presence of ions that are free to move. Therefore, all ionic compounds are electrolytes. Also, some polar covalent compounds form ions and conduct electricity when dissolved in water. For example, HCl and HBr. However, nonelectrolytes, such as organic solvents, do not conduct electricity.

Weak electrolytes in aqueous solution attain an equilibrium between ions and the undisassociated compound. The equilibrium constant for such systems is called the dissociation constant. The value of the dissociation constant changes with a change of temperature.

A - ACIDS & BASES

One means of defining a substance is to list its properties and reactions. This form of definition is called an **operational definition** and is based on experimental observations, which include a set of conditions.

As the understanding of acid-base reactions has grown, conceptual definitions (those that try to answer the questions: Why? How?) of acids and bases have been extended. These conceptual definitions have also been applied to reactions that do not necessarily take place in aqueous solutions.

UNIT 9 - MAJOR UNDERSTANDINGS (CONTINUED)

☆ 3.1ss The acidity or alkalinity of an aqueous solution can be measured by its pH value. The relative level of acidity or alkalinity of these solutions can be shown by using indicators.

☆ 3.1tt On the pH scale, each decrease of one unit of pH represents a tenfold increase in hydronium ion concentration.

ACIDS

Acids may be defined in terms of their characteristic properties. These properties can be observed experimentally and form the basis of the operational definition of an acid. They include:

CONCEPTUAL DEFINITION OF ACIDS

Arrhenius' Theory – An acid is a substance that yields hydrogen ions in aqueous solutions. This conceptual definition is adequate when considering reactions in aqueous solutions. As knowledge of the mechanism of chemical reactions has increased, more inclusive definitions have been advanced. The characteristic properties of acids in aqueous solution are due to an excess of hydrogen ions (hydronium ions) which combine with water molecules to become H_3O^+ (hydronium ion).

Brönsted-Lowry Theory – An acid is any species (molecule or ion) that can donate a proton to another species. The *Brönsted-Lowry Theory* does not replace the *Arrhenius' Theory*, but extends it. The Brönsted-Lowry definition of an acid includes all substances that are acids according to the Arrhenius definition.

In addition, some molecules and ions are classified as acids under the Brönsted-Lowry definition that are not acids in the Arrhenius sense. For example, in the reaction:

$$NH_3 + H_2O \leftrightarrow NH_4^+ + OH^-$$

The water molecule donates a proton to the ammonia and is considered an acid in the Brönsted-Lowry sense. In the reverse reaction, the ammonium ion will donate a proton and act as the acid, while the hydroxide ion accepts the proton and acts as a base.

OPERATIONAL DEFINITION OF ACIDS

- **Aqueous solutions of acids conduct electricity** – They conduct electricity in relation to the degree of their ionization. A few acids ionize almost completely in aqueous solution and are strong electrolytes (strong acids). Others ionize only to a slight degree and are weak electrolytes (weak acids).

- **Acids will react with certain active metals to liberate hydrogen gas** – Those metals above hydrogen as shown in *Reference Table J*, *Activity Series*, will react with acids to produce a salt of the metal and hydrogen gas.

Note: Some acids, in addition to their acid properties, have strong oxidizing ability. Therefore, except in very dilute solution, they do not release hydrogen gas on reaction with metals. For example, nitric acid and concentrated sulfuric acid have strong oxidizing properties.

- Acids cause color changes in acid-base indicators. Acid-base indicators are substances that have different colors in acid and basic solutions. Two common indicators are litmus which is blue in basic solution and red in acid solution, and phenolphthalein which is pink in basic solution and colorless in acid solution.

  Note: These indicators do not change color exactly at pH 7. Different indicators change color at different concentrations of hydrogen ions.

- Acids react with hydroxides to form water and a salt. When hydrogen ions react with hydroxide ions, water is formed. This reaction is called **neutralization**. For example:

$$HCl + NaOH \rightarrow NaCl + H_2O$$

- Dilute aqueous solutions of acids have a sour taste, such as vinegar and acetic acid.

- Acids react with metallic oxides to form salts and water.

BASES

Bases may be defined in terms of their characteristic properties. These properties can be observed experimentally and form the basis of the operational definition of a base. They include:

CONCEPTUAL DEFINITION OF BASES

Arrhenius' Theory – A base is a substance that yields hydroxide ions as the only negative ions in aqueous solution. According to the Arrhenius definition, the only bases are hydroxides. The characteristic properties of bases in an ion aqueous solution are due to the hydroxide ion.

Brönsted-Lowry Theory – A base is any species (molecule or ion) that can accept a proton. The Brönsted-Lowry definition extends the Arrhenius' definition to include many species in addition to the OH^- that can accept a proton. For example, in the reaction:

$$H_2O + HCl \rightarrow H_3O^+ + Cl^-$$

The water molecule combines with a proton to form the hydronium ion and is here considered a base in the Brönsted-Lowry sense. In the reverse reaction, the hydronium ion will donate a proton and act as an acid. While the chloride ion, which accepts the proton, acts as a base.

✰ CONJUGATE ACID-BASE PAIR

According to the *Brönsted-Lowry Theory*, acid-base reactions involve a transfer of protons from the acid to the base. To accept a proton, a base must have at least one pair of unshared electrons. The proton (H^+) will share a pair of electrons belonging to the base, forming a coordinate covalent bond.

In an acid-base reaction, an acid transfers a proton to become a conjugate base. This acid and its newly formed base form a **conjugate acid-base pair**. A base gains a proton to become a conjugate acid, forming a second acid-base pair. Each pair, made up of an acid and its base, is related by the transfer of a proton.

In the following reactions, the two conjugate pairs are identified by subscripts.

$$Base_1 + Acid_2 \leftrightarrow Acid_1 + Base_2$$

$$H_2O + HCl \leftrightarrow H_3O^+ + Cl^-$$

$$NH_3 + H_2O \leftrightarrow NH_4^+ + OH^-$$

The same form of identification of acid and base pairs can be done using brackets.

$$H_2O + H_2SO_4 \leftrightarrow H_3O^+ + HSO_4^-$$

$Base_1 \quad Acid_2 \quad\quad Acid_1 \quad Base_2$

Note: The strongest acids have the weakest conjugate bases, and the strongest bases have the weakest conjugate acids.

PRACTICE

1   What is a conjugate acid-base pair in the reaction $H_2O + HI \rightarrow H_3O^+ + I^-$?
   (1) H_2O and HI
   (2) H_2O and I^-
   (3) HI and I^-
   (4) HI and H_3O^+

2   In the reaction $CH_3COOH + H_2O \leftrightarrow CH_3COO^- + H_3O^+$, a conjugate acid-base pair is
   (1) CH_3COOH and H_3O^+
   (2) CH_3COO^- and H_2O
   (3) CH_3COOH and CH_3COO^-
   (4) CH_3COO^- and H_3O^+

3   In the reaction: $H_3PO_4 + H_2O \leftrightarrow H_2PO_4^- + H_3O^+$, a conjugate acid-base pair is
   (1) H_3PO_4 and H_2O
   (2) H_3PO_4 and $H_2PO_4^-$
   (3) $H_2PO_4^-$ and H_2O
   (4) $H_2PO_4^-$ and H_3O^+

Operational Definitions of Bases

- **Aqueous solutions of bases conduct electricity.**

- **Bases cause color changes in acid-base indicators** – They cause red litmus to turn blue and phenolphthalein (a weak, colorless acid) to turn pink.

- **Bases react with acids to form water and a salt.**

- **Aqueous solutions of bases feel slippery.**

- **Strong bases have a caustic action on the skin.**

Interpreting Acid-Base Indicators

Certain dyes in solutions are sensitive to changes in hydrogen ion concentration. This sensitivity causes visible reactions when the indicator is combined with a substance to be tested. The chart below lists some indicators and the color changes they undergo [see *Reference Table M*].

dye	acidic color	basic color
litmus	red	blue
phenolphthalein	colorless	red
methyl red	red	yellow
bromthymol blue	yellow	blue

SKILLS 3.1XXXIII *INTERPRET CHANGES IN ACID-BASE INDICATOR COLOR.*

4 Both $HNO_3(aq)$ and $CH_3COOH(aq)$ can be classified as
   (1) Arrhenius acids that turn blue litmus red
   (2) Arrhenius bases that turn blue litmus red
   (3) Arrhenius acids that turn red litmus blue
   (4) Arrhenius bases that turn red litmus blue

5 Phenolphthalein remains colorless in a aqueous solution of
   (1) $NaOH(aq)$
   (2) $HCl(aq)$
   (3) $Ca(OH)_2(aq)$
   (4) $NH_4OH(aq)$

6 Red litmus will turn blue when placed in a aqueous solution of
   (1) HCl   (3) CH_3OH
   (2) CH_3COOH (4) NaOH

☆ AMPHOTERIC (AMPHIPROTIC) SUBSTANCES

An amphoteric (amphiprotic) substance is one that can act either as an acid or as a base, depending on its chemical environment. Common amphiprotic substances include H_2O and NH_3, and polyatomic negative ions containing hydrogen. For example H_2O, NH_3, HSO_4^-, HCO_3^- are considered amphiprotic substances.

$$H_2O + H_2O = H_3O^+ + OH^-$$

The above equation illustrates that water (H_2O) is amphiprotic and therefore can act as either a Brönsted-Lowry acid or base.

SKILLS 3.1XXXI *GIVEN PROPERTIES, IDENTIFY SUBSTANCES AS ARRHENIUS ACIDS OR ARRHENIUS BASES.*

Directions: Underline the <u>acid</u> and (circle) the base in the following reactions.

7 Question: $KOH(aq) + HNO_3(aq) \rightarrow KNO_3(aq) + H_2O(l)$

8 Question: $Ca(OH)_2(aq) + H_2SO_4(aq) \rightarrow CaSO_4(aq) + 2H_2O(l)$

9 Question: $NaOH(aq) + HCl(aq) \rightarrow NaCl(aq) + H_2O$

B – ACID-BASE REACTIONS

NEUTRALIZATION

Acid-base neutralization pertains to the reaction that occurs when equivalent quantities of an acid and a hydroxide are mixed. One mole of hydrogen ions will react with one mole of hydroxide ions to form water.

$$H^+ + OH^- \rightarrow H_2O$$

In acid-base neutralization reactions, the products are a salt and water.

$$NaOH + HCl \rightarrow NaCl + H_2O$$

ACID-BASE TITRATION

The molarity of an acid (or base) of unknown concentration can be determined by slowly combining it with a base (or acid) of known molarity. The acid or base solution of a known molarity is called the **standard solution**. This process of metering a standard solution into a solution of unknown concentration is called **titration**. During titration, when the molar quantities of acid and base mixed are equal, neutralization has occurred. This point of neutralization is called the "equivalence point."

The molarity of a solution of unknown concentration can be calculated from an understanding of the molar relationship involved. By knowing the concentration of the standard solution and the volumes of both solutions needed to reach the equivalence point, the following procedure is used to find the molarity of the unknown solution:

- After writing the balanced equation, the molar ratio of the reactants and products can be determined from the coefficients.

- By using the following equation, the number of moles of standard solution required to neutralize the solution of unknown concentration can be determined.

moles of known solute = volume of solution in liters x molarity

- By molar ratios, determine the moles of the solution of unknown concentration that were used.

$$\frac{\textbf{moles of known}}{\textbf{moles of unknown}} = \frac{\textbf{liters of known x molarity of known}}{\textbf{liters of known x molarity of unknown}}$$

- By substituting in the above equation, find the molarity of the solution of unknown concentration. When **monoprotic acids**, which provide one proton per molecule, or bases which can accept one proton per molecule are used, the following titration equation, as stated in *Reference Table T* is used: $M_A V_A = M_B V_B$

molarity of acid x volume of acid = molarity of base x volume of base

SAMPLE PROBLEM
How many milliliters of 0.5 M NaOH solution are required to neutralize 50 ml of 0.2 M HCl solution?

SOLUTION
Since both the acid and base are monoprotic, the volumes (given in milliliters) can be convert to liters and use the equation.

liters of acid x molarity of acid = liters of base x molarity of base

$$0.050 \text{ L} \times 0.2 \text{ M} = V_B \times 0.5 \text{ M}$$

$$\frac{\overset{0.1}{\cancel{0.050} \text{ L} \times 0.2 \cancel{\text{M}}}}{\underset{1}{\cancel{0.5 \text{ M}}}} = V_B$$

$$V_B = \textbf{0.002 liters} \text{ (answer)}$$

10 If 50 milliliters (mL) of a 0.01 M HCl solution is required to neutralize exactly 25 milliliters (mL) of NaOH, what is the concentration of the base?
   (1) 0.01 M   (2) 0.02 M   (3) 0.00005 M   (4) 0.04 M

11 How many moles of NaOH are required to exactly neutralize 0.50 liter of 2.0 M HCl?
   (1) 1.0   (2) 2.0   (3) 0.50   (4) 4.0

12 How many milliliters of 2.0 M HCl are required to exactly neutralize 10. milliliters of 3.0 M NaOH?
   (1) 5.0   (2) 15   (3) 20   (4) 30

13 As 0.1 M HCl is added to 0.1 M KOH, the pH of the basic solution
   (1) decreases and basicity decreases
   (2) increases and basicity decreases
   (3) decreases and basicity increases
   (4) increases and basicity increases

14 If 50. milliliters of a 1.0 M NaOH solution is needed to exactly neutralize 10. milliliters of an HCl solution, the molarity of the HCl solution is
   (1) 1.0 M   (2) 0.20 M   (3) 5.0 M   (4) 10. M

15 If 50. milliliters of 0.50 M HCl is used to completely neutralize 25 milliliters of KOH solution, what is the molarity of the base?
   (1) 1.0 M   (2) 0.25 M   (3) 0.50 M   (4) 2.5 M

16 Which equation represents a neutralization reaction?
   (1) $CaO + H_2O \rightarrow Ca(OH)_2$
   (2) $2HCl + Zn \rightarrow ZnCl_2 + H_2$
   (3) $H_2SO_4 + CaCO_3 \rightarrow CaSO_4 + H_2O + CO_2$
   (4) $HNO_3 + KOH \rightarrow KNO_3 + H_2O$

Directions: Complete the following simple neutralization reactions.

17 Question: $NaOH(aq) + HCl(aq) \rightarrow$

18 Question: $Ca(OH)_2(aq) + H_2SO_4(aq) \rightarrow$

19 Question: $KOH(aq) + HNO_3(aq) \rightarrow$

C – SALTS

A **salt** is an ionic compound containing positive ions other than hydrogen and negative ions other than hydroxide. Most salts are strong electrolytes and are considered to be completely dissociated in aqueous solution. Some salts in aqueous solution react with the water to form solutions that are acidic or basic.

This process is called **hydrolysis**, and it is considered to be the opposite of a **neutralization reaction**. For example, in a neutralization reaction, an acid and base react to form a salt and water. In hydrolysis, the salt is added to the water to form the acid and base, which originally formed the salt. Of the various reactions that occur when salts react with water, four cases may be distinguished. They are:

- A salt of a strong acid and a strong base forms a neutral solution with a pH of about 7. An example is NaCl, formed from the strong acid, HCl, and the strong base NaOH.

- A salt of a weak acid and a strong base forms a basic solution with a pH of greater than 7. An example is $NaC_2H_3O_2$, which is formed from acetic acid, $HC_2H_3O_2$ (acetic acid is also shown as CH_3COOH), a weak acid, and the strong base NaOH.

- A salt of a strong acid and a weak base forms an acidic solution with a pH of less than 7. An example is NH_4Cl, which is formed from the strong acid, HCl, and the weak base, NH_4OH.

- A salt of a weak acid and base forms a solution that may be acidic or basic, or neutral, depending on the ionization constants of the products. An example is $NH_4C_2H_3O_2$ which is formed from the weak acid, acetic acid, $HC_2H_3O_2$, and the weak base ammonium hydroxide, NH_4OH.

🌐 **REAL WORLD CONNECTIONS**

SWIMMING POOL CHEMISTRY

Chemical treatment of swimming pools to control bacteria is usually done by the use of the addition of halogen salts. The salts of chlorine, bromine, and iodine are commonly dissolved in pools in parts per million (ppm). pH regulation at about 7.2 to 7.6 is usually required to keep pools slightly alkaline. This is accomplished by the addition of sodium carbonate. In order to lower the pH the addition of sodium acid sulfate ($NaHSO_4$) in small amounts.

pH

The logarithm (exponent) of the reciprocal (negative logarithm) of the hydrogen ion concentration is called **pH**. Therefore, if the hydrogen ion concentration is 1 x 10^{-5}, its reciprocal would be 1 x 10^5, and its logarithm (exponent) is 5. Its pH is expressed as 5. The pH of a solution indicates the concentration of hydrogen ions (acid strength) in a solution.

A pH of 7 is neutral. A pH of less than 7 is acidic; pH greater than 7 is basic. Pure water has a pH of 7 at 25°C. Mathematically, pH is expressed as pH $-\log[H_3O^+]$. On the pH scale, each decrease of one unit of pH represents a ten-fold increase in hydronium ion concentration.

SKILLS 3.1XXXII *IDENTIFY SOLUTIONS AS ACID, BASE, OR NEUTRAL BASED UPON pH.*

20 Which statement best describes a solution with a pH of 3?
  (1) It has an H_3O^+ ion concentration of 1 x 10^3 mol/L and is acidic.
  (2) It has an H_3O^+ ion concentration of 1 x 10^{-3} mol/L and is acidic.
  (3) It has an H_3O^+ ion concentration of 1 x 10^3 mol/L and is basic.
  (4) It has an H_3O^+ ion concentration of 1 x 10^{-3} mol/L and is basic.

pH SCALE
Acid & Base Identification

	14	
BASES	13 **13.0**	lye
	12.2	lime
	12 **12.0**	ammonia
	11 **11.1**	Milk of Magnesia
	10	
	9	
	8.5	sea water
	8 **8.1**	Baking Soda
	8.0	Lake Ontario water
NEUTRAL	7 **7.0**	distilled water
	6	
	5.6	unpolluted rain
	5 **5.0**	tomatoes
	4	
ACIDS	**3.5**	orange juice
(Acid Rain)	3 **3.0**	carbonated drinks
	2.8	vinegar
	2 **2.0**	lemon juice
	1.2	sulfuric acid
	1 **1.0**	hydrochloric acid
	1.0	battery acid
	0	

21 Phenolphthalein has a pink color in solution which has a pH of
  (1) 1   (2) 5   (3) 7   (4) 11

22 In a solution with a pH of 3, the color of
  (1) litmus is red   (3) phenolphthalein is red
  (2) litmus is blue   (4) phenolphthalein is blue

23 Which relationship between ion concentrations always exists in an aqueous solution that is basic?
  (1) $[H^+]$ equals zero   (3) $[H^+]$ is less than $[OH^-]$
  (2) $[H^+]$ equals $[OH^-]$ (4) $[H^+]$ is greater than $[OH^-]$

24 Which pH value represents a solution with the lowest OH^- ion concentration?
  (1) 1   (2) 7   (3) 10   (4) 14

REAL WORLD CONNECTIONS

Cleaning agents loosen or dissolve fats and oils which bind dirt to surfaces. Sanitation requires the control of bacteria, mold, and virus growth which may endanger the health of the individual. Water alone is not a good cleaning agent since it is a polar solvent and grease is non-polar. Soaps or detergents and disinfectant added to water make an effective solution for cleaning and sanitation.

Soaps are the metallic salts of fatty acids having a chain of 10-18 carbon atoms. The most common soaps are sodium and potassium soaps of stearic or palmitic acids. Sodium soaps, like sodium stearate, are hard and widely used. The potassium soaps tend to lather easily and are used in creams and cosmetics. Soap is produced in the process of **saponification**. Melted fats react with strong alkali to produce glycerol and soap.

©Stich

melted fats	+	strong bases	→	glycerol	+	soap
(glycerol stearate)		(sodium hydroxide)	→	(sodium stearate)		$CH_3(CH_2)_{16}COO^-Na^+$

Acid rain results from the wastes. Industrial smoke and exhaust emissions (mostly sulfur dioxide and nitrogen oxide) pollute the air so much that precipitation becomes acid. This acidic rain falls into the lakes and surrounding water sheds, lowering the pH of the water making it impossible for animals and plants to survive.

INTERNATIONAL EFFECTS OF ACID RAIN

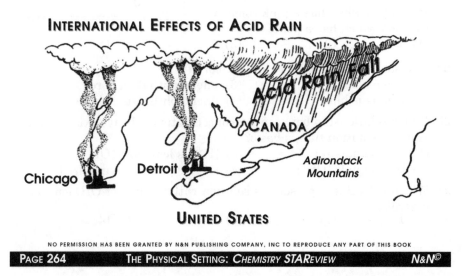

Household chemicals used to unclog drains contain both potassium hydroxide (KOH) and sodium hypochlorite (NaOCl). These substances are very caustic, and small children are known to swallow them. Some cleaning agents contain quaternary ammonium compounds.

- Commercial **drain cleaners** use the saponification reaction to remove grease that collects in drain pipes. These products contain lye (sodium hydroxide) which, when added to the grease in the drain should convert the fats to soap. They are extremely corrosive and must be handled carefully.

- **Bleaching** – NaOCl and CaOCl$_2$ are the most common chlorine compounds used. Chlorine, in the presence of a strong soap, ammonia, or an acid like vinegar forms a poisonous chlorine gas. Peroxide bleaches are mild and easily decompose to release oxygen. They are used to bleach protein and cellulose fibers.

Buffers – If the proper ions are present in a weakly acidic or basic solution, the pH of those solutions tend to remain the same regardless of the addition of other ion; e.g. a solution of acetic acid with a high concentration of sodium acetate also in an ammonium water solution with a high concentration of ammonium chloride. These salts are called buffer salts.

Blood acidosis/alkalosis – Both pulmonary (lungs) and renal (kidneys) functions act to compensate for disturbances in acid/base balance to maintain blood pH at 7.37 to 7.43 by altering the plasma concentration of the HCO$_3^-$ (bicarbonate) ion.

D – NORMALITY

In solving titration problems, as long as the acid and base are monoprotic, (by using the above equation), the concentration of either can easily be determined, if the concentration of one of them is known. However, if one of the two (either the acid or base) are diprotic (H$_2$SO$_4$), or triprotic (H$_3$PO$_4$), a complication arises.

To overcome this complication, chemists have devised an expression of concentration, which is concerned with the amount of hydrogen ions given off by an acid or accepted by a base. For example, since a mole of HCl molecules can donate a mole of H$^+$ (recall that one mole of H$^+$ weighs 1g.), it is called a monoprotic acid. It is capable of supplying 1 gram-equivalent of H^+. A solution of one mole of a monoprotic acid would be called a 1 molar solution (1M) or a 1 normal solution (1N). A mole of a diprotic acid, such as H_2SO_4, is considered 2 normal (2N) and can supply 2 gram equivalents of H^+. H_3PO_4 is a triprotic acid. It can supply 3 gram equivalents of H^+ per mole of acid molecules and is considered 3N.

25 Question: What is the normality of 1 liter of a 3 molar solution of H_3PO_4?

The normality of bases is classified in the same manner. For example, NaOH will break up so that one OH^- ion is produced for every molecule broken up. Therefore, NaOH is called a **monoprotic base**, and a mole of this base will be capable of accepting 1 mole of H^+, so it is considered a 1 gram-equivalent base. A 1M solution of $Mg(OH)_2$ is 2 normal (2N). Mathematically, the relationship between reacting acids and bases includes their volumes and their concentrations expressed in normality, similar to monoprotic acids and bases. For example:

Acid Vol. x Acid Normality = Base Vol. x Base Normality

Expressing the concentration in normality allows the use of diprotic and triprotic acids or bases in the equation. Although normality is no longer a suggested way to express concentration, it will probably be in common usage for some time. A limitation of the normality scale is that a given solution may be more than one normality, depending on the reaction for which it is used and how much it ionizes in solution.

IONIZATION CONSTANT

☆ The equilibrium constant for the ionization of acids (K_a) is a convenient method for comparing the relative strength of acids. For the reaction:

$$HB(aq) = H^+(aq) + B^-(aq)$$

$$K_a = \frac{[H^+][B^-]}{[HB]}$$

Ionization constants can be calculated for all acids that are not completely ionized. For acids that are completely ionized there is no equilibrium. The denominator [HB] approaches zero and K_a approaches infinity. Ionization constants such as those used in the *Handbook for Chemistry and Physics* can be used in comparing the relative strength of acids. Note: The magnitude of the number indicates the strength of the acid.

For example, an acid with a $K_a = 1.8 \times 10^{-5}$ (although a weak acid) is stronger than an acid with $K_a = 1.0 \times 10^{-6}$.

The Ionization Constant For Water — K_w

Only 1×10^{-7} moles per liter of water molecules ionize at room temperature and standard pressure. When that small amount of water molecules do ionize, they break up into equal portions of hydrogen and hydroxide ions:

$$H_2O \rightarrow H^+ + OH^- \qquad \text{also} \qquad 2\,H_2O \rightarrow H_3O^+ + OH^-$$

The molar proportions of the equation above are: $1 \rightarrow 1 + 1$. Therefore, if 1×10^{-7} moles per liter of water molecules ionizes, it will form 1×10^{-7} moles per liter H^+ and 1×10^{-7} moles per liter OH^-. Since water is such a weak electrolyte, its concentration is considered a constant. The equilibrium constant expression for water would be:

$$K_{eq} = \frac{[H^+]\,[OH^-]}{[H_2O]}$$

However, as stated above, for practical purposes, the concentration of water is a constant. Since the product of two constants is another constant, (in this case called K_w) the equilibrium expression for water is written as follows:

$$K_w = [H^+]\,[OH^-]$$

Therefore, as shown above, it follows that in water and aqueous solutions the product of the hydrogen ion concentration and the hydroxide ion concentration is a constant at constant temperature. This constant, K_w, is useful in solving problems involving hydrogen ion and hydroxide ion concentrations.

Substituting the molar concentrations of hydrogen and hydroxide ions into the formula, a numerical constant at 25°C for the ionization of water per liter can be derived.

$$K_w = [H^+]\,[OH^-]$$
$$K_w = [1 \times 10^{-7}]\,[1 \times 10^{-7}] = 1.0 \times 10^{-14}$$

Note: in pure water, $[H^+] = [OH^-] = 1.0 \times 10^{-7}$ at 25° C

$$pH = -\log[H^+]$$
$$= -\log[1.0 \times 10^{-7}]$$
$$pH = 7$$

Note: As the H^+ increases, the OH^- decreases. For Example:

$H^+ = 1 \times 10^{-2}$ moles/liter $\qquad\qquad OH^- = 1 \times 10^{-12}$ moles/liter

$$H^+ + OH^- = 1 \times 10^{-14} \text{ moles/liter}$$

PERFORMANCE INDICATOR 3.1
ASSESSMENTS

PART A – MULTIPLE CHOICE

1 Given the reaction:

$$2NaOH + H_2SO_4 \rightarrow Na_2SO_4 + 2H_2O$$

How many milliliters of 1 M NaOH are needed to exactly neutralize 100 milliliters of 1 M H_2SO_4?
(1) 50 mL   (3) 300 mL
(2) 200 mL   (4) 400 mL

2 According to the *Brönsted-Lowry Theory*, H_2O is considered to be a base when it
(1) donates an electron   (3) donates a proton
(2) accepts an electron   (4) accepts a proton

3 Given the neutralization reaction:

$$H_2SO_4 + 2KOH \rightarrow K_2SO_4 + 2HOH$$

Which compound is a salt?
(1) KOH   (3) K_2SO_4
(2) H_2SO_4 (4) HOH

4 According to the *Arrhenius Theory*, which list of compounds includes only bases?
(1) KOH, $Ca(OH)_2$, and CH_3OH
(2) KOH, NaOH, and LiOH
(3) LiOH, $Ca(OH)_2$, and $C_2H_4(OH)_2$
(4) NaOH, $Ca(OH)_2$, and CH_3COOH

5 Given the reaction:

$$NH_3(g) + H_2O(l) \leftrightarrow NH_4^+(aq) + OH^-(aq)$$

Which is a conjugate acid-base pair?
(1) $H_2O(l)$ and $NH_4^+(aq)$ (3) $NH_3(g)$ and $OH^-(aq)$
(2) $H_2O(l)$ and $NH_3(g)$ (4) $NH_3(g)$ and $NH_4^+(aq)$

6 Which compound reacts with an acid to form a salt and water?
(1) CH3Cl   (3) KCl
(2) CH_3COOH (4) KOH

7 How many milliliters of 0.20 M HCl are needed to exactly neutralize 40. milliliters of 0.40 M KOH?
(1) 20. mL   (2) 40. mL   (3) 80. mL   (4) 160 mL

8 Which compound is a salt?
(1) CH_3OH (2) $C_6H_{12}O_6$ (3) $H_2C_2O_4$ (4) $KC_2H_3O_2$

9 Given the equation: $H^+ + OH^- \rightarrow H_2O$
Which type of reaction does the equation represent?
(1) esterification   (3) hydrolysis
(2) decomposition   (4) neutralization

10 What is the pH of a 0.00001 molar HCl solution?
(1) 1   (2) 9   (3) 5   (4) 4

11 According to the *Brönsted-Lowry Theory*, an acid is any species that can
(1) donate a proton   (3) accept a proton
(2) donate an electron   (4) accept an electron

12 A salt of a strong acid and a strong base forms a
(1) acetic solution with a pH of less than 7
(2) neutral solution with a pH of about 7
(3) basic solution with a pH of more than 7
(4) basic solution with a pH of less than 7

13 In an aqueous solution, which substance yields hydrogen ions as the only positive ions?
(1) C_2H_5OH (3) KH
(2) CH_3COOH (4) KOH

14 What is the pH of a solution that results from the complete neutralization of an HCl solution with a NaOH solution?
(1) 1   (2) 7   (3) 10   (4) 4

15 How many milliliters of 0.20 M KOH are needed to completely neutralize 90.0 milliliters of 0.10 M HCl?
(1) 25 mL   (2) 45 mL   (3) 90. mL   (4) 180 mL

Indicator	Result
red litmus	blue
blue litmus	blue
phenolphthalein	pink

16 The results of testing a colorless solution with three indicators are shown in the table at the right. Which formula could represent the solution tested?
(1) NaOH(aq)   (3) $C_6H_{12}O_6(aq)$
(2) HCl(aq)   (4) $C_{12}H_{22}O_{11}(aq)$

17 What is the pH of a 0.001 M HCl solution?
(1) 14   (2) 11   (3) 3   (4) 7

18 In an acid solution, the $[H^+]$ ion is found to be 1×10^{-2} mole per liter. What is the $[OH^-]$ ion in moles per liter?
(1) 1×10^{-2} (2) 1×10^{-7} (3) 1×10^{-12} (4) 1×10^{-14}

19 Which of the following 0.1 M solutions has the *lowest* pH?
  (1) 0.1 M NaOH
  (2) 0.1 M CH_3OH
  (3) 0.1 M NaCl
  (4) 0.1 M HCl

20 The diagram at the right shows an apparatus used to test the conductivity of various materials. Which aqueous solution will cause the bulb to light? 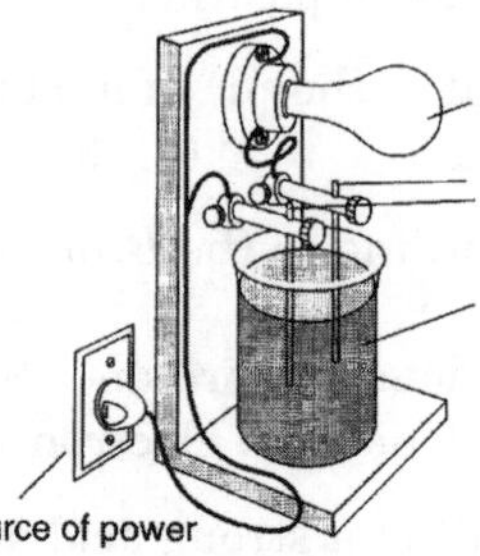
  (1) $C_6H_{12}O_6(aq)$
  (2) $C_{12}H_{22}O_{11}(aq)$
  (3) $CH_3OH(aq)$
  (4) $LiOH(aq)$

Bulb

Electrodes

Aqueous solution

Source of power

21 Which 0.1 M solution will turn phenolphthalein pink?
  (1) $HBr(aq)$
  (2) $CO_2(aq)$
  (3) $LiOH(aq)$
  (4) $CH_2OH(aq)$

22 Which compound is an electrolyte?
  (1) CH_3OH
  (2) CH_3COOH
  (3) $C_3H_5(OH)_3$
  (4) $C_{12}H_{22}O_{11}$

23 Which substance is classified as an Arrhenius base?
  (1) HCl   (2) NaOH   (3) $LiNO_3$ (4) $KHCO_3$

24 As the hydrogen ion concentration of an aqueous solution increases, the hydroxide ion concentration of this solution will
  (1) decrease
  (2) increase
  (3) remain the same

PART B - CONSTRUCTED-RESPONSE

Directions: Refer to the *Chemistry Reference Tables K, L,* and *M* to answer the following constructed-response questions.

Table K
Common Acids

Formula	Name
$HCl(aq)$	hydrochloric acid
$HNO_3(aq)$	nitric acid
$H_2SO_4(aq)$	sulfuric acid
$H_3PO_4(aq)$	phosphoric acid
$H_2CO_3(aq)$ or $CO_2(aq)$	carbonic acid
$CH_3COOH(aq)$ or $HC_2H_3O_2(aq)$	ethanoic acid (acetic acid)

Table L
Common Bases

Formula	Name
$NaOH(aq)$	sodium hydroxide
$KOH(aq)$	potassium hydroxide
$Ca(OH)_2(aq)$	calcium hydroxide
$NH_3(aq)$	aqueous ammonia

Table M
Common Acid–Base Indicators

Indicator	Approximate pH Range for Color Change	Color Change
methyl orange	3.2–4.4	red to yellow
bromthymol blue	6.0–7.6	yellow to blue
phenolphthalein	8.2–10	colorless to pink
litmus	5.5–8.2	red to blue
bromcresol green	3.8–5.4	yellow to blue
thymol blue	8.0–9.6	yellow to blue

1 Question: Write the balanced formula equation for the neutralization reaction that takes place between NaOH and H_2SO_4. [1]

2 Question: Using mole equivalents, describe how acids and bases neutralize each other. [1]

3 Question: State how the concentration of H_3O^+ ions compares to the concentration of OH^- ions in a solution that has a pH of 5. [1]

4 Question: State how the concentration of H_3O^+ ions change as solutions treated with bromcresol green change from yellow to blue. [1]

5 Question: A solution tested with litmus paper turned the litmus paper blue. Describe how the concentration of the hydronium ion compares to the concentration of the hydroxide ion in the solution. [1]

PART C – EXTENDED CONSTRUCTED-RESPONSE

Statement A: Electrolytes are substances that will conduct an electric current when dissolved into solution. Soluble salts and aqueous solutions of acids and bases are electrolytes. A substance that produces a large number of ions in solution is said to be a strong electrolyte and will conduct electricity more readily than a weak electrolyte that only produces a relatively few ions in solution.

1   **Question**: Illustrate the dissociation of HCl and NaOH into their component ions and tell why they are considered to be electrolytes. [2]

2   **Question**: Explain why a 2-M solution of HCl will be a better conductor of electricity than a 1-M solution of HCl. [1]

3   **Question**: When glucose ($C_6H_{12}O_6$) and methanol (CH_3OH) are dissolved into water the resulting solutions do not conduct an electric current. State one reason why they are not considered to be electrolytes. [1]

Statement B: As the result of acid rain, many of the lakes in the Adirondack region of New York State are now "dead" lakes because the pH of the water is too acidic to support freshwater aquatic life. This same acid rain falls on the lakes of the Hudson Valley, yet these lakes are not in danger of becoming acidic due to the fact that the calcium carbonate that makes up the limestone of the region helps to neutralize the acid in the rain.

4   **Question**: Explain how the H_3O^+ ion concentration in the lake water of the Adirondacks compares to the H_3O^+ ion concentration of the lake water in the Hudson Valley? [1]

5   **Question**: Describe one procedure that you might do to make the lake water in the Adirondacks less acidic. [1]

Statement C: Arrhenius acids are substances that produce H^+ ions in aqueous solution and Arrhenius bases are substances that produce OH^- ions in aqueous solution. Neutralization occurs when an Arrhenius acid reacts with an Arrhenius base to produce a salt plus water.

6 Questions:

    a   Write a balanced equation using the reactants HCl and NaOH. [1]

    b   Identify the Arrhenius acid, base, and salt by writing the correct formulas in the space provided. [2]

    c   Write a balanced equation to illustrate how the H^+ of the Arrhenius acid and OH^- ion of the Arrhenius base react together to neutralize each other and form water. [1]

Statement D: Titration is a laboratory process in which a volume of solution of known concentration is used to determine the concentration of another solution.

7 Question: During a titration in the laboratory, 200.0 mL of a .6 M HCl solution was used to neutralize 500.0 mL of a NaOH solution. Determine the molarity of the NaOH solution. [1]

Statement E: The *Brönsted-Lowry Theory* of acids and bases states that an acid is a proton (H^+) donor and a base is a proton acceptor.

8 Question: Using this criterion, identify an acid and a base in the following reaction and write their formulas in the space provided. [1]

$$NH_3 + HCl = NH_4^+ + Cl^-$$

Statement F: The acidity or alkalinity of a solution can be measured by its pH value which is equal to the negative log of the $[H_3O^+]$. On the pH scale, each decrease of one unit of pH represents a tenfold increase in the hydronium ion concentration.

9   **Question**: Three solution samples were tested and their pH values are recorded in the accompanying table. Identify the solution that is most acidic and describe one procedure you could do to make it less acidic. [2]

Solution Sample	pH
1	8.1
2	6.5
3	4.3

Statement G: A solution was measured to have a $[H_3O^+]$ concentration equal to 1.0×10^{-9}.

10 **Question**: Calculate the pH of this solution and state whether it is acidic or basic. [2]

11 **Question**: Will this solution have a $[H_3O^+]$ concentration that is greater or less than a solution which has a pH equal to 6 and how many times greater is the $[H_3O^+]$ of this solution compared to a solution that has a pH equal to 10? [2]

Statement H: A solution was tested with the indicators listed in the chart on page 275. The following results were observed: it turned blue with methyl violet, orange with methyl orange, and remained colorless with phenolphthalein.

12 **Question**: Based on the information presented, state whether there are more H_3O^+ or OH^- ions present in the solution. [1]

13 Question: Based upon the results recorded below, predict what color you think the solution would turn upon the addition of bromthymol blue. [1]

Indicator	Acid	Color Transition	Base	Transition Interval pH
Methyl violet	yellow	aqua	blue	0.0 – 1.6
Methyl orange	red	orange	yellow	3.2 – 4.4
Phenolphthalein	colorless	pink	red	8.2 – 10.6
Bromthymol blue	yellow	green	blue	3.0 – 4.6

PART D – LABORATORY SKILLS

ACID-BASE TITRATION

Acid-base titration is a form of volumetric analysis by which the unknown concentration of an acid (or base) solution by neutralizing it with a known concentration of base (or acid) can be determined.

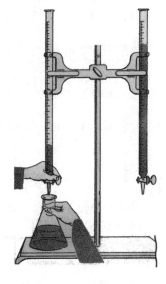

Recall that one reason for a reaction to "go to an end or to completion" is that water appears as a product. Also recall that acids increase the amount of hydrogen ions (H^+) as they ionize in water, and most bases increase the amount of hydroxide ions (OH^-) as they ionize in water. So that, when an acid solution is neutralized by a basic solution, the net ionic equation is:

$$H^+ + OH^- \rightarrow H_2O$$

When excess hydrogen ions are neutralized by hydroxide ions, the point of neutralization is reached ("equivalent point"). This point may be determined by use of an indicator whose end point (the pH at which it has a color change) is close to the pH at the equivalent point. Dilute solutions of sodium hydroxide or potassium hydroxide may be titrated against dilute hydrochloric or acetic acids. If burets are not available, calibrated medicine droppers or pipettes can be used. An example of an acid-base titration experiment is to find the unknown concentration of acetic acid in a vinegar solution.

After thoroughly cleaning the equipment, a few drops of phenolphthalein is added to the vinegar solution. A standardized solution of sodium hydroxide is titrated into the vinegar solution until the mixed solution just starts to turn pink for 30 seconds. At this point the volumes of both the acid and the base of known concentration are both noted, and the figures are keyed into the following formula:

$$\frac{\text{molarity}}{\text{of the acid}} \times \frac{\text{volume}}{\text{of the acid}} = \frac{\text{molarity}}{\text{of the base}} \times \frac{\text{volume}}{\text{of the base}}$$

$$N_a \times V_a = N_b \times V_b$$

The concentration of the acetic acid is calculated.

1   **Question**: If 50.0 milliliters of 3.0 M HNO_3 completely neutralized 150.0 milliliters of KOH, what was the molarity of the KOH solution?
(1) 1.0 M   (2) 4.5 M   (3) 3.0 M   (4) 6.0 M

2   **Question**: How many milliliters of 0.20 M HCl are needed to exactly neutralize 40. milliliters of 0.40 M KOH?
(1) 20. mL   (2) 40. mL   (3) 80. mL   (4) 160 mL

3   **Question**: If 20. milliliters of 1.0 M HCl was used to completely neutralize 40. milliliters of an NaOH solution, what was the molarity of the NaOH solution?
(1) 0.50 M   (2) 20. M   (3) 1.5 M   (4) 4.0 M

4   **Question**: What can be determined by acid-base titration?

5   **Question**: Why is it important that an acid-base titration go to completion?

6   **Question**: How is the "equivalent point" reached?

UNIT 10
NUCLEAR
CHEMISTRY

KEY IDEA 4 ENERGY EXISTS IN MANY FORMS, AND WHEN THESE FORMS CHANGE ENERGY IS CONSERVED.

PERFORMANCE INDICATOR 3.1

PERFORMANCE INDICATOR
4.4 *EXPLAIN THE BENEFITS AND RISKS OF RADIOACTIVITY.*

PERFORMANCE INDICATOR 5.3
COMPARE ENERGY RELATIONSHIPS WITHIN AN ATOM'S NUCLEUS TO THOSE OUTSIDE THE NUCLEUS.

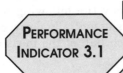

UNIT 10 – MAJOR UNDERSTANDINGS

☆ 3.1o Stability of an isotope is based on the ratio of neutrons and protons in its nucleus. Although most nuclei are stable, some are unstable and spontaneously decay, emitting radiation.

☆ 4.4a Each radioactive isotope has a specific mode and rate of decay (half-life).

☆ 5.3a A change in the nucleus of an atom that converts it from one element to another is called transmutation. This can occur naturally or can be induced by the bombardment of the nucleus with high-energy particles.

☆ 3.1p Spontaneous decay can involve the release of alpha particles, beta particles, positrons, and/or gamma radiation from the nucleus of an unstable isotope. These emissions differ in mass, charge, ionizing power, and penetrating power.

☆ 4.4b Nuclear reactions include natural and artificial transmutation, fission, and fusion.

☆ 4.4f There are benefits and risks

UNIT 10
NUCLEAR CHEMISTRY

This unit is related to Key Idea 4 for the text and Performance
Indicators 3.1, 4.4, and 5.3 for the assessments

INTRODUCTION

Isotopes of atoms can be stable or unstable. Stability of isotopes is
based on the number of protons and neutrons in an atom's nucleus. Some
nuclei are unstable and spontaneously decay, emitting radiation.

A – HALF-LIFE

The half-life of a radioactive isotope is the time required for one-half
of the nuclei of a given sample of that isotope to disintegrate. The decay
of radioactive elements occurs erratically, so that a small amount might
decay one day and a large amount might decay the following month.
Scientists, knowing that the mass of an atom is essentially derived from
its nucleus, have picked a span of time in which half of the mass of the
sample has decayed.

UNIT 10 – MAJOR UNDERSTANDINGS (CONTINUED)

associated with fission and
fusion reactions.

☆ 4.4c Nuclear reactions can be
represented by equations that
include symbols which
represent atomic nuclei (with
mass number and atomic
number), subatomic particles
(with mass number and
charge), and/or emissions such
as gamma radiation.

☆ 5.3b Energy released in a
nuclear reaction (fission or
fusion) comes from the
fractional amount of mass that
is converted into energy.
Nuclear changes convert
matter into energy.

☆ 5.3c Energy released during
nuclear reactions is much

greater than the energy
released during chemical
reactions.

☆ 4.4e There are inherent risks
associated with radioactivity
and the use of radioactive
isotopes. Risks can include
biological exposure, long-term
storage and disposal, and
nuclear accidents.

☆ 4.4d Radioactive isotopes
have many beneficial uses.
Radioactive isotopes are used
in medicine and industrial
chemistry for radioactive
dating, tracing chemical and
biological processes, industrial
measurement, nuclear power,
and detection and treatment
of diseases.

Sample Problem:
If the half-life of the isotope ^{42}K is 12.4 hours, and if you had 100 grams of the isotope, how much would you have left after 37.2 hours?

Solution:

Divide the total time by $\dfrac{37.2 \text{ hours}}{12.4 \text{ hours}}$ = **3 half-life periods**

During the first half-life period,
the following would occur: **100 g → 50.0 g**

During the second half-life period,
the following would occur: **50 g → 25.0 g**

During the third half-life period,
the following would occur: **25 g → 12.5 g**

        Answer: **12.5 grams**

Note: It is strongly suggested that you should know the definition for half-life and then use your own good reasoning power, instead of using equations or formulas, to solve such problems.

Always Make A chart

SKILLS 4.4I *CALCULATE THE INITIAL AMOUNT, THE FRACTION REMAINING, OR THE HALF-LIFE OF A RADIOACTIVE ISOTOPE, GIVEN TWO OF THE THREE VARIABLES.*

1   At the end of 12 days, $^1/_4$ of an original sample of a radioactive element remains. What is the half life of the element?
   (1) 24 days   (2) 48 days   (3) 3 days   ④ 6 days

2   An original sample of a radioisotope had a mass of 10 grams. After 2 days, 5 grams of the radioisotope remains unchanged. What is the half-life of this radioisotope?
   (1) 1 day   ② 2 days   (3) 5 days   (4) 4 days

3   What is the number of hours required for potassium-42 to undergo 3 half-life periods? [Refer to *Reference Table N.*]
   (1) 6.2 hours   (2) 12.4 hours   (3) 24.8 hours   (4) 37.2 hours

4   After 3 half-life periods, 12.5 grams of an original sample of radioisotope remains unchanged. What was the mass of the original sample?
   (1) 250.0 g   (2) 50.0 g   ③ 100. g   (4) 200. g

5   How many grams of a 32-gram sample of ^{32}P will remain after 71.5 days?
                               14.3days
   ① 1   (2) 2   (3) 8   (4) 4

6   A radioactive isotope has a half-life of 10 years. What fraction of the original mass will remain unchanged after 50 years?
   (1) $^1/_2$ (2) $^1/_8$ (3) $^1/_{16}$ (4) $^1/_{32}$

B – NATURAL RADIOACTIVITY

Radioactivity is the spontaneous disintegration of the nucleus of an atom with the emission of particles and/or radiant energy. Some naturally occurring elements are radioactive. Therefore, the term **natural radioactivity** is used.

When the nucleus of an element contains a disproportionate amount of neutrons, as compared to protons, the nucleus starts to emit particles. It is then classified as radioactive. Elements with an atomic number of higher than 82 (Lead) fall into this category. When one element is changed to another element because of change in the nucleus, the change is called **transmutation**.

DIFFERENCE IN EMANATIONS

Emanations differ from each other in mass, charge, penetrating power, and ionizing power. The nuclear disintegration of naturally radioactive atoms produces alpha particles, beta particles and gamma radiation.

Alpha decay – When an alpha particle is given off as the result of nuclear disintegration, the reaction is called alpha decay. Alpha particles can be considered helium nuclei because they consist of 2 protons and 2 neutrons. Therefore, they have a mass of four **amu** (atomic mass unit). An atom that emits an alpha particle is called an **alpha emitter**.

When an atom emits an alpha particle, the atomic number is reduced by 2 and the mass number is reduced by 4.

Example: $^{226}_{88}\text{Ra} \rightarrow {}^{4}_{2}\text{He} + {}^{222}_{86}\text{Rn}$

Beta decay – Beta particles are high-speed electrons. When a beta particle is given off as the result of neutron disintegration, the reaction is called beta decay. The atom that emits a beta particle is called a **beta emitter**.

When an atom emits a beta particle, the atomic number is increased by 1 and the mass number remains the same.

Example: $^{234}_{90}\text{Th} \rightarrow {}^{234}_{91}\text{Pa} + {}^{0}_{-1}\text{e}$

7   **Question**: If a beta particle is a fast moving electron and electrons are found outside of the nucleus, what is the beta particle doing in the nucleus, in the first place?

REAL WORLD CONNECTIONS
ELECTROMAGNETIC SPECTRUM

The **electromagnetic spectrum** includes the entire range of radiation – extending in frequency from approximately 10^{23} hertz to 0 hertz or, in corresponding wavelengths, from 10^{-13} centimeter to infinity. The forms of radiation include (in order of decreasing frequency) cosmic-ray photons, gamma rays, X-rays, ultraviolet radiation, visible light, infrared radiation, microwaves, and radio waves.

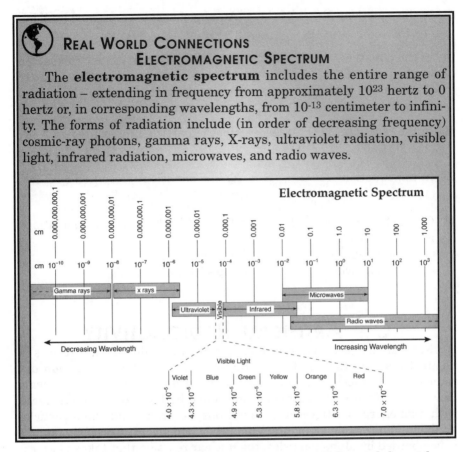

Gamma radiation – Gamma rays are not particles and do not have mass or charge. They are similar to high energy X-rays. Most nuclear changes involve the emission of gamma rays, reducing the energy content of the nucleus without affecting its charge or mass. The detection and study of radioactivity is made possible by its ionizing, fluorescent, and photographic effects.

Separation of emanations is possible by an electric field or magnetic field. In such an electric field, alpha particles are deflected toward the negative electrode, beta particles toward the positive electrode, but gamma rays are not affected by the field.

SKILLS 3.1 IX *DETERMINE THE DECAY MODE AND WRITE NUCLEAR EQUATIONS SHOWING ALPHA AND BETA DECAY.*

8 Given the equation: $X \rightarrow {}^{4}_{2}He + {}^{222}_{86}Rn$, the nucleus represented by X is

(1) ${}^{218}_{84}Po$ (2) ${}^{218}_{88}Po$ (3) ${}^{218}_{84}Ra$ (4) ${}^{226}_{88}Ra$

9 In the equation: $X \rightarrow {}_{2}^{4}\text{He} + {}_{85}^{216}\text{At}$, the element represented by X is

(1) Fr   (2) Bi   (3) Rn   (4) Ra

10 In the equation: ${}_{90}^{232}\text{Th} \rightarrow {}_{88}^{228}\text{Ra} + X$, which particle is represented by the letter X?

(1) an alpha particle   (3) a positron

(2) a beta particle   (4) a deuteron

11 In the reaction: ${}_{92}^{238}\text{U} \rightarrow X + {}_{2}^{4}\text{He}$, the particle represented by X is

(1) ${}_{90}^{234}\text{Th}$ (2) ${}_{92}^{234}\text{U}$ (3) ${}_{93}^{238}\text{Np}$ (4) ${}_{94}^{242}\text{Pu}$

12 In the equation: ${}_{15}^{31}\text{P} \rightarrow {}_{16}^{31}\text{S} + X$, the particle represented by X is

(1) ${}_{2}^{4}\text{He}$ (2) ${}_{0}^{1}\text{n}$ (3) ${}_{1}^{1}\text{H}$ (4) ${}_{-1}^{0}\text{e}$

13 Given the reaction: ${}_{88}^{226}\text{Ra} \rightarrow {}_{86}^{222}\text{Rn} + X$, which type of emanation is represented by X?

(1) alpha particle   (3) proton

(2) beta particle   (4) positron

C – ARTIFICIAL RADIOACTIVITY

Natural radioactivity occurs under natural conditions and results in natural transmutation. The products of natural transmutation are radioactive isotopes, which decay finally into a stable isotope of lead. However, elements can be made radioactive by bombarding their nuclei with high energy particles such as protons, neutrons, and alpha particles producing man-made elements. When the element nitrogen, for example, is bombarded by alpha particles, the nuclear reaction that takes place is:

alpha particle + nitrogen → proton + oxygen

$${}_{2}^{4}\text{He} + {}_{7}^{14}\text{N} \rightarrow {}_{1}^{1}\text{H} + {}_{8}^{17}\text{O}$$

As noted from the above reaction, isotopes of two new elements are formed. This is called **artificial transmutation.** The process includes the bombardment of nuclei by accelerated particles which cause nuclei to become unstable and may result in the formation of radioactive isotopes, or radioactive isotopes of new elements called **radioisotopes**. Another example follows:

$${}_{13}^{27}\text{Al} + {}_{2}^{4}\text{He} \rightarrow {}_{15}^{30}\text{P} + {}_{0}^{1}\text{n}$$

In the both of the above equations, note the following:

- The sum of the atomic masses (the superscripts) on the left must equal the total of atomic masses (the superscripts) on the right.

- The sum of the atomic numbers (the subscripts) on the left must equal the total of the atomic numbers (the subscripts) on the right.

- In an equation depicting artificial radioactivity, there are at least two reactants on the left side of the equation. In natural radioactivity equations, there appears only one reactant on the left side of the equation. The following example points out how the above suggestions work.

Problem: In the following reaction what nucleus is represented by X?

$$X + {}_{1}^{1}H \rightarrow {}_{3}^{6}Li + {}_{2}^{4}He$$

Solution: Noting that the sums of both superscripts of the completed right side of the equation are 10 and 5, respectively, and the sums on the incomplete left side are 1 and 1, respectively, the atomic mass and number of element X can be easily determined.

Since the atomic number identifies the element, this element with an atomic number of 4 is Beryllium, which has an atomic mass of 9.

Therefore, the answer is written (at right): ${}_{4}^{9}X = {}_{4}^{9}Be$

Accelerators – Accelerators are used to give charged particles sufficient kinetic energy to overcome electrostatic forces and penetrate the nucleus. Electric and magnetic fields are used to accelerate these charged particles.

🌍 REAL WORLD CONNECTIONS

"MAN-MADE" ELEMENTS

The last element to be discovered in nature was francium (Fr-87). It was discovered at the Curie Laboratory in Paris, France in 1939 by **Marguerite Perey**. Its longest lived isotope lasted 22 minutes. All of the elements above 87 in the periodic table were discovered by bombarding and splitting heavier, more unstable elements, such as uranium. These "man-made" elements are still being discovered. However, their half-lives range from a few seconds to milliseconds in quantities of fewer than 100 atoms. In the years since Madam Perey's discovery, the positive identification of newly discovered elements has become increasingly difficult. IUPAC has the responsibility to either reject or accept a new element's identification and name.

Source: *Chemical & Engineering News*, July 17, 1995

D – NUCLEAR ENERGY

In nuclear reactions, mass is converted to energy. Nuclear reactions involve energies a million or more times greater than ordinary chemical reactions. The energy changes are due to the the changes in binding energy as a result of what is called **mass defect**. In order to understand these reactions, it is necessary to clarify these terms.

MASS DEFECT

The mass of a free proton $(1.6725 \times 10^{-24}g)$ and the mass of a free neutron $(1.6748 \times 10^{-24}g)$ is known. Knowing that the nucleus of elements represents the total number of protons and neutrons, the mass of an element should be easily predicted by adding together the total mass of all neutrons and protons in the nucleus.

REAL WORLD CONNECTIONS

MANHATTAN PROJECT
CHEMICAL & ENGINEERING NEWS
JULY 17, 1995

Copyright © 1995 by theAmerican Chemical Society.

The first atomic bomb was tested at the Trinity site, Alamogordo, NM, on July 16, 1945. The development of the atomic bomb was the culmination of the Manhattan Project, an organized effort to develop the most powerful weapons ever known for use in ending World War II. A key event in the development of this weapon was the discovery of plutonium in 1941 by **Glenn T. Seaborg**, graduate student Arthur C. Wahl, and research fellow and chemistry instructor Joseph W. Kennedy.

"We discovered the isotope plutonium-238 first," said Seaborg. "But we were able to show after we produced the longer lived isotope plutonium-239 that it was fissionable with slow neutrons and hence was eligible material to be the explosive material in an atomic bomb. This led to the plutonium part of the Manhattan Project." The 1951 Nobel Laureate Seaborg also later developed a process for separating weapons-grade plutonium from uranium and fission products in nuclear reactors.

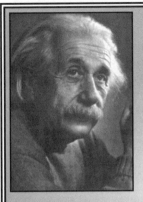
In the case of Helium with 2 neutrons and 2 protons in its nucleus, consider the following:

Mass of 2 free neutrons $= 1.6748 \times 10^{-24}g \times 2 = 3.3496 \times 10^{-24}g$

Mass of 2 free protons $\quad = 1.6725 \times 10^{-24}g \times 2 = 3.3450 \times 10^{-24}g$

Total Mass of 2 free protons and neutrons $= 6.6946 \times 10^{-24}g$

However, the sum of the masses of the nucleons in the Helium nucleus was found to be $6.641236 \times 10^{-24}g$. If one total is subtracted from the other, a total mass deficiency of $0.053364 \times 10^{-24}g$ for every Helium atom is found.

If this value is substituted for the mass factor in Einstein's equation, **E=mc²**, it can be shown that when nuclear particles merge to make up a nucleus, a great deal of energy is released. This occurs as this small amount of mass is changed into energy. The amount of energy released is called the **binding energy**. It is a measure of the stability of the atom formed. The greater the amount of energy released in the formation of the nucleus, the greater will be the amount of energy required to separate the nucleus into separate particles.

FISSION REACTION

A fission reaction results in the "splitting" of heavier nuclei into lighter ones. Fission is brought about by a nucleus capturing slow moving neutrons, which results in the nucleus becoming very unstable. The unstable nucleus splits to form fission fragments of elements of lighter weight, liberation of energy, and release of two or more neutrons. The liberation of energy is the result of conversion of mass into energy.

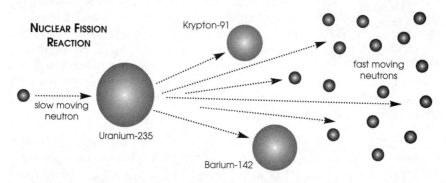

Only unstable elements of high atomic numbers can be fissioned. When a heavy element fissions, the new elements formed have a more stable configuration because of the greater binding energy per nucleon. In a nuclear reactor, the chain reaction can be controlled with control rods which limit the amount of interacting neutrons. In an atomic bomb, the chain reaction is not controlled.

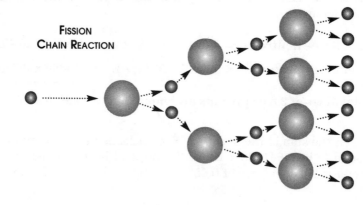

REAL WORLD CONNECTIONS
FISSION REACTORS

The energy of fission reactions is related directly with the decrease of mass that occurs. For every gram of uranium-235 that reacts, 80,000 kJ of energy is given off. This amount of energy compares with 30 kilojoule per gram for coal and 2.8 kilojoule per gram for exploding TNT.

However, fission reactions present many complications. First, is the concern with the process itself. During a fission reaction, a slow moving neutron splits a uranium-235 atom into two unequal pieces forming two different elements. In the process, it also produces neutron and beta particles. It is unknown what radioactive elements will be produced because each uranium-235 atom will split in different ways. The result may produce isotopes of rubidium (at number 37) and cesium (at number 55), while another breaks up into isotopes of bromine (at number 35) and lanthanum (at number 57). Yet another may yield isotopes of zinc (at number 530) and samarium (at number 62).

Second, there is concern with the products of the fission reaction. Of the 35 identified elements formed more than 200 isotopes have been identified as products of the fission of uranium-235. These products represent a dangerous hazard, especially strontium-90. In the form of strontium carbonate ($SrCO_3$), it is incorporated in the bones of animals and human beings.

Third, there is concern with the storage of these radioactive products. The amounts produced each month are staggering, and accidents have occurred despite all the precautions taken by the nuclear regulatory agencies. Beyond that, there is danger of fire, earthquakes, and explosion which could cause a "melt-down" with a release of deadly radiation.

BREEDER REACTORS

The supply of uranium-235 in Earth is finite. An alternative source would be to convert the more abundant isotope, uranium-238 into plutonium-239 (1) which can also undergo fission (2). This is shown in the following summary reaction [bracket denotes intermediate step].

Reaction 1: $^{238}_{92}U + ^{1}_{0}n \rightarrow \left[^{239}_{92}U \rightarrow ^{239}_{93}Np + ^{0}_{-1}e \right] \rightarrow ^{239}_{94}Pu + 2\,^{0}_{-1}e$

Reaction 2: $^{239}_{94}Pu + ^{1}_{0}n \rightarrow ^{90}_{38}Sr + ^{147}_{56}Ba + 3\,^{1}_{0}n$

Since the above produces more neutrons than it consumes, a fission reaction can then follow producing additional energy.

THE "TYPICAL" NUCLEAR REACTOR

The following represent a list of requirements for the operation of a nuclear reactor:

- **Fuels** – Uranium-233, uranium-235, and plutonium-239 are fissionable. Natural uranium (99.3% uranium-238 and 0.7% uranium-235), and enriched uranium (3 to 4 percent enrichment with uranium - 235) are commonly used as fuels. Uranium-233 produced from thorium-232 and plutonium-239 produced from uranium-238, are obtained as fuels in breeder reactors. Breeder reactors produce more

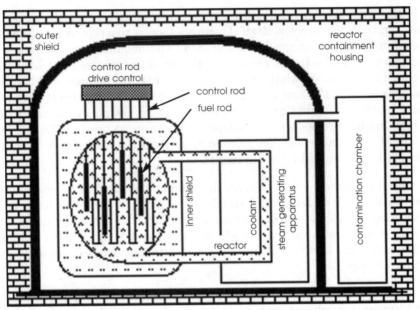

GENERAL NUCLEAR REACTOR AND POWER GENERATING SYSTEM

fuel than is consumed. Through a complex process, these fuels are used to make the uranium oxide which is packed in the fuel rods made of stainless steel.

- **Moderators** – For efficient nuclear fission, it is necessary to slow down the speed of the neutrons. Moderators are materials that have the ability to slow down neutrons quickly with little tendency to absorb them. Particles of similar mass such as hydrogen and its isotope deuterium have been found effective as moderators. The neutrons are slowed down most effectively by a head-on collision with a particle of similar mass. Water, heavy water, beryllium, and graphite are commonly used as moderators, which slow down the neutrons without capturing them.

- **Control rods** – The fission process in a reactor can be controlled by adjusting the number of neutrons available. Boron and cadmium are commonly used in control rods because they absorb neutrons very well. They are placed alongside the fuel rods and by withdrawing and inserting these rods the amount of neutrons available for fission is controlled. In the event of an emergency, these rods are inserted to completely absorb the neutrons needed for fission; and thereby, shut down the fission reaction.

- **Coolants** – Coolants are used to keep the temperatures generated by fission at reasonable levels within the reactor and to carry heat to heat exchanges and turbines so that it can be utilized in the production of energy. Water, heavy water, air, helium, carbon dioxide, molten sodium and molten lithium are examples of coolants. In some

reactors, the coolants also serve as a help to the moderator in the removal of heat from the reactor core, where the fuel rods are located, and help prevent a core melt down.

- **Shielding** – There are two shields used in nuclear reactors. The **internal shield**, made of a steel lining, protects the walls of the reactor from radiation damage. The **external shield**, made of high density concrete, acts as a radiation containment vessel in the event of a nuclear accident.

FUSION REACTION

When two light nuclei fuse into a heavier nucleus at high temperatures and pressures, an element of more stable configuration (with greater binding energy per nucleon) is formed. The mass of the heavier nucleus formed is less than the sum of the masses of the lighter nuclei. The difference in mass is converted into energy.

Fusion is the process of combining two light nuclei to form a heavier one. The energy released in a fusion reaction is much greater than in a fission reaction. Solar energy is probably the result of the fusion of ordinary hydrogen atoms to form helium. The nuclear reaction of a hydrogen bomb utilizes fission as a trigger for fusion. A typical fusion reaction occurs on the Sun and is represented by the following formula:

$$\,^2_1H + \,^2_1H \rightarrow \,^4_2He$$

The energy released by this fusion reaction has been calculated as 57.1 x 10^7 kJ per gram of reactant compared to 8.21 x 10^7 kJ per gram of reactant for a fission reaction. The energy produced in a fusion reaction would be about seven times the energy produced through fission. Nuclear fusion presents the most appealing method of producing great amounts of energy for many reasons.

- **Production** – The production process is safe and does not present a threat. That is, it can be much more easily controlled than other forms of energy producing and shuts down automatically. Also, the isotopes produced are not radioactive but "clean," stable isotopes, that reduce the pollution threat to life.

- **Fuels** – The isotopes of hydrogen, ^2_1H (**deuterium**) and ^3_1H (**tritium**), are used as fuels. Heavy water (deuterium oxide) is obtained by concentrating the trace qualities present in water. Tritium is made by a nuclear reaction shown below:

$$^6_3Li + {}^1_0n \rightarrow {}^3_1H + {}^4_2He$$

The fuel deuterium is abundant and can be obtained cheaply from sea water. Tritium, another isotope of hydrogen is also used.

There are a number of considerations that must be addressed concerning fusion reactors including:

- There is a high energy requirement – Since each nucleus carries a positive charge, all nuclei repel one another with increasing strength as they are moved closer together. Consequently, for the nuclei to interact, they must have enough kinetic energy to overcome this repulsion.

- The magnitude of repulsion increases with charge. Therefore, only the nuclei of lowest possible charge can be used. Fusion with ordinary hydrogen, however, is very slow. Fusion reactions involving deuterium, or deuterium and tritium, are useful sources for the release of energy. Of these, the most rapid reaction is between deuterium and tritium. The thermonuclear approach, through the use of very high temperatures, appears to be very promising for controlled fusion. However, this requires temperatures of several million degrees Celsius.

Technical problems with nuclear fusion, such as the requirement of extremely high temperatures and their containment, continue to challenge nuclear scientists and engineers. Once begun, the containment of the reaction with such high temperatures is extremely difficult.

NO PERMISSION HAS BEEN GRANTED BY N&N PUBLISHING COMPANY, INC TO REPRODUCE ANY PART OF THIS BOOK

In order that the reaction be carried on in an area where it does not come in contact with materials which can break down, "magnetic bottles" were designed to contain the reaction. "Magnetic bottles" make use of strong magnetic fields and confine the reaction to an area where it does not come in contact with any materials except the magnetic field itself.

SKILLS 4.4II *COMPARE AND CONTRAST FISSION AND FUSION REACTIONS.*

14 During a nuclear reaction
(1) mass is gained
(2) mass is lost
(3) mass is converted to energy
(4) energy is converted to mass

15 Question: The Sun's energy is produced by what type of reaction?

16 Question: What is the reactant that produces the Sun's energy?

17 Question: Name one constructive use of radioactive energy.

18 Question: Name one pollution problem that results from nuclear fission.

SKILLS 4.4III *COMPLETE NUCLEAR EQUATIONS; PREDICT MISSING PARTICLES FROM NUCLEAR EQUATIONS.*

19 In the reaction: $^{6}_{3}Li + ^{1}_{0}n \rightarrow ^{4}_{2}He + ^{3}_{1}X$
The species represented by X is
(1) $^{2}_{1}H$ (2) $^{3}_{1}H$ (3) $^{3}_{2}He$ (4) $^{4}_{3}He$

20 In the reaction: $^{27}_{13}Al + ^{4}_{2}He \rightarrow ^{30}_{15}P + X$
The particle represented by X is
(1) a neutron
(2) a beta particle
(3) an electron
(4) an alpha particle

21 What is represented by X in the reaction? $X \rightarrow ^{14}_{7}N + ^{0}_{-1}e$

(1) $^{14}_{6}C$ (2) $^{13}_{6}C$ (3) $^{12}_{6}C$ (4) $^{11}_{6}C$

Directions: Complete the following nuclear equations:

22 Question: $^{238}_{92}U + ^{2}_{1}H \rightarrow$ _____ $+ ^{0}_{-1}e$

23 Question: $^{238}_{92}U + ^{14}_{7}N \rightarrow ^{251}_{99}Es +$ _____

24 Question: $^{59}_{27}Co +$ _____ $\rightarrow ^{56}_{25}Mn + ^{4}_{2}He$

25 Question: $^{23}_{11}Na + ^{2}_{1}H \rightarrow$ _____ $+ ^{1}_{1}H$

RADIOACTIVE WASTES

Environmental ecosystems which are finely balanced are threatened by the presence of radioactive wastes. The nuclear energy industry is working on this problem.

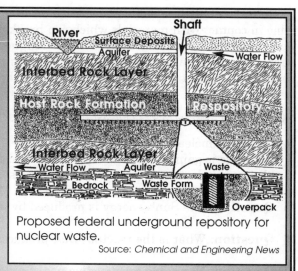

Proposed federal underground repository for nuclear waste.

Source: *Chemical and Engineering News*

However, serious problems still plague the safe disposal of such products as radioactive strontium-90, which has a half-life of 28.1 years. Even after 6 half-life periods, 168.6 years, enough will remain to cause great harm if it is not contained. The problem is that fission products from nuclear reactors are intensely radioactive and cannot be discarded. They must be stored for a long time or disposed of in special ways. Solid and liquid wastes, such as strontium-90 and cesium-137, are encased in special containers for permanent storage underground or in isolated areas.

Low level radioactive wastes may be diluted and released directly into the environment. Gaseous radioactive wastes such as radon-222, krypton-85, and nitrogen-16, are stored at safe levels for decay and then dispersed into the air.

USES OF RADIOISOTOPES

Radioactive Isotopes have the same physical and chemical properties as nonradioactive isotopes. The only difference is the instability of their nuclei. In physical and chemical reactions, they are both expected to behave the same way. This is the fundamental principle for the use of "tagged" or **tracer** isotopes. Age determination of both living and nonliving specimens, diagnosing, and treating diseases, and analytical biology and chemistry are just a few of the uses for radioactive isotopes.

In transmutation, when a neutron collides with an $^{238}_{92}U$ atom, it causes the atom to change into a new radioactive element as shown below:

$$^{238}_{92}U + ^{1}_{0}n \rightarrow ^{239}_{92}U \rightarrow ^{239}_{93}Np + ^{0}_{-1}e$$

Chemical reactivity – Since **radioisotopes** are chemically similar to stable isotopes of the same element, they can be used as tracers to follow the course of a reaction without seriously altering the chemical conditions. Many organic reaction mechanisms are studied by the use of carbon-14 as a tracer.

🌍 REAL WORLD CONNECTIONS

Radioactive Detectives – Rosalyn S. Yalow, born in New York City, was awarded the 1977 Nobel Prize in medicine for developing the technique called radioimmunoassay (RIA). The technique is an extraordinarily sensitive method of using radiotracers to detect the presence of minute amounts of drugs, hormones, antibiotics, and many other organic and inorganic substances. The process is used to provide early indications of disease and can be carried out on small amounts of tissue, blood, or other bodily fluids. A few examples of the use of radioactive tracers in medicine include:

- Red blood cells contain hemoglobin which contains iron. The rate at which injected ^{59}Fe appears in the blood provides a measurement of red blood cell production.

- Blood serum with ^{131}I injected into the body with the use of a detector placed over the heart, can determine the amount of blood pumped per minute.
- Fibrinogen, a soluble protein found in the blood tagged with radioactive iodine, can detect clots and embolisms (bubbles) by piling up against them to signal above average blood activity at that spot in a blood vessel or organ.

- Tagged tetrahydrocannabinol (marijuana's active component) shows that this product stays in the blood stream for 3-days, and its byproducts can be detected in the urine for 8 days.

Based on radioactivity – Radioisotopes are used in medical diagnosis, therapy, food preservation, and as a means of measuring the physical dimensions of many industrial products.

Isotopes with very short half-lives and which will be quickly eliminated from the body are used for diagnostic injections. Technetium-99 is used for pinpointing brain tumors. Iodine-131 is used for diagnosing thyroid disorders. Radium and cobalt-60 are used in cancer therapy. Radiation kills bacteria, yeasts, molds, and insect eggs in foods, permitting the food to be stored for a much longer time.

Based on half-life – Radioisotopes give a fairly consistent method of dating some geologic events. The ratio of uranium-238 to lead-206 in a mineral can be used to determine the age of the mineral. C-14 to C-12 ratio is used in dating living organisms

🌐 REAL WORLD CONNECTIONS

Carbon-14 has a half-life of approximately 5,568 years. Part of the CO_2 in the air is carbon-14. Plants take in CO_2 from the air, consequently fixing a quantity in its protoplasm. A gram of carbon from a living plant will radiate about 15 beta particles per minute. When the plant dies, it no longer takes in carbon-14. Scientists determine the age of old trees by comparing the radiation of beta particles of the old materials with that of present plants. In this manner, they can very accurately determine their age.

SKILLS 4.4IV *IDENTIFY SPECIFIC USES OF SOME RADIOISOTOPES SUCH AS I-131 IN DIAGNOSING AND TREATING THYROID DISORDERS; C-14 TO C-12 RATIO IN DATING LIVING ORGANISMS; U-238 TO PB-206 RATIO IN DATING GEOLOGICAL FORMATIONS; CO-60 IN TREATING CANCER.*

26 **Question**: Write a paragraph identifying and describing at least two (2) specific uses for radioisotopes in the health care field (medicine).

27 **Question**: Using complete sentences, describe the process and explain the value of radioactive dating. Also, provide at least two (2) specific examples.

ASSESSMENTS
PART A - MULTIPLE CHOICE

1   Which substance can be used as both a coolant and a moderator in a nuclear reactor?
    (1) heavy water   (3) graphite
    (2) carbon dioxide   (4) helium

2   A radioactive isotope used in the study of many organic reaction mechanisms is
    (1) carbon-12 (2) carbon-14 (3) oxygen-16   (4) oxygen-18

3   High energy is a requirement for fusion reactions to occur because the nuclei involved
    (1) attract each other because they have like charges
    (2) attract each other because they have unlike charges
    (3) repel each other because they have like charges
    (4) repel each other because they have unlike charges

4   Organic molecules react to form a product. These reactions may be studied by using
    (1) Sr-90   (2) Co-60   (3) N-16   (4) C-14

5   Which statement explains why fusion reactions are difficult to initiate?
    (1) Positive nuclei attract each other.
    (2) Positive nuclei repel each other.
    (3) Neutrons prevent nuclei from getting close enough to fuse.
    (4) Electrons prevent nuclei from getting close enough to fuse.

6   The radioisotope I-131 is used to
    (1) control nuclear reactors
    (2) determine the age of fossils
    (3) diagnose thyroid disorders
    (4) trigger fusion reactors

7   In which list can all particles be accelerated by an electric field?
    (1) alpha particles, beta particles, and neutrons
    (2) alpha particles, beta particles, and protons
    (3) alpha particles, protons, and neutrons
    (4) beta particles, protons, and neutrons

8   Given the nuclear reaction:

$$_{4}^{9}\text{Be} + X \rightarrow {}_{6}^{12}\text{C} + {}_{0}^{1}\text{n}$$

What is the identity of particle X?
    (1) alpha particle   (3) proton
    (2) beta particle   (4) neutron

9 A particle accelerator can increase the kinetic energy of
   (1) an alpha particle and a beta particle
   (2) an alpha particle and a neutron
   (3) a gamma ray and a beta particle
   (4) a neutron and a gamma ray

10 To make nuclear fission more efficient, which device is used in a nuclear reactor to slow the speed of neutrons?
   (1) internal shield   (3) control rod
   (2) external shield   (4) moderator

11 Which equation is an example of artificial transmutation?

   (1) $^{238}_{92}U \rightarrow \, ^4_2He + \, ^{234}_{90}Th$ (3) $^{14}_{6}C \rightarrow \, ^{14}_{7}N + \, ^0_{-1}e$

   (2) $^{27}_{13}Al + \, ^4_2He \rightarrow \, ^{30}_{15}P + \, ^1_0n$ (4) $^{226}_{88}Ra \rightarrow \, ^4_2He + \, ^{222}_{86}Rn$

12 Which reaction illustrates fusion?

   (1) $^2_1H + \, ^2_1H \rightarrow \, ^4_2He$ (3) $^{27}_{13}Al + \, ^4_2He \rightarrow \, ^{30}_{15}P + \, ^1_0n$

   (2) $^1_0n + \, ^{27}_{13}Al \rightarrow \, ^{24}_{11}Na + \, ^4_2He$ (4) $^{14}_{7}N + \, ^4_2He \rightarrow \, ^1_1H + \, ^{17}_{8}O$

13 An accelerator can *not* be used to speed up
   (1) alpha particles   (3) protons
   (2) beta particles   (4) neutrons

14 Question: In the reaction $^9_4Be + \, ^4_2He \rightarrow X + \, ^1_0n$, the X represents what element?

15 In a fission reactor, the speed of the neutrons may be decreased by
   (1) a moderator   (3) a fuel rod
   (2) an accelerator   (4) shielding

16 A particle accelerator is used to provide charged particles with sufficient
   (1) kinetic energy to penetrate a nucleus
   (2) kinetic energy to penetrate an electron cloud
   (3) potential energy to penetrate a nucleus
   (4) potential energy to penetrate an electron cloud

17 Which nuclide is a radioisotope used in the study of organic reaction mechanisms?
   (1) carbon-12   (3) uranium-235
   (2) carbon-14   (4) uranium-238

18 Fissionable uranium-233, uranium-235, and plutonium-239 are used in a nuclear reactor as
   (1) coolants   (3) moderators
   (2) control rods   (4) fuels

19 The diagram below represents a nuclear reaction in which a neutron bombards a heavy nucleus.

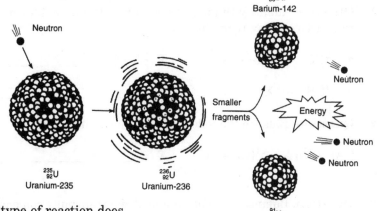

Which type of reaction does the diagram illustrate?
(1) fission
(2) fusion
(3) alpha decay
(4) beta decay

20 Within a nuclear reactor, the purpose of the moderator is to
(1) absorb neutrons in the reactor core
(2) absorb neutrons in the outer containment structure
(3) slow down neutrons in the reactor core
(4) slow down neutrons in the outer containment structure

21 In a fusion reaction, reacting nuclei must collide. Collisions between two nuclei are difficult to achieve because the nuclei are
(1) both negatively charged and repel each other
(2) both positively charged and repel each other
(3) oppositely charged and attract each other
(4) oppositely charged and repel each other

22 Brain tumors can be located by using an isotope of
(1) carbon-14
(2) iodine-131
(3) technetium-99
(4) uranium-238

23 Which isotope is used in geological dating?
(1) uranium-238
(2) iodine-131
(3) cobalt-60
(4) technetium-99

24 Control rods in nuclear reactors are commonly made of boron and cadmium because these two elements have the ability to
(1) absorb neutrons
(2) emit neutrons
(3) decrease the speed of neutrons
(4) increase the speed of neutrons

25 Which substance is used as a coolant in a nuclear reactor?
(1) neutrons
(2) plutonium
(3) hydrogen
(4) heavy water

PART B – CONSTRUCTED-RESPONSE

1 Question: Identify the particle resulting from the following natural radioactive decay reactions. [2]

a $^{238}_{92}U \rightarrow {}^4_2He + X$ $X =$ _$^{234}_{90}Th$_

b $^{214}_{83}Bi \rightarrow X + {}^0_{-1}e$ $X =$ _$^{214}_{84}Po$_

2 Question: Balance the following artificial transmutation equation. [1]

$^{27}_{13}Al + {}^1_0n \rightarrow {}^{24}_{11}Na + X$ $X =$ _^4_2He_

3 Question: Balance the following artificial transmutation equation. [1]

$^7_3Li + X \rightarrow {}^4_2He + {}^4_2He$ $X =$ _^1_1H_

4 Question: Carbon-14, a radioactive isotope, can be used to trace the chemical pathway of photosynthesis. Explain why this radioactive isotope can be used instead of the non radioactive isotope, Carbon-12, in these reactions. [2] It's easier to trace thru the body

5 Question: Using the information on *Reference Table N*, write a balanced nuclear equation that shows the transmutation of Cobalt-60 into its more stable nuclide. [1]

$^{60}_{27}Co \longrightarrow {}^{60}_{28}Ni + {}^0_{-1}e$

6 Question: Using the information on *Reference Table N*, write a balanced nuclear equation that shows the transmutation of thorium-232 into its more stable nuclide. [1]

$^{232}_{90}Th \rightarrow {}^4_2He + {}^{228}_{88}Ra$

7 Question: As a nuclide undergoes alpha decay, explain how the mass number and atomic number of the nucleus is changed. [1]

The numbers are reduced

PART C – EXTENDED CONSTRUCTED-RESPONSE

Article A: Converting nuclear energy into electrical energy has many advantages as well as disadvantages. People have different opinions as to whether the advantages outweigh the disadvantages. The advantage of using nuclear energy is that it is more powerful than other conventional sources of energy. Nuclear power plants are also cleaner, in that they do not produce any air pollution in the form of carbon dioxide and smoke particles. The disposal of radioactive wastes, however, presents a serious problem. The fission products from nuclear reactors are very radioactive and cannot be discarded. Also, many of the waste products have very long half-lives and must be isolated and stored for extremely long periods of time or disposed of in special ways. Strontium-90, for instance, has a half-life of 28.1 years. Even after 6 half-life periods, enough will remain to be harmful to any living organism that is exposed to the beta negative particles that are given off from the waste products.

1   **Question**: List two advantages of using nuclear energy as compared to the burning of fossil fuels. [2] *Nuclear power plants are cleaner, & it is more powerful than other sources.*

2   **Question**: State one disadvantage of using nuclear energy. [1] *One disadvantage is the disposal of radioactive wastes, have very long half-lives making the radioactivity dangerous*

3   **Question**: Calculate and write the number of years that corresponds to six half-life periods for strontium-90. [2] *28.1 × 6 = 168.6*

4   **Question**: Write a balanced nuclear equation that shows the transmutation of strontium-90, and name the more stable nuclide that is produced. [2] *Beta - Decay → $_{-1}^{0}e$*

$$_{38}^{90}Sr \longrightarrow \ _{-1}^{0}e + \ _{39}^{90}Y$$

Article B: Radioactive dating is the process of determining the age of an object by comparing the percentage of a radioactive isotope to the percentage of its decay product in a given sample of matter. Different radioactive isotopes are used to date different things. For example, uranium-238, which has a half-life of 4.51 billion years, is used to date the ancient rocks of Earth's crust.

Potassium-40, on the other hand, has a shorter half-life, and is useful for dating rocks and minerals that are fifty million to fifty thousand years old. The potassium-40 gives off a positron and is converted into argon-40. Over time, the proportion of potassium-40 decreases and the proportion of argon-40 increases. By knowing the half-life of potassium-40 and the percentage of the nuclide remaining in the rock, it is possible to determine the age of the rock.

Finally, carbon-14 is a radioactive nuclide that only has a half-life of 5,730 years. It is not useful in dating rocks, but is very useful in dating things that were at one time living. For example, the age of a piece of wood which has only half the amount of carbon-14 in it compared to that which is found in living plants today would be estimated to be about 5,730 years old.

5 Question: Based upon the information contained in the article above, state how the half-life of a radioactive isotope determines its usefulness in dating different objects. [1]

6 Question: Of the different radioactive isotopes listed in the article above, state which one might be used to identify the age of rocks containing large amounts of orthoclase feldspar that has the formula of $KAlSi_3O_8$. [1]

7 Question: Write a balanced nuclear equation that shows the transmutation of C-14 into its more stable nuclide. [1]

8 Question: Write a balanced nuclear equation that shows the transmutation of U-238 into its more stable nuclide. [1]

9 Question: The amount of C-14 contained in an object has been reduced to 25 percent of what it was in the original sample. Calculate the age of the object. [1]

PART D – LABORATORY SKILLS

CHEMISTRY LAB: RADIOACTIVE DECAY

Purpose: To determine the half-life of a radioactive substance.

Materials: Box with cover, 100 pennies.

Procedure:

1 Put the 100 pennies into the box with a cover on it. Decide which orientation of the pennies represent "decay" (for example, heads represents decay).

2 Cover the box and shake thoroughly.

3 Remove from the box the pennies that have "decayed" and count them.

4 Record the number of "decayed" pennies in the Data Table.

5 Calculate the number of pennies remaining undecayed and calculate the percentage that decayed from the formula:

$$\% \text{ decaying} = \frac{\text{number of pennies removed}}{\text{number of pennies before shaking}} \times 100$$

6 Repeat the procedure for additional trials until all the pennies have "decayed."

7 Construct a graph with the number of pennies before shaking on the ordinate and the trial number on the abscissa.

Observations: See Data Table below & Graph (page 302).

Toss Number or Half-Life	Trial 1		Trial 2		Trial 3		Average	
	Active	Decay	Active	Decay	Active	Decay	Active	Decay
0	100	0	100	0	100	0	100	0
1								
2								
3								
4								
5								
6								
7								
8								
9								

Conclusion and Review Questions:

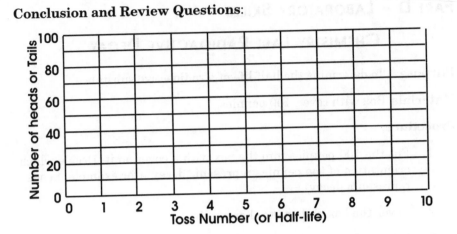

1 Based upon your graph, what is the half-life (the number of trials for half the pennies to decay)?

2 Using the information recorded in your Data Table, explain what happens to the percent decaying with succeeding trials.

3 Would the rate of decay be affected if you changed the amount of undecayed material? Explain.

4 Would the half-life be affected if you changed the amount of undecayed material? Explain.

UNIT 11
MATH & LAB
SKILLS

STANDARD 1: MATHEMATICAL ANALYSIS: KEY IDEA 1: ABSTRACTION AND SYMBOLIC REPRESENTATION ARE USED TO COMMUNICATE MATHEMATICALLY.

STANDARD 1: MATHEMATICAL ANALYSIS: KEY IDEA 2: DEDUCTIVE AND INDUCTIVE REASONING ARE USED TO REACH MATHEMATICAL CONCLUSIONS.

STANDARD 1: SCIENTIFIC INQUIRY: KEY IDEA 1: THE CENTRAL PURPOSE OF SCIENTIFIC INQUIRY IS TO DEVELOP EXPLANATIONS OF NATURAL PHENOMENA IN A CONTINUING, CREATIVE PROCESS.

STANDARD 1: ENGINEERING DESIGN: KEY IDEA 1: ENGINEERING DESIGN IS AN ITERATIVE PROCESS INVOLVING MODELING AND OPTIMIZATION (FINDING THE BEST SOLUTION WITHIN GIVEN CONSTRAINTS); THIS PROCESS IS USED TO DEVELOP TECHNOLOGICAL SOLUTIONS TO PROBLEMS WITHIN GIVEN CONSTRAINTS.

STANDARD 2: INFORMATION SYSTEMS: KEY IDEA 1: INFORMATION TECHNOLOGY IS USED TO RETRIEVE, PROCESS, AND COMMUNICATE INFORMATION AS A TOOL TO ENHANCE LEARNING.

STANDARD 2: INFORMATION SYSTEMS: KEY IDEA 2: KNOWLEDGE OF THE IMPACTS AND LIMITATIONS OF INFORMATION SYSTEMS IS ESSENTIAL TO ITS EFFECTIVENESS AND ETHICAL USE.

STANDARD 6: SYSTEMS THINKING: KEY IDEA 1: THROUGH SYSTEMS THINKING, PEOPLE CAN RECOGNIZE THE COMMONALITIES THAT EXIST AMONG ALL SYSTEMS AND HOW PARTS OF A SYSTEM INTERRELATE AND COMBINE TO PERFORM SPECIFIC FUNCTIONS.

STANDARD 6: MODELS: KEY IDEA 2: MODELS ARE SIMPLIFIED REPRESENTATIONS OF OBJECTS, STRUCTURES, OR SYSTEMS USED IN ANALYSIS, EXPLANATION, INTERPRETATION, OR DESIGN.

STANDARD 6: MAGNITUDE & SCALE: KEY IDEA 3: THE GROUPING OF MAGNITUDES OF SIZE, TIME, FREQUENCY, AND PRESSURES OR OTHER UNITS OF MEASUREMENT INTO A SERIES OF RELATIVE ORDER PROVIDES A USEFUL WAY TO DEAL WITH THE IMMENSE RANGE AND THE CHANGES IN SCALE THAT AFFECT THE BEHAVIOR AND DESIGN OF SYSTEMS.

UNIT 11
MATH & LAB SKILLS

This unit is related to Standards 1, 2, 6, and 7 for the Skills sections.

INTRODUCTION

Chemistry describes both chemical and physical phenomena and relationships in the world around us. Since mathematics is the most precise way of expressing these relationships, it is used extensively in the high school chemistry course. Students should have a basic knowledge of algebra and general problem solving.

A – MATH SKILLS

A chemical equation differs from a pure mathematical equation because the chemical formula is based on measurement. No measurement can be "exactly" correct. Each measurement consists of three parts:

First, there is a number reading, read off the measuring device.

Second, there is a unit.

Third, there is a statement of the measurement's accuracy. This accuracy is determined by the number of significant digits.

STANDARD 6: EQUILIBRIUM & STABILITY: KEY IDEA 4: EQUILIBRIUM IS A STATE OF STABILITY DUE EITHER TO A LACK OF CHANGE (STATIC EQUILIBRIUM) OR A BALANCE BETWEEN OPPOSING FORCES (DYNAMIC EQUILIBRIUM).

STANDARD 6: PATTERNS OF CHANGE: KEY IDEA 5: IDENTIFYING PATTERNS OF CHANGE IS NECESSARY FOR MAKING PREDICTIONS ABOUT FUTURE BEHAVIOR AND CONDITIONS.

STANDARD 7: CONNECTIONS: KEY IDEA 1: THE KNOWLEDGE AND SKILLS OF MATHEMATICS, SCIENCE, AND TECHNOLOGY ARE USED TOGETHER TO MAKE INFORMED DECISIONS AND SOLVE PROBLEMS, ESPECIALLY THOSE RELATING TO ISSUES OF SCIENCE, TECHNOLOGY, SOCIETY, CONSUMER DECISION MAKING, DESIGN, AND INQUIRY INTO PHENOMENA.

STANDARD 7: STRATEGIES: KEY IDEA 2: SOLVING INTERDISCIPLINARY PROBLEMS INVOLVES A VARIETY OF SKILLS AND STRATEGIES, INCLUDING EFFECTIVE WORK HABITS; GATHERING AND PROCESSING INFORMATION; GENERATING AND ANALYZING IDEAS; REALIZING IDEAS; MAKING CONNECTIONS AMONG THE COMMON THEMES OF MATHEMATICS, SCIENCE, AND TECHNOLOGY; AND PRESENTING RESULTS.

A measurement taken with a meter stick might be read as, 5.17 cm. The last digit is an estimate to the nearest tenth of a scale division and is considered significant. This measurement has three significant digits. This reading is the same as 0.0517 meters. The zero (0) simply locates the decimal point. The reading still has the same accuracy and three significant digits. When measurements combine arithmetically, the accuracy of the answer depends on both the accuracy of the measurements and the way in which they are combined.

RULES FOR SIGNIFICANT FIGURES

Students should apply the following rules for determining the number of significant digits (figures):

- **Initial zeros** are never significant. Since they are only used to locate a decimal point, the number 0.0203 has three significant figures.

- Zeros between two non-zero digits are significant. Example: 104.002 contains six significant figures.

- **Final zeros** Zeros to the right of nonzero digits are significant only if a decimal point is present. If a decimal point is not present, then the zeros are not significant.

   Examples:

2500	only contains 2 significant figures
25.00	contains 4 significant figures
250.00	contains 5 significant figures
2.50×10^2	contains 3 significant figures

- In addition and subtraction of measured quantities, first perform the designated function, then round the answer to the appropriate number of places past the decimal point. The number is expressed to the same number of places past the decimal point where there is a significant digit in each one of the measured quantities of the problem.

   Examples:

   $$14.32 + 3.144$$
   $$17.464 = 17.46$$

   $$14.3 + 3.146$$
   $$17.446 = 17.4$$

- In **multiplying** or **dividing** two measured numbers, the product or quotient should have the same number of significant digits as the least significant quantity in the problem.

Examples:

Multiplying: $3.4 \times 2.62 = 8.908 = 8.9$

Dividing: $4.124 \div 2.35 = 1.7548936 = 1.75$

- **Rounding off**: When rounding to the proper number of significant figures, numbers less than 5 are dropped and numbers greater than 5 are rounded up. If the number is 5, however, remember that 5s are only rounded up to an even integer. It is dropped if it is rounded up to an odd integer.

Examples:
> 2.375 rounded to three significant figures becomes 2.38
> (the five is rounded up to an even integer)

> 2.365 rounded to three significant figures becomes 2.36
> (the five would have been rounded up to an odd integer; therefore, is dropped)

SCIENTIFIC NOTATION

To simplify working with very large and very small numbers, scientists usually write numbers in **scientific notation**. The general procedure for writing any number in scientific notation is listed below.

- Move the decimal point of the given number to the right or left until there is only one digit to the left of the decimal point.

- Count the number of places you moved the decimal point. Raise ten to the power of this number. Moving the decimal point to the left is positive, while moving the decimal point to the right is negative.

ADDITION AND SUBTRACTION

Steps to add or subtract numbers in scientific notation, for example:
$$2.34 \times 10^3 + 1.33 \times 10^5$$

1) Make sure the powers of ten are equal:
$$.0234 \times 10^5 + 1.33 \times 10^5$$

2) Add or subtract the numbers before the power of ten:
$$.0234 + 1.33 = 1.3535$$

3) Retain the same power of ten in the answer:
$$1.35 \times 10^5$$

Steps to multiply numbers in scientific notation:
$$2.3 \times 10^4 \cdot 1.2 \times 10^3$$

1) Multiply the two numbers preceding the power of ten:
$$2.3 \times 1.2 = 2.76$$

2) Multiply the powers of ten by adding the exponent:
$$10^4 + 10^3 = 10^7$$

3) The answer includes both steps (1) and (2):
$$2.76 \times 10^7$$

Steps to divide numbers expressed in scientific notation:

$$4.9 \times 10^5 / 2.3 \times 10^2$$

1) Divide the number preceding the power of ten in the numerator, by the number preceding the power of ten in the denominator:

$$4.9 / 2.3 = 2.13$$

2) Subtract the exponent of the power of ten in the numerator. This gives the exponent of the power of ten in the answer:

$$10^5 / 10^2 = 10^3$$

3) The answer includes both steps (1) and (2):

$$2.13 \times 10^3$$

ORDER OF MAGNITUDE

Orders of magnitude are useful when it is desired to make a quick estimate of the measurements of some quantity. The power of ten that is the nearest approximation of a measurement is defined as the order of magnitude of that measurement.

DIMENSIONAL ANALYSIS (FACTOR - LABEL METHOD)

Measurements in chemistry always have units associated with them. Addition and subtraction are only possible if the quantities have the same units. It is possible to multiply or divide quantities with different units and come out with still another kind of unit. In these cases, the units should be treated as algebraic quantities. For example:

$$2.2 \text{ lbs/kg} \times 0.5 \text{ kg} = 1.1 \text{ lbs}$$

In addition, mathematical expressions can be simplified by manipulating units. Units can be cancelled out if they appear in both the numerator and denominator or combined into other units.

Problem: Sulfuric acid is used in automobile batteries. It has a density of 1.2 g/cm³. What is the mass (in grams) of 400 mL (4.0 x 10² mL) of this acid?

Solution: In liquid measure, 1 cm³ = 1 mL. Therefore, the following equation can be set up:

$$x \text{ number of grams} = (4.0 \times 10^2 \text{ mL}) \left(\frac{1 \text{ cm}^3}{1 \text{ mL}} \right) \left(\frac{1.2 \text{ g}}{\text{cm}^3} \right)$$

$$\text{number of grams} = 4.8 \times 10^2 \text{ g} \text{ (answer)}$$

B – LAB ACTIVITIES

The skills and activities in this unit should be developed and reinforced throughout the year by your laboratory experiences. Note: It is most important that a student should be familiar with general laboratory safety procedures [☆ pgs 312-316].

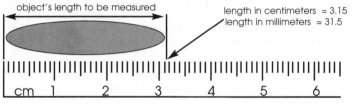

Metric Scale Measurement

MEASUREMENT

The following rules should be used when measuring in the lab.

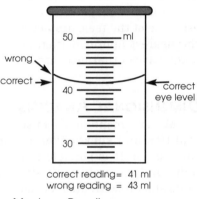

- Use common measuring devices: balance, graduated cylinder, thermometer, buret, etc.

- Interpolate to 1/10th of the smallest scale division of a measuring device.

- Round off numbers according to the correct number of significant figures. The accuracy of a measurement or calculated result can be indicated by the use of significant figures.

correct reading= 41 ml
wrong reading = 43 ml

Meniscus Reading on a graduated cylinder

- Use of a buret can improve and provide more precise measurements of the volume of acids, bases, and other liquids.

CALCULATIONS

- When adding or subtracting, as well as other mathematical solutions, use the decimal position of the number which contains the least accurately known figure to round off the final answer.

Add:		Subtract:	
	32.6		
	431.33		531.46
	6,144.212		– 86.3
	————————		————————
(answers)	6,608.14 = **6,608.1**		445.16 = **445.2**

- When multiplying or dividing, as well as other mathematical solutions, use the decimal position of the number which contains the least accurately known figure to round off the final answer.

Multiply:
$$\begin{array}{r} 1.336 \\ \times \ 4.2 \\ \hline \end{array}$$

Divide:
$$\begin{array}{r} 5.1 \\ \div \ 2.13 \\ \hline \end{array}$$

(answers) $5.712 = \mathbf{5.7}$ $2.39 = \mathbf{2.4}$

When the number dropped is 5 or more, the preceding number is increased by one. For example, 2.4179 taken to three significant figures becomes 2.42.

- Determine percent error whenever applicable by using the following equation:

$$\textbf{Actual Error} = \left(\begin{array}{c}\textbf{Experimental or} \\ \textbf{Observed Value}\end{array}\right) - \left(\begin{array}{c}\textbf{Theoretical or} \\ \textbf{Accepted Value}\end{array}\right)$$

$$\begin{array}{c}\textbf{Percent} \\ \textbf{Error}\end{array} = \frac{\textbf{Actual Error}}{\textbf{Theoretical or Accepted Value}} \ \text{x } 100\%$$

- **Observed value** is the experimentally measured value or the value calculated from the experimental results. The **accepted value** is the most probable value taken from generally accepted references. The following is an example of how to report percentage error.

Example: You are told to weigh a specific mass of $BaCl_2 \cdot 2H_2O$ and to find the percent by mass of water in the crystal. After heating the mass of hydrated crystal to constant mass in a crucible, you obtain the following results:

mass of the hydrated crystal . . . . .10.0 g
mass of the product after heating . . . . .8.8 g
mass of water . . . . 1.2 g
experimental percentage of water . . . . .12.0 %
theoretical percentage of water . . . . .14.0 %
actual error (step 4 - step 5) . . . .-2.0 %

Substituting in the above equation, the percent error can be found:

$$\begin{array}{c}\textbf{Percent} \\ \textbf{Error}\end{array} = \frac{\textbf{(Actual Error) -2\%}}{\textbf{(Theoretical Percent) 14\%}} = \textbf{- 0.143 x 100\% = - 14.3\%}$$

C – Lab Skills

Students should acquire at least the following basic skills for using lab burners, haldling glass, use of filters and funnels, pouring liquids and solids, heating materials, and conducting evaporations and drying.

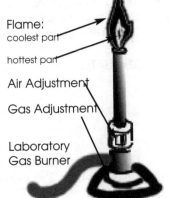

Flame:
coolest part

hottest part

Air Adjustment

Gas Adjustment

Laboratory
Gas Burner

Lab Burners

The proper adjustment and use of the burner or heat source follows:

- Make sure all connections are secure and do not allow for gas leakage.

- Understand the controls of the gas valve is in the "off" position when the valve handle is at a right angle to the outlet. It is in the "on" position when the valve handle is parallel to the outlet.

- Know how to adjust the gas supply with the burner gas adjustment device. In this manner, you can adjust the amount of gas supplied directly from the burner and not the gas valve.

- Know which part of the burner will adjust the amount of air intake so that the gas-air mixture will be at its optimum efficiency. If the air supply is too low, you will get a tall yellow flame which will blacken the piece of equipment you are using for heating purposes. This is due to the incomplete combustion of the gas.

- Know that once the air-gas mixture is adjusted, the flame will produce two cones. It is the tip of the inner cone which is the hottest part of the flame.

- Know that if too much air is present in the line, a "flutter" or "roaring" noise will be heard.

Handling Glass

How to cut, firepolish, and bend glass tubing. In the laboratory, two types of glass are used. "Hard" glass softens at about 800°C and is used to make pyrex test tubes. "Soft" glass is the glass that is used for glass tubing, and it melts at about 600°C.

1 **Cutting glass tubing** – (figure **a** on page 313) Using a flat surface on which to lay the glass and a triangular file, make a deep scratch at the desired point on the tubing. Holding the tubing so that the cut is away from the body, grasp the glass so that the thumbs are behind the scratch. Using the thumbs as a fulcrum, gently pull the ends of the glass towards the body. The glass should break easily at the scratch mark (figure **b** on page 313).

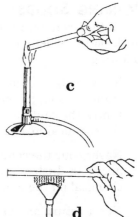

2. **Firepolishing glass tubing** – Glass tubing, when cut, will have sharp, cutting edges. Holding the tubing so that one end is just above the hot, inner blue cone of the bunsen burner flame, rotate it. When the flame gives off a yellow color, and the end appears smooth, remove it from the flame. If the tubing is left in the flame too long, the end will begin to close. Place the glass on a fireproof surface and allow it to cool.

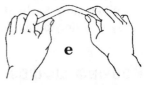

Caution: Normally glass looks the same if hot or cold. Make sure that is has cooled down before touching it.

3 **Bending glass tubing** – Before bending a piece of glass tubing (figure **c**) make sure that the ends are firepolished. (figure **d**) With a "wing top" to spread the flame of the burner, take the piece of glass in both hands and rotate it above the spread-out flame until a yellow color appears, and the glass turns soft and pliable. (figure **e**) Remove it from the flame and bend it to form the desired angle.

FILTER AND FUNNEL

When filtering a solid from a liquid, a good grade of filter paper should be used. Fold the filter paper many times to obtain a fluted filter. A fluted filter will more efficiently displace the air in the vessel into which the liquid is filtered, and the filtering process will proceed faster. The illustration below is the most commonly used method of folding filter paper.

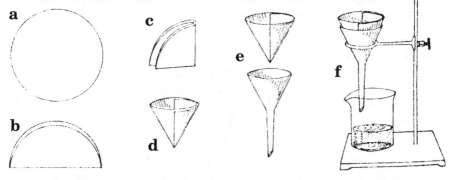

POURING SOLIDS

Before removing any chemical from its stock bottle, whether a solid or liquid, do the following:

- Read the label information concerning its identification, its purity, and most importantly, the caution information concerning the chemical inside.

- Never pour the solid chemical onto the balance pan. Instead, weigh a piece of weighing paper, then pour the chemical on the paper.

- Never return any excess to the stock bottle. Instead, discard it in a safe place, designated by your instructor.

- When pouring a chemical onto a piece of weighing paper which is on a balance, revolve the stock bottle in a forward and reverse manner. When close to the desired weight, tap the outer lip of the bottle lightly in order to have more control of the quantity of chemical poured.

POURING LIQUIDS

After reading the stock bottle for identification, purity, and caution information, grasp the stock bottle by the label and pour with the unlabeled side next to the container into which you are pouring. In this way, if there is excess dripping from the bottle, it will not drip onto the label.

- In transferring liquids into wide mouth bottles, pour the liquid onto a clean stirring rod so that the liquid clings to the stirring rod. This will minimize any splattering.

- When pouring into a test tube or other small mouthed container, pour along the inner edge in order to avoid splattering.

- When making a dilute acid solution, always add the acid to the water.

- When using a reagent bottle, grasp the flanged top with the back of the forefinger and middle fingers, holding it there while pouring, as shown in the illustration below.

Note: Do not set the stopper on a table; instead put it back directly onto the reagent bottle when you are finished pouring.

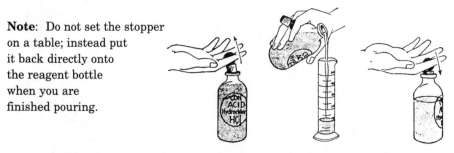

HEATING MATERIALS

To help prevent accidents, follow some common sense rules when heating materials in the laboratory. They include:

- Use some protective device for the eyes.
- Never heat stoppered liquids or solids.
- Never heat a test tube containing any substance (including water) while it is pointed toward you or anyone else.
- Always use a holder while heating any substance.
- Place beakers, flasks, and evaporating dishes on a wire gauze to spread the heat when using a ring stand.
- Use a water bath to evaporate liquids that will catch fire easily.
- Use a crucible and support the crucible on a clay triangle when heating a substance with direct heat (flame or electric)

Note: The formation of large bubbles in boiling, due to local super-heating and referred to as "bumping," can sometimes be prevented by the addition of a few glass beads or boiling chips

EVAPORATION AND DRYING

When evaporating a liquid or drying a solid do the following:

- Use a fume hood when evaporating hazardous solvents or materials.
- In situations where the temperature must be controlled with a high degree of precision, the use of drying ovens, heating mantle, or electric heater will be necessary. **Note**: In the presence of flammable materials, do not use an open flame.
- In drying a solid, heat gently so that you do not lose some of your sample as the result of superheating in spots with the resultant popping out of some of the material being heated.

COMMON LABORATORY APPARATUS

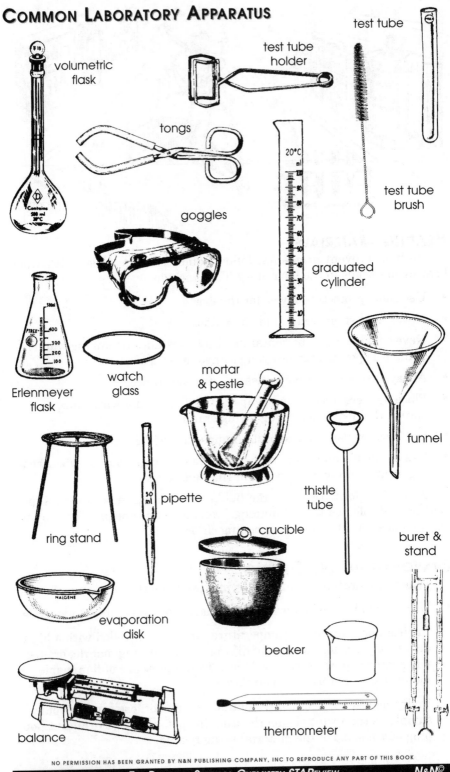

test tube

test tube
holder

volumetric
flask

tongs

test tube
brush

goggles

20°C
ml

graduated
cylinder

watch
glass

mortar
& pestle

Erlenmeyer
flask

funnel

pipette

thistle
tube

ring stand

crucible

buret &
stand

evaporation
disk

beaker

balance

thermometer

LABORATORY SKILLS QUESTIONS

1 The process of filtration is performed in the laboratory to
   (1) form precipitates
   (2) remove water from solutions
   (3) separate dissolved particles from the solvent
   (4) separate insoluble substances in an aqueous mixture

2 The volume of an acid required to neutralize exactly 15.00 milliliters
   (mL) of a base could be measured most precisely if it were added to
   the base solution from a
   (1) 100. mL graduate   (3) 50. mL buret
   (2) 125 mL Erlenmeyer flask   (4) 50. mL beaker

3 Using the rules for significant figures, the sum of 0.027 gram and
   0.0023 gram should be expressed as
   (1) 0.029 gram   (3) 0.03 gram
   (2) 0.0293 gram   (4) 0.030 gram

4 The diagram at the right represents a portion of a buret.
   What is the reading of the meniscus?
   (1) 39.2 mL   (3) 40.7 mL
   (2) 39.5 mL   (4) 40.9 mL

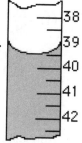

5 A bunsen burner flame is sooty black and mixed with an orange-yel-
   low color. Which is the probable reason for this condition?
   (1) No oxygen is mixing with the gas.
   (2) No gas is mixing with the oxygen.
   (3) Insufficient oxygen is mixing with the gas.
   (4) Insufficient gas is mixing with the oxygen.

6 In an experiment the gram atomic mass of magnesium was determined to be 24.7. Compared to the accepted value 24.3, the percent
   error for this determination was
   (1) 0.400   (2) 1.65   (3) 2.47   (4) 98.4

7 Which piece of laboratory apparatus would most likely be used to
   evaporate a 1-milliliter sample of a solution to dryness?
   (1) volumetric flask   (3) pipette
   (2) buret   (4) watch glass

8 A student determined the melting point of a substance to be 55.2°C.
   If the accepted value is 50.1°C, the percent error is
   (1) 5.10   (2) 9.24   (3) 10.2   (4) 120

9 A cube has a volume of 8.0 cm³ and a mass of 216 grams. The density of the cube, in grams per cubic centimeter, is best expressed as
   (1) 27   (2) 270   (3) 0.37   (4) 0.370

10 Which diagram to the right represents a pipette?

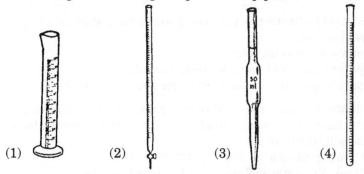

(1)   (2)   (3)   (4)

11 In an experiment, a student found that the percent of oxygen in a sample of $KClO_3$ was 42.3%. If the accepted value is 39.3%, the experimental percent error is

(1) $\dfrac{42.3}{39.3} \times 100\%$

(2) $\dfrac{39.3}{42.3} \times 100\%$

(3) $\dfrac{3.0}{42.3} \times 100\%$

(4) $\dfrac{3.0}{39.3} \times 100\%$

D – LABORATORY REPORTS

You should be able to write concise reports of laboratory experiences. The student should be able to:

- Organize information in a logical manner.

- Put appropriate data in tables and graphs whenever possible.

- Make a list of observations.

- Draw conclusions based on observations.

Laboratory reports may seem tedious and redundant, but they are the expression of your personality. They convey in your words a concise form of communication which reflects the way that you work. If your laboratory report is sloppy, with misspelled words, and shows poor organization, it is an indication of your manner, and you will be judged by these criteria. The most important discovery is not a contribution to science until it has been communicated to others.

In short, like any other form of communication, the laboratory report should include the following:

- The content is factual, objective, and easily read.

- All observations and conclusions are supported by evidence.

- The correct word is used. Knowledge of language is evident, and spelling is flawless.

- The scientific apparatus is accurately described, and the working details of the experiment are complete.

- Self devised graphs and their interpretation.

ADDITIONAL PRACTICE FOR LABORATORY SKILLS

12 As a result of dissolving a salt in water, a student found that the temperature of the water increased. From this observation alone, the student should conclude that the dissolving of the salt
(1) produced an acid solution   (3) was endothermic
(2) produced a basic solution   (4) was exothermic

13 How many milliliters of 0.4 M HCl are required to completely neutralize 200 milliliters of 0.16 M potassium hydroxide?
(1) 500   (2) 200   (3) 80   (4) 30

14 During a titration, a student used 50. milliliters of 0.1 M acid. How many moles of acid, expressed to proper significance, were used?
(1) 0.005   (3) 0.00500
(2) 0.0050   (4) 0.005000

Base your answers to questions 15 and 16 on the table at the right which shows the data collected during the heating of a 5.0 gram sample of a hydrated salt.

Mass of Salt (g)	Heating Time (minutes)
5.0	0.0
4.1	5.0
3.1	10.
3.0	15.
3.0	30.
3.0	60.

15 After 60. minutes, how many grams of water appear to remain in the salt?
(1) 0.00   (3) 19
(2) 20   (4) 0.90

16 What is the percent of water in the original sample?
(1) 82. %   (2) 60. %   (3) 30. %   (4) 40. %

17 Given the following titration data:

         Volume of base (KOH) = 40.0 mL
         Molarity of base = 0.20 M
         Volume of acid (HCl) added = 20.0 mL

The concentration of HCl required for the acid to neutralize the base is
(1) 10. M   (2) 0.20 M   (3) 0.10 M   (4) 0.40 M

18 A student obtained the data at the right in determining the solubility of $NaNO_3$.

Which set of coordinates would graphically present the data in the table at the right most clearly?

Temp. ($°C$)	Solubility (g $NaNO_3$ /100 g H_2O)
0	73
10	80
20	88
30	97
40	105
50	115
60	124
70	134
80	145

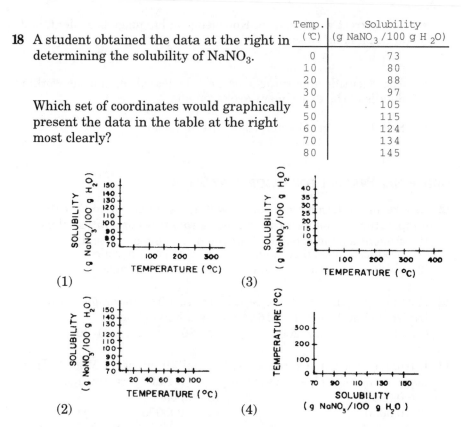

(1)   (3)

(2)   (4)

19 Which graph shown below could represent the uniform cooling of a substance, starting with the gaseous phase and ending with the solid phase?

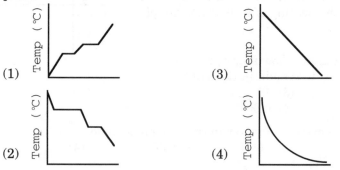

(1)   (3)

(2)   (4)

20 Which milligram quantity contains a total of four significant figures?
(1) 0.3010 mg   (2) 3010. mg   (3) 3100. mg   (4) 30001 mg

21 The volume of acid used to neutralize 15.00 milliliters of a base solution can be measured most precisely by the use of a
(1) beaker   (3) graduated cylinder
(2) buret   (4) volumetric flask

22 A student has to measure the diameter of a test tube in order to calculate the tube's volume. Based on the diagram, the tube's diameter is closest to

(1) 1.25 cm
(2) 2.32 cm
(3) 3.25 cm
(4) 12.5 cm

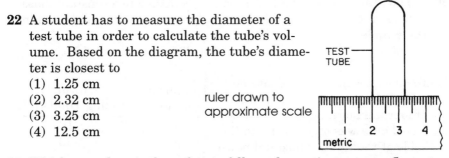

ruler drawn to approximate scale

TEST TUBE

23 Which procedure is the safest to follow when using an open flame to heat the contents of a test tube that contains a flammable mixture?
(1) Cork the test tube and then heat it gently near the bottom only.
(2) Heat the open test tube gently near the bottom only.
(3) Cork the test tube and place it in a beaker of water, then heat the water in the beaker.
(4) Place the open test tube in a beaker of water, then heat the water in the beaker.

24 In the laboratory, a student determined the percent by mass of water in a hydrated salt to be 17.3 percent. If the accepted value is 14.8 percent, the percent error is
(1) 2.50 %   (2) 5.92 %   (3) 16.9 %   (4) 27.1 %

25 Expressed to the correct number of significant figures, what is the correct sum of (3.04 g + 4.134 g + 6.1 g)?
(1) 13 g   (2) 13.3 g   (3) 13.27 g   (4) 13.274 g

26 Which diagram represents a graduated cylinder?

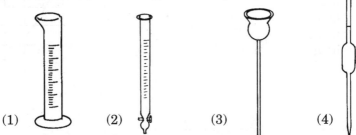

(1)   (2)   (3)   (4)

27 Which procedure represents the safest technique to use for diluting a concentrated acid?
(1) Add the acid to the water quickly.
(2) Add the water to the acid quickly.
(3) Add the acid slowly to the water with steady stirring.
(4) Add the water slowly to the acid with steady stirring.

28 Which measurement contains three significant figures?
(1) 0.05 g   (2) 0.050 g   (3) 0.056 g   (4) 0.0563 g

29 A 9.90-gram sample of a hydrated salt is heated to a constant mass of 6.60 grams. What was the percent by mass of water contained in the sample?

(1) 66.7   (2) 50.0   (3) 33.3   (4) 16.5

30 In an experiment, a student determined the normal boiling points of four unknown liquids. The collected data was organized into the table at the right. Which unknown liquid has the weakest attractive forces between its molecules?

Unknown Liquids	Normal Boiling Points (°C)
A	10
B	33
C	78
D	100

(1) A   (3) C
(2) B   (4) D

31 A student collected data in an experiment in which the uniform cooling of a water sample was observed from 50°C to -32°C. Which graph most likely represents the results obtained by the student?

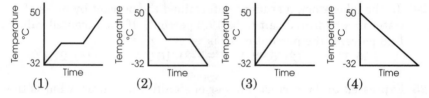

(1)   (2)   (3)   (4)

32 The graph at the right represents the decay of a radioactive isotope. What is the half-life of this isotope?

(1) 1 hour
(2) 2 hours
(3) 3 hours
(4) 6 hours

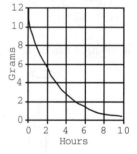

33 The graph at the right represents four solubility curves. Which curve best represents the solubility of a gas in water?

(1) A
(2) B
(3) C
(4) D

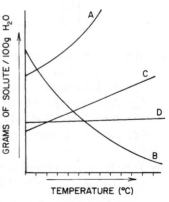

UNIT 12

REFERENCE TABLES
FOR
PHYSICAL SETTING: CHEMISTRY

UNIVERSITY OF THE STATE OF NEW YORK • THE STATE EDUCATION DEPARTMENT
2002 EDITION (AS REVISED FOR JUNE 2003)

LIST OF REFERENCE TABLES

PERIODIC TABLE OF ELEMENTS

REVISED FOR JUNE 2003

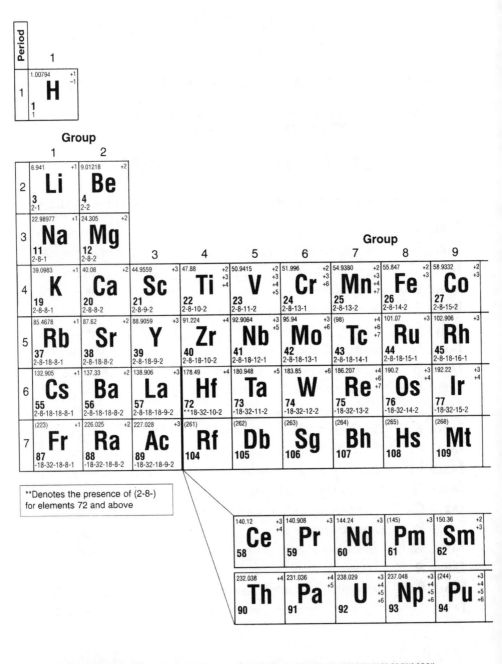

**Denotes the presence of (2-8-) for elements 72 and above

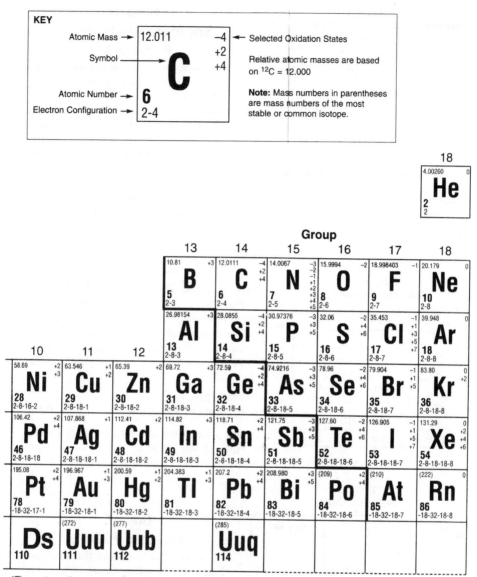

Group

18
4.00260   0
He
2
2

			13	14	15	16	17	18
			10.81 +3 **B** 5 2-3	12.0111 -4,+2,+4 **C** 6 2-4	14.0067 -3,-2,-1,+1,+2,+3,+4,+5 **N** 7 2-5	15.9994 -2 **O** 8 2-6	18.998403 -1 **F** 9 2-7	20.179 0 **Ne** 10 2-8
10	11	12	26.98154 +3 **Al** 13 2-8-3	28.0855 -4,+2,+4 **Si** 14 2-8-4	30.97376 -3,+3,+5 **P** 15 2-8-5	32.06 -2,+4,+6 **S** 16 2-8-6	35.453 -1,+1,+3,+5,+7 **Cl** 17 2-8-7	39.948 0 **Ar** 18 2-8-8
58.69 +2,+3 **Ni** 28 2-8-16-2	63.546 +1,+2 **Cu** 29 2-8-18-1	65.39 +2 **Zn** 30 2-8-18-2	69.72 +3 **Ga** 31 2-8-18-3	72.59 -4,+2,+4 **Ge** 32 2-8-18-4	74.9216 -3,+3,+5 **As** 33 2-8-18-5	78.96 -2,+4,+6 **Se** 34 2-8-18-6	79.904 -1,+1,+5 **Br** 35 2-8-18-7	83.80 0,+2 **Kr** 36 2-8-18-8
106.42 +2,+4 **Pd** 46 2-8-18-18	107.868 +1 **Ag** 47 2-8-18-18-1	112.41 +2 **Cd** 48 2-8-18-18-2	114.82 +3 **In** 49 2-8-18-18-3	118.71 +2,+4 **Sn** 50 2-8-18-18-4	121.75 -3,+3,+5 **Sb** 51 2-8-18-18-5	127.60 -2,+4,+6 **Te** 52 2-8-18-18-6	126.905 -1,+1,+5,+7 **I** 53 2-8-18-18-7	131.29 0,+2,+4,+6 **Xe** 54 2-8-18-18-8
195.08 +2,+4 **Pt** 78 -18-32-17-1	196.967 +1,+3 **Au** 79 -18-32-18-1	200.59 +1,+2 **Hg** 80 -18-32-18-2	204.383 +1,+3 **Tl** 81 -18-32-18-3	207.2 +2,+4 **Pb** 82 -18-32-18-4	208.980 +3,+5 **Bi** 83 -18-32-18-5	(209) +2,+4 **Po** 84 -18-32-18-6	(210) **At** 85 -18-32-18-7	(222) 0 **Rn** 86 -18-32-18-8
(272) **Ds** 110	(277) **Uuu** 111	(285) **Uub** 112		(285) **Uuq** 114				

*The systematic names and symbols for elements of atomic numbers above 109 will be used until the approval of trivial names by IUPAC.

151.96 +2,+3 **Eu** 63	157.25 +3 **Gd** 64	158.925 +3 **Tb** 65	162.50 +3 **Dy** 66	164.930 +3 **Ho** 67	167.26 +3 **Er** 68	168.934 +3 **Tm** 69	173.04 +2,+3 **Yb** 70	174.967 +3 **Lu** 71
(243) +3,+4,+5,+6 **Am** 95	(247) +3 **Cm** 96	(247) +3,+4 **Bk** 97	(251) +3 **Cf** 98	(252) **Es** 99	(257) **Fm** 100	(258) **Md** 101	(259) **No** 102	(260) **Lr** 103

Table A
Standard Temperature and Pressure

Name	Value	Unit
Standard Pressure	101.3 kPa 1 atm	kilopascal atmosphere
Standard Temperature	273 K 0°C	kelvin degree Celsius

Table B
Physical Constants for Water

Heat of Fusion	334 J/g
Heat of Vaporization	2260 J/g
Specific Heat Capacity of H_2O (ℓ)	4.18 J/g•°C

Table C
Selected Prefixes

Factor	Prefix	Symbol
10^3	kilo-	k
10^{-1}	deci-	d
10^{-2}	centi-	c
10^{-3}	milli-	m
10^{-6}	micro-	μ
10^{-9}	nano-	n
10^{-12}	pico-	p

Table D
Selected Units

Symbol	Name	Quantity
m	meter	length
g	gram	mass
Pa	pascal	pressure
K	kelvin	temperature
mol	mole	amount of substance
J	joule	energy, work, quantity of heat
s	second	time
L	liter	volume
ppm	part per million	concentration
M	molarity	solution concentration

TABLE A
STANDARD TEMPERATURE & PRESSURE

Standard temperature and pressure (STP) are used when working with gas law problems.

The volume occupied by gases is very much dependent on temperature and pressure. Oftentimes problems will be given where you have to correct to STP.

Example: A gas sample occupies 40.0 mL at 325 K and 103.5 kPa. What volume will the gas occupy at STP? [Ans.: 34.3 mL]

TABLE B
PHYSICAL CONSTANTS FOR WATER

The Physical Constants for Water contains three values. The specific heat capacity of water is used when you are calculating the amount of heat that is gained or lost by a given mass of water that is changing temperature.

Example:
heat gained or lost = g x ΔT x specific heat

The values for the Heat of Fusion and the Heat of Vaporization will be used when you are given a change of phase problem.

TABLE C
SELECTED PREFIXES

This table contains the prefixes, their corresponding power of ten, and the symbol used to represent the prefix.

TABLE D
SELECTED UNITS

This table contains several of the SI units, their symbols, names and quantity. Be sure to familiarize yourself with the information included on this table.

H_3O^+	hydronium	CrO_4^{2-}	chromate
Hg_2^{2+}	dimercury (I)	$Cr_2O_7^{2-}$	dichromate
NH_4^+	ammonium	MnO_4^-	permanganate
$C_2H_3O_2^-$ } CH_3COO^- }	acetate	NO_2^-	nitrite
		NO_3^-	nitrate
CN^-	cyanide	O_2^{2-}	peroxide
CO_3^{2-}	carbonate	OH^-	hydroxide
HCO_3^-	hydrogen carbonate	PO_4^{3-}	phosphate
$C_2O_4^{2-}$	oxalate	SCN^-	thiocyanate
ClO^-	hypochlorite	SO_3^{2-}	sulfite
ClO_2^-	chlorite	SO_4^{2-}	sulfate
ClO_3^-	chlorate	HSO_4^-	hydrogen sulfate
ClO_4^-	perchlorate	$S_2O_3^{2-}$	thiosulfate

TABLE E
SELECTED
POLYATOMIC IONS

The polyatomic ions and their names in this table are used when writing formulas and naming compounds. Polyatomic ions bond with metals or other polyatomic ions by means of an ionic bond.

Table F
Solubility Guidelines for Aqueous Solutions

Ions That Form *Soluble* Compounds	Exceptions	Ions That Form *Insoluble* Compounds	Exceptions
Group 1 ions (Li^+, Na^+, etc.)		carbonate (CO_3^{2-})	when combined with Group 1 ions or ammonium (NH_4^+)
ammonium (NH_4^+)		chromate (CrO_4^{2-})	when combined with Group 1 ions, Ca^{2+}, Mg^{2+}, or ammonium (NH_4^+)
nitrate (NO_3^-)			
acetate ($C_2H_3O_2^-$ or CH_3COO^-)		phosphate (PO_4^{3-})	when combined with Group 1 ions or ammonium (NH_4^+)
hydrogen carbonate (HCO_3^-)		sulfide (S^{2-})	when combined with Group 1 ions or ammonium (NH_4^+)
chlorate (ClO_3^-)		hydroxide (OH^-)	when combined with Group 1 ions, Ca^{2+}, Ba^{2+}, Sr^{2+}, or ammonium (NH_4^+)
perchlorate (ClO_4^-)			
halides (Cl^-, Br^-, I^-)	when combined with Ag^+, Pb^{2+}, and Hg_2^{2+}		
sulfates (SO_4^{2-})	when combined with Ag^+, Ca^{2+}, Sr^{2+}, Ba^{2+}, and Pb^{2+}		

TABLE F
SOLUBILITY GUIDELINES

These two tables are for use when predicting whether or not a compound is soluble or not. Generalizations and exceptions can quickly be observed when determining the solubility of compounds.

Example: Which of the following compounds is insoluble?
(1) NaCl
(2) AgCl
(3) KCl
(4) $CaCl_2$

Table G   Solubility Curves

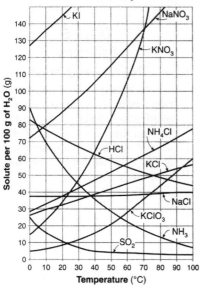

Solute per 100 g of H₂O (g) vs Temperature (°C)

TABLE G
SOLUBILITY CURVES

This table shows how the solubility of substances in a given mass of water is affected by a change in temperature. A curve with a positive slope represents a solute that has a positive heat of solution. This means that in the dissolving process, as the temperature increases, so does the solubility. Notice that all solubility curves with a negative slope represent gases. This shows you that the heat of solution is negative and the dissolving process is exothermic. Notice, as the temperature increases, the solubility of a gas decreases.

Every point on a line represents a saturated solution. A saturated solution is one in which the maximum amount of solute is dissolved into the given mass of solvent. It also represents a solution in which an equilibrium exists between the dissolved and undissolved solute that is in solution. A solution is said to be unsaturated if it has less solute dissolved in it than that which could be dissolved in it at a given temperature. On the other hand, if the dissolved amount is noted to be above the solubility curve of the substance, the solution is said to be supersaturated.

Table H
Vapor Pressure of Four Liquids

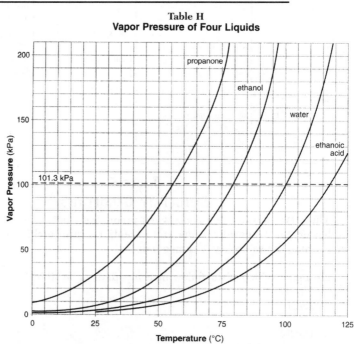

Table I
Heats of Reaction at 101.3 kPa and 298 K

Reaction	ΔH (kJ)*
$CH_4(g) + 2O_2(g) \longrightarrow CO_2(g) + 2H_2O(\ell)$	–890.4
$C_3H_8(g) + 5O_2(g) \longrightarrow 3CO_2(g) + 4H_2O(\ell)$	–2219.2
$2C_8H_{18}(\ell) + 25O_2(g) \longrightarrow 16CO_2(g) + 18H_2O(\ell)$	–10943
$2CH_3OH(\ell) + 3O_2(g) \longrightarrow 2CO_2(g) + 4H_2O(\ell)$	–1452
$C_2H_5OH(\ell) + 3O_2(g) \longrightarrow 2CO_2(g) + 3H_2O(\ell)$	–1367
$C_6H_{12}O_6(s) + 6O_2(g) \longrightarrow 6CO_2(g) + 6H_2O(\ell)$	–2804
$2CO(g) + O_2(g) \longrightarrow 2CO_2(g)$	–566.0
$C(s) + O_2(g) \longrightarrow CO_2(g)$	–393.5
$4Al(s) + 3O_2(g) \longrightarrow 2Al_2O_3(s)$	–3351
$N_2(g) + O_2(g) \longrightarrow 2NO(g)$	+182.6
$N_2(g) + 2O_2(g) \longrightarrow 2NO_2(g)$	+66.4
$2H_2(g) + O_2(g) \longrightarrow 2H_2O(g)$	–483.6
$2H_2(g) + O_2(g) \longrightarrow 2H_2O(\ell)$	–571.6
$N_2(g) + 3H_2(g) \longrightarrow 2NH_3(g)$	–91.8
$2C(s) + 3H_2(g) \longrightarrow C_2H_6(g)$	–84.0
$2C(s) + 2H_2(g) \longrightarrow C_2H_4(g)$	+52.4
$2C(s) + H_2(g) \longrightarrow C_2H_2(g)$	+227.4
$H_2(g) + I_2(g) \longrightarrow 2HI(g)$	+53.0
$KNO_3(s) \xrightarrow{H_2O} K^+(aq) + NO_3^-(aq)$	+34.89
$NaOH(s) \xrightarrow{H_2O} Na^+(aq) + OH^-(aq)$	–44.51
$NH_4Cl(s) \xrightarrow{H_2O} NH_4^+(aq) + Cl^-(aq)$	+14.78
$NH_4NO_3(s) \xrightarrow{H_2O} NH_4^+(aq) + NO_3^-(aq)$	+25.69
$NaCl(s) \xrightarrow{H_2O} Na^+(aq) + Cl^-(aq)$	+3.88
$LiBr(s) \xrightarrow{H_2O} Li^+(aq) + Br^-(aq)$	–48.83
$H^+(aq) + OH^-(aq) \longrightarrow H_2O(\ell)$	–55.8

*Minus sign indicates an exothermic reaction.

TABLE I
HEATS OF REACTION
at 101.3 kPa and 298 K
(Standard Pressure and
Temperature)

This table shows the heats of reaction for various chemical reactions at STP. The heats of reaction are measured in kilojoules (kJ). A positive heat of reaction indicates that the reaction is endothermic, and the heat value is added to the reactant side in a thermo-chemical equation. A negative heat of reaction indicates that the reaction is exothermic, and the heat value is added to the product side in a thermo-chemical equation. Also, the greater the negative value for the heat of reaction, the greater the stability of the products.

TABLE H (on left page)
VAPOR PRESSURE OF FOUR LIQUIDS

This table shows the relationship between the vapor pressure of four different liquids, and how the vapor pressure changes with temperature. In general, it can be seen that, as the temperature increases, the vapor pressure of a liquid also increases. This table can also be used for boiling point questions. Remember that the boiling point of a liquid is the temperature at which the vapor pressure of the liquid equals the atmospheric pressure on it. The makers of the table have conveniently marked the vapor pressure at sea level (101.3 kPa) with a dashed line. The temperature at which any one of the vapor pressure lines crosses the 101.3 kPa line is the boiling point of that liquid.

This table can also be used to compare the intermolecular forces of attraction that exists between the molecules of the sub stance. At any given temperature, the substance that has the highest vapor pressure has the weakest intermolecular forces of attraction, and the substance that has the lowest vapor pressure has the strongest intermolecular forces of attraction holding it together.

PAGE 328

Table J
Activity Series**

Most	Metals	Nonmetals	Most
	Li	F_2	
	Rb	Cl_2	
	K	Br_2	
	Cs	I_2	
	Ba		
	Sr		
	Ca		
	Na		
	Mg		
	Al		
	Ti		
	Mn		
	Zn		
	Cr		
	Fe		
	Co		
	Ni		
	Sn		
	Pb		
	**H_2		
	Cu		
	Ag		
	Au		
Least			Least

**Activity Series based on hydrogen standard
Note: H_2 is *not* a metal

Table K
Common Acids

Formula	Name
HCl(aq)	hydrochloric acid
HNO_3(aq)	nitric acid
H_2SO_4(aq)	sulfuric acid
H_3PO_4(aq)	phosphoric acid
H_2CO_3(aq) or CO_2(aq)	carbonic acid
CH_3COOH(aq) or $HC_2H_3O_2$(aq)	ethanoic acid (acetic acid)

Table L
Common Bases

Formula	Name
NaOH(aq)	sodium hydroxide
KOH(aq)	potassium hydroxide
$Ca(OH)_2$(aq)	calcium hydroxide
NH_3(aq)	aqueous ammonia

TABLE J – ACTIVITY SERIES

This table can be used for single replacement reactions and to predict the spontaneity of redox reactions. In single replacement reactions, a more active metal (above on the table) will replace a less active metal (below on the table) from a compound.

Example 1: $Mg + Zn(NO_3)_2 \rightarrow Mg(NO_3)_2 + Zn$

Likewise, a more active nonmetal will replace a less active nonmetal from a compound.

Example 2: $F_2 + 2KCl \rightarrow 2KF + Cl_2$

The spontaneity of redox reactions involving metals can be predicted in the same manner as the single replacement reactions.

Example: Will a reaction occur spontaneous between Mg and Zn^{+2} ion? In this case the ion is represented as being dissolved into an aqueous solution instead of bonded in a compound: $Zn(NO_3)_2$ as in Example 1 above. In either case, Mg is above the Zn and, therefore, will replace it in chemical reactions.

TABLE K – COMMON ACIDS

This table simply lists the formulas and names of the more common acids that are most used in inorganic chemistry. Remember that the formulas for acids are written in two different ways. In inorganic chemistry, an acid is indicated when hydrogen is written first in the formula of the compound. (Ex: HNO_3) In organic chemistry, an acid is indicated by adding the formula of the carboxyl group (COOH) to the hydrocarbon chain (Ex: CH_3COOH)

TABLE L – COMMON BASES

This table lists the formulas and names of a few of the more common bases used in inorganic chemistry. Remember that a substance is a base when the hydroxide ion is chemically bonded to a metal ion or to a positively charged polyatomic ion. Ammonia is unique in that $NH_3(g)$, when bubbled through water, will produce a basic solution.

Table M
Common Acid–Base Indicators

Indicator	Approximate pH Range for Color Change	Color Change
methyl orange	3.2–4.4	red to yellow
bromthymol blue	6.0–7.6	yellow to blue
phenolphthalein	8.2–10	colorless to pink
litmus	5.5–8.2	red to blue
bromcresol green	3.8–5.4	yellow to blue
thymol blue	8.0–9.6	yellow to blue

Table N
Selected Radioisotopes

Nuclide	Half-Life	Decay Mode	Nuclide Name
^{198}Au	2.69 d	β^-	gold-198
^{14}C	5730 y	β^-	carbon-14
^{37}Ca	175 ms	β^+	calcium-37
^{60}Co	5.26 y	β^-	cobalt-60
^{137}Cs	30.23 y	β^-	cesium-137
^{53}Fe	8.51 min	β^+	iron-53
^{220}Fr	27.5 s	α	francium-220
^{3}H	12.26 y	β^-	hydrogen-3
^{131}I	8.07 d	β^-	iodine-131
^{37}K	1.23 s	β^+	potassium-37
^{42}K	12.4 h	β^-	potassium-42
^{85}Kr	10.76 y	β^-	krypton-85
^{16}N	7.2 s	β^-	nitrogen-16
^{19}Ne	17.2 s	β^+	neon-19
^{32}P	14.3 d	β^-	phosphorus-32
^{239}Pu	2.44×10^4 y	α	plutonium-239
^{226}Ra	1600 y	α	radium-226
^{222}Rn	3.82 d	α	radon-222
^{90}Sr	28.1 y	β^-	strontium-90
^{99}Tc	2.13×10^5 y	β^-	technetium-99
^{232}Th	1.4×10^{10} y	α	thorium-232
^{233}U	1.62×10^5 y	α	uranium-233
^{235}U	7.1×10^8 y	α	uranium-235
^{238}U	4.51×10^9 y	α	uranium-238

ms = milliseconds; s = seconds; min = minutes;
h = hours; d = days; y = years

TABLE M
COMMON ACID-BASE INDICATORS

An acid-base indicator is one which changes color based upon the acidity or basicity of the solution. This table contains some acid base indicators, the approximate pH range, and the corresponding color change. Remember that a pH of 7 is neutral, meaning that there are equal amounts of H_3O^+ ions and OH$^-$ ions present in solution. If a solution has a pH less than 7, the solution is acidic, and contains more H_3O^+ ions than OH$^-$ ions. (The lower the number on the pH scale, the greater the concentration of H_3O^+ ions, and the more acidic the solution. If a solution has a pH greater than 7, the solution is basic, and contains more OH$^-$ ions than H_3O^+ ions. (The higher the number on the pH scale, the greater the concentration of OH$^-$ ions, and the more basic the solution).

TABLE N
SELECTED RADIOISOTOPES

This table lists some representative radioisotopes, their symbols, half-life, decay mode and name. The table will be used when working on half-life problems and looking up decay modes which can be used when balancing nuclear equations.

Table O
Symbols Used in Nuclear Chemistry

Name	Notation	Symbol
alpha particle	$_2^4He$ or $_2^4\alpha$	α
beta particle (electron)	$_{-1}^0e$ or $_{-1}^0\beta$	β^-
gamma radiation	$_0^0\gamma$	γ
neutron	$_0^1n$	n
proton	$_1^1H$ or $_1^1p$	p
positron	$_{+1}^0e$ or $_{+1}^0\beta$	β^+

TABLE O
SYMBOLS USED IN NUCLEAR CHEMISTRY

This table lists the different types of radioactive emissions, and gives their notation and symbols. The notation and symbols are used when balancing nuclear equations.

Table P
Organic Prefixes

Prefix	Number of Carbon Atoms
meth-	1
eth-	2
prop-	3
but-	4
pent-	5
hex-	6
hept-	7
oct-	8
non-	9
dec-	10

TABLE P
ORGANIC PREFIXES

This is a handy table to have when naming organic compounds. The prefixes are used to indicate the number of carbons present in a molecule or parent chain. (Ex: methane, ethane, propane). They are also used when indicating the number of carbons contained in a radical attached to the parent chain (Ex: methyl, ethyl, propyl).

TABLE Q
HOMOLOGOUS SERIES OF HYDROCARBONS

This table lists the first three homologous series of hydrocarbons, gives their general formulas, and provides an example of their names and structural formulas. Remember, alkanes are saturated hydrocarbons with single bonds connecting the carbon atoms together. Alkenes are unsaturated hydrocarbons which contain only one double bond in the carbon chain. Alkynes are unsaturated hydrocarbons that contain a triple bond in the carbon chain.

Table Q
Homologous Series of Hydrocarbons

Name	General Formula	Examples	
		Name	Structural Formula
alkanes	C_nH_{2n+2}	ethane	H—C—C—H (ethane structure)
alkenes	C_nH_{2n}	ethene	C=C (ethene structure)
alkynes	C_nH_{2n-2}	ethyne	$H-C\equiv C-H$

n = number of carbon atoms

Class of Compound	Functional Group	General Formula	Example
halide (halocarbon)	$-F$ (fluoro-) $-Cl$ (chloro-) $-Br$ (bromo-) $-I$ (iodo-)	$R-X$ (X represents any halogen)	$CH_3CHClCH_3$ 2-chloropropane
alcohol	$-OH$	$R-OH$	$CH_3CH_2CH_2OH$ 1-propanol
ether	$-O-$	$R-O-R'$	$CH_3OCH_2CH_3$ methyl ethyl ether
aldehyde	$\overset{\displaystyle O}{\overset{\|}{-C-H}}$	$\overset{\displaystyle O}{\overset{\|}{R-C-H}}$	$\overset{\displaystyle O}{\overset{\|}{CH_3CH_2C-H}}$ propanal
ketone	$\overset{\displaystyle O}{\overset{\|}{-C-}}$	$\overset{\displaystyle O}{\overset{\|}{R-C-R'}}$	$\overset{\displaystyle O}{\overset{\|}{CH_3CCH_2CH_2CH_3}}$ 2-pentanone
organic acid	$\overset{\displaystyle O}{\overset{\|}{-C-OH}}$	$\overset{\displaystyle O}{\overset{\|}{R-C-OH}}$	$\overset{\displaystyle O}{\overset{\|}{CH_3CH_2C-OH}}$ propanoic acid
ester	$\overset{\displaystyle O}{\overset{\|}{-C-O-}}$	$\overset{\displaystyle O}{\overset{\|}{R-C-O-R'}}$	$\overset{\displaystyle O}{\overset{\|}{CH_3CH_2COCH_3}}$ methyl propanoate
amine	$\overset{\|}{-N-}$	$\overset{R'}{\overset{\|}{R-N-R''}}$	$CH_3CH_2CH_2NH_2$ 1-propanamine
amide	$\overset{\displaystyle O\ \ }{\overset{\|\ \ }{-C-NH}}$	$\overset{\displaystyle O\ \ R'}{\overset{\|\ \ \|}{R-C-NH}}$	$\overset{\displaystyle O}{\overset{\|}{CH_3CH_2C-NH_2}}$ propanamide

R represents a bonded atom or group of atoms.

TABLE R
ORGANIC FUNCTIONAL GROUPS

A functional group is a characteristic group of atoms that attach to a carbon chain in order to form a specific class of organic compounds. These classes of organic compounds are named in accordance with the IUPAC system of nomenclature. Table R lists several classes of organic compounds, their functional group, general formula, and an example of how each class of compound is named using the IUPAC system of nomenclature.

Atomic Number	Symbol	Name	First Ionization Energy (kJ/mol)	Electro-negativity	Melting Point (K)	Boiling* Point (K)	Density** (g/cm³)	Atomic Radius (pm)
1	H	hydrogen	1312	2.1	14	20	0.00009	37
2	He	helium	2372	—	1	4	0.000179	32
3	Li	lithium	520	1.0	454	1620	0.534	155
4	Be	beryllium	900	1.6	1551	3243	1.8477	112
5	B	boron	801	2.0	2573	3931	2.340	98
6	C	carbon	1086	2.6	3820	5100	3.513	91
7	N	nitrogen	1402	3.0	63	77	0.00125	92
8	O	oxygen	1314	3.5	55	90	0.001429	65
9	F	fluorine	1681	4.0	54	85	0.001696	57
10	Ne	neon	2081	—	24	27	0.0009	51
11	Na	sodium	496	0.9	371	1156	0.971	190
12	Mg	magnesium	736	1.3	922	1363	1.738	160
13	Al	aluminum	578	1.6	934	2740	2.698	143
14	Si	silicon	787	1.9	1683	2628	2.329	132
15	P	phosphorus	1012	2.2	317	553	1.820	128
16	S	sulfur	1000	2.6	386	718	2.070	127
17	Cl	chlorine	1251	3.2	172	239	0.003214	97
18	Ar	argon	1521	—	84	87	0.001783	88
19	K	potassium	419	0.8	337	1047	0.862	235
20	Ca	calcium	590	1.0	1112	1757	1.550	197
21	Sc	scandium	633	1.4	1814	3104	2.989	162
22	Ti	titanium	659	1.5	1933	3580	4.540	145
23	V	vanadium	651	1.6	2160	3650	6.100	134
24	Cr	chromium	653	1.7	2130	2945	7.190	130
25	Mn	manganese	717	1.6	1517	2235	7.440	135
26	Fe	iron	762	1.8	1808	3023	7.874	126
27	Co	cobalt	760	1.9	1768	3143	8.900	125
28	Ni	nickel	737	1.9	1726	3005	8.902	124
29	Cu	copper	745	1.9	1357	2840	8.960	128
30	Zn	zinc	906	1.7	693	1180	7.133	138
31	Ga	gallium	579	1.8	303	2676	5.907	141
32	Ge	germanium	762	2.0	1211	3103	5.323	137
33	As	arsenic	944	2.2	1090	889	5.780	139
34	Se	selenium	941	2.6	490	958	4.790	140
35	Br	bromine	1140	3.0	266	332	3.122	112
36	Kr	krypton	1351	—	117	121	0.00375	103
37	Rb	rubidium	403	0.8	312	961	1.532	248
38	Sr	strontium	549	1.0	1042	1657	2.540	215
39	Y	yttrium	600	1.2	1795	3611	4.469	178
40	Zr	zirconium	640	1.3	2125	4650	6.506	160

Note: Table S continues on the next page

TABLE S
PROPERTIES OF SELECTED ELEMENTS

Table S is a useful table for several pieces of information pertaining to the many elements listed. The table is self-explanatory as it provides a listing of elements and a number of their properties. The element's atomic number, symbol, and name are the first three pieces of information listed in the table. Next to each element are listed the 1st Ionization Energy, Electronegativity, Melting Point, Boiling Point, Density, and Atomic Radius. Note: Not all elements have been selected for this table.

Atomic Number	Symbol	Name	First Ionization Energy (kJ/mol)	Electro-negativity	Melting Point (K)	Boiling* Point (K)	Density** (g/cm³)	Atomic Radius (pm)
41	Nb	niobium	652	1.6	2741	5015	8.570	146
42	Mo	molybdenum	684	2.2	2890	4885	10.220	139
43	Tc	technetium	702	1.9	2445	5150	11.500	136
44	Ru	ruthenium	710	2.2	2583	4173	12.370	134
45	Rh	rhodium	720	2.3	2239	4000	12.410	134
46	Pd	palladium	804	2.2	1825	3413	12.020	137
47	Ag	silver	731	1.9	1235	2485	10.500	144
48	Cd	cadmium	868	1.7	594	1038	8.650	171
49	In	indium	558	1.8	429	2353	7.310	166
50	Sn	tin	709	2.0	505	2543	7.310	162
51	Sb	antimony	831	2.1	904	1908	6.691	159
52	Te	tellurium	869	2.1	723	1263	6.240	142
53	I	iodine	1008	2.7	387	458	4.930	132
54	Xe	xenon	1170	2.6	161	166	0.0059	124
55	Cs	cesium	376	0.8	302	952	1.873	267
56	Ba	barium	503	0.9	1002	1910	3.594	222
57	La	lanthanum	538	1.1	1194	3730	6.145	138
Elements 58–71 have been omitted.								
72	Hf	hafnium	659	1.3	2503	5470	13.310	167
73	Ta	tantalum	728	1.5	3269	5698	16.654	149
74	W	tungsten	759	2.4	3680	5930	19.300	141
75	Re	rhenium	756	1.9	3453	5900	21.020	137
76	Os	osmium	814	2.2	3327	5300	22.590	135
77	Ir	iridium	865	2.2	2683	4403	22.560	136
78	Pt	platinum	864	2.3	2045	4100	21.450	139
79	Au	gold	890	2.5	1338	3080	19.320	146
80	Hg	mercury	1007	2.0	234	630	13.546	160
81	Tl	thallium	589	2.0	577	1730	11.850	171
82	Pb	lead	716	2.3	601	2013	11.350	175
83	Bi	bismuth	703	2.0	545	1833	9.747	170
84	Po	polonium	812	2.0	527	1235	9.320	167
85	At	astatine	—	2.2	575	610	—	145
86	Rn	radon	1037	—	202	211	0.00973	134
87	Fr	francium	393	0.7	300	950	—	270
88	Ra	radium	—	0.9	973	1413	5.000	233
89	Ac	actinium	499	1.1	1320	3470	10.060	—
Elements 90 and above have been omitted.								

*Boiling point at standard pressure
**Density at STP

Table T
Important Formulas and Equations

Density	$d = \dfrac{m}{V}$	d = density m = mass V = volume
Mole Calculations	number of moles = $\dfrac{\text{given mass (g)}}{\text{gram-formula mass}}$	
Percent Error	% error = $\dfrac{\text{measured value} - \text{accepted value}}{\text{accepted value}} \times 100$	
Percent Composition	% composition by mass = $\dfrac{\text{mass of part}}{\text{mass of whole}} \times 100$	
Concentration	parts per million = $\dfrac{\text{grams of solute}}{\text{grams of solution}} \times 1\,000\,000$	
	molarity = $\dfrac{\text{moles of solute}}{\text{liters of solution}}$	
Combined Gas Law	$\dfrac{P_1 V_1}{T_1} = \dfrac{P_2 V_2}{T_2}$	P = pressure V = volume T = temperature (K)
Titration	$M_A V_A = M_B V_B$	M_A = molarity of H^+ M_B = molarity of OH^- V_A = volume of acid V_B = volume of base
Heat	$q = mC\Delta T$ $q = mH_f$ $q = mH_v$	q = heat H_f = heat of fusion m = mass H_v = heat of vaporization C = specific heat capacity ΔT = change in temperature
Temperature	K = °C + 273	K = kelvin °C = degrees Celsius
Radioactive Decay	fraction remaining = $\left(\dfrac{1}{2}\right)^{\frac{t}{T}}$ number of half-life periods = $\dfrac{t}{T}$	t = total time elapsed T = half-life

TABLE T
IMPORTANT FORMULAS & EQUATIONS

This table is also self-explanatory. However, the student should become familiar with the different formulas and equations listed on the table and how they apply to solving problems in basic inorganic chemistry.

Index & Glossary

The following is a listing of terms and other items relevant to *Physical Setting: Chemistry*. Page numbers follow the words and/or phrases in order that students can check the context in which the term is used.

Absolute reducing tendency: (234) total amount by which a substance gains electrons and loses oxygen.

Absolute temperature scale: (131) see Kelvin.

Absolute zero: (131) the temperature at which substances possess no thermal energy, equal to -273.15°C, or -459.67°F.

Absorption: (113, 171) to take in; assimilate

Accelerators: (283) a device, such as a cyclotron or linear accelerator, that accelerates charged subatomic particles or nuclei to high energies; also called atom smasher.

Accepted value: (311) most probable value taken from generally accepted references.

Acetic acid: (196, 262, 265) CH_3COOH or ethanoic acid; used as a solvent and in the manufacture of rubber, plastics, acetate fibers, pharmaceuticals, and photographic chemicals; chief acid of vinegar.

Acetylene series: (193) see Alkyne.

Acid-base indicator: (256, 258, 331) any of various substances, such as litmus or phenolphthalein, that indicate the presence, absence, or concentration of another substance or the degree of reaction between two or more substances by means of a characteristic change, especially in color; see *Reference Table M*.

Acidosis: (265) abnormal increase in the acidity of the body's fluids, caused either by accumulation of acids or by depletion of bicarbonates.

Acid rain: (264) environmental pollution caused when sulfur and nitrogen dioxides combine with atmospheric moisture to produce highly precipitation falling as rain.

Acids: (66, 196, 198, 205, 255-276, 265, 310, 330) any species that can donate a proton to another substance; a molecule or ion that can combine with another by forming a covalent bond with two electrons of the other; see *Reference Table K*.

Activated complex: (159, 161, 163, 189) intermediate species formed when reactants form products in a reaction.

Activation energy: (159, 161, 162, 164, 204) minimum energy required to initiate a reaction.

Adage: (123) a saying that sets forth a general truth and that has gained credit through long use.

Addition polymerization: (206) a reaction in which monomers of unsaturated compounds join together.

Addition: (206) reactions generated by addition of one or more atoms to an unsaturated organic molecule at the double or triple bond; results in saturation of the compound.

Adsorption: (119) accumulation of gases, liquids, or solutes on the surface of a solid or liquid.

Alcohols: (196-198, 197) hydrocarbons in which one of the hydrogen atoms is replaced by one or more hydroxyl groups (O-H).

Aldehydes: (198) hydrocarbons in which an end carbon contains a functional group (CHO).

Alkadienes: (194) homologous series of hydrocarbons containing two double bonds.

Alkali metals: (44) common name for Group 1 metals.

Alkaline earth metals: (44) common name for Group 2 metals.

Alkalosis: (265) Abnormally high alkalinity of the blood and body fluids.

Alkanes: (192, 332) homologous of hydrocarbons having the general formula C_nH2_{n+2}.

Alkenes: (193, 332) any of a series of unsaturated, open chain hydrocarbons with one or more carbon-carbon double bonds, having the general formula C_nH_{2n}.

Alkyl radicals: (195) an alkane which has lost a hydrogen atom, resulting in an open bond structure.

Alkynes: (194, 332) homologous series of hydrocarbons having the general formula C_nH_{2n-2}.

Allotrope: (40, 45, 47,51) chemical element in two or more forms with differing physical properties; e.g., carbon exists as graphite and diamond.

Alloy: (37, 51, 120, 243) homogeneous mixture or solid solution of two or more metals, the atoms of one replacing or occupying interstitial positions between the atoms of the other.

Alpha decay: (280) result which occurs when a nucleus disintegrates with the emission of alpha particles.

Alpha emitter: (280) atom that emits an alpha particle.

Alpha particles: (280, 281, 282) consists of two neutron and two protons and can be considered Helium nuclei.

Amides: (199-200) organic compound, such as acetamide, containing the $CONH_2$ radical.

Amines: (199) any of a group of organic compounds of nitrogen, such as ethylamine, that may be considered ammonia derivatives in which one or more hydrogen atoms have been replaced by a hydrocarbon radical.

Amino Acids: (200, 208, 209) organic compound containing both an amino group (NH_2) and a carboxylic acid group (COOH), especially any of the 20 compounds that have the basic formula $NH_2CHRCOOH$, and that link together by peptide bonds to form proteins.

Amphiprotic (amphoteric) substances: (259) substance which can act either as an acid or as a base.

Amorphous: (40, 51, 109) lacking definite form or structure; shapeless.

amu: see atomic mass unit.

Angstrom unit: (19, 24, 42, 94) unit of length equal to one hundred-millionth of a centimeter, used especially to specify radiation wavelengths atomic and ionic radii. (1 Å = 1 x 10^{-10} meter)

Anode: (231, 239, 241) pole where oxidation takes place in a chemical cell.

Antibiotic: (293) substance, such as penicillin or streptomycin, produced by or derived from certain fungi, bacteria, and other organisms, that can destroy or inhibit the growth of other microorganisms. Antibiotics are widely used in the prevention and treatment of infectious diseases.

Apparatus, laboratory: (203-204) common laboratory apparatus pictured and uses discussed.

Aqueous: (53, 67, 96, 163, 196, 239, 254, 255, 256, 258, 262, 267) relating to dissolved in water.

Aromatic: (195) relating to, or containing one or more six-carbon rings characteristic of the benzene series and related organic groups.

Arrhenius' Theory: (255, 256) aqueous solutions, acids yield hydrogen ions, bases yield hydroxide ions; after Svante August Arrhenius (1859-1927), Swedish physicist and chemist; 1903 Nobel Prize for electrolytic theory of dissociation.

Artificial radioactivity: (282) radioactive isotopes which result from artificial transmutation.

Artificial transmutation: (282) bombarding nuclei with high energy particles resulting in transmutations into new, usually stable, nuclei.

Asymmetric: (87, 94) having no balance or symmetry.

Atom: (10-34, 37, 41, 42, 62, 64, 65, 67, 70, 84, 85, 86, 90, 94, 117, 130, 175, 195, 197, 199, 202, 221, 222, 264, 278) smallest elemental particle which retains all of the characteristics of that element.

Atomic Absorption Analysis (24). process vaporizes a solution and measures the intensity of excited sodium atoms to determine the concentration of sodium in the solution.

Atomic energy: see nuclear energy.

Atomic bomb: (284, 286) explosive weapon of great destructive power derived from the rapid release of energy in the fission of heavy atomic nuclei, as of uranium 235.

Atomic mass: (13, 14, 69, 282, 283) the weighted average quantity of matter that the naturally occurring isotopes of an element contain.

Atomic Mass Unit (amu): (13, 30, 72, 73, 81, 280) unit of measure which is standardized as 1/12 of the mass of a carbon atom.

Atomic number: (12, 36, 39, 41, 42, 45, 47, 48, 50, 117, 280, 283, 334) indicates the number of protons in the nucleus; see *Reference Table S*.

Atomic orbital model: (18) the average region of most probable electron location defined by quantum mechanics so that no two electrons will have the same energy level.

Atomic radius: (41-42, 94, 95, 334) one-half of the measured internuclear distance between atoms in the solid phase or in a crystalline metal; see *Reference Table S*.

Atomic structure: (12-15) a nuclear model of an atom using quantum mechanical theory to account for probable energy levels of its electrons.

Atomic weight (72) average mass of an atom of an element, usually expressed relative to the mass of carbon 12, which is assigned 12 atomic mass units.

Avogadro's Law or hypothesis: (15, 139) equal volumes of gases, under the same conditions of temperature and pressure, contain equal numbers of particles; named for Italian physicist Amedeo Avogadro (1776-1856), a founder of physical chemistry.

Avogadro's number: (15, 62, 69, 79, 139) 6.02 x 10^{23}; particles in a mole of matter; a mole of any substance always contains the same number of molecules; also Avogadro constant.

Azo: (209) prefix for substances containing a nitrogen group, especially N=N.

Bacteria: (204, 262, 264) any of the unicellular, prokaryotic microorganisms of the class Schizomycetes, which vary in terms of morphology, oxygen and nutritional requirements, and motility, and may be free-living, saprophytic, or pathogenic, the latter causing disease in plants or animals.

Balancing simple redox reactions: (224) determining the loss and gain of electrons.

Bases: (66, 196, 205, 255-276, 310, 330) any species (molecule or ion) which can accept a proton in the form of a H^+ ion; see *Reference Table L*.

Basicity: (261, 330) producing, resulting from, or relating to a base; containing a base, especially in excess of acid.

Battery: (238) spontaneous chemical cells in which spontaneous redox reactions are used to provide a source of electrical energy.

Beaker: (205) wide cylindrical glass vessel with a pouring lip, used as a laboratory container and mixing jar.

Benzene series: (195) cyclic homologous series with a general formula of C_nH_{2n-6} called the aromatic hydrocarbons.

Beta decay: (280) reaction which results in neutron disintegration and the emission of a high speed electron called a beta particle.

Beta particle: (280, 287, 295) high-speed electron or positron, especially one emitted in radioactive decay.

Binary acid: (65) acid in which there are only two elements in the formula, hydrogen being one of them.

Binary compounds: (117) compounds made up of just two elements.

Binary salts: (66) two element-compound formed by replacing part of the hydrogen ions of an acid with metal ions or electropositive radicals.

Binding energy: (285) energy released when the fusion of two particles occurs; a measure of the stability of the atom.

Biodegrade: (209) capable of being decomposed by biological agents, especially bacteria.

Bleach: (265) to remove the color from, as by means of chemical agents or sunlight.

Blocks – Periodic Table: (66-73) division of elements in some forms of the Periodic Table.

Bohr, Niels H.: (11, 15) Danish physicist (1885-1962); helped to develop quantum theories; Nobel Prize in 1922; developed the atomic bomb.

Bohr model: (15, 16, 18) shows structure of the atom, preceded the orbital structure.

Boiling point: (109, 113, 117, 129, 130, 192, 334) temperature at which the vapor pressure of a liquid equals the pressure on the liquid.

Bonds: (41, 42, 46, 66, 84-104, 111, 112, 158, 163, 175, 189, 190, 191) the simultaneous attraction of electrons by two or more atoms.

Boyle's Law: (134-135, 137) at constant temperatures, the volume of a given mass of a gas varies inversely with the pressure exerted on it.

Boyle, Robert, (10, 135) English natural philosopher and chemist (1627-1691); important contributions to experimental chemistry; known for his ideal-gas law.

Breeder reactor: (287) nuclear reactor that produces as well as consumes fissionable material, especially one that produces more fissionable material than it consumes.

Bromthymol blue: (258) common acid-base indicator.

Brönsted-Lowry Theory: (255, 256, 257) a conceptual definition for acids and bases wherein acids are proton donors and bases are proton acceptors; after Danish chemist Johannes Nicolaus Brønsted (1879-1947) ,known for his theory of acids and bases (1923).

Buckminsterfullerene: (52) see fullerenes.

Bucky balls: (52) see fulerenes.

Bucky tubes: (52) variation of buckyballs – long, hollow carbon tubes, successfully introduced into scanning and tunneling microscopy as "sharp needles" for probing surfaces.

Buffers: (265) substance that minimizes change in the acidity of a solution when an acid or base is added to the solution.

Bunsen burner use: (312) illustration of the proper adjustment and use of the bunsen burner or heat source.

Buret: (310) uniform-bore glass tube with fine gradations and a stopcock at the bottom, used especially in laboratory procedures for accurate fluid dispensing and measurement.

Calorie: (132, 142) unit of heat equal to 1/100 the quantity of heat required to raise the temperature of 1 gram of water from 0 to 100°C at 1 atmosphere pressure.

Calorimeter: (142) apparatus for measuring the heat generated by a chemical reaction, change of state, or formation of a solution.

Calorimetry: (142) study of energy changes involved in chemical reactions.

Carbohydrate: (97, 208) any of a group of organic compounds that includes sugars, starches, celluloses, and gums and serves as a major energy source in the diet of animals.; produced by photosynthetic plants and contain only carbon, hydrogen, and oxygen.

Carboxyl: (208) univalent radical, COOH, the functional group characteristic of all organic acids.

Capillary action: (110) interaction between contacting surfaces of a liquid and a solid that distorts the liquid surface from a planar shape.

Catalysts: (161, 163, 164, 171, 172, 203) used in a reaction to change the rate of the reaction and are removed from the reaction intact.

Cathode: (231, 239, 240, 241) pole in a chemical cell where reduction occurs.

Cathode protection: (226) protecting by plating with a more active metal.

Cation: (50) an ion or group of ions having a positive charge and characteristically moving toward the negative electrode in electrolysis.

Caustic: (265) capable of burning, corroding, dissolving, or eating away by chemical action.

Cellulose: (206, 208) complex carbohydrate that is composed of glucose units, forms the main constituent of the cell wall in most plants, and is important in the manufacture of numerous products, such as paper, textiles, pharmaceuticals, and explosives.

Celsius: (131, 135-136) a temperature scale with fixed points at 0°C at ice water equilibrium and 100°C at steam water equilibrium.

Chadwick, James: (11) English physicist (1891-1974); experiments on the bombardment of certain light elements with alpha particles led to the discovery of the neutron (1932);awarded the 1935 Nobel Prize for physics; during World War II, Chadwick worked on the atomic bomb.

Charles' Law: (135, 137) at constant pressure, the volume of a given mass of gas varies directly with the Kelvin (Absolute) temperature; after Jacques Alexandre César Charles (1746-1823), the French physicist and inventor who was the first to use hydrogen in balloons (1783).

Chaos Theory: (174) uncertainty in the initial state of the given system, no matter how small, will lead to rapidly growing errors in any effort to predict the future behavior.

Chemical cells: (232) an electrochemical cell in which a spontaneous chemical reaction is used to produce an electric current.

Chemical change: (111, 220) transition of matter in which properties and identity are altered.

Chemical equilibrium: (170) a reversible reaction at a given temperature in which the products of the molar concentrations of the products divided by the product of the molar concentrations of the reactants is a constant.

Chemical formula: see formulas.

Chemistry: study of composition, structure, and properties of matter; changes which matter undergoes; energy accompanying these changes.

Chemical properties: (40, 107, 107) characteristics that change due to molecular changes (burning, interaction with air, water, acids, solvents, etc.).

Chloroplasts: (97) chlorophyll-containing plastid found in algal and green plant cells.

Chromatography: (119) techniques for the separation of complex mixtures that rely on the differential affinities of substances for a gas or liquid mobile medium and for a stationary adsorbing medium through which they pass, such as paper, gelatin, or magnesia.

Coefficient: (67, 75, 172, 260) number or symbol multiplying a variable or an unknown quantity in an algebraic term

Colligative properties: (128) properties which depend on the relative number of particles rather than on the nature of the particles.

Collision Theory: (133, 159) gas particles produce reactions if they hit each other with proper energy and orientation.

Colloids: (120, 207) suspension of finely divided particles in a continuous medium in which the particles are approximately 5 to 5,000 angstroms in size, do not settle out of the substance rapidly, and are not readily filtered.

Combined gas laws: (137) Boyle's and Charles' Laws used together.

Combustion: (202, 204, 205) chemical change, especially oxidation, accompanied by the production of heat and light.

Common ion effect: (177) the addition of a ion that is common to a chemical species found in an equilibrium system.

Composition reactions: (223) category of redox reactions.

Compounds: (62, 70, 117, 188-217, 221-222, 241, 330) two or more different substances, chemically combined in a definite ratio by weight.

Concentration: (166, 169, 170, 173, 177, 205, 236, 240, 259-260, 263, 265, 266, 267, 331) amount of a specified substance in a unit amount of another substance.

Concentrated solution: (124-125, 126, 169) solution in which a large amount of solute can be dissolved in a small amount of solvent.

Conceptual definitions: (254, 255, 256) definitions that attempt to answer the why and how statements of acids and bases.

Condensation: (166) chemical reaction in which water or another simple substance is released by the combination of two or more molecules.

Condensation polymerization: (206) bonding of monomers into polymers by a dehydration reaction.

Conductivity: (37) ability or power to conduct or transmit heat, electricity, or sound.

Conjugate acid-base pair: (257) in an acid-base reaction, an acid transfers a proton to become a conjugate base, this acid and the newly formed base form an acid-base pair.

Constant: (172, 173, 176-177) experimental condition, factor, or quantity that does not vary or that is regarded as invariant in specified circumstances.

Control rods: (288) see nuclear control rods.

Coolants: (288) see nuclear coolants.

Coordinate covalent bonds: (41, 87, 88, 257) occurs when the two shared electrons forming a covalent bond are both donated by one of the atoms.

Corrosion: (226, 265) gradual oxidation of a metal which results in the metal returning to its ionic form.

Covalent atomic radius: (41) effective distance from the center of the nucleus to outer valence shell of that atom in a typical or covalent bond.

Covalent bonds: (41, 42, 52, 84, 86, 87, 91, 92, 93, 95, 96, 97, 189, 190) bond in which the atoms share electrons in an overlapping manner.

Cracking: (214) a process by which large molecules are broken down to smaller molecules.

Crick, Francis: (98) British biologist (1916-) proposed a spiral model, the double helix, for the molecular structure of DNA;1962 Nobel Prize for advances in the study of genetics.

Crookes, William: (11) British chemist and physicist (1832-1919); discovered (1861) the element thallium and research in vacuum physics; invented the radiometer in 1875; investigated electrical discharges; laid the foundation for J.J. Thomson's research in the late 1890s concerning discharge-tube phenomena.

Crystals (crystalline structures): (40, 85, 89, 107, 08-109, 120, 174, 203) homogenous solid formed by a repeating, three-dimensional pattern of atoms, ions, or molecules and having fixed distances between constituent parts; solids in which atoms are arranged in a regular geometric pattern.

Cyclic hydrocarbons: (195) hydrocarbons arranged in a ring structure.

Dalton, John: (10-11, 138) English chemist and physicist (1766-1844); developed the ancient concept of atoms into a scientific theory that became a foundation of modern chemistry.

Dalton's Law of Partial Pressures: (138) pressure exerted by a gaseous mixture is equal to the sum of the partial pressures of its components.

Daniell electrochemical cell: zinc-copper battery; after English meteorologist, chemist, and inventor John Frederic Daniell (1790-1845).

de Broglie, Louis: (11) French physicist (1892-1987); known for theory that matter has the properties of both particles and waves, derived from the work of Albert Einstein and Max Planck; received the 1929 Nobel Prize for physics.

Decomposition reactions: (76) category of redox reactions.

Dehydration: (206) process of removing water from a substance or compound.

Delta: (10) Greek letter sign (Δ) used in reactions to indicate change.

Democritius: (10) Ancient Greek scholar (460-370 BC); first used the term "atom" -"uncuttable" particles.

Density: (118, 334) mass of unit volume of a substance.

Deoxyribonucleic acid: see DNA.

Deposition: (114) phase change in which a gas moves directly to a solid.

Desalinization: (119) removal salts and other chemicals.

Deuterium: (13) isotope of hydrogen with one proton and one neutron.

Diatomic: (46, 92, 159) made up of two atoms.

Dielectric effect: (122) the ability of a solvent to reduce the force of attraction between charged particles.

Diffusion: (139) spontaneous intermingling of the particles of two or more substances as a result of random thermal motion.

Dihydroxy alcohols: (198) compounds containing two hydroxyl (O-H) groups.

Dilute solution: (126) solution in which a large amount of solvent is required to dissolve a small amount of solute.

Dimensional analysis: (309) measurements treated as algebraic quantities.

Dipole moment: (87) product of a charge and the distance of partial separation in asymmetrical molecules

Dipole: (87, 94-95, 96, 121) results from the asymmetric distribution of electron charges in a molecule, and is polar in nature.

Diprotic: (265) having two hydrogen ions to donate to bases in an acid-base reaction.

Dissociation: (122, 130, 177, 262) chemical process by means of which a change in physical condition, as in pressure or temperature, or the action of a solvent causes a molecule to split into simpler groups of atoms, single atoms, or ions; immediate reverse association begins to occur and there is established a dynamic equilibrium between the reactants and the product.

Dissociation constant: (254) equilibrium constant for weak electrolytes in aqueous solution.

Dissolution: (123) decomposition into fragments or parts; disintegration; see dissociation.

Distillation: (118) extraction of the volatile components of a mixture by the condensation and collection of the vapors that are produced as the mixture is heated.

DNA: (98, 209) a nucleic acid that carries the genetic information in the cell and is capable of self-replication and synthesis of RNA; sequence of nucleotides determines individual hereditary characteristics.

Double bond: (91, 191, 205) binding of carbon atoms through sharing of two pairs of electrons.

Ductility: (37, 89, 107) substance easily molded or shaped.

Dynamic: (166, 167) relating to energy or to objects in motion or characterized by continuous change, activity, or progress.

Dynamic equilibrium: (166) state of balance in which the reaction rates are for opposing reactions are equal.

Effective collisions: (159) reacting particles smash into each other with enough force to break old bonds and form new ones.

Einstein, Albert: (11, 285) German-American physicist (1879-1955), contributed 20th-century vision of physical reality; and elaborated quantum mechanics and relativity.

Electric furnace process: (243) easily controlled arc furnace used in the production of high-quality steel; see open hearth process.

Electrochemical cells: (229, 232) apparatus for producing electric current by chemical action; also called voltaic cells.

Electrochemistry: (204, 227, 229, 231, 232, 235, 240) study of the relationship between electricity and chemistry.

Electrodes: (229, 231, 232, 243, 281) conductor used to attract cations to the cathode and anions to the anode.

Electrodialysis: (119) increasing the rate of separation of smaller molecules from larger molecules by selective diffusion through a semipermeable membrane by the application of an electric potential across the dialysis membrane.

Electrolysis: (45, 48, 236, 241) chemical change, especially decomposition, produced in an electrolyte by an electric current.

Electrolytes: (129, 130, 189, 254, 255, 262, 267) substance whose water solution conducts an electrical current.

Electrolytic cell: (229, 231, 236, 237, 240) chemical compound that ionizes when dissolved or molten to produce an electrically conductive medium.

Electromagnetic radiation: (130) magnetic energy rays, waves, or particles produced by electric charge in motion.

Electromagnetic spectrum: (280) entire range of radiation extending in frequency from approximately 10^{23} hertz to 0 hertz or, in corresponding wavelengths, from 10^{-13} centimeter to infinity and including, in order of decreasing frequency, cosmic-ray photons, gamma rays, x-rays, ultraviolet radiation, visible light, infrared radiation, microwaves, and radio waves.

Electron: (11, 21-23, 48, 50, 85, 86, 87, 88, 90, 93, 96, 204, 220-221, 223, 224, 229, 232, 240, 241, 257, 280) fundamental, negatively charged subatomic particle; a constituent of all ordinary matter; responsible for many physical and chemical properties of matter, such as the formation of chemical compounds.

Electron configuration: (22) distribution of the electrons among the various orbitals of an atom.

Electron density formulas: (91) of H_2O, CO_2, and carbon tetrafluoride.

Electron-dot diagrams: (21) diagram showing the valence electrons of an atom by using the elements letter representation and the number of valence electrons in dots.

Electronegativity: (37, 42, 44, 45, 47, 48, 50, 64; 86, 87, 91, 92, 93-95, 204, 220, 221, 228, 334) measure of the ability of an atom to attract the electrons that form a bond between it and another atom.

Electroplating: (240) when the surface of an item has been coated with a thin layer of metal usually by the process of electrolysis.

Electrostatic force: (22, 85, 96, 283) forces of attraction and repulsion acting between particles due to the close proximity of electrons and protons

Element: (11, 36, 40, 43-52, 117, 221, 280, 283, 286, 287, 334-335) substance that cannot be decomposed into two or more substances by means of chemical change; see *Reference Table S* for names.

Emanations: (280, 281) any of several radioactive gases that are isotopes of radon and are products of radioactive decay.

Empirical formula: (63) verifiable or provable by means of observation or experiment, and represents the simplest ratio in which elements combine to form a compound.

Emulsion: (120) suspension of small globules of one liquid in a second liquid with which the first will not mix.

Endothermic reaction: (112, 113, 160, 161, 162, 163, 171, 173, 176, 177, 329) reaction that absorbs heat from its surroundings.

Energy, conservation law: (130) energy may be converted from one form to another but is never created nor destroyed.

Energy forms: (130) include mechanical, heat, electrical, radiant, chemical, and nuclear energy.

Energy and chemical bonds: (111) potential energy associated with changes in chemical bonds (chemical energy).

Energy (nuclear): (130, 284) reactions that involve a great amount of energy.

Energy and spontaneous reactions: (173) energy changes in reactions.

Enthalpy: (162) thermodynamic function of a system, equivalent to the sum of the internal energy of the system plus the product of its volume multiplied by the pressure exerted on it by its surroundings.

Entropy: (110, 122-123, 174, 175, 176) randomness or disorder of regularity in a system.

Enzymes: (161, 208) any of numerous proteins or conjugated proteins produced by living organisms and functioning as biochemical catalysts.

Enzyme substrate complex:(161) association between the catalyst and the material on which it acts.

Equations, balanced: (67, 224, 225, 260) representation of a chemical reaction usually written as a linear array equal in reactants and products.

Equations, chemical: (66-67, 70, 124, 172, 177, 234, 235, 239, 259, 282, 283, 336) a representation of a chemical reaction, usually written as a linear array in which the symbols and quantities of the reactants are separated from those of the products by an equal sign, an arrow, or a set of opposing arrows.

Equilibrium: (114, 131, 166, 167, 168, 169, 170, 171, 172, 177, 232, 235, 254) the state of a chemical reaction in which its forward and reverse reactions occur at equal rates so that the concentration of the reactants and products does not change with time.

Equilibrium constants (Keq): (172, 267) ratio between the concentration of products divided by the concentration of reactants.

Equilibrium shift: (170) is the change in equilibrium in response to a stress.

Equivalence point: (259, 260) point of neutralization.

Erlenmeyer flask: (316) conical laboratory flask with a narrow neck and flat, broad bottom; after German chemist Richard Erlenmeyer (1825-1909).

Esterification: (204-205) reaction of acid with alcohol to give an ester and water.

Esters: (199) covalent compounds with pleasant odors made by reacting organic acids with alcohols.

Ethanol: (196, 203) a hydrocarbon consisting of two carbon atoms to which an hydroxyl group is attached.

Ethers: (199) two primary alcohols that are treated with a dehydrating agent, water is removed from the molecules and the two alcohol chains are joined by an oxygen bridge.

Ethylene series: see Alkenes.

Evaporation: (109, 166, 315) to convert or change into a vapor or gas from a liquid.

Excited state: (18) occurs when atoms absorb energy and electrons shift to a higher energy level; unstable

Exothermic reaction: (112, 113, 160, 162, 171, 173, 176, 204, 328, 329) reaction that releases heat into its surroundings.

Experimental mass ratio: (319) mass of the substance in grams divided by the mass of the residue in grams.

External shield: (289) see nuclear reactors, made of high density concrete, acts as a radiation containment vessel.

Fats: (191, 205, 208) esters made up of glycerine and of higher fatty acids.

Fatty acids: (191) long-chain carboxylic acids.

Fermentation: (203) any of a group of chemical reactions induced by living or nonliving ferments that split complex organic compounds into relatively simple substances, especially the anaerobic conversion of sugar to carbon dioxide and alcohol by yeast.

Ferrous corrosion: see rust.

Filtration: (118, 313) process used to separate suspended matter in a liquid usually through filter paper.

Final zero: (305) significant figures only if a decimal point is present.

Firepolishing: (313) preparing glass tubing in lab experiments.

Fission: (284, 286-287, 288) nuclear reaction in which an atomic nucleus, especially a heavy nucleus such as an isotope of uranium, splits into fragments, usually two fragments of comparable mass, with the evolution of from 100 million to several hundred million electron volts.

Flame tests: (23) test used to identify metallic ions, through exciting electrons.

Fluorescent: (281) emission of electromagnetic radiation, especially of visible light, stimulated in a substance by the absorption of incident radiation and persisting only as long as the stimulating radiation is continued.

Fluorine: (47) element with highest electronegativity in Group 17 of Periodic Table.

Forensic analysis: (24) relating to research used in courts of law or for public discussion or argumentation.

Formic acid: (196) HCOOH or methanoic acid.

Formula (chemical general): (62-63, 65, 72, 190, 192-196) statements that use chemical symbols to represent the composition of a substance.

Formula (mathematics): (125, 129, 142, 336) statement, especially an equation, of a fact, rule, principle, or other logical relation.

Formula (structural): (63, 156, 190-191, 192-194, 198, 199, 336) chemical formula, indicates arrangement of atoms in a molecule by using connecting lines from one atom to another.

Formula mass: see gram formula mass.

Fourth quantum number: (17) see atomic structure models.

Fractional distillation: (214) utilizing the differences in the boiling points of two or more liquids in order to separate them from one another.

Free energy: (175) tendency for a change to occur spontaneously.

Free energy change: (175) energy released or absorbed which can be used to do work for every mole of the compound formed.

Free radicals: (97) uncharged atom or molecule that has an odd number of electrons—i.e., one electron is unpaired; highly reactive and thus have only a temporary existence.

Freezing point: (129, 130, 192) temperature at which a liquid becomes a solid.

Freezing point depression: (129) lowering of the freezing point of a solvent.

Fullerenes: (40, 52) "buckyballs;" more or less spherical molecules made up of an allotropic form of carbon atoms; named after American designer Buckminster Fuller (1895-1983), creator of the geodesic dome.

Functional groups: (195-196) particular arrangement of a few atoms which gives characteristic properties to an organic molecule.

Funnel and filter paper: (313) use in a laboratory activity; illustrated.

Fuse: (241) liquefy or reduce to a plastic state by heating; melt.

Fusion reaction: (289) when two light nuclei fuse into a heavier nucleus at high temperature and pressure, usually an element of more stable configuration is formed.

Fusion reactor: (289) where fusion reactions can be completed at a controlled rate, wherein two atoms are fused into one element.

Gamma radiation: (280, 281) extremely high frequency electromagnetic waves which do not have mass or charge.

Gases and gaseous state of matter: (107, 108, 110, 141-144, 167) in this phase all molecules in a species have vibrating, rotating, and translating motions.

Gases behavior: (108, 167) manner in which certain gases behave in reactions and takes into account certain variables which include temperature, pressure, and volume.

Giauque, William: (174) American chemist (1895-1982); 1949 Nobel Prize for his research in low-temperature thermodynamic chemistry.

Glass tubing: (312-313) handling and preparing glass tubes used in experiments.

Global Warming: (140) popular term in environmental science for the effect that certain variable constituents of the Earth's lower atmosphere have on surface temperatures; also known as the greenhouse effect.

Glycerol: (205, 208, 264) syrupy, sweet, colorless or yellowish liquid, $C_3H_8O_3$, obtained from fats and oils as a byproduct of saponification and used as a solvent, an antifreeze, a plasticizer, and a sweetener and in the manufacture of dynamite, cosmetics, liquid soaps, inks, and lubricants.

Graham, Thomas (139) Scottish inorganic and physical chemist (1805-1869) founder of colloid chemistry and one of the chief founders of physical chemistry.

Graham's Law: (139) relationship between mass and velocity; theory - "Under the same conditions of temperature and pressure, gases diffuse at a rate inversely proportionate to the square roots of their molecular masses," therefore, H_2 diffuses faster than O_2.

Gram atomic mass: (69) quantity of an element that has a mass in grams equal to its atomic mass in atomic mass units.

Gram formula mass: (69, 72) sum of the gram atomic masses.

Gram molecular mass: (69) quantity of substance that has a mass in grams equal to its molecular mass in atomic mass units.

Graphite: (52) soft, steel-gray to black, hexagonally crystallized allotrope of carbon with a metallic luster and a greasy feel, used in lead pencils, lubricants, paints, and coatings, that is fabricated into a variety of forms such as molds, bricks, electrodes, crucibles, and rocket nozzles.

Greenhouse Effect (140) phenomenon whereby the Earth's atmosphere traps solar radiation, caused by the presence in the atmosphere of gases such as carbon dioxide, water vapor, and methane that allow incoming sunlight to pass through but absorb heat radiated back from the Earth's surface; also known as the global warming.

Ground state atoms: (18) atoms whose electrons are not in an excited state; lowest energy state of an atom.

Groups of the Periodic Table: (40, 43) vertical columns of the Periodic Table; elements with similar properties that fall into the same column.

Haber process: (170, 171) chemical process in which nitrogen and hydrogen are combined to make ammonia; after German chemist Fritz Haber (1868-1934); 1918 Nobel Prize for the synthetic production of ammonia.

Half-cell: (230, 232, 234) each vessel in which one half-reaction is taking place during a redox reaction.

Half-life: (278, 279, 294, 331) time required for a radioactive isotope nuclei to disintegrate to one half its mass.

Half-reactions: (228, 234) reaction either representing a loss of electrons or the gain of electrons.

Half-cell electrode potential: (234) comparison of the driving force of a half-reaction with that of the hydrogen standard to establish a scale of voltages.

Halogen substitution (halogenation): (202) replacement of the hydrogen atoms in saturated hydrocarbons by an active halogen atom producing any of a group of five chemically related nonmetallic elements including fluorine, chlorine, bromine, iodine, and astatine.

Halogen derivatives: (202, 203) products of halogenation.

Halogen group: (47) elements in Group 17 of the Periodic Table.

Hamilton, William: (11) Irish mathematician (1805-1865); developed the famous *Theory of Systems of Rays* (1827); work on optics showed how the methods of algebra could be brought to bear on the problems of optics; developed quaternions—couplets of complex numbers that were of great importance in the later development of vector analysis.

Heat energy: (130) energy associated with the temperature of a body or system of bodies.

Heat of fusion: (113-114, 326) amount of energy required to convert one gram of any solid substance to a liquid at its melting point.

Heat of reaction: (162, 329) heat energy released or absorbed in the formation of the products; see *Reference Table I*.

Heat of vaporization: (114, 117, 326) energy needed to vaporize a unit mass of a liquid at a constant temperature.

Heating: (315) techniques for accident prevention during heating.

Heisenberg, Werner K.: (11) German theoretical physicist (1901-1976); developed quantum mechanics and the uncertainty principle in book, *The Physical Principles of Quantum Theory* (1928); awarded the Nobel Prize for physics in 1932.

Hemoglobin: (293) iron-containing respiratory pigment in red blood cells of vertebrates.

Heterogeneous mixture: (118, 120) mixture samples that are not uniform in composition throughout; see solutions.

Homogeneous mixture: (118) mixture samples that are uniform in composition throughout.

Homologous series: (192, 332) classification of related structures and properties into groups, in which each member of the group differs from its neighbor by a definite increment.

Hydrated crystal: (311) a crystal in which water molecules are attached by coordinate covalent bonds to a central metallic ion or ionic compound.

Hydration: (121) solute particle dissociation when water is the solvent.

Hydride (42, 64, 222) compound of hydrogen with another, more electropositive element or group.

Hydrocarbons: (191-209, 332) compounds containing only carbon and hydrogen; see *Reference Table Q*.

Hydroelectric cell (235-236) single unit for electrolysis or conversion of chemical into electric energy, usually consisting of a container with electrodes and an electrolyte.

Hydrogenation: (203) addition of hydrogen to an unsaturated substance.

Hydrogen bond: (95, 98) bond formed between a hydrogen atom in one molecule and a highly electronegative atom in another molecule.

Hydrolysis: (161, 199, 205, 262) a process by which some salts react with water to form solutions that are acidic or basic.

Hydronium ion: (263) results when a water molecule forms a coordinate covalent bond with a proton (or hydrogen ion).

Hydroxyl group: (197) -OH group that replace hydrogen atoms of hydrocarbons.

Ideal gas model: (133-134, 269) see Kinetic Molecular Theory of Gases.

Immiscible solution: (126) a mixture of two liquids which do not dissolve in one another.

Increment: (192) a small positive or negative change in the value of a variable

Indian Point: (289) nuclear power plant in Buchanan, NY; operated by the New York Power Authority; on line in 1976.

Indicators: (258, 331) substances (usually weak acids) which have difference colors in acid and base solutions.

Inert: (46, 84, 85) not readily reactive with other elements; forming few or no chemical compounds.

Inert gases: (48) not readily reactive with other elements; forming few or no chemical compounds; also noble or rare gases, common name for Group 18 elements.

Initial zero: (307) locator for decimals; not significant figures.

Inhibitor: (172) substance that retards or stops a chemical reaction.

Inorganic compounds: (188, 330, 336) relating to compounds not containing hydrocarbon groups.

Internal shield: (289) see nuclear reactors, made of a steel lining, protects walls of reactor from radiation damage.

International Union of Pure and Allied Chemistry: see IUPAC.

Intermolecular bonds: see bonds.

Intermolecular forces (94- 98, 114, 329) energy between two molecules that form a compound.

Intramolecular bond: (42) attractive forces inside molecules.

Ion: (44, 48, 64, 65, 70, 87, 88, 122, 129, 203, 221, 222, 224, 230, 232, 239, 240, 241, 254, 255, 259, 262, 263, 265, 266, 267, 331) an atom or a group of atoms that has acquired a net electric charge by gaining or losing one or more electrons.

Ionic bonds: (42, 84, 97, 163) occurs when the atoms of two or more different elements combine, resulting in the transfer of one or more electrons from one element to another, so that when the bond is broken, ions are formed.

Ionic compounds: (96, 163, 205, 254) hetero-nuclear compound containing ionic bonds.

Ionic radius: (42-43, 94) radii of ions in solid state.

Ionic solids: (85) solid compound containing ionic bonds.

Ionization constant: (266, 267) reaction by which ions are formed resulting in equilibrium condition.

Ionization energy: (37, 44, 45, 47, 50, 228, 255, 280, 334) energy required to remove an electron from an atom.

Isomers: (190, 192-193) any of two or more substances that are composed of the same elements in the same proportions but differ in properties because of differences in the arrangement of atoms.

Isotopes: (12, 13, 14, 36, 278, 279, 282, 284, 287, 290, 292, 294) atoms of one element with the same number of protons but a different number of neutrons.

IUPAC: (38, 51, 61, 62, 192, 193, 194, 196, 198, 200, 283, 333) International Union of Pure and Applied Chemistry; 74- nation organization formed in 1919, recognized as the world authority on chemical nomenclature, terminology, standardized methods for measurement, atomic weights and many other critically evaluated data; (www.iupac.org).

Joule: (15, 132, 142) basic SI unit of energy; International System unit of electrical, mechanical, and thermal energy equal to the work done when a force of 1 newton acts through a distance of 1 meter; after British physicist James Prescott Joule (1818-1889) who established the mechanical theory of heat and discovered the first law of thermodynamics.

Kelvin scale: (131, 135-136, 137) temperature scale with fixed points at 273 K at ice water equilibrium and 1 atmosphere of pressure, and 373 K at the steam water equilibrium and 1 atmosphere of pressure; also Absolute Temperature; after British physicist William Thomson (1st Baron Kelvin, 1824-1907)

Ketones: (198-199) organic compounds which contain a carbonyl (CO) functional group and hydrocarbon side groups.

Kernel: (21, 42, 44, 93) refers to the atom exclusive of the valence electrons.

Key Ideas: (7-8, 9-10, 35-36, 61-62, 83-84, 105-107, 157-158, 187-188, 219-220, 253-254, 277-278 305-306, 323) broad, unifying, general statements from the core curriculum of what students have to know.

Kilocalorie (kcal.): (142) one thousand calories; unit of heat equal to the amount of heat required to raise the temperature of 1 kilogram of water by 1°C at 1 atmosphere pressure.

Kilojoules: (329) units of one thousand joules; J x 10^3; see joules

Kinetic energy (K.E.): (114, 130, 134, 139, 164, 166, 176, 283, 290) energy of motion or reaction.

Kinetics, chemical: (158-186) branch of chemistry concerned with the rates of chemical reactions, and the mechanisms by which these reactions occur.

Kinetic Molecular Theory of Gases: (133-134) the "ideal gas model" holds that gas particles have little volume, move in random straight lines, are separated by great distances, and have no attraction to each other.

Laboratory activities: (310-316) measurements, skills, safety, & reports.

Laboratory apparatus: (317) illustrations of common equipment for experiments, safety, & reports.

Laser: (23) any of several devices that convert incident electromagnetic radiation of mixed frequencies to one or more discrete frequencies of highly amplified and coherent ultraviolet, visible, or infrared radiation.

Lavoisier, Antoine Laurent: (10) French chemist (1743-1794); revolutionary textbook, *Elements of Chemistry* (1789) presented a new system of chemistry based on concept of chemical elements and made extensive use of the conservation of mass in chemical reactions.

Law of chemical equilibrium: (172) see chemical equilibrium.

Law of the conservation of energy: (130) energy may be converted from one form to another but is never created or destroyed.

Lead-storage battery: (239-240) produced electricity using voltaic cells with lead oxide and sulfuric acid; automotive application.

Leaching: (242) removal of soluble or other constituents from a substance by the action of a percolating liquid.

LeChatelier's principle: (169, 177) thermodynamic principle that every change in a system in stable chemical equilibrium results in a rearrangement of the system so that the original change is minimized; after French chemist and metallurgist Henri Louis Le Châtelier (1850-1936).

Length: (107) measurement of the extent of something along its greatest dimension.

Lewis electron dot diagrams: (21, 86) notations for valence electrons originated by American chemist Gilbert Newton Lewis (1875-1946);

contributed to the study of thermodynamics, atomic structure, and bonding, as well as to the theory of acids and bases; see electron-dot diagrams; book, *Thermodynamics and the Free Energy of Chemical Substances* (1923).

Light: (19) electromagnetic radiation that has a wavelength in the range from about 4,000 (violet) to about 7,700 (red) angstroms and may be perceived by the normal unaided human eye; see spectrum; visible radiant energy.

Lipids: see fats.

Liquids: (40, 107, 107, 109, 209, 314) phase of matter; has a definite volume but an indefinite shape.

Litmus: (258) pH indicator, blue in basic solution and red in acid solution.

Logarithm: (263) power to which a base, usually 10, must be raised to produce a given number.

Luster (37, 89) soft, reflected light; sheen.

Macromolecule: (97) very large molecule, such as a polymer or protein, consisting of many smaller structural units linked together; also called supermolecule.

Magnetic bottles: (291) designed to confine nuclear fusion through the use of strong magnetic fields.

Major Understandings: (7-8, 9-10, 35-36, 61-62, 83-84, 105-106, 157-158, 187-188, 219-220, 253-254, 277-278) statements of specific detail on concepts underlying the chemistry core curriculum's performance indicators.

Malleability: (37, 89, 107) capable of being shaped or formed, as by hammering or pressure.

Manhattan Project: (284) World War II code name for the U.S. effort to produce the atomic bomb; named for the Manhattan Engineer District of the U.S. Army Corps of Engineers, because much of the early research was done in New York City.

Mass: (107, 124, 125, 136, 139, 278, 281, 284, 285, 286, 288, 289) measure of the quantity of matter that a body or an object contains.

Mass defect: (284) energy equal to the binding energy when the fusion of two or more particles occur.

Mass number: (13) number which indicates the total number of protons and neutrons in the nucleus of an atom.

Math skills: (305-309) significant figures, scientific notation, order of magnitude.

Mendeleev, Dmitri Ivanovich: (11, 36), Russian scientist (1834-1907); formulated the Periodic Table (also spelled Mendeleyev).

Matter: (11, 107-156) something that has mass and exists as a solid, liquid, or gas.

Measurement: (307, 310) dimension, quantity, or capacity determined by measuring; laboratory devices to determine size, weight, etc.

Mechanism of a chemical reaction: (158): sequence of steps in a reaction by which the over all reaction takes place.

Melting: (242) to be changed from a solid to a liquid state by application of heat, or pressure, or both.

Melting point: (113, 114, 117, 120, 334) temperature at which a solid and liquid are in equilibrium.

Meniscus: (95, 310) curved upper surface of a nonturbulent liquid in a container that is concave if the liquid wets the container walls and convex if it does not.

Methane series: (192) see also alkanes; odorless, colorless, flammable gas, CH_4, the major constituent of natural gas, that is used as a fuel and is an important source of hydrogen and a wide variety of organic compounds.

Metal ion: (42) see stock system; examples: FeO - iron (II) oxide and Fe_2O_3 - iron (III) oxide.

Metallic bonding: (89) force or mechanism joining the atoms of metals.

Metallic solids: (108) electropositive elements that usually have a shiny surface, are generally good conductors of heat and electricity, and can be melted or fused; having firm or compact physical properties

Metalloids (semimetals): (38, 39, 45, 46) nonmetallic element, such as arsenic, that has some of the chemical properties of a metal.

Metals: (37-38, 39, 42, 44, 45, 46, 50, 51, 85, 93, 97, 255, 330) any of a category of electropositive elements that usually have a shiny surface, generally good conductors of heat and electricity, and can be melted or fused, hammered into thin sheets, or drawn into wires; their atoms tend to lose electrons when combining with other atoms.

Metallurgy: (242) science that deals with procedures used in extracting metals from their ores, purifying and alloying metals, and creating useful objects from metals.

Methyl red: (258) acid-base indicator of univalent hydrocarbon radical, CH_3-, derived from methane.

Microorganisms: (204(organism of microscopic or submicroscopic size, especially a bacterium or protozoan.

Miscible solution: (126) solution of liquid solutes - soluble in liquid solvents.

Millikan, Robert A.: (11) American physicist (1868-1953); determined the value of the charge on an electron; demonstrated the charge was a discrete constant rather than a statistical average; Nobel Prize for physics in 1923.

Mixtures: (118) varying amounts of two or more distinct substances which differ in properties and composition.

Moderators: (288) see nuclear moderators, materials that have the ability to slow down neutrons quickly.

Molality: (129) expression of solution concentration which indicates the number of moles of solute in 1 kilogram of solvent.

Molar volume of a gas: (139) 22.4 liters of any gas at STP.

Molarity: (124, 259-260) expression of solution concentration which indicates the number of moles of solute in one liter of solution.

Mole: (15, 43, 62, 67, 69, 70, 73, 74, 75, 124-125, 129, 130, 139, 162, 163, 171, 240, 259, 266, 267) that quantity of a substance weighing (in grams) the same as its molecular weight (see also Avogardo's number of particles).

Molecular attraction: see dipoles and bonding.

Molecular formula: (63, 191, 195) symbolic representation of a structure of a covalently bonded particle; whole number multiple of the empirical formula.

Molecular substances: (88, 209) structural matter (possessing mass and occupying space) based on bond pairs and lone pairs of molecules

Molecular solids: (88) substance composed of molecules.having a definite shape and volume; one that is neither liquid nor gaseous.

Molecules: (64, 66, 67, 70, 73, 74, 87, 91, 96, 97, 110, 122, 130, 134, 139, 161, 172, 189, 191, 192, 195, 196, 197, 200, 206, 224, 255, 266. 267) two definitions: 1) a discrete particle formed by covalently bonded atoms; 2) The smallest particle of an element or compound capable of independent existence.

Monatomic gases: (48, 50) Group 18 elements in the Periodic Table.

Monatomic ion: (96, 221) a single atom with a charge.

Monohydroxy alcohols: (197) alcohols which have 1 hydroxyl (-O-H) group.

Monomer: (206) repeating chemical units which make up a polymer.

Monoprotic: (260, 265-266) having only one hydrogen ion to donate to a base in an acid-base reaction or having only one metal ion or positive radical.

Moseley, Henry Gwyn Jeffreys: (36) English physicist (1887- 1915); first to identify experimentally the nuclear charge of an element with what he called the atomic number.

Nanometer: (120) one billionth (10^{-9}) of a meter.

Natural radioactivity: (280, 282) the spontaneous disintegration of the nucleus of an atom with the emission of subatomic particles, usually occurs in nature in elements with an atomic number higher than 82.

Negative oxidation state: (47, 50) see oxidation state.

Negligible bond rearrangements: (163) often rapid reactions at room temperature, such as reactions of ionic substances in aqueous solutions.

Net reaction: (158) summation of all the changes that occur in a chemical reaction.

Network solids: (88) solid molecular substance consisting of covalently bonded atoms linked into a network which extends throughout the sample with an absence of simple discrete particles.

Neutralization: (256, 259, 260, 262) , occurs when in acid-base reactions equal quantities of an acid and base are mixed.

Neutrons: (12, 278, 280, 282, 284, 285, 286, 287, 288) subatomic particle with a mass of approximately one atomic mass unit and a unit charge of zero.

Noble gases: (48) see inert gases; common name for Group 18 elements.

Nomenclature: (192, 193, 196) procedure of assigning names to the kinds and groups of organisms listed in a taxonomic classification.

Nonaqueous: (189) not watery or easily dissolved in water.

Nonelectrolytes: (189) substances which when dissolved in solution form molecules which are not charged and will not conduct electricity.

Nonmetals: (37, 42, 50, 85, 93, 94, 97, 242) any of a number of elements, such as oxygen or sulfur, that lack the physical and chemical properties of metals; atoms which tend to gain electrons when in combination with other atoms.

Nonpolar covalent bond: (86) the equal sharing of electrons between atoms of the same element.

Nonpolar molecules: (91, 96, 189) symmetrical molecule composed of more than two atoms maintaining a uniform charge; example: CO_2.

Nonvolatile solute: (129) component of a solution present in the lesser amount but more resistant to evaporation at normal temperatures and pressures which raises the boiling point of the solution.

Normality: (265-266) manner of expressing concentration which is concerned with the gram equivalent weight of H+ ions supplied or accommodated.

Nuclear control rods: (288) boron and cadmium rods which absorb neutrons in a fission reactor.

Nuclear coolants: (288) water, heavy water, air, helium, carbon dioxide, molten sodium, and molten lithium are used to keep the temperatures generated in fission reactions at reasonable levels within the reactor and to carry heat to heat exchanges and turbines.

Nuclear energy: (284) energy released when mass is converted to energy.

Nuclear fission: (288, 289, 290) "splitting" of heavier nuclei into lighter ones with the release of energy; also see fission.

Nuclear fuels: fuels used in nuclear reactors and include: uranium-233, uranium-235, and plutonium - 239.

Nuclear fusion: (289, 290) the fusion of two lighter nuclei into a heavier nucleus at high temperatures and pressures.

Nuclear moderators: (288, 289) materials which slow down the speed of neutrons; they include: water, heavy water, beryllium, and graphite.

Nuclear reactors: (51, 286, 287, 288, 289) any of several devices in which a chain reaction is initiated and controlled, with the resulting heat typically used for power generation and the neutrons and fission products used for military, experimental, and medical purposes.

Nuclear shielding: (288) internal and external barriers used in reactors.

Nucleic acid: (97, 209) group of complex compounds found in all living cells and viruses; composed of purines, pyrimidines, carbohydrates, and phosphoric acid; in the form of DNA and RNA, they control cellular function and heredity.

Nucleotide: (98) any of various compounds consisting of a nucleotide combined with a phosphate group and forming the basic constituent of DNA and RNA.

Nucleons: (12, 286, 289) any particle located in the nucleus (protons, neutrons).

Nucleus: (11, 12-13, 44, 280, 281, 283, 284, 286, 289, 290) core of an atom in which are located the protons and neutrons.

Observed value: (311) experimentally measured value, value calculated from experimental results.

Olefin series: (193) common name for the Alkene series of hydrocarbons.

Open hearth process: (243) reverberatory furnace used in the production of high-quality steel.

Open system: (169) product removal from the reaction "go to completion."

Operational definition: (254, 255, 256) properties and reactions of substances based on experimental observation which includes a set of conditions.

Orbital blocks: (43) grouping of elements by electron configuration used as a designation on some forms of the Periodic Table.

Orbital notation: (16) depiction of orbital electron configuration.

Orbitals: (17, 18, 22, 89) the average region of the most probable electron location.

Order of magnitude: (309) number assigned to a quantity so that it may be compared with other quantities; example $5,000 = 5.0 \times 10^3$ therefore, the order of magnitude is 10.

Organic acids: (196) acids contain an carboxyl (-COOH) functional group.

Organic chemistry: (188-218, 330, 332) analysis of substances generally characterized by chains of connected carbon atoms; substances derived from plant and animal (organic) sources as opposed to those derived from inanimate (inorganic) materials.

Organic compounds: (188, 189, 191, 333) discussion of compounds of carbon; see *Reference Table R*.

Organic isomers: (190) compounds that have the same molecular formula in the same proportions, but different structures.

Organic reactions: (202) substitution, addition, fermentation, and esterification.

Osmosis: (119) diffusion of fluid through a semipermeable membrane until there is an equal concentration of fluid on both sides of the membrane.

Oxidation: (45, 47, 48, 50, 64, 67, 198-199, 204, 205, 220-243) reaction in which the atoms in an element lose electrons and the valence of the element is correspondingly increased; combustion or burning with oxygen.

Oxidation number: (64, 65, 221) see oxidation state.

Oxidation state: (64) number (or state) of an atom, which represents the charge which that atom has, or appears to have, when electrons are counted according to certain arbitrary rules.

Oxidizing agents: (198, 220, 255-256) species in a redox reaction which is reduced.

Palmitic acid: (264) fatty acid, $C_{15}H_{31}COOH$, occurring in many natural oils and fats and used in making soaps.

Paraffin series: (192) see Alkane series.

Particle (69, 70, 109, 114, 118, 128, 129, 139, 164, 166, 220, 280, 281, 283, 285, 288) any of various units of matter below the size of an atom, including the elementary particles and hadrons.

Patina: (242) thin greenish layer, usually basic copper sulfate, that forms on copper or copper alloys, such as bronze, as a result of corrosion.

Pauling, Linus C.: (94) American physical chemist (1901-1994); extensive contributions to structural chemistry and molecular biology; Nobel Prizes in 1954 and 1962.

Peptide: (200, 208) any of various natural or synthetic compounds containing two or more amino acids linked by the carboxyl group of one amino acid and the amino group of another.

Percent by mass: (126) number of grams of solute in 100 grams of solvent.

Percent by volume: (126) portion of volume of a solution that is solute

Percent composition: (72) formula for determination of the proportion of an element in a compound.

Percent error: (311) actual error divided by the the accepted value x 100%.

Perey, Marguerite: (283) French physicist isolated francium from uranium ore (1939).

Performance Indicators: (7-8, 9-10, 35-36, 61-62, 83-84, 105-107, 157-158, 187-188, 219-220, 253-254, 277-278, 323) criteria for how students should be able to demonstrate their understanding of the chemistry core curriculum's key ideas.

Periodic law: (36) Moseley's idea that properties of elements are periodic functions of the atomic number.

Periodic Table of the Elements: (36-60) a classification and tabulation of the chemical elements in the order of their atomic numbers that permits systematic explanation and prediction of many of the elements' chemical and physical properties.

Periodic Table key: (43) instruction on how to read and use the Periodic Table.

Periods of the Periodic Table: (40) horizontal rows of the Periodic Table, also called "rows" or "series."

pH: (262, 263, 331) measure of the acidity or alkalinity of a solution, numerically equal to 7 for neutral solutions, increasing with increasing alkalinity and decreasing with increasing acidity.

Phase change: see phases of matter.

Phase equilibrium: (166) dynamic conditions in a closed system allow for reversible phase changes.

Phases of matter: (107-116) an expression which refers to the state in which matter exists; they include: gases, liquids, and solids.

Phenolphthalein: (258) pH indicator, pink in basic solution and colorless in acid solution.

Photography: (227, 281) process of producing images of objects on photosensitive surfaces.

Photons: (19) also called quantum, is a unit of electromagnetic radiation.

Photosynthesis: (97, 177, 208) process in green plants and certain other organisms by which carbohydrates are synthesized from carbon dioxide and water using light as an energy source.

Physical properties: (40, 107) aspects or traits of a substance discernible by the senses.

Physical change: (111) transition of matter in which properties are altered, but identity remains.

Pi bond: (191): second, weaker and more reactive bond (after sigma) in an unsaturated organic compound.

Pipette: (318) narrow, usually calibrated glass tube into which small amounts of liquid are suctioned for transfer or measurement.

Planck, Max Ernst Ludwig: (11, 15) German physicist (1858-1947), developed the concept of the quantum, or fundamental increment of energy — that became a cornerstone of modern physics; Nobel Prize for quantum theory, 1918.

Planck's constant: (15) radiation of frequency v comes in quanta, or packages, with an energy E determined by $E = hv$. In mks units, h is about equal to 6.6261 x (10^{-34}) joule-sec, an extremely small quantity. The constant appears in every description of matter and radiation.

Plasma: (265) The clear, yellowish fluid portion of blood, lymph, or intramuscular fluid in which cells are suspended.

Platelet: (172) minute, disklike cytoplasmic body found in the blood plasma of mammals that promotes blood clotting.

Plating: (226) thin layer of metal, such as gold or silver, deposited on or applied to a surface.

Polar covalent bonds: (86, 93) molecules resulting from unequal sharing of electrons.

Polarity: (86, 95, 189) intrinsic separation, alignment, or orientation, especially of a physical property.

Polyatomic ion: (64, 65, 66, 67, 87, 93, 96-97, 222, 327, 330) see *Reference Table E*, compound of two or more covalently bonded atoms with a charge; suffixes:"-ate" and "-ite."

Polymers: (206, 209) long chain molecules made up of repeating smaller molecules called monomers; an example is polyethylene.

Polymerization: (206) formation of large molecules from smaller ones.

Potential energy: (114, 130, 160-161, 162) energy of position.

Pouring liquids: (314) see laboratory safety skills.

Precipitate (169, 177) product resulting from a process, an event, or a course of action.

Precipitation reaction: (76) process of separating a substance from a solution as a solid.

Prefixes: (326) word part put before a measurement to indicate its numerical power; see *Reference Table C*.

Pressure: (136, 139, 166, 168, 170, 267) force applied uniformly over a surface, measured as force per unit of area.

Primary alcohols: (196) alcohols in which the hydroxyl group is attached to an end carbon atom.

Primary battery: (238) can supply energy but cannot be recharged.

Principal energy levels: (16, 17, 39) see atomic structure models.

Principal quantum number: (16, 17) see Atomic Orbital Model.

Products: (66, 67, 96, 160, 162, 169, 172, 208, 260, 262) substance resulting from a chemical reaction.

Properties of Matter: (107) characteristic traits that serve to define or describe one type of substance and distinguish it from others.

Protein: (97, 200, 206, 208, 209) group of complex organic macromolecules; contain carbon, hydrogen, oxygen, nitrogen, and usually sulfur; composed of one or more chains of amino acids; fundamental components of all living cells and include many substances, such as enzymes, hormones, and antibodies, necessary for the proper functioning of an organism.

Protium: (13) isotope of hydrogen which contains one proton in its nucleus with a mass of 1 amu.

Protons: (12, 88, 95, 255, 256, 257, 278, 280, 282, 284, 285, 289) subatomic particle, found in the nucleus, with a unit positive charge of one and a mass of one atomic mass unit.

Quanta: (15, 19) smallest amount of a physical quantity that can exist independently, especially a discrete quantity of electromagnetic radiation.

Quantum: (11, 15, 32) distinct, discrete amount of energy.

Quantum number: (16-18) numerical designation of the rules of quantum mechanics which refer to the probable location and energy level of the electron.

Quaternary: (265) relating to an atom bonded to four carbon atoms.

Radiant energy: (130) energy transferred by radiation, especially by an electromagnetic wave; see photons.

Radioactive element: (47) having spontaneous emission of radiation, either directly from unstable atomic nuclei or as a consequence of a nuclear reaction.

Radioactive dating: (294-295) dating based on the radioactive decay of elements, also see half-life.

Radioactive isotopes: see radioisotopes.

Radioactive tracers: (292, 293) radioactive isotopes such as Carbon-14 used in tracing the course of a reaction without altering the chemical conditions.

Radioactive wastes: (292) discussion of nuclear energy industrial wastes.

Radioactivity: (280, 281, 282, 283, 287, 293, 294, 332) spontaneous disintegration of the nucleus of an atom with the emission of particles and/or radiant energy.

Radiation: (289, 295) stream of particles or electromagnetic waves emitted by the atoms and molecules of a radioactive substance as a result of nuclear decay.

Radioimmunoassay: (293) immunoassay of a radiolabeled substance, such as a hormone or an enzyme (RIA); developed by American physicist Rosalyn Yalow (1921-).

Radioisotopes: (292-294, 331) radioactive isotopes of an element; see *Reference Table N.*

Rate of chemical reaction: (158) measure, in terms of the number of moles of reactant consumed (or moles of products formed) per unit volume in a unit of time.

Rare earth series: (51) Lanthanoid Series of elements; they are difficult to extract from the "earth" or oxide salt, hence the term "rare earth."

Rare gases: (48) see inert gases; Group 18 elements.

Reactants: (66, 67, 93, 96, 160-161, 162, 164, 169, 171, 172, 175, 204, 260, 283, 290) substance participating in a chemical reaction, especially a directly reacting substance present at the initiation of the reaction.

Reactions: (69, 75, 85, 112, 158, 159, 160, 166, 189, 202, 204, 254, 255, 259, 265, 280, 284, 291, 293) change or transformation in which a substance decomposes, combines with other substances, or interchanges constituents with other substances.

Reactivity: (42, 44, 45, 46, 48) tending to be responsive or to react to a stimulus.

Reactors, nuclear: (289) see fission.

Reagent bottle: (314) stoppered container for substances used in a chemical reactions.

Real World Connections: (7-8, 23-24, 43-44, 51-52, 76, 97-98, 108-109, 110, 111, 119, 122, 124, 127, 128, 129, 133, 139, 140, 142, 160, 161, 169, 170, 172, 174, 176, 177, 188, 190, 191, 203, 205, 207, 208, 226, 227, 237, 241-242, 262, 264-265, 281, 283, 284, 285, 286, 289, 292, 293) practical applications of theoretical chemistry in everyday existence.

Reciprocal: (263) number related to another in such a way that when multiplied together their product is 1.

Redox reactions: (204, 220-243, 330) abbreviation for reduction-oxidation reactions: reactions in which atoms and ions compete for electrons, resulting in the reduction or oxidation of these particles. This process is referred to as redox.

Reducing agents: (220, 228) agent which supplies electrons in a redox reaction.

Reduction: (220-243) gain or apparent gain of electrons.

Reference Tables for Physical Setting / Chemistry: (list: 323; Tables A – T: 324-336).

Refraction index: (107) measure of the extent that light is bent as it passes through the substance.

Relative reducing tendency: (234) comparative amount (to hydrogen ions) by which ions a substance gains electrons and loses oxygen.

Replacement: (76, 330) displacement of one substance in a compound by another substance.

Residue: (319) matter remaining after completion of an abstractive chemical or physical process, such as evaporation, combustion, distillation, or filtration.

Resistance: (120) opposition of a body or substance to current passing through it, resulting in a change of electrical energy into heat or another form of energy.

Ribonucleic acid (RNA): (209) polymeric constituent of all living cells and many viruses, consisting of a long, usually single-stranded chain of alternating phosphate and ribose units with the bases adenine, guanine, cytosine, and uracil bonded to the ribose.

"Roasting" of metallic ores: (241) reaction of a metallic ore with oxygen in order to form the oxide of the ore.

Rotational movement: (134, 139, 175) spinning or revolving, electron motion; as in gas and liquid.

Rows: (40) see periods of the Periodic Table.

Rust: (227) any of various powdery or scaly reddish-brown or reddish-yellow hydrated ferric oxides formed on iron and iron-containing materials by low-temperature oxidation in the presence of water.

Rutherford, Ernest: (11, 12, 30) British physicist (1871-1937); identified the phenomenon of radioactive half-life and formulated the still-accepted explanation of radioactivity; created gold foil experiments which indicated the atom to be mostly empty space; nucleus very small compared to the size of atom.

Salt bridge: (230, 232) structure containing a solution of a salt which allows the migration of ions in a Daniell electrochemical cell.

Salts: (66, 253-276) ionic compound containing positive ions other than hydrogen ions and negative ions other than hydroxide ions.

Saponification: (205, 264, 265) hydrolysis of fats by bases.

Saturated compounds: (90, 202) organic compounds in which the carbon atoms are bonded by the sharing of a single pair of electrons.

Saturation of solutions: (126, 127, 168, 169, 328) solution in which the maximum amount of solute is dissociated or dissolved by a solvent at a specific temperature and pressure.

Schrodinger, Erwin: (11) Austrian theoretical physicist (1887-1961); published (1926) four papers that laid the foundation of the wave-mechanics approach to quantum theory and set forth his now-famous wave equation; shared the Nobel Prize for physics in 1933.

Scientific notation: (308-309) method of writing or displaying numbers in terms of a decimal number between 1 and 10 multiplied by a power of 10.

Screening (shielding) effect: (44) causes the inner shell electrons to reduce the force of attraction between the positively charged nucleus and the valence electrons.

Seaborg, Glenn T.: (284) American chemist (1912-); shared a 1951 Nobel Prize for the discovery of plutonium.

Second quantum number: (16) see atomic structure models.

Secondary alcohols: (197) occurs when a hydroxyl (O-H) group is attached to a carbon atom which is attached to two other carbon atoms.

Secondary battery: (239) can supply energy and be recharged

Semiconductor: (46, 51) any of various solid crystalline substances, such as germanium or silicon, having electrical conductivity greater than insulators but less than good conductors.

Semimetals: (37) term preferred by IUPAC to denote metalloids.

Series: (40) see periods of the Periodic Table.

Shielding effect: see screening effect.

SI units: (326) International System of Units, or the SI (from the original Système International d'Unites); forms the basis for both international commerce and communication in science and technology.

Sigma bond: (191) lone, but strong bond between carbon atoms in a saturated organic compound.

Significant figures: (307, 210) digits of the decimal form of a number beginning with the left-most non-zero digit and extending to the right to include all digits warranted by the accuracy of measuring devices used to obtain the numbers; also called significant digits.

Single bond: (90, 191) binding of carbon atoms sharing one pair of electrons.

Single replacement reactions: (223, 330) category of redox reactions.

Slag (242, 243) vitreous mass left as a residue by the smelting of metallic ore.

Smelting: (242) to melt or fuse (ores) in order to separate the metallic constituents.

Soap: (205, 264) results from the combination of a glycerol ester and a base.

Solar energy: (289) fusion energy created by the Sun.

Solids: (40, 85, 88, 107, 108, 314) phase of matter in which particles are aligned in a definite pattern, and possess vibrational motion.

Solid state of matter: (40, 107, 108) in this state, the atoms are only vibrating and do not possess any other form of motion.

Solubility: (168, 177, 189, 241, 328-329) expression of the concentration of a solute in a solvent, which is given under certain conditions; see *Reference Table F*.

Solubility curves: (126, 328) measure saturation; see *Reference Table G*.

Solubility guidelines: (327) predictions of solubility of compounds; see *Reference Table F*.

Solubility product constant: (176) *Ksp* – measure of the concentration of slightly soluble salts in a solvent, usually water.

Solutes: (121, 124, 126, 129, 169, 328) internal component in a solution which is dissociated by the external or solvent phase.

Solutions: (118, 121-130, 168-169, 232, 239, 240,254, 258, 262, 263, 265-266, 328, 331) homogeneous mixture of two or more substances, the composition of which may vary within certain limits; one substance is uniformly dispersed throughout another in particles that are molecular in size; if the particles are larger than this, the solution is not a true solution but a mixture.

Solvation: (121) dissociation of solute particle by a solvent.

Solvents: (119, 121, 126, 128, 169, 189, 254) a substance, usually a liquid, capable of dissolving another substance.

Spatial: (189-190) of or relating to space – the infinite extension of the three-dimensional field in which all matter exists.

Specific heat: (132) see calorie; in a material, amount of heat energy required to raise the temperature of 1g. of material, 1°C.

Spectral lines: (19) characteristic wave lengths of radiant energy given off when excited electrons return to a ground state.

Spectroscope: (19) a visual optical instrument that separates a beam of radiation into its component wavelengths.

Spectrum: (19) specific bright line bands of color resulting from the separation of light by a spectroscope.

Spontaneous reaction: (173, 175, 232, 235, 330) reaction that having once been initiated will continue under the existing conditions.

Standard electrode potential: (229-230, 234-235, 236, 240) potential differences in a specified half-reaction, using the hydrogen half-reaction as a reference.

Standard solutions: (259) acid or base whose molarity is known.

Standard Temperature and Pressure (STP): (40, 51, 136-137, 139, 326) an acknowledged measure of comparison for quantitative or qualitative value; for gas: 0°C or 273 K and 760mm of mercury (760 torr.) at 1 atm pressure; for non-gas: 25°C or 298 K; see *Reference Table A*.

Standard units: (326) see *Reference Table D*.

Starches: (206) naturally abundant nutrient carbohydrate, $(C_6H_{10}O_5)_n$, found chiefly in the seeds, fruits, tubers, roots, and stem pith of plants, notably in corn, potatoes, wheat, and rice, and varying widely in appearance according to source but commonly prepared as a white, amorphous, tasteless powder.

State of Equilibrium: (108) state of a chemical reaction in which its forward and reverse reactions occur at equal rates so that the concentration of the reactants and products does not change with time.

Stearic: (264) colorless, odorless, tasteless ester of glycerol and stearic acid, $CH_3(CH_2)_{16}COOH$, found in most animal and vegetable fats

Stock system: (65) naming of compounds of metals with more than one oxidation state, Roman numerals denote the oxidation state of the metal.

Stoichiometry: (62, 70) study of quantitative relationships implied by chemical formulas and chemical equations.

Stoney, G. D.: (11) named electrons with Sir John Joseph Thomson c. 1874

STP: see Standard Temperature and Pressure.

Structural formula: see formula (structural)

Subatomic particles: (11) particles smaller than an atom.

Sublevels: (16,17) second quantum numbers.

Sublimation: (114) direct phase change from solid to a gaseous state.

Substance: (113, 117, 118, 175, 254, 258, 259) homogeneous matter having identical properties and composition.

Substitution reactions: (202, 203) replacement of one kind of atom or group with another kind of atom or group.

Substrate: (161) material or substance on which an enzyme acts.

Super–cooled liquids: (108) materials that behave as highly viscous liquids with crystalline structures.

Superconductor: (51) apparatus allowing the flow of electric current without resistance in certain metals, alloys, and ceramics at temperatures near absolute zero, and in some cases at temperatures hundreds of degrees above absolute zero.

Supersaturated solution: (126, 127, 328) solution in which more solute is dissolved than can be dissolved under normal conditions.

Surface area: (164) reactive area of a substance, when increased, the rate of reaction increases.

Surface tension: (110) phenomenon associated with the interface between a fluid and another phase; most familiar example involves the water-air interface.

Suspension: (120) relatively coarse, non-colloidal dispersion of solid particles in a liquid.

Symbol: (62, 324-325, 3334-335) see Periodic Table; a representation of one atom or one mole of atoms of an element, see *Reference Table S*.

Symbols used in nuclear chemistry: (332) see *Reference Table O*.

Symmetrical: (86, 87, 91) exact correspondence of form and configuration about a center.

Synthesis: (75) formation of a compound from simpler compounds or elements.

Synthetic: (169, 207, 209) produced by synthesis, especially not of natural origin.

Table of Standard Electrode Potentials: (229-230, 234, 235, 236) aids in determining the spontaneous nature of a reaction.

Temperature, defined (thermometry): (130, 139, 166, 168, 171, 175, 267) measure of the average kinetic energy in a system.

Temperature and pressure relationship: (139, 168, 329) at constant volume, in a direct proportion, if temperature increases, pressure increases; see *Reference Table H*.

Tertiary alcohols: (197) hydroxyl group in the alcohol is attached to a carbon atom which is in turn attached to three other carbon atoms.

Ternary acids: (66) acids which combine hydrogen with a polyatomic ion and contain three elements in their formulas.

Ternary compounds: (117) compounds with three elements.

Tetrahedron bonds: (189) four equidistant bonds whose vertices form a tetrahedron.

Tetratomic: (46) having four atoms per molecule; having four replaceable univalent atoms or radicals.

Third quantum number: (17) see atomic structure models.

Thermal decomposition: (202) separation into constituents by heat reaction.

Thermite reaction: (242) leaching bauxite with strong solution of sodium hydroxide to yield pure aluminum oxide to ready for reduction

Thermochemical: (329) chemistry of heat and heat-associated chemical phenomena.

Thermodynamics: (174) relationships between heat and other forms of energy.

Thermometer: (130) instrument used to measure temperature.

Thermonuclear: (290) derived from the fusion of atomic nuclei at high temperatures.

Thomson, Sir John Joseph: (11) British chemist/physicist (1856-1940); identified the electron, c. 1897.

Thomson, William: (131, 135-136, 137) British physicist (1st Baron Kelvin, 1824-1907); see Kelvin

Titration: (259-260, 265) process of metering a standard solution into a solution of unknown concentration.

Torr: (143) unit of pressure that is equal to approximately $1.316 fl10^{-3}$ atmosphere or 1,333 pascals.

Tracers, radioactive: (292) radioisotopes used to follow the course of a reaction without seriously altering any chemical conditions which exist.

Transition elements: (50) elements found in Groups 3 through 12 of the Periodic Table.

Translational movement: (134, 139, 166, 175) changing or transforming, as in gases.

Transmutation: (280, 282, 292) when one element is changed to another as a result of changes in the nucleus.

Transmutation, artificial: (280) when one element is bombarded with subatomic particles forming newer elements.

Trihydroxy alcohols: (198) compounds containing three hydroxyl groups (O-H) in their formulas.

Triple bond: (91, 191, 205) bond formed between carbon atoms by the sharing of three pairs of electrons.

Triprotic: (265, 266) having three hydrogen ions to donate to bases in an acid-base reaction.

Tritium: (13) an isotope of hydrogen in which the nucleus contains one proton and two neutrons.

Tyndall effect: (120) analyzing chemical mixtures by using dispersion of light scattering through a colloid (suspension of finely divided particles in a continuous medium in which the particles do not settle out of the substance and are not readily filtered); after Irish physicist John Tyndall (1820-1893).

Unsaturated compounds: (91, 191, 192, 193, 203) organic compounds with one or more double or triple bonds between carbon atoms.

Unsaturated solution: (126) solution in which less solute is dissolved than is capable of being dissolved under normal conditions.

Valence electrons: (21, 43, 93) electrons found in the outermost principal energy level of an atom.

Van der Waals Radius: (41,) half the internuclear distance of the closest approach of atoms that form no bonds; after Dutch physicist Johannes Diderik van der Waals (1837-1923); known for his work in physical chemistry that led to the equation of state of gases and liquids.

Van der Waal's forces: (48, 92, 95-96, 192) weak intermolecular forces of attraction between molecules based upon the shifting of the electrons within the molecule.

Vapor pressure: (109) pressure exerted by the vapor escaping from a liquid or solid in equilibrium.

Vapor pressure (328) see *Reference Table H.*

Vaporiztion: (111, 166) gaseous state of a substance that is liquid or solid under ordinary conditions.

Velocity: (139) rapidity or speed of motion; swiftness.

Vibration: (111, 134, 139, 175) shaking of particles as in solids, liquids, and gases.

Viscosity: (110) property of fluids (liquids or gases) that is a measure of a fluid's resistance to flow.

Volatile: (38) evaporating readily at normal temperatures and pressures.

Volta(ic) cells: (229, 232) apparatus for producing electric current by chemical action; also called electrochemical cells; after Count Alessandro Volta (1745-1827), Italian physicist who invented the first electric battery (1800).

Voltage: (233) electromotive force or potential difference, usually expressed in volts.

Voltmeter: (232) instrument, such as a galvanometer, for measuring potential differences in volts.

Volume: (107) amount of space occupied by a three-dimensional object or region of space.

Volume-volume problems: (75) problems concerning reacting gases at the same temperature and pressure.

Wastes, radioactive: (292) radioactive material no longer be usable.

Water, ionization constant of: (267) for practical purposes of comparison, water is considered a constant.

Watson, James: (98) American biologist (1928-) proposed a spiral model, the double helix, for the molecular structure of DNA;1962 Nobel Prize for advances in the study of genetics.

Wave-Mechanical Model: (18) accounts for the spectra of heavier and more complicated atoms; also called electron cloud model.

Width: (107) measurement of the extent of something from side to side.

Xenon: (23) colorless, odorless, highly unreactive gaseous element found in minute quantities in the atmosphere, extracted commercially from liquefied air and used in stroboscopic, bactericidal, and laser-pumping lamps. (Symbol: Xe – atomic number 54).

Zincs: (226) magnesium blocks used to reduce corrosion on the "in water" metal parts of boats.

Zymase: (203) catalyst used in the fermentation of carbohydrates to alcohol and carbon dioxide.

PHYSICAL SETTING: CHEMISTRY PRACTICE TEST #1 – JUNE 2003

PART A

Answer all questions in this part.

Directions (1–30): For *each* statement or question, write the *number* of the word or expression that, of those given, best completes the statement or answers the question. Some questions may require the use of the *Reference Tables for Physical Setting/Chemistry*.

1 The atomic number of an atom is always equal to the number of its
   (1) protons, only
   (2) neutrons, only
   (3) protons plus neutrons
   (4) protons plus electrons

2 Which subatomic particle has no charge?
   (1) alpha particle
   (2) beta particle
   (3) neutron
   (4) electron

3 When the electrons of an excited atom return to a lower energy state, the energy emitted can result in the production of
   (1) alpha particles
   (2) isotopes
   (3) protons
   (4) spectra

4 The atomic mass of an element is calculated using the
   (1) atomic number and the ratios of its naturally occurring isotopes
   (2) atomic number and the half-lives of each of its isotopes
   (3) masses and the ratios of its naturally occurring isotopes
   (4) masses and the half-lives of each of its isotopes

5 The region that is the most probable location of an electron in an atom is
   (1) the nucleus
   (2) an orbital
   (3) the excited state
   (4) an ion

6 Which is a property of most nonmetallic solids?
   (1) high thermal conductivity
   (2) high electrical conductivity
   (3) brittleness
   (4) malleability

7 Alpha particles are emitted during the radioactive decay of
   (1) carbon-14   (2) neon-19   (3) calcium-37   (4) radon-222

8 Which is an empirical formula?
   (1) P_2O_5 (2) P_4O_6 (3) C_2H_4 (4) C_3H_6

9 Which substance can be decomposed by a chemical change
   (1) Co   (2) CO   (3) Cr   (4) Cu

10 The percent by mass of calcium in the compound calcium sulfate ($CaSO_4$) is approximately
   (1) 15%   (2) 29%   (3) 34%   (4) 47%

11 What is represented by the dots in a Lewis electron-dot diagram of an atom of an element in Period 2 of the Periodic Table?
   (1) the number of neutrons in the atom
   (2) the number of protons in the atom
   (3) the number of valence electrons in the atom
   (4) the total number of electrons in the atom

12 Which type of chemical bond is formed between two atoms of bromine?
(1) metallic   (2) hydrogen   (3) ionic   (4) covalent

13 Which of these formulas contains the most polar bond?
(1) H–Br   (2) H–Cl   (3) H–F   (4) H-I

14 According to Table F, which of these salts is *least* soluble in water?
(1) LiCl   (2) RbCl   (3) $FeCl_2$ (4) $PbCl_2$

15 Which of these terms refers to matter that could be heterogeneous?
(1) element   (2) mixture   (3) compound   (4) solution

16 In which material are the particles arranged in a regular geometric pattern?
(1) $CO_2(g)$ (2) $NaCl(aq)$ (3) $H_2O(l)$ (4) $C_{12}H_{22}O_{11}(s)$

17 Which change is exothermic?
(1) freezing of water   (3) vaporization of ethanol
(2) melting of iron   (4) sublimation of iodine

18 Which type of change must occur to form a compound?
(1) chemical   (2) physical   (3) nuclear   (4) phase

19 Which formula correctly represents the composition of iron (III) oxide?
(1) FeO_3 (2) Fe_2O_3 (3) Fe_3O (4) Fe_3O_2

20 Given the reaction: $PbCl_2(aq) + Na_2CrO_4(aq) \rightarrow PbCrO_4(s) + 2\ NaCl(aq)$
What is the total number of moles of NaCl formed when 2 moles of Na_2CrO_4 react completely?
(1) 1 mole   (2) 2 moles   (3) 3 moles   (4) 4 moles

21 Which hydrocarbon is saturated?
(1) propene   (2) ethyne   (3) butene   (4) heptane

22 Which statement correctly describes an endothermic chemical reaction?
(1) The products have higher potential energy than the reactants, and the ΔH is negative.
(2) The products have higher potential energy than the reactants, and the ΔH is positive.
(3) The products have lower potential energy than the reactants, and the ΔH is negative.
(4) The products have lower potential energy than the reactants, and the ΔH is positive.

23 At standard pressure when NaCl is added to water, the solution will have a
(1) higher freezing point and a lower boiling point than water
(2) higher freezing point and a higher boiling point than water
(3) lower freezing point and a higher boiling point than water
(4) lower freezing point and a lower boiling point than water

24 Which element has atoms that can form single, double, and triple covalent bonds with other atoms of the same element?
(1) hydrogen   (2) oxygen   (3) fluorine   (4) carbon

25 Which compound is an isomer of pentane?
(1) butane   (3) methyl butane
(2) propane   (4) methyl propane

26 In which substance does chlorine have an oxidation number of +1?
(1) Cl_2 (2) HCl   (3) HClO   (4) $HClO_2$

27 Which statement is true for any electrochemical cell?
  (1) Oxidation occurs at the anode, only.
  (2) Reduction occurs at the anode, only.
  (3) Oxidation occurs at both the anode and the cathode.
  (4) Reduction occurs at both the anode and the cathode.

28 Given the equation: $2\,Al + 3\,Cu^{2+} \rightarrow 2\,Al^{3+} + 3\,Cu$
  The reduction half-reaction is
  (1) $Al \rightarrow Al^{3+} + 3e^-$ (3) $Al + 3e^- \rightarrow Al^{3+}$
  (2) $Cu^{2+} + 2e^- \rightarrow Cu$ (4) $Cu^{2+} \rightarrow Cu + 2e^-$

29 Which 0.1 M solution contains an electrolyte?
  (1) $C_6H_{12}O_6(aq)$ (3) $CH_3OH(aq)$
  (2) $CH_3COOH(aq)$ (4) $CH_3OCH_3(aq)$

30 Which equation represents a neutralization reaction?
  (1) $Na_2CO_3 + CaCl_2 \rightarrow 2\,NaCl + CaCO_3$
  (2) $Ni(NO_3)_2 + H_2S \rightarrow NiS + 2\,HNO_3$
  (3) $NaCl + AgNO_3 \rightarrow AgCl + NaNO_3$
  (4) $H_2SO_4 + Mg(OH)_2 \rightarrow MgSO_4 + 2\,H_2O$

31 An Arrhenius acid has
  (1) only hydroxide ions in solution
  (2) only hydrogen ions in solution
  (3) hydrogen ions as the only positive ions in solution
  (4) hydrogen ions as the only negative ions in solution

32 Which type of radioactive emission has a positive charge and weak penetrating power?
  (1) alpha particle   (3) gamma ray
  (2) beta particle   (4) neutron

33 Which substance contains metallic bonds?
  (1) Hg(*l*)   (2) $H_2O(l)$ (3) NaCL(*s*)   (4) $C_6H_{12}O_6(s)$

34 What is the name of the process in which the nucleus of an atom of one element is changed into the nucleus of an atom of a different element?
  (1) decomposition   (3) substitution
  (2) transmutation   (4) reduction

Note that question 35 has only three choices.

35 A catalyst is added to a system at equilibrium. If the temperature remains constant, the activation energy of the forward reaction
  (1) decreases   (2) increases   (3) remains the same

PART B-1
Answer all questions in this part.
Directions (36–50): For *each* statement or question, write the *number* of the word or expression that, of those given, best completes the statement or answers the question. Some questions may require the use of the *Reference Tables for Physical Setting/Chemistry*.

36 The nucleus of an atom of K-42 contains
  (1) 19 protons and 23 neutrons   (3) 20 protons and 19 neutrons
  (2) 19 protons and 42 neutrons   (4) 23 protons and 19 neutrons

37 What is the total number of electrons in a Cu^+ ion?
(1) 28   (2) 29   (3) 30   (4) 36

38 Which list of elements is arranged in order of increasing atomic radii?
(1) Li, Be, B, C   (3) Sc, Ti, C, Cr
(2) Sr, Ca, Mg, Be   (4) F, Cl, Br, I

39 Which isotope is most commonly used in the radioactive dating of the remains of organic materials?
(1) ^{14}C (2) ^{16}N (3) ^{32}P (4) ^{37}K

40 According to Reference Table H, what is the vapor pressure of propanone at 45°C?
(1) 22 kPa   (2) 33 kPa   (3) 70. kPa   (4) 98 kPa

41 The freezing point of bromine is
(1) 539°C   (2) −539°C   (3) 7°C   (4) −7°C

42 Hexane (C_6H_{14}) and water do *not* form a solution. Which statement explains this phenomenon?
(1) Hexane is polar and water is nonpolar.
(2) Hexane is ionic and water is polar.
(3) Hexane is nonpolar and water is polar.
(4) Hexane is nonpolar and water is ionic.

43 The potential energy diagram at the right represents a reaction. Which arrow represents the activation energy of the forward reaction?
(1) A
(2) B
(3) C
(4) D

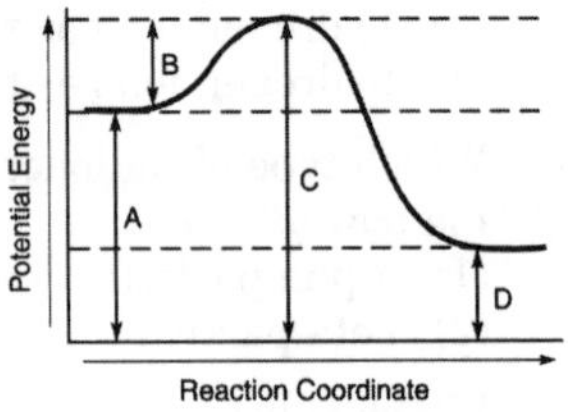

Reaction Coordinate

44 Given the formulas of four organic compounds at the right: Which pair below contains an alcohol and an acid?
(1) a and b
(2) a and c
(3) b and d
(4) c and d

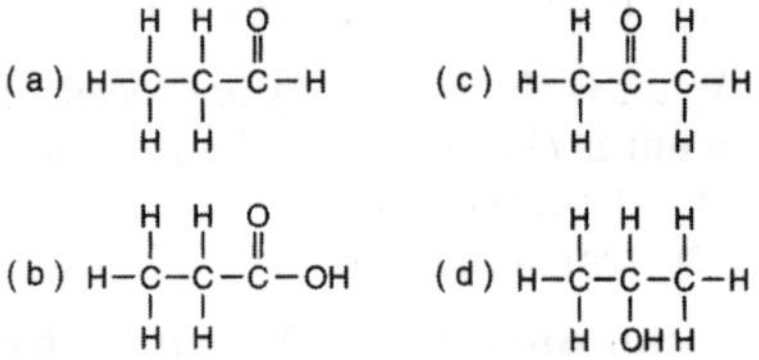

45 Which type of reaction is represented by the equation at the right? Note: **n** and n are very large numbers equal to about 2000.
(1) esterification
(2) fermentation
(3) saponification
(4) polymerization

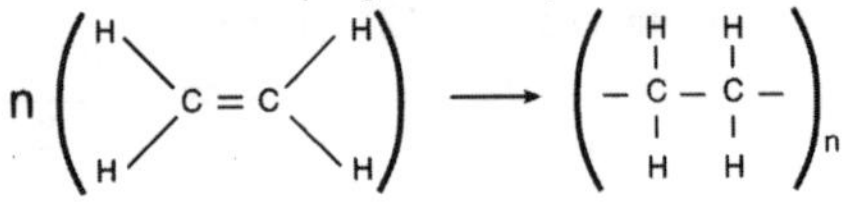

46 A diagram of a chemical cell and an equation are shown at the right. When the switch is closed, electrons will flow from
(1) the Pb(s) to the Cu(s)
(2) the Cu(s) to the Pb(s)
(3) the Pb^{2+}(aq) to the Pb(s)
(4) the Cu^{2+}(aq) to the Cu(s)

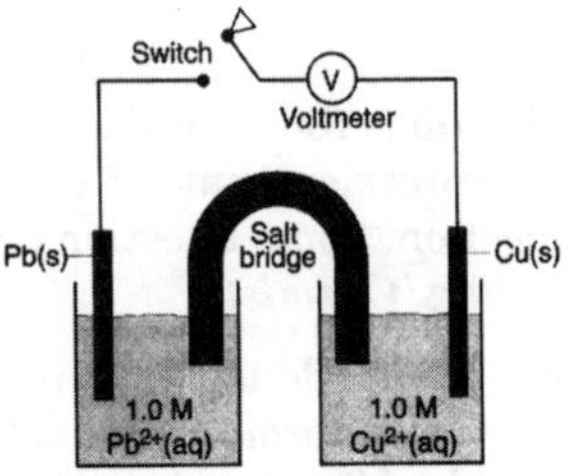

$Pb(s) + Cu^{2+}(aq) \longrightarrow Pb^{2+}(aq) + Cu(s)$

47 Which ion has the same electron configuration as an atom of He?
    (1) H–   (2) O²⁻   (3) Na⁺   (4) Ca²⁺

48 Each student was given four unknown
    solutions. Each solution was checked for
    conductivity and tested with phenolph-
    thalein. The results are shown in the table
    at the right. Based on the data table,
    which unknown solution could be
    0.1 M NaOH?

Solution	Conductivity	Color with Phenolphthalein
A	Good	Colorless
B	Poor	Colorless
C	Good	Pink
D	Poor	Pink

    (1) A   (3) C
    (2) B   (4) D

49 In the reaction $^{239}_{93}Np \rightarrow {}^{239}_{94}Pu + X$, what does X represent?
    (1) a neutron   (3) an alpha particle
    (2) a proton   (4) a beta particle

Note that question 50 has only three choices.

50 As carbon dioxide sublimes, its entropy
    (1) decreases   (2) increases   (3) remains the same

PART B-2

Answer all questions in this part.

Directions (51–63): Record your answers in the spaces provided. Some questions
may require the use of the *Reference Tables for Physical Setting/Chemistry*.

Base your answers to questions 51 and 52 on the electron
configuration table show at the right.

Element	Electron Configuration
X	2–8–8–2
Y	2–8–7–3
Z	2–8–8

51 What is the total number of valence electrons in an
    atom of electron configuration X? [1]

_____

52 Which electron configuration represents the excited state of a calcium atom?
    [1]

_____

Base your answers to questions 53 and 54 on the information below.

Given: Samples of Na, Ar, As, Rb

53 Which *two* of the given elements have the most similar chemical properties?
    [1]
    _____ and _____

54 Explain your answer in terms of the Periodic Table of the Elements. [1]

_____

_____

Base your answers to questions 55 and 56 on the information below.

Diethyl ether is widely used as a solvent.

55 In the space provided,
    draw the structural formu-
    la for diethyl ether. [1]

56 In the space provided,
    draw the structural formu-
    la for an alcohol that is an
    isomer of diethyl ether. [1]

Base your answers to questions 57 and 58 on the information below.

Two chemistry students each combine a different metal with hydrochloric acid. Student A uses zinc, and hydrogen gas is readily produced.
Student B uses copper, and no hydrogen gas is produced.

57 State one chemical reason for the different results of students A and B. [1]

_____

58 Using Reference Table J, identify another metal that will react with
    hydrochloric acid to yield hydrogen gas. [1]

_____

59 Given the reaction between two different
    elements in the gaseous state:

    Box A at the right represents a
    mixture of two reactants before
    the reaction occurs. The product
    of this reaction is a gas. In Box B
    provided at the right, draw the
    system after the reaction has
    gone to completion, based on the
    Law of Conservation of Matter.
    [2]

    Box A   Box B
    System Before Reaction   System After Reaction Has
                             Gone to Completion

60 As a neutral sulfur atom gains two electrons, what happens to the radius of
    the atom? [1]

_____

61 After a neutral sulfur atom gains two electrons, what is the resulting charge
    of the ion? [1]

_____

62*a* In the space provided, calculate the heat released when 25.0 grams of water freezes at 0°C. Show all work. [1]

b Record your answer with an appropriate unit. [1] _____

63 State one difference between voltaic cells and electrolytic cells. Include information about *both* types of cells in your answer. [1]

_____

_____

_____

PART C
Answer all questions in this part.

Directions (64–79): Record your answers in the spaces provided in your answer booklet. Some questions may require the use of the *Reference Tables for Physical Setting/Chemistry.*

Base your answers to questions 64 and 65 on the diagram at the right, which shows a piston confining a gas in a cylinder.

64 Using the set of axes provided at the right, sketch the general relationship between the pressure and the volume of an ideal gas at constant temperature. [1]

65 The gas volume in the cylinder is 6.2 milliliters and its pressure is 1.4 atmospheres. The piston is then pushed in until the gas volume is 3.1 milliliters while the temperature remains constant.

a In the space provided, calculate the pressure, in atmospheres, after the change in volume. Show all work. [1]

b Record your answer. [1]

_____ **atm**

66 A student recorded the following buret readings during a titration of a base
    with an acid:

	Standard 0.100 M HCl	Unknown KOH
Initial reading	9.08 mL	0.55 mL
Final reading	19.09 mL	5.56 mL

   a   In the space provided, calcu-
       late the molarity of the
       KOH. Show all work. [1]

   b   Record your answer to the
       correct number of significant
       figures. [1]

   _____ M

67 John Dalton was an English scientist who proposed that atoms were hard,
    indivisible spheres. In the modern model, the atom has a different internal
    structure.

   a   Identify one experiment that led scientists to develop the modern model
       of the atom. [1]

   _____

   b   Describe this experiment. [1]

   _____

   _____

   c   State one conclusion about the internal structure of the atom, based on
       this experiment. [1]

   _____

   _____

Base your answers to questions 68 through 73 on the information below and on
your knowledge of chemistry.

Nuclear Waste Storage Plan for Yucca Mountain

    In 1978, the U.S. Department of Energy began a study of Yucca
Mountain which is located 90 miles from Las Vegas, Nevada. The study was
to determine if Yucca Mountain would be suitable for a long-term burial site
for high-level radioactive waste. A three-dimensional (3-D) computer scale
model of the site was used to simulate the Yucca Mountain area. The computer model study for Yucca Mountain included such variables as: the possibility
of earthquakes, predicted water flow through the mountain, increased rain-
fall due to climate changes, radioactive leakage from the waste containers,
and increased temperatures from the buried waste within the containers.

    The containers that will be used to store the radioactive waste are
designed to last 10,000 years. Within the 10,000-year time period, cesium
and strontium, the most powerful radioactive emitters, would have decayed.
Other isotopes found in the waste would decay more slowly, but are not powerful radioactive emitters.

In 1998, scientists discovered that the compressed volcanic ash making up Yucca Mountain was full of cracks. Because of the arid climate, scientists assumed that rainwater would move through the cracks at a slow rate. However, when radioactive chlorine-36 was found in rock samples at levels halfway through the mountain, it was clear that rainwater had moved quickly down through Yucca Mountain. It was only 50 years earlier when this chlorine-36 isotope had contaminated rainwater during atmospheric testing of the atom bomb.

Some opponents of the Yucca Mountain plan believe that the uncertainties related to the many variables of the computer model result in limited reliability of its predictions. However, advocates of the plan believe it is safer to replace the numerous existing radioactive burial sites around the United States with the one site at Yucca Mountain. Other opponents of the plan believe that transporting the radioactive waste to Yucca Mountain from the existing 131 burial sites creates too much danger to the United States. In 2002, after years of political debate, a final legislative vote approved the development of Yucca Mountain to replace the existing 131 burial sites.

68 State one uncertainty in the computer model that limits the reliability of this computer model. [1]

_____

_____

69 Scientists assume that a manufacturing defect would cause at least one of the waste containers stored in the Yucca Mountain repository to leak within the first 1,000 years. State one possible effect such a leak could have on the environment near Yucca Mountain. [1]

_____

_____

70 State one risk associated with leaving radioactive waste in the 131 sites around the country where it is presently stored. [1]

_____

_____

71 If a sample of cesium-137 is stored in a waste container in Yucca Mountain, how much time must elapse until only $\frac{1}{32}$ of the original sample remains unchanged? [1]

_____

72 The information states "Within the 10,000-year time period, cesium and strontium, the most powerful radioactive emitters, would have decayed." Use information from Reference Table N to support this statement. [1]

_____

_____

73 Why is water flow a crucial factor in deciding whether Yucca Mountain is a suitable burial site? [1]

_____

_____

Base your answers to questions 74 through 76 on the information below.

A student wishes to investigate how the reaction rate changes with a change in concentration of HCl(aq).

Given the reaction: $Zn(s) + HCl(aq) \rightarrow H_2(g) + ZnCl_2(aq)$

74 Identify the independent variable in this investigation. [1]

_____

75 Identify one other variable that might affect the rate and should be held constant during this investigation. [1]

_____

76 Describe the effect of increasing the concentration of HCl(aq) on the reaction rate and justify your response in terms of *collision theory*. [1]

_____

_____

Base your answers to questions 77 through 79 on the information below.

A truck carrying concentrated nitric acid overturns and spills its contents. The acid drains into a nearby pond. The pH of the pond water was 8.0 before the spill. After the spill, the pond water is 1,000 times more acidic.

77 Name an ion in the pond water that has increased in concentration due to this spill. [1]

_____

78 What is the new pH of the pond water after the spill? [1]

_____

79 What color would bromthymol blue be at this new pH? [1]

_____

PART A
Answer all questions in this part.

Directions (1–31): For *each* statement or question, write the *number* of the word or expression that, of those given, best completes the statement or answers the question. Some questions may require the use of the *Reference Tables for Physical Setting / Chemistry*.

1   A neutral atom contains 12 neutrons and 11 electrons. The number of protons in this atom is
    (1) 1   (2) 11   (3) 12   (4) 23

2   Isotopes of an element must have different
    (1) atomic numbers   (3) numbers of protons
    (2) mass numbers   (4) numbers of electrons

3   Which element is a noble gas?
    (1) krypton   (2) chlorine   (3) antimony   (4) manganese

4   On the present Periodic Table of the Elements, the elements are arranged according to increasing
    (1) number of oxidation states   (3) atomic mass
    (2) number of neutrons   (4) atomic number

5   What is a property of most metals?
    (1) They tend to gain electrons easily when bonding.
    (2) They tend to lose electrons easily when bonding.
    (3) They are poor conductors of heat.
    (4) They are poor conductors of electricity.

6   What is the correct formula for iron (III) phosphate?
    (1) FeP (2) Fe_3P_2 (3) $FePO_4$ (4) $Fe_3(PO_4)_2$

7   The bond between Br atoms in a Br_2 molecule is
    (1) ionic and is formed by the sharing of two valence electrons
    (2) ionic and is formed by the transfer of two valence electrons
    (3) covalent and is formed by the sharing of two valence electrons
    (4) covalent and is formed by the transfer of two valence electrons

8   The amount of energy required to remove the outermost electron from a gaseous atom in the ground state is known as
    (1) first ionization energy   (3) conductivity
    (2) activation energy   (4) electronegativity

9   What occurs when an atom of chlorine and an atom of hydrogen become a molecule of hydrogen chloride?
    (1) A chemical bond is broken and energy is released.
    (2) A chemical bond is broken and energy is absorbed.
    (3) A chemical bond is formed and energy is released.
    (4) A chemical bond is formed and energy is absorbed.

10 Which molecule is nonpolar?
   (1) H_2O (2) NH_3 (3) CO   (4) CO_2

11 Which must be a mixture of substances?
   (1) solid   (2) liquid   (3) gas   (4) solution

12 A bottle of rubbing alcohol contains both 2-propanol and water. These liquids can be separated by the process of distillation because the 2-propanol and water
   (1) have combined chemically and retain their different boiling points
   (2) have combined chemically and have the same boiling point
   (3) have combined physically and retain their different boiling points
   (4) have combined physically and have the same boiling point

13 Compared to pure water, an aqueous solution of calcium chloride has a
   (1) higher boiling point and higher freezing point
   (2) higher boiling point and lower freezing point
   (3) lower boiling point and higher freezing point
   (4) lower boiling point and lower freezing point

14 Under which conditions does a real gas behave most like an ideal gas?
   (1) at low temperatures and high pressures
   (2) at low temperatures and low pressures
   (3) at high temperatures and high pressures
   (4) at high temperatures and low pressures

15 What is the IUPAC name of the compound with the structural formula at the right?

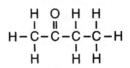

   (1) propanone   (3) butanone
   (2) propanal   (4) butanal

16 Which statement best explains the role of a catalyst in a chemical reaction?
   (1) A catalyst is added as an additional reactant and is consumed but not regenerated.
   (2) A catalyst limits the amount of reactants used.
   (3) A catalyst changes the kinds of products produced.
   (4) A catalyst provides an alternate reaction pathway that requires less activation energy.

17 Given the reaction at equilibrium:

$$H_2(g) + Br_2(g) \rightleftharpoons 2\ HBr(g)$$

   The rate of the forward reaction is
   (1) greater than the rate of the reverse reaction
   (2) less than the rate of the reverse reaction
   (3) equal to the rate of the reverse reaction
   (4) independent of the rate of the reverse reaction

18 Which statement best explains why most atomic masses on the Periodic Table are decimal numbers?
   (1) Atomic masses are determined relative to an H–1 standard.
   (2) Atomic masses are determined relative to an O–16 standard.
   (3) Atomic masses are a weighted average of the naturally occurring isotopes.
   (4) Atomic masses are an estimated average of the artificially produced isotopes.

19 All organic compounds must contain the element
(1) phosphorus　　　　　　　(3) carbon
(2) oxygen　　　　　　　　　(4) nitrogen

20 Which of the following compounds has the highest boiling point?
(1) H_2O　　(2) H_2S　　　(3) H_2Se　　　(4) H_2Te

21 The functional group —COOH is found in
(1) esters　　(2) aldehydes　　(3) alcohols　　　(4) organic acids

22 Which of these elements is the best conductor of electricity?
(1) S　　　(2) N　　　　(3) Br　　　　(4) Ni

23 Given the reaction: $2\,Al(s) + Fe_2O_3(s) \xrightarrow{\text{heat}} Al_2O_3(s) + 2\,Fe(s)$

Which species undergoes reduction?
(1) Al　　　(2) Fe　　　(3) Al^{3+}　　　(4) Fe^{3+}

24 Which energy transformation occurs when an electrolytic cell is in operation?
(1) chemical energy → electrical energy
(2) electrical energy → chemical energy
(3) light energy → heat energy
(4) light energy → chemical energy

25 Which of these pH numbers indicates the highest level of acidity?
(1) 5　　　(2) 8　　　(3) 10　　　(4) 12

26 According to the Arrhenius theory, when a base dissolves in water it produces
(1) CO_3^{2-} as the only negative ion in solution
(2) OH^- as the only negative ion in solution
(3) NH_4^+ as the only positive ion in solution
(4) H^+ as the only positive ion in solution

27 Which compound is an electrolyte?
(1) $C_6H_{12}O_6$　(2) CH_3OH　　(3) $CaCl_2$　　　(4) CCl_4

28 Which equation represents a spontaneous nuclear decay?

(1) $C + O_2 \rightarrow CO_2$　　　(3) $^{27}_{13}Al + ^4_2He \rightarrow ^{30}_{15}P + ^1_0n$

(2) $H_2CO_3 \rightarrow CO_2 + H_2O$　　(4) $^{90}_{38}Sr \rightarrow ^{0}_{-1}e + ^{90}_{39}Y$

29 The stability of an isotope is based on its
(1) number of neutrons, only　(3) ratio of neutrons to protons
(2) number of protons, only　(4) ratio of electrons to protons

Note that questions 30 and 31 have only three choices.

30 As the temperature of a substance *decreases*, the average kinetic energy of its particles
(1) decreases　(2) increases　　(3) remains the same

31 When an atom of phosphorus becomes a phosphide ion (P^{3-}), the radius
(1) decreases　(2) increases　　(3) remains the same

PART B-1

Answer all questions in this part.

Directions (32–50): For *each* statement or question, write the *number* of the word or expression that, of those given, best completes the statement or answers the question. Some questions may require the use of the *Reference Tables for Physical Setting / Chemistry.*

32 The data table below represents the properties determined by the analysis of substances A, B, C, and D.

Substance	Melting Point (°C)	Boiling Point (°C)	Conductivity
A	−80	−20	none
B	20	190	none
C	320	770	as solid
D	800	1250	in solution

Which substance is an ionic compound?
(1) A (2) B (3) C (4) D

33 What is the total number of electrons in a Cr^{3+} ion?
(1) 18   (2) 21   (3) 24   (4) 27

34 As the atoms of the Group 17 elements in the ground state are considered from top to bottom, each successive element has
(1) the same number of valence electrons and similar chemical properties
(2) the same number of valence electrons and identical chemical properties
(3) an increasing number of valence electrons and similar chemical properties
(4) an increasing number of valence electrons and identical chemical properties

35 Which solution when mixed with a drop of bromthymol blue will cause the indicator to change from blue to yellow?
(1) 0.1 M HCl   (3) 0.1 M CH_3OH
(2) 0.1 M NH_3 (4) 0.1 M NaOH

36 What is the empirical formula of a compound with the molecular formula N_2O_4?
(1) NO   (2) NO_2 (3) N_2O (4) N_2O_3

37 What is the correct Lewis electron-dot structure for the compound magnesium fluoride?

Mg : F :   Mg⁺[: F :]   [: F :]⁻ Mg²⁺ [: F :]   : F : Mg : F :
(1)   (2)   (3)   (4)

38 Given the reaction: $Mg(s) + 2\,AgNO_3(aq) \rightarrow Mg(NO_3)_2(aq) + 2\,Ag(s)$

Which type of reaction is represented?
(1) single replacement   (3) synthesis
(2) double replacement   (4) decomposition

39 Which equation shows conservation of both mass and charge?
(1) $Cl_2 + Br^- \rightarrow Cl^- + Br_2$
(3) $Zn + Cr^{3+} \rightarrow Zn^{2+} + Cr$
(2) $Cu + 2 Ag^+ \rightarrow Cu^{2+} + Ag$
(4) $Ni + Pb^{2+} \rightarrow Ni^{2+} + Pb$

40 The volume of a gas is 4.00 liters at 293 K and constant pressure. For the volume of the gas to become 3.00 liters, the Kelvin temperature must be equal to

(1) $\dfrac{3.00 \times 293}{4.00}$

(3) $\dfrac{3.00 \times 4.00}{293}$

(2) $\dfrac{4.00 \times 293}{3.00}$

(4) $\dfrac{293}{3.00 \times 4.00}$

41 What is the molarity of a solution containing 20 grams of NaOH in 500 milliliters of solution?
(1) 1 M   (2) 2 M   (3) 0.04 M   (4) 0.5 M

42 Which graph best represents the pressure-volume relationship for an ideal gas at constant temperature?

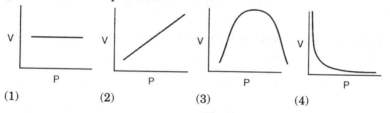

(1)   (2)   (3)   (4)

43 Given the equation: $C_2H_6 + Cl_2 \rightarrow C_2H_5Cl + HCl$
This reaction is best described as
(1) addition involving a saturated hydrocarbon
(2) addition involving an unsaturated hydrocarbon
(3) substitution involving a saturated hydrocarbon
(4) substitution involving an unsaturated hydrocarbon

44 The diagram at the right shows a key being plated with copper in an electrolytic cell. Given the reduction reaction for this cell:

$$Cu^{2+}(aq) + 2e^- \rightarrow Cu(s)$$

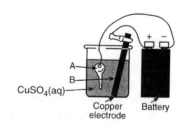

This reduction occurs at
(1) A, which is the anode
(2) A, which is the cathode
(3) B, which is the anode
(4) B, which is the cathode

45 A student neutralized 16.4 milliliters of HCl by adding 12.7 milliliters of 0.620 M KOH. What was the molarity of the HCl acid?
(1) 0.168 M   (2) 0.480 M   (3) 0.620 M   (4) 0.801 M

46 Nuclear fusion *differs* from nuclear fission because nuclear fusion reactions
    (1) form heavier isotopes from lighter isotopes
    (2) form lighter isotopes from heavier isotopes
    (3) convert mass to energy
    (4) convert energy to mass

47 After 32 days, 5 milligrams of an 80-milligram sample of a radioactive iso-
    tope remains unchanged. What is the half-life of this element?
    (1) 8 days   (2) 2 days   (3) 16 days   (4) 4 days

48 Which electron configuration represents an atom of chlorine in an excited
    state?
    (1) 2–8–7   (2) 2–8–8   (3) 2–8–6–1   (4) 2–8–7–1

Note that questions 49 and 50 have only three choices.

49 As each successive element in Group 15 of the Periodic Table is considered in
    order of increasing atomic number, the atomic radius
    (1) decreases   (2) increases   (3) remains the same

50 Given the equation: $KNO_3(s) \xrightarrow{H_2O(l)} KNO_3(aq)$

    As $H_2O(l)$ is added to $KNO_3(s)$ to form $KNO_3(aq)$, the entropy of the system
    (1) decreases   (2) increases   (3) remains the same

PART B–2
Answer all questions in this part.
Directions (51–62): Record your answers in the spaces provided. Some questions
may require the use of the *Reference Tables for Physical Setting / Chemistry*.

**Base your answers to questions 51 and 52 on the unbalanced equation
provided.**

    _____ $C_5H_{12}(g)$ + _____ $O_2(g) \rightarrow$ _____ $CO_2(g)$ + _____ $H_2O(g)$

51 Balance the equation, using the smallest whole-number coefficients. [1]

52 *a*   Using your balanced equation, show a correct numerical setup for calcu-
         lating the total number of moles of $H_2O(g)$ produced when 5.0 moles of $O_2(g)$
         are completely consumed. Use the space provided. [1]

    b   Record your answer. [1] _____ **mol H_2O**

Base your answers to questions 53 through 55 on the data table provided.

53 On the table provided, record the electronegativity for the elements with atomic numbers 11 through 17. [1]

Atomic Number	Electronegativity
11	
12	
13	
14	
15	
16	
17	

54 On the grid provided, mark an appropriate scale on the axis labeled "Electronegativity." [1]

55 On the same grid, plot the data from the data table. Circle and connect the points. [1]

Example:

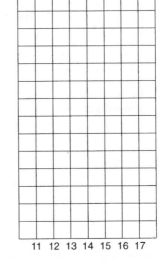

Base your answers to questions 56 through 58 on the information below.

A student uses 200 grams of water at a temperature of 60°C to prepare a saturated solution of potassium chloride, KCl.

56 Identify the solute in this solution. [1]

_____

57 According to *Reference Table G*, how many grams of KCl must be used to create this saturated solution? [1]

_____ **grams**

58 This solution is cooled to 10°C and the excess KCl precipitates (settles out). The resulting solution is saturated at 10°C. How many grams of KCl precipitated out of the original solution? [1]

_____ **grams**

Base your answers to questions 59 through 61 on the diagram of the voltaic cell at the right.

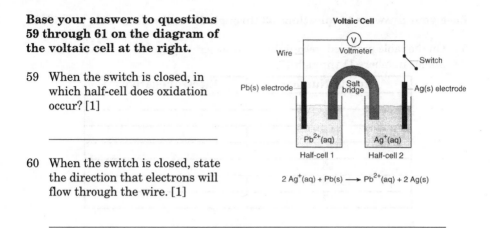

Voltaic Cell

59 When the switch is closed, in which half-cell does oxidation occur? [1]

_____

60 When the switch is closed, state the direction that electrons will flow through the wire. [1]

_____

61 *Based on the given equation*, write the balanced half-reaction that occurs in half-cell 1. [1]

_____

62 In the space provided, draw a Lewis electron-dot structure for an atom of phosphorus. [1]

PART C
Answer all questions in this part.

Directions (63–81): Record your answers in the spaces provided. Some questions may require the use of the *Reference Tables for Physical Setting / Chemistry.*

Base your answers to questions 63 and 81 on the information and the bright-line spectra represented at the right.

Many advertising signs depend on the production of light emissions from gas-filled glass tubes that are subjected to a high-voltage source. When light emissions are passed through a spectroscope, bright-line spectra are produced.

Gas A

Gas B

Gas C

Gas D

Unknown mixture

63 Identify the *two* gases in the unknown mixture. [2]

_____ and _____

64 Explain the production of an emission spectrum in terms of the *energy states of an electron*. [1]

_____

_____

_____

Base your answers to questions 65 through 67 on the particle diagrams below, which show atoms and/or molecules in three different samples of matter at STP.

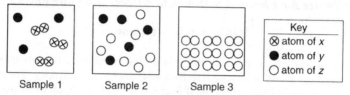

Sample 1   Sample 2   Sample 3

Key
⊗ atom of *x*
● atom of *y*
○ atom of *z*

65 Which sample represents a pure substance? [1] _____

66 When two atoms of *y* react with one atom of *z*, a compound forms. Using the number of atoms shown in sample 2, what is the maximum number of molecules of this compound that can be formed? [1]

_____

67 Explain why ⊗⊗⊗ does *not* represent a compound. [1]

_____

_____

Base your answers to questions 68 through 70 on the information below.

Many artificial flavorings are prepared using the type of organic reaction shown below.

$$\underset{\text{Reactant 1}}{\overset{\displaystyle H \quad O}{H-\underset{\displaystyle H}{\overset{\displaystyle |}{C}}-\overset{\displaystyle \|}{C}-OH}} \; + \; \underset{\text{Reactant 2}}{\overset{\displaystyle H \; H \; H}{HO-\underset{\displaystyle H \; H \; H}{\overset{\displaystyle | \; | \; |}{C-C-C}}-H}} \longrightarrow H-\underset{\displaystyle H}{\overset{\displaystyle H \quad O}{C}}-C-O-C-C-C-H \; + \; HOH$$

68 What is the name of this organic reaction? [1]

_____

69 To what class of organic compounds does reactant 2 belong? [1]

_____

70 In the space provided, draw the structural formula of an isomer of reactant 2. [1]

Base your answers to questions 71 through 74 on the article below, the Reference Tables for Physical Setting/Chemistry, and your knowledge of chemistry.

Radioactivity at home

You may be surprised to learn that you do not need to visit a nuclear power plant or a hospital X-ray laboratory to find sources of radioactivity. They are all around us. In fact, it is likely that you'll find a few at home. Your front porch may incorporate cinder blocks or granite blocks. Both contain uranium. Walk through the front door, look up, and you'll see a smoke detector that owes its effectiveness to the constant source of alpha particle emissions from Americium-241. As long as the gases remain ionized within the shielded container, electricity flows, and all is calm. When smoke enters the chamber, it neutralizes the charges on these ions. In the absence of these ions, the circuit breaks and the alarm goes off.

Indicator lights on your appliances may use Krypton-85; electric blankets, promethium- 147; and fluorescent lights, thorium-229. Even the food we eat is radioactive. The more potassium-rich the food source, the more potassium-40—a radioactive isotope that makes up about 0.01% of the natural supply of this mineral—is present. Thus, brazil nuts, peanuts, bananas, potatoes, and flour, all rich in potassium, are radiation sources.

—*Chem Matters*
April 2000

71 Write the equation for the alpha decay that occurs in a smoke detector containing Americium-241 (Am-241). [2]

_____

72 How is the radioactive decay of Krypton-85 different from the radioactive decay of Americium-241? [1]

_____

_____

73 State one benefit or useful application of radioactivity not mentioned in this article. [1]

_____

_____

74 State one risk or danger associated with radioactivity. [1]

_____

_____

Base your answers to questions 75 and 76 on the information below.

Gypsum is a mineral that is used in the construction industry to make dry-wall (sheetrock). The chemical formula for this hydrated compound is $CaSO_4 \cdot 2\ H_2O$. A hydrated compound contains water molecules within its crystalline structure. Gypsum contains 2 moles of water for each 1 mole of calcium sulfate.

75 What is the gram formula mass of $CaSO_4 \cdot 2\ H_2O$? [1]

_____ g/mol

76 *a* In the space provided, show a correct numerical setup for calculating the percent composition by mass of water in this compound. [1]

b Record your answer. [1]

_____ %

Base your answers to questions 77 through 79 on the information and potential energy diagram below.

Chemical cold packs are often used to reduce swelling after an athletic injury. The diagram represents the potential energy changes when a cold pack is activated.

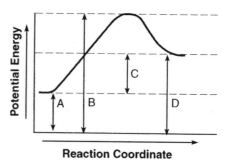

77 Which lettered interval on the diagram represents the potential energy of the products? [1]

_____

78 Which lettered interval on the diagram represents the heat of reaction? [1]

_____

79 Identify a reactant listed in *Reference Table I* that could be mixed with water for use in a chemical cold pack. [1]

_____

Base your answers to questions 80 and 81 on the information below.

Calcium hydroxide is commonly known as agricultural lime and is used to adjust the soil pH. Before the lime was added to a field, the soil pH was 5. After the lime was added, the soil underwent a 100-fold decrease in hydronium ion concentration.

80 What is the new pH of the soil in the field? [1]

_____

81 According to *Reference Table F*, calcium hydroxide is soluble in water. Identify another hydroxide compound that contains a Group 2 element and is also soluble in water. [1]

_____

PHYSICAL SETTING: CHEMISTRY PRACTICE TEST #3 – JUNE 2004

PART A
Answer all questions in this part.

Directions (1–33): For *each* statement or question, write the *number* of the word or expression that, of those given, best completes the statement or answers the question. Some questions may require the use of the *Reference Tables for Physical Setting/Chemistry*.

1 The modem model of the atom is based on the work of
   (1) one scientist over a short period of time
   (2) one scientist over a long period of time
   (3) many scientists over a short period of time
   (4) many scientists over a long period of time

2 Which statement is true about the charges assigned to an electron and a proton?
   (1) Both an electron and a proton are positive.
   (2) An electron is positive and a proton is negative.
   (3) An electron is negative and a proton is positive.
   (4) Both an electron and a proton are negative.

3 In the wave-mechanical model, an orbital is a region of space in an atom where there is
   (1) a high probability of finding an electron
   (2) a high probability of finding a neutron
   (3) a circular path in which electrons are found
   (4) a circular path in which neutrons are found

4 What is the charge of the nucleus in an atom of oxygen-17?
   (1) 0   (2) –2   (3) +8   (4) +17

5 Which pair of symbols represents a metalloid and a noble gas?
   (1) Si and Bi   (3) Ge and Te
   (2) As and Ar   (4) Ne and Xe

6 Which statement describes a chemical property of iron?
   (1) Iron can be flattened into sheets.
   (2) Iron conducts electricity and heat.
   (3) Iron combines with oxygen to form rust.
   (4) Iron can be drawn into a wire.

7 Given the reaction: $N_2(g) + 3 H_2(g) \rightleftharpoons 2 NH_3(g)$

   What is the mole-to-mole ratio between nitrogen gas and hydrogen gas?
   (1) 1:2   (2) 1:3   (3) 2:2   (4) 2:3

8 What is the percent by mass of oxygen in propanal, CH_3CH_2CHO?
   (1) 10.0%   (2) 27.6%   (3) 38.1%   (4) 62.1%

9   Covalent bonds are formed when electrons are
    (1) transferred from one atom to another
    (2) captured by the nucleus
    (3) mobile within a metal
    (4) shared between two atoms

10 Which type of molecule is CF_4?
    (1) polar, with a symmetrical distribution of charge
    (2) polar, with an asymmetrical distribution of charge
    (3) nonpolar, with a symmetrical distribution of charge
    (4) nonpolar, with an asymmetrical distribution of charge

11 Which change occurs when a barium atom loses two electrons?
    (1) It becomes a negative ion and its radius decreases.
    (2) It becomes a negative ion and its radius increases.
    (3) It becomes a positive ion and its radius decreases.
    (4) It becomes a positive ion and its radius increases.

12 Conductivity in a metal results from the metal atoms having
    (1) high electronegativity
    (2) high ionization energy
    (3) highly mobile protons in the nucleus
    (4) highly mobile electrons in the valence shell

13 Which of these elements has the *least* attraction for electrons in a chemical
    bond?
    (1) oxygen   (2) fluorine   (3) nitrogen   (4) chlorine

14 Recovering the salt from a mixture of salt and water could best be accomplished by
    (1) evaporation   (3) paper chromatography
    (2) filtration   (4) density determination

15 The average kinetic energy of water molecules is greatest in which of these
    samples?
    (1) 10 g of water at 35ºC   (3) 100 g of water at 25ºC
    (2) 10 g of water at 55ºC   (4) 100 g of water at 45ºC

16 Helium is most likely to behave as an ideal gas when it is under
    (1) high pressure and high temperature
    (2) high pressure and low temperature
    (3) low pressure and high temperature
    (4) low pressure and low temperature

17 At STP, the element oxygen can exist as either O_2 or O_3 gas molecules. These
    two forms of the element have
    (1) the same chemical and physical properties
    (2) the same chemical properties and different physical properties
    (3) different chemical properties and the same physical properties
    (4) different chemical and physical properties

18 Which sample contains particles in a rigid, fixed, geometric pattern?
    (1) $CO_2(aq)$ (2) $HCl(g)$ (3) $H_2O(l)$ (4) $KCl(s)$

19 Given the reaction at 25ºC:

$$Zn(s) + 2\ HCl(aq) \rightarrow ZnCl_2(aq) + H_2(g)$$

The rate of this reaction can be increased by using 5.0 grams of powdered zinc instead of a 5.0-gram strip of zinc because the powdered zinc has
(1) lower kinetic energy   (3) more surface area
(2) lower concentration   (4) more zinc atoms

20 Which statement about a system at equilibrium is true?
(1) The forward reaction rate is less than the reverse reaction rate.
(2) The forward reaction rate is greater than the reverse reaction rate.
(3) The forward reaction rate is equal to the reverse reaction rate.
(4) The forward reaction rate stops and the reverse reaction rate continues.

21 A catalyst increases the rate of a chemical reaction by
(1) lowering the activation energy of the reaction
(2) lowering the potential energy of the products
(3) raising the temperature of the reactants
(4) raising the concentration of the reactants

22 Which element must be present in an organic compound?
(1) hydrogen   (2) oxygen   (3) carbon   (4) nitrogen

23 Which compound is a saturated hydrocarbon?
(1) hexane   (2) hexene   (3) hexanol   (4) hexanal

24 Given the reaction:

$$CH_3\overset{O}{\overset{\|}{C}}{-}OH + HOC_2H_5 \rightleftharpoons CH_3\overset{O}{\overset{\|}{C}}{-}O{-}C_2H_5 + H_2O$$

This reaction is an example of
(1) fermentation   (2) saponification
(3) hydrogenation   (4) esterification

25 Which of these compounds has chemical properties most similar to the chemical properties of ethanoic acid?
(1) C_3H_7COOH (3) $C_2H_5COOC_2H_5$
(2) C_2H_5OH (4) $C_2H_5OC_2H_5$

26 Given the reaction that occurs in an electrochemical cell:

$$Zn(s) + CuSO_4(aq) \rightarrow ZnSO_4(aq) + Cu(s)$$

During this reaction, the oxidation number of Zn changes from
(1) 0 to +2   (2) 0 to –2   (3) +2 to 0   (4) –2 to 0

27 A voltaic cell spontaneously converts
(1) electrical energy to chemical energy
(2) chemical energy to electrical energy
(3) electrical energy to nuclear energy
(4) nuclear energy to electrical energy

28 Which pair of formulas represents two compounds that are electrolytes?
    (1) HCl and CH_3OH (3) C_5H_{12} and CH_3OH
    (2) HCl and NaOH   (4) C_5H_{12} and NaOH

29 Hydrogen chloride, HCl, is classified as an Arrhenius acid because it produces
    (1) H^+ ions in aqueous solution   (3) OH^- ions in aqueous solution
    (2) Cl^- ions in aqueous solution   (4) NH_4^+ ions in aqueous solution

30 Which compound could serve as a reactant in a neutralization reaction?
    (1) NaCl   (2) KOH   (3) CH_3OH (4) CH_3CHO

31 Which of these particles has the greatest mass?
    (1) alpha   (2) beta   (3) neutron   (4) positron

32 In a nuclear fusion reaction, the mass of the products is
    (1) less than the mass of the reactants because some of the mass has been
         converted to energy
    (2) less than the mass of the reactants because some of the energy has been
         converted to mass
    (3) more than the mass of the reactants because some of the mass has been
         converted to energy
    (4) more than the mass of the reactants because some of the energy has
         been converted to mass

33 Which of these types of radiation has the greatest penetrating power?
    (1) alpha   (2) beta   (3) neutron   (4) positron

PART B-1
Answer all questions in this part.

Directions (34–50): For *each* statement or question, write the *number* of the word or expression that, of those given, best completes the statement or answers the question. Some questions may require the use of the *Reference Tables for Physical Setting / Chemistry*.

34 How many electrons are contained in an Au^{3+} ion?
    (1) 76   (2) 79   (3) 82   4) 197

35 Which electron configuration represents the electrons of an atom in an excited state?
    (1) 2–4   (2) 2–6   (3) 2–7–2   (4) 2–8–2

36 In comparison to an atom of $^{19}_{9}F$ in the ground state, an atom $^{12}_{6}C$ in the ground state has
    (1) three fewer neutrons   (3) three more neutrons
    (2) three fewer valence electrons (4) three more valence electrons

37 Element X is a solid that is brittle, lacks luster, and has six valence electrons. In which group on the Periodic Table would element X be found?
(1) 1   (2) 2   (3) 15   (4) 16

38 What is the empirical formula for the compound $C_6H_{12}O_6$?
(1) CH_2O (2) $C_2H_4O_2$ (3) $C_3H_6O_3$ (4) $C_6H_{12}O_6$

39 The bonds between hydrogen and oxygen in a water molecule are classified as
(1) polar covalent   (3) ionic
(2) nonpolar covalent   (4) metallic

40 The graph below represents the uniform heating of a substance, starting with the substance as a solid below its melting point.

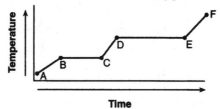

Which line segment represents an increase in potential energy and no change in average kinetic energy?
(1) $\overline{AB}$ (2) $\overline{BC}$ (3) $\overline{CD}$ (4) $\overline{EF}$

41 Using your knowledge of chemistry and the information in *Reference Table H*, which statement concerning propanone and water at 50ºC is true?
(1) Propanone has a higher vapor pressure and stronger intermolecular forces than water
(2) Propanone has a higher vapor pressure and weaker intermolecular forces than water.
(3) Propanone has a lower vapor pressure and stronger intermolecular forces than water.
(4) Propanone has a lower vapor pressure and weaker intermolecular forces than water.

42 A solution that is at equilibrium must be
(1) concentrated   (3) saturated
(2) dilute   (4) unsaturated

43 Given the reaction: $N_2(g) + O_2(g) + 182.6 \text{ kJ} \rightleftharpoons 2 \text{ NO}(g)$

Which change would cause an immediate increase in the rate of the forward reaction?
(1) increasing the concentration of NO(g)
(2) increasing the concentration of N_2(g)
(3) decreasing the reaction temperature
(4) decreasing the reaction pressure

44 Which 10-milliliter sample of water has the greatest degree of disorder?
   (1) $H_2O(g)$ at 120°C   (3) $H_2O(l)$ at 20°C
   (2) $H_2O(l)$ at 80°C   (4) $H_2O(s)$ at 0°C

45 Which pH indicates a basic solution?
   (1) 1   (2) 5   (3) 7   (4) 12

46 Which structural formula represents 2-pentyne?

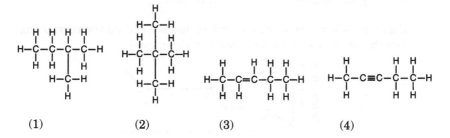

   (1)   (2)   (3)   (4)

47 Which structural formula represents an ether?

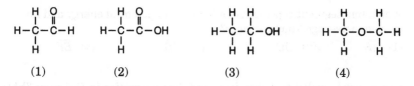

   (1)   (2)   (3)   (4)

48 Given the reaction for the corrosion of aluminum:

   $$4\,Al + 3\,O_2 \rightarrow 2\,Al_2O_3$$

   Which half-reaction correctly represents the oxidation that occurs?
   (1) $Al + 3e^- \rightarrow Al^{3+}$ (3) $O_2 + 4e^- \rightarrow 2\,O^{2-}$
   (2) $Al \rightarrow Al^{3+} + 3e^-$ (4) $O_2 \rightarrow 2\,O^{2-} + 4e^-$

49 Based on *Reference Table N*, what fraction of a sample of gold-198 remains radioactive after 2.69 days?

   (1) $\frac{1}{4}$ (3) $\frac{3}{4}$

   (2) $\frac{1}{2}$ (4) $\frac{7}{8}$

Note that question 50 has only three choices.

50 As the elements of Group 1 on the Periodic Table are considered in order of increasing atomic radius, the ionization energy of each successive element generally
   (1) decreases   (2) increases   (3) remains the same

PART B-2

Answer all questions in this part.

Directions (51–64): Record your answers in the spaces provided. Some questions may require the use of the *Reference Tables for Physical Setting/Chemistry*.

Base your answers to questions 51 through 53 on the balanced chemical equation below.

$$2 H_2O \rightarrow 2 H_2 + O_2$$

51 What type of reaction does this equation represent? [1]

_____

52 How does the balanced chemical equation show the Law of Conservation of Mass? [1]

_____

_____

53 What is the total number of moles of O_2 produced when 8 moles of H_2O is completely consumed? [1]

_____mol

Base your answers to questions 54 and 55 on the unbalanced redox reaction below.

$$Cu(s) + AgNO_3(aq) \rightarrow Cu(NO_3)_2(aq) + Ag(s)$$

54 Write the reduction half-reaction. [1]

_____

55 Balance the redox equation using the smallest whole-number coefficients. [1]

_____Cu(s) + _____AgNO$_3$(aq) → _____Cu(NO$_3$)$_2$(aq) + _____ Ag(s)

Base your answers to questions 56 through 58 on the information below.

A student titrates 60.0 mL of HNO$_3$(aq) with 0.30 M NaOH(aq). Phenolphthalein is used as the indicator. After adding 42.2 mL of NaOH(aq), a color change remains for 25 seconds, and the student stops the titration.

56 What color change does phenolphthalein undergo during this titration? [1]

_____ to _____

57 In the space provided, show a correct numerical setup for calculating the molarity of the $HNO_3(aq)$. [1]

58 According to the data, how many significant figures should be present in the calculated molarity of the $HNO_3(aq)$? [1]

_____

Base your answers to questions 59 through 61 on the data table below, which shows three isotopes of neon.

Isotope	Atomic Mass (atomic mass units)	Percent Natural Abundance
^{20}Ne	19.99	90.9%
^{21}Ne	20.99	0.3%
^{22}Ne	21.99	8.8%

59 In terms of *atomic particles*, state one difference between these three isotopes of neon. [1]

_____

_____

60 Based on the atomic masses and the natural abundances shown in the data table, in the space provided, show a correct numerical setup for calculating the average atomic mass of neon. [1]

61 Based on natural abundances, the average atomic mass of neon is closest to which whole number? [1]

_____

62 Based on the Periodic Table, explain why Na and K have similar chemical properties. [1]

_____

_____

_____

63 In the space to the right of the reactants and arrow provided, draw the structural formula for the product of the reaction shown. [1]

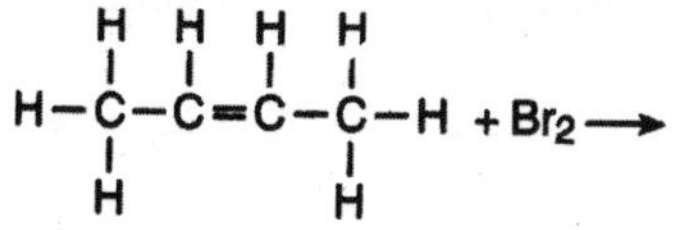

$$H-\overset{\overset{\displaystyle H}{|}}{C}-\overset{\overset{\displaystyle H}{|}}{C}=\overset{\overset{\displaystyle H}{|}}{C}-\overset{\overset{\displaystyle H}{|}}{C}-H + Br_2 \longrightarrow$$

64 Given the nuclear equation:

$$^{58}_{29}CU \rightarrow {}^{58}_{28}Ni + X$$

What nuclear particle is represented by X? [1] _____

PART C
Answer all questions in this part.

Directions (65–85): Record your answers in the spaces provided. Some questions may require the use of the *Reference Tables for Physical Setting / Chemistry*.

Base your answers to questions 65 through 67 on the information and equation below.

Antacids can be used to neutralize excess stomach acid. Brand *A* antacid contains the acid-neutralizing agent magnesium hydroxide, $Mg(OH)_2$. It reacts with HCl(aq) in the stomach, according to the following balanced equation:

$$2\ HCl(aq) + Mg(OH)_2(S) \rightarrow MgCl_2(aq) + 2\ H_2O(l)$$

65 In the space provided, show a correct numerical setup for calculating the number of moles of $Mg(OH)_2$ (gram-formula mass = 58.3 grams/mole) in an 8.40-gram sample. [1]

66 If a person produces 0.050 mole of excess HCl in the stomach, how many moles of $Mg(OH)_2$ are needed to neutralize this excess hydrochloric acid? [1]

_____ **mol**

67 Brand B antacid contains the acid-neutralizing agent sodium hydrogen carbonate. Write the chemical formula for sodium hydrogen carbonate. [1]

_____

Base your answers to questions 68 through 70 on the information below.

Naphthalene, a nonpolar substance that sublimes at room temperature, can be used to protect wool clothing from being eaten by moths.

68 Explain, in terms of *intermolecular forces*, why naphthalene sublimes. [1]

_____

_____

_____

69 Explain why naphthalene is *not* expected to dissolve in water. [1]

_____

_____

_____

70 The empirical formula for naphthalene is C_5H_4 and the molecular mass of naphthalene is 128 grams/mole. What is the molecular formula for naphthalene? [1]

_____

Base your answers to questions 71 through 74 on the data table below, which shows the solubility of a solid solute.

Temperature	Solute per 100 g of H2O(g)
0	18
20	20
40	24
60	29
80	36
100	49

71   On the grid provided, mark an appropriate scale on the axis labeled "Solute per 100 g of $H_2O(g)$." An appropriate scale is one that allows a trend to be seen. [1]

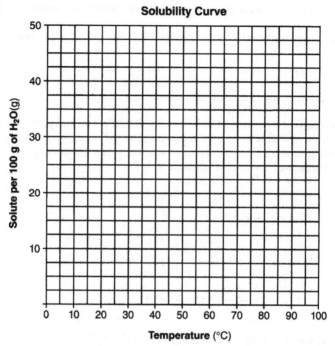

Solubility Curve

(y-axis: Solute per 100 g of $H_2O(g)$ — 10, 20, 30, 40, 50)

(x-axis: Temperature (°C) — 0, 10, 20, 30, 40, 50, 60, 70, 80, 90, 100)

72   On the same grid, plot the data from the data table. Circle and connect the points. [1]

     Example:

73   Based on the data table, if 15 grams of solute is dissolved in 100 grams of water at 40°C, how many *more* grams of solute can be dissolved in this solution to make it saturated at 40°C? [1]

     _____ **g**

74   According to *Reference Table G*, how many grams of KClO must be dissolved in 100 grams of H_2O at 10°C to produce a saturated solution? [1]

     _____ **g**

Base your answers to questions 75 through 78 on the information below.

A weather balloon has a volume of 52.5 liters at a temperature of 295 K. The balloon is released and rises to an altitude where the temperature is 252 K.

75 How does this temperature change affect the gas particle motion? [1]

_____

_____

76 The original pressure at 295 K was 100.8 kPa and the pressure at the higher altitude at 252 K is 45.6 kPa. Assume the balloon does not burst. In the space provided, show a correct numerical setup for calculating the volume of the balloon at the higher altitude. [1]

77 What Celsius temperature is equal to 252 K? [1]

_____ °C

78 What pressure, in atmospheres (atm), is equal to 45.6 kPa? [1]

_____ atm

Base your answers to questions 79 and 80 on the information and equation below.

Human blood contains dissolved carbonic acid, H_2CO_3, in equilibrium with carbon dioxide and water. The equilibrium system is shown below.

H_2CO_3,(aq) CO_2(aq) + H_2O(l)

79 Explain, using LeChatelier's principle, why decreasing the concentration of CO_2 decreases the concentration of H_2CO_3.

_____

_____

80 What is the oxidation number of carbon in H_2CO_3(aq)? [1]

_____

Base your answers to questions 81 through 84 on the information below.

A safe level of fluoride ions is added to many public drinking water supplies. Fluoride ions have been found to help prevent tooth decay. Another common source of fluoride ions is toothpaste. One of the fluoride compounds used in toothpaste is tin(II) fluoride.

A town located downstream from a chemical plant was concerned about fluoride ions from the plant leaking into its drinking water. According to the Environmental Protection Agency, the fluoride ion concentration in drinking water cannot exceed 4 ppm. The town hired a chemist to analyze its water. The chemist determined that a 175-gram sample of the town's water contains 0.000 250 gram of fluoride ions.

81 In the box provided, draw a Lewis electron-dot diagram for a fluoride ion. [1]

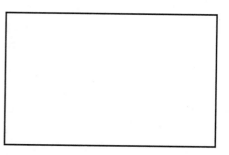

82 What is the chemical formula for tin(II) fluoride? [1]

_____

83 How many parts per million of fluoride ions are present in the analyzed sample? [1]

_____ **ppm**

84 Is the town's drinking water safe to drink? Support your decision using information in the passage and your calculated fluoride level in question 83. [1]

_____

_____

_____

_____

85 A plan is being developed for an experiment to test the effect of concentrated strong acids on a metal surface protected by various coatings. Some safety precautions would be the wearing of chemical safety goggles, an apron, and gloves. State one additional safety precaution that should be included in the plan. [1]

_____

_____

_____

_____